Keir Hardie

Keir Hardie
radical and socialist

Kenneth O. Morgan

Weidenfeld & Nicolson
London

for Jane

© 1975 Kenneth O. Morgan

First published 1975
Paperback edition first published 1984

George Weidenfeld and Nicolson Ltd
91 Clapham High Street London SW4 7TA

British Library Cataloguing in Publication Data

Morgan, Kenneth O.
  Keir Hardie.
  1. Hardie, Keir   2. Statesmen—Great Britain
  —Biography
  I. Title
  941.081′092′4   HD8393.H3

ISBN 0-279-78440-4

Printed and bound in Great Britain by
Butler and Tanner Ltd
Frome and London

Contents

Preface

Keir Hardie is by any test a decisive figure in the making of twentieth-century Britain. More than any other man, he was the maker of the modern Labour Party. Since his death he has been its folk-hero and inspiration. Yet already he seems an elusive, almost forgotten figure, utterly remote from the Britain of the 1970s. More than most Labour leaders, he has not been fortunate in his biographers. While some of them, particularly David Lowe, William Stewart and Emrys Hughes, provide much valuable personal information on their subject, none of them can reasonably be said to offer a satisfactory historical assessment. Neither is there any adequate study of the early growth of the Independent Labour Party, Hardie's main political instrument. The real Hardie, it seems, is rapidly sliding into premature oblivion; only the deceptive legend of the cloth cap survives. In this book, I have tried to fill this gaping void in British political historiography. Naturally, I have attempted to provide an account of the main events of Hardie's life, and to explain his personality. Much more important, I have sought to explore the nature of his influence on the formation and the ideas of the Labour movement. It seems to me that his career has all too often been interpreted in simplistic class terms, and that the kaleidoscopic quality of his socialism has all too seldom been subjected to close examination. The main theme underlying this book is the nature of Hardie's unique fusion of late nineteenth-century radicalism and socialism. This seems to me the essence of his political faith. Hardie is treated here as a figure from the past. I have not intended to draw any comparisons between the Labour movement of his day and the political and industrial tensions of Britain in the early 1970s. No doubt it is naïve to believe that I have wholly succeeded.

Writing the life of Keir Hardie poses special problems for the biographer. There survives no large cache of 'Hardie Papers', usually the staple raw material for the political historian. The research for this book has entailed an unusually wide-ranging amount of quarrying in various sources, in public and private hands, in different parts of England, Wales and Scotland, on the continent and across the Atlantic. Throughout, I have been heavily dependent on primary published material, particularly the Labour newspaper press through which Hardie communicated so freely for most of his career. However, I have also discovered very large quantities of Hardie's private correspondence, far more than I could have suspected to exist when I began my research. His letters to contemporaries such as Glasier and MacDonald have proved especially valuable. So too have the archives of institutions such as the Independent Labour Party, the Labour Party and the Socialist International. My search for material ended in success in almost every case; the one exception concerned the Norman Angell Papers which, for some reason, are located in South Bend College, Indiana, USA, and where the officials in charge declined to acknowledge my correspondence. Apart from this, the major problem concerning the source material for Hardie's career, as it emerged during the many years which this book took to prepare, was one not of dearth but of almost overwhelming abundance.

Uncovering material on Hardie has left me with many deep debts of gratitude to different people and institutions. I am particularly indebted to Mr A.F. Thompson of Wadham College, Oxford, for originally proposing that I undertake a project which has given me such enjoyment, and for much wise and friendly counsel along the way. Another friend, Dr Henry Pelling of St John's College, Cambridge, kindly lent me transcripts of some of the Francis Johnson Papers; this would, perhaps, be the occasion to underline the immense value of his writings for all students of recent British Labour history. Mr Malcolm Bruce Glasier of West Kirby most generously gave me full and free access to the massive papers of his fascinating parents, Bruce and Katherine Glasier, while his wife provided superb hospitality. Mr David Marquand MP equally generously allowed me to work on the papers of Ramsay MacDonald at his home; his own eagerly-awaited biography of MacDonald will surely be a landmark in the study of Labour's recent past. Mr Bruce Aubry of Bristol was most kind and helpful in guiding me through parts of the archive of the Independent Labour Party, and freely shared with me his immense bibliographical knowledge of Hardie. I am also indebted to the National Administrative Council of the ILP, and its secretary, Mr Donald Bateman, for allowing me access to parts of the archive that related to Hardie. It is to be hoped that all historians will be permitted to work on the entire archive in future, now that it has been so expertly and fully scheduled. Dr Fred Reid of the University of Warwick kindly made available his Oxford doctoral thesis on Hardie's early life, which is most informative on the Scottish phase of Hardie's career up to Mid-Lanark; it is much to be hoped that it will be published some day.

I am also much indebted to Mr Hedley Dennis of Abercynon for giving me access to the interesting papers of his late wife, Agnes; to Mrs Martha Hughes, Cumnock, for allowing me to use the papers of her late husband, Mr Emrys Hughes MP; to Mrs Irene Wagner of the Transport House library for much kindness to me when I worked on the Labour Party's early records there; to Miss E.M.H. Schreuder of the Institute of Social History, Amsterdam, for guidance on the sources there and for sharing with me her expert knowledge of Sylvia Pankhurst; to Mr Hywel Francis of the University College of Swansea for help on the South Wales records; to Mr Ian MacDougall of the Scottish Society of Labour History, Edinburgh, for similar assistance on the Scottish materials; to Professor John Vincent for helpful negotiations on the materials at Bristol; and to Professor Michael Fry of Carleton University, Ottawa, for guidance on Canadian sources. Inquiries about sources were also helpfully answered by Miss Lilian Fluger of Arbejderbevaegelsens Bibliothek og Arkiv, Copenhagen; Mr A. Belcher of the Colne Valley Labour Party; Mr A. Bromley Davenport of the Skipton Labour Party; Dr Cameron Hazlehurst of the Australian National University, Canberra; Professor John Saville, University of Hull; Mr Chris Cook of the Political Records Project, London School of Economics; Mr Deian Hopkin of the University College of Wales; and Mr Walter Morgan of the National Library of Wales, Aberystwyth. All the libraries and record offices visited were, without exception, unfailingly courteous and helpful. In addition to those listed in the bibliography, the British Museum Newspaper Library at Colindale ought also to be recorded. I would like to thank the following for permission to quote from papers in their keeping: the Trustees of the British Museum, the British

Library of Political and Economic Science, the National Library of Scotland and the President and Fellows of Corpus Christi College, Oxford. I also wish to thank Mrs Martha Hughes, Mr Malcolm Bruce Glasier and the Rt Hon. Malcolm MacDonald for permission to quote from private papers of which they own the copyright. I have also benefited from interviews with Lord Brockway, the Rt Hon. James Griffiths, Mr Emrys Thomas of the ILP, and the late Rev. T.E. Nicholas, Aberystwyth. Mr Benjamin Buchan of Weidenfeld and Nicolson was most helpful in preparing the book for publication. Of course, none of the people or institutions listed here is in any way responsible for the views expressed in this book, or for any errors of fact or of interpretation that doubtless remain.

I have also much cause to be grateful to the two British universities in which I have worked. At the University College of Swansea, under the enthusiastic and kindly guidance of Professor Glanmor Williams, I first developed an interest in Welsh and English Labour history. The Provost and Fellows of the Queen's College, Oxford, generously provided financial assistance from their research fund, an expert typist in Miss Pat Lloyd and a sabbatical year without which my research could hardly have been completed. I have also learnt much from undergraduates whom I have taught at Oxford over the years, particularly for a PPE special subject on British Labour History, now regrettably a casualty of syllabus reform.

My final indebtedness is the most profound of all. My father gave me constant help in my research, particularly on the Welsh sources; I suspect that his labours were spurred on as much by affection for Keir Hardie as for me! He and my mother gave my work every encouragement throughout. My wife, Jane, unselfishly helped with research and with checking the manuscript, patiently tolerated the intrusion of Keir Hardie into the first year of our marriage and made it all seem worthwhile. Finally, thanks are due to David Keir, whose appearance greatly enlivened the correction of proofs.

Kenneth O. Morgan

'Stonecroft',
East End, North Leigh,
Oxfordshire

October 1974

I The Legend and the Reality (1856–87)

The life of James Keir Hardie is one of the legends of modern British politics. Long ago the symbol of the 'man in the cloth cap' passed from history into romance. Many years before his death in 1915 – and he was only fifty-nine when he died – he had attained a kind of heroic stature amongst working-class people. By his late forties even, he was already enthroned in the affections of his disciples as 'our Grand Old Man'. His portrait had replaced those of the Queen or of Gladstone on the walls of miners' cottages. A Welsh admirer, Wil Jon Edwards, saw him as a messianic figure, a latter-day Jesus: 'he and his gospel were indivisible'.[1] Ramsay MacDonald, writing (somewhat unwillingly) an introduction to William Stewart's official biography of Hardie in 1921, continued the biblical analogies. He compared Hardie with Moses, leading the children of the labour and socialist movements out of bondage towards the promised land.[2] In later decades Hardie retained his stature as the one undisputed folk-hero of the British Labour Party, a memorial of an earlier, crusading era, when the party was suffused with idealism and a sense of mission. He provided Christian names for the only son of the suffragette, Sylvia Pankhurst, and for the TUC general secretary, Victor Grayson Hardie Feather. Even after the second world war, even after the internal divisions that rent the Labour Party from 1951 onwards, the party's annual conference could still revere Hardie's name. The very phrase, 'If Keir Hardie were alive today', was guaranteed to restore even the most fractious delegates to comradeship and unity. Left and Right could be reconciled in recognition of a common tradition and martyrology. Even in the disillusion and despair that beset the Labour Party in the late 1960s and earlier seventies, Hardie still served as a touchstone of an earlier, purer tradition, much as the early Christian Fathers inspired nineteenth-century Evangelicals, repelled by the

worldliness and materialism of modern clerical institutions. Beyond
fear of reclaim, it seems, the legend of Keir Hardie has made him no
longer a pragmatic politician, but rather one of the saints who from
their labours rest.

While his disciples in all parties revere the memory of Hardie as an
incorruptible idealist, so his detractors have viewed him as an extremist. The two interpretations are of course complementary. The
Labour Party since 1915 has invariably seen Hardie as the very model
of uncompromising, red-blooded socialism, the antithesis of the
empirical, 'untheological' outlook inculcated by Labour leaders from
Attlee to Harold Wilson. The Independent Labour Party, disaffiliated from the Labour Party in 1932 and a dwindling minority
since then, continued to claim Hardie as one of their own, their only
true begetter. The Communist Party, in a *Keir Hardie Special* published during the lifetime of the first Labour government in 1924,
depicted Hardie as the prototype of socialist class-consciousness, the
complete contrast to the opportunism and office-seeking of Ramsay
MacDonald and the other Labour Cabinet ministers.[3] Hardie's battle
against the 'Lib-Labs' in the TUC in the late 1880s was compared
with the Communist-led Minority Movements within the unions
after 1919. The Communists, too, created a Hardie in their own
image. But to the political Right, by contrast, Hardie was the epitome
of the irreconcilable, impractical doctrinaire, the ardent ally of every
quixotic minority, the friend of every nation and race save his own.
The Liberal editor, A.G. Gardiner of the *Daily News*, not an entirely
hostile observer by any means, considered Hardie the one leading figure
in the Labour Party who was manifestly not equipped to lead it.[4]
Hardie's flamboyant appearances in parliament, his melodramatic
entry into the Commons in 1892, his unconventional attire (later
transmuted into the legend of the 'cloth cap'), his daring attacks on the
royal family, his truculent rejection of party alliances and affiliations—
all this prejudiced conservative minds against him from the start. For
much of the rest of his career he was a hated as well as a revered figure,
who was freely compared with 'wild animals' and other disagreeable
species. In Baron Corvo's work, *Hadrian VII*, Hardie appears, thinly-
disguised as Jerry Sant, a treacherous Aberdonian anarchist who
assassinates the Pope. Biography after biography, from William
Stewart's authorized book in 1921 to Emrys Hughes's attractive work

of filial piety in 1956 has added layers to the legend.[5] It seems now almost futile to protest that the real Hardie was infinitely more complex. The reality of Hardie as a pragmatic, calculating, sometimes self-contradictory politician, deeply immersed in late nineteenth-century radicalism, a product of the Progressive alliance, who at various times looked to John Morley or Lloyd George as leaders of a new broad-based popular front, the advocate of a wide-ranging 'labour alliance' of socialists and trade unionists rather than of a rigid doctrinaire sect—this reality seems lost in the swirling mists of legend perpetuated through the years by disciples and detractors alike. Hardie, it appears, has passed from history into pre-history.

Nevertheless, a rescue operation is far from impossible. Even though no major archive of Hardie letters has survived, substantial collections of his correspondence with individuals like Bruce Glasier and Ramsay MacDonald are accessible. So are the records of bodies like the Labour Representation Committee, the Second International and (to some extent) the Independent Labour Party. In addition Hardie gave of himself so freely in print, in the *Miner*, the *Labour Leader*, the Merthyr *Pioneer*, and countless other newspapers, tracts and pamphlets, that there is no dearth of hard evidence for his political outlook and methods. The reinterpretation of his career in historical terms need not be an unduly detached one. His early years in particular will always retain their heroic and moving quality, as a saga of how a poor working-class boy could survive to remould the political world around him. Hardie's achievement remains immense. He is amongst the handful of figures in British history to have forged a new national party, with an abiding mass appeal. Further, he combined practical achievement with a power of prophetic insight and imagination unique in his own time. No historical treatment of his career is adequate unless it ranges beyond the hothouse world of the academic seminar or the research institute and takes account of the emotional core of Hardie's life. He had a rare capacity to inspire devotion from humbler supporters, to an extent that the researcher can easily forget when Hardie's disagreeable disputes with prominent colleagues such as MacDonald, Glasier and Snowden are laid bare. Hardie brings the historian close to the enduring base of the Labour Party whose architect he largely was. At the same time his career was so kaleidoscopic, so unpredictable, so different from the rigid, uncompromising saint of legend, that it illustrates, too, many of the more ambiguous and erratic features of that party. He takes us close to its abiding weaknesses as well as its enduring strengths. A study of Keir Hardie must be more than a biography of a highly individual offspring of late nineteenth-century *fin-de-siècle* radical-socialism. It serves to illustrate the paradoxes and ironies of that protean creed. It helps to show both how the Labour Party emerged as a party of protest and how it has too often failed as a party of power.

The early life of Keir Hardie has been retailed often enough by chroniclers of the British labour movement. He himself seems to have drafted fragments of an autobiography: several versions of his childhood were set down in his journalistic writings from the *Ardrossan and Saltcoats Herald* in 1882 down to the Merthyr *Pioneer* in 1914. Some of the details of these early years changed subtly with each account and the overlay of sentimental nostalgia is immense, but the broad outlines are clear enough. Hardie was born on 15 August 1856, in a one-room house at Legbrannock near Holytown in Lanarkshire, in the western Scottish coalfield. He was to be the eldest of seven sons and two daughters. His mother was Mary Keir (or Kerr), a devout farm servant of remarkable strength of character, to whose memory Hardie was always devoted. The father is uncertain. A collier, William Aitken, was declared to be the father in the local register in March 1857. However, a manuscript account written years later by Allan A. Durward, a socialist from Aberdeen, claimed that Aitken had been bribed by a local doctor to claim paternity.[6] At all events, Hardie (like Ramsay MacDonald) was an illegitimate child; at some later stage he discovered this and divulged the fact to Sylvia Pankhurst.[7] In 1859 his mother married David Hardie, a ship's carpenter who had in turn been a sailor and a miner. Their boy was known as James Keir Hardie henceforth. David Hardie, tough and hard-working as he could be, was not a wholly satisfactory father. He drank freely in his earlier years and was said to have taunted his wife about the 'bastard' she had begotten. A major legacy of these years was Hardie's detestation of liquor as a factor making for social disruption and domestic poverty. It was the temperance movement that helped to steer him in his early twenties from the stern agnosticism, in which his parents reared him, into extreme evangelicalism.

By any standards Hardie's early years were scarred by poverty and distress. He once wrote of himself: 'I am of the unfortunate class who never knew what it was to be a child – in spirit, I mean. Even the memories of boyhood and young manhood are gloomy.'[8] As the Hardie family expanded, young James became the major breadwinner at a tender age. He began work early in 1865, at the age of eight years and nine months and went through a series of bleak and unrewarding employments. He was employed variously in a printing office, in the brass-finishing shop of the Anchor Shipping Line, as a rivet heater in a boatyard. At the end of 1866 there took place an incident to which Hardie frequently reverted in his later writings. At the time, his father was again out of work, owing to a lock-out in the Clyde shipbuilding yards, and strike benefits had been reduced to 2s a week. Hardie at the time was employed by a baker in central Glasgow. He earned 3s 6d each week for a day of twelve and a half hours, from 7.0 am to 7.30 pm. At the time, his younger brother was suffering from a fever which eventually proved fatal. Hardie arrived fifteen minutes late for work, two days running. His later description of events lacked nothing in pathos: 'Round a great mahogany table sat the members of the family, with the father at the top. In front, there was a very wonderful-looking coffee boiler, in the great glass bowl of which the coffee was bubbling. The table was loaded with dainties.'[9] In an amiable tone of voice, his employer told the young Hardie that he was dismissed. That night a baby was born to the Hardie household, deprived as they were of fuel and food. The year 1867 came, with the family on the brink of destitution. There seems no reason to doubt that such an incident occurred or that it deeply affected his youthful revulsion against injustice and persecution. The fact that this unknown employer was an active churchgoer no doubt added something to Hardie's distinction between institutional Christianity, which was organized hypocrisy, and 'real religion' which emanated from the heart of the people. Most important of all, perhaps, incidents such as this served to give a highly personal flavour of persecution to Hardie's social and political outlook, to kindle the belief that in a very special sense he was an outcast and an outsider, destined to plough his furrow alone.

Early in 1867 the Hardie family left Glasgow and moved to Newarthill, a depressed mining area in eastern Lanarkshire. At the age of ten, Hardie went down the pit, the No. 18 at Newarthill. Soon

after, they moved to Quarter, near Hamilton. Here, as a miner in the
No. 4 pit at Quarter, Hardie was to grow to manhood. He was to
remain a working collier until he was twenty-three. This was, without
doubt, a formative period. His dawning awareness of the reality of
community and of class, of the struggle and hardships of working-class
life, was essentially a product of his years at the coal-face. The
working-class world that he knew, in Quarter and later in Merthyr,
was a miners' world, with its private, close-knit loyalties. It was the
miners' cause that led him into trade union activity, into the movement
for an eight-hour day, and ultimately into a kind of socialism. He began
work as a 'trapper' at a wage of one shilling a day, with the responsibility of tending the trap that ventilated the mine. 'Trapper' was his
soubriquet in the press later on. Here, as he frequently and eloquently
recalled in later years, he experienced all the terrors of life underground, the rockfalls and explosions that killed without warning.[10] On
one occasion a boy working with him was killed, leaving Hardie,
terrified, alone in the darkness. Miners' lives were cheap in the
western Scottish coalfield and safety provisions scandalously negligent.
Hardie, like his comrades, was especially moved by the catastrophe at
the Blantyre pit on 22 October 1877, which cost the lives of over two
hundred miners. His subsequent columns in the Scottish press often
contained cogent and well-documented discussions of pit safety precautions and the inadequacies of inspection procedures. He showed
that the callous indifference of the mineowners was a root cause of
these repeated disasters. At the same time, he acknowledged that the
inadequate education of the colliers in elementary safety procedures
and their reluctance to turn informers, when confronted by the human
errors of their fellow workmen, played their part also. Self-help, he
concluded, was as important as safety legislation. In this primitive
almost pre-industrial world, scarred by human suffering, with mineowners and ironmasters fiercely resistant to trade unions being formed
amongst their men and all too prone to bring in blackleg labour,
frequently Irish, Hardie grew into his early twenties, apparently
destined for the conventional, unremarkable career of a poor Scottish
miner.

Even at this early stage, however, there were indications that he
was far from being the typical working man. He was never submissive,
always proudly ambitious. He had a powerful urge for self-improvement

and self-education unusual even amongst Scottish miners at the time. He attended night school at Fraser's school, Holytown, where he learnt the rudiments of grammar and syntax. He acquired the passion, though not yet the discipline, for wide reading. By the early 1880s he noted in his diary that he had made some acquaintance with Latin and French also. 'Of Arithmetic I know next to nothing.'[11] In the darkness of the mine, he learnt Pitman's shorthand, picking out the characters on a blackened slate with the wire used by miners to adjust the wicks of their lamps.[12] Hardie himself left many accounts of the books that fired his youthful imagination: they largely follow the same lines.[13] Literary and historical themes attracted him most. Books on political and economic questions played by contrast almost no part in his early education. The writings of Marx, indeed of any socialist, were unknown to him at this stage. As Hardie repeatedly claimed, it was the folk poetry of Burns to which he often turned; its simple message of human comradeship and equality was easily adapted to the world he knew. He read widely in Scottish history and fable. Wilson's *Tales of the Borders*, the Wallace uprising of 1297–8, the ballad of Chevy Chase, all stimulated his enthusiasm for the Scottish patriotic cause and for home rule; in Scotland, as in Wales, nationalism and democracy went hand in hand. He read avidly, too, the biographies of eminent men: that of President Garfield of the USA (assassinated after a brief presidency in 1881, when Hardie was twenty-five) served as a moral precept for hard work and integrity finding their own reward. Of all these early books, however, perhaps two above all stand out in their influence on Hardie's later rhetoric and writings. Carlyle's *Sartor Resartus*, through the musings of the whimsical Professor Teufelsdröchk (Devilsdung), described vividly the division of society into 'Dandies and Drudges' and the apocalyptic revolution that would result. Its mystical evocation of the regeneration of man was a theme to fire the imagination of the young Hardie, as it did that of another unknown Celtic rebel, David Lloyd George, at much the same time. Finally, Ruskin's essays entitled *Unto This Last*, with their passionate critique of self-interest and of the values of commercial society, provided something of the moral framework for Hardie's shadowy political philosophy. For Hardie, as for Ruskin, the quality of living was to be the ultimate touchstone for any creed and any society: 'there is no wealth but life'.

The other aspect of Hardie's early years which marked him out, to
some extent, as a man apart, was his sudden embrace of the twin
causes of evangelical Christianity and of temperance. Brought up by
his parents in a sternly rational creed of agnosticism, Hardie became
converted to Christianity in 1877. As a result he joined the Evangelical
Union, an offshoot of the United Secession Church, which had been
founded by the Reverend James Morison in 1841 and was popularly
known as the 'Morisonians'.[14] This church in vital respects reflected
and reinforced the outlook of the young Hardie. Certainly Morison
himself was no socialist. He once declined to put up Robert Owen at
his manse in Kilmarnock, on the grounds that since he could do
nothing for Owen's soul he did not see why he should accommodate
his body. Still, Morison's theology carried some politically radical implications. It was universalist in creed: Morison argued that Christ's
atonement was for all mankind since Christ had died for the whole of
humanity, not just for a small 'elect', as strict Calvinists believed. The
Morisonians thus broke entirely with the predestinarian creed of the
established Presbyterian Kirk and of the Secessionists as well, since the
latter insisted that grace was withheld from most of the human race.
Further, the Evangelical Union was intensely democratic in ethos. It
claimed that salvation was the gift of every man. It made, therefore, a
ready appeal to working-class adherents, particularly in the west of
Scotland, repelled by the bourgeois character of the established Kirk.
Finally, the Morisonians were remarkably flexible in their tenets and
in the forms of ecclesiastical organization. They existed 'not so much
to construct a theology as to win souls', wrote Morison;[15] it could have
been Keir Hardie addressing a Labour Party rally. The Evangelical
Union was a religious version of Hardie's 'labour alliance', including
as it did a wide range of Congregationalists and Presbyterians in
association against the doctrinaire rigidity of the Calvinistic orthodoxy.
In the event, many of the Morisonians merged with the Congregational
Union in 1896, shortly after their founder's death. Hardie himself was
to join the local Congregational Church in Cumnock when he moved
from Lanarkshire to Ayrshire in 1881. Here he did battle on behalf
of the minister, the Reverend Andrew Noble Scott, who fell foul of
the local deacons as a result of his intense evangelicalism. Scott was
dismissed and Hardie promptly resigned in sympathy with him, early
in 1884. He was never a regular churchgoer again.

Even so, he continued to regard himself as a Christian, however hard to locate in a specific denomination. He took the opportunity in 1892 to attend the Congregational Union of England and Wales, with dramatic impact at their conference at Bradford.[16] His conversion to Christianity, in revulsion against the severe agnosticism of his youth, was evidently a decisive experience in his early years, one that deeply influenced his mind thereafter. In personal behaviour, it left a legacy of intense puritanism, later reflected in his scorn for the Court and for polite society. He applauded measures to restrict dancing at public houses: 'immorality is apt to be great on such occasions'.[17] At the same time, he rebelled against the intolerant fanaticism of the dogmatists, whether the official Calvinist establishment or the deacons of Cumnock. Later on, the Marxists of the Social Democratic Federation seemed to Hardie to exhibit many of the same narrow qualities. Above all, Hardie's conversion to Christianity emphasized for him the supreme need for personal salvation. Theology was unimportant: 'other things will follow in good time'. His Christianity was highly flexible, a religion of humanity with little doctrinal content, utopian, romantic, outward-looking, democratic and egalitarian. Its ultimate justification lay in the vision of the true believer and in the priesthood of all man-kind, pledged to the coming of 'the Christ that is to be'. On such a basis, rather than on hard-headed economic analysis, was Hardie's socialism to be founded.

Hardie's faith, however, was always intimately related to character, conduct and good works. Grace for the believer was always con-ditional; it could be lost through anti-social or selfish behaviour. With his experience of his father it was a natural transition for Hardie to transfer his new-found spiritual zeal into the cause of temperance, a theme dear to the heart of Morison himself. Hardie had joined the Good Templars in 1873 at the age of seventeen. For the next few years, at least until 1884, Hardie's public activity was strongly geared towards the temperance movement. He was a leading lecturer and organizer for the Good Templars and in 1883 became District Deputy for the movement in Ayrshire.[18] To him, the evil of drink was all-pervasive. It was the root cause of human weakness, of poverty and social degradation. His advice to miners, anxious for self-improvement, was to 'drink less, read more and think more'.[19] He dismissed the social critique of thinkers such as Henry George, the advocate of a single tax

on land. This programme was useless 'as long as the traffic in intoxi-
cating drink is allowed to remain'.[20] It was hardly surprising that
Hardie was never able to strike up a satisfactory relationship later on
with an earthy humanist like Robert Blatchford. By the early 1880s,
then, Hardie's personal philosophy had apparently been shaped. He
was, it appeared, the very prototype of the Victorian virtues of the
aspiring artisan. Self-educated, self-improved, fired with missionary
zeal to redeem humanity in the light of his own blinding experience of
salvation, he was the symbol of self-help rather than of social re-
organization. He epitomized the 'labour aristocrat' as delineated by
Marx. No-one, it seemed, could have been further in the early 1880s
than was Keir Hardie from an understanding of, or sympathy with,
the message of socialism.

This philosophy survived Hardie's first dramatic acquaintance with
the realities of industrial confrontation. In 1878 he had become
involved with trade unionism for the first time, when he became agent
in the Hamilton district of the Lanarkshire Miners' Union, newly
formed by Alexander McDonald. It was a period of severe depression
and of falling wages in the western Scottish coalfield. McDonald, the
very prototype of the Lib-Lab, urged his men that the only feasible
basis for a stable wage was to reduce output in the hope that a sliding
scale might be accepted, as it had been in South Wales in 1875.
Hardie, who at this time deeply admired McDonald (even comparing
him with Martin Luther), accepted this policy without demur. But in
the autumn of 1879 there came a sharp division between them. Faced
with widespread wage reductions, the Hamilton miners, led by Hardie,
rejected McDonald's advice and went on strike.[21] This stoppage was
followed by another, general throughout all the Lanarkshire pits,
which lasted for six weeks in August and September 1880. It became
hallowed in local legend as the 'tattie strike', as the miners managed to
eke out an existence by picking potatoes (or 'tatties') during the summer
days. The outcome was fore-ordained. The coalowners and ironmasters of Lanarkshire were far too powerful for the breakaway union
which Hardie helped to form. They were all too well equipped with
Irish and other blacklegs as strike-breakers. The 'tattie strike' collapsed
as it had always seemed certain to do. A later venture in the autumn
of 1881 in Ayrshire (with 'James Hardie, Hamilton' as secretary) was
also a total failure. The five thousand Ayrshire men, who demanded

a ten per cent wage increase, had to return to work after a ten weeks' stoppage. Hardie emerged from the fires with his early reputation as a labour organizer apparently in ruins. He was expelled from the Hamilton pits and had to move permanently from Lanarkshire to Ayrshire: 'we'll ha' no more damned Hardies in our pits'. More seriously, he had fallen out with McDonald, who had opposed the 'tattie strike' and with whom he had several angry exchanges in public. There was a fierce clash over the depletion of the union funds – conflicts over money matters were to dog Hardie throughout his career. The breach between the older and the younger miners' leaders was never completely healed, despite Hardie's later avowals to the contrary.[22] He left the pits at the age of twenty-six with a local reputation as a fiery and dogged protagonist of the miners' grievances, but a wider reputation as a somewhat impractical and hot-headed industrial rebel. His record during the 'tattie strike' and his public quarrel with McDonald continued to dog him, to his disadvantage, at least until the Mid-Lanark by-election in 1888. The first phase of Hardie's career, somewhat ignominiously, had ended. It was the end of his practical experience as a working man in the coal pits of Lanarkshire. In 1882 he left his cloth cap behind.

Hardie now faced a period of acute financial crisis. He was no longer a single man. In 1879 he had married Lillie Wilson, a dark-haired Lanarkshire girl he had met during work with the Good Templars. They now lived together in a two-roomed cottage in Cumnock, in Ayrshire. It cannot be said to have been an entirely fortunate marriage for either side. Mrs Hardie was patient, devoted, endlessly brave in the face of repeated personal crises and near-tragedies. She struggled to keep the Cumnock household going on a small financial allowance. Hardie paid her a deeply-felt tribute at the 'coming of age' ILP conference at Bradford in 1914. On the other hand, Mrs Hardie had little real understanding of her husband's political ambitions and played virtually no part in his career. Indeed, they preyed on her nerves. She was 'temperamentally unfitted for the storms and vicissitudes of her husband's public life', wrote Mrs Katherine Glasier.[23] It was usually poised middle-class women such as Mrs Pankhurst or Mrs Cobden Sanderson who were more often associated with Hardie in public after he entered parliament. Nor, one may surmise, was Mrs Hardie particularly satisfying to Hardie's highly-developed emotional needs.

Throughout his career, he had a series of usually innocent and brief affaires with young left-wing girls he encountered in the socialist movement, from the 1890s down to 1914. With Annie Hines of Oxford in 1893 and with Sylvia Pankhurst after 1910 his relations were the most passionate of all. Hardie was, without doubt, highly responsive to women: 'distant fields look greenest', he wrote enigmatically on meeting 'Mrs W.' in the Glasgow temperance movement in 1884.[24] One of the many sources of tension in his later career was that his marriage failed to satisfy him either physically or intellectually. Their family, however, had to be fed and cared for. Their first son, James (whose sad later career, marred by fecklessness and gambling debts, added a further dimension of sorrow to his father's life) was the eldest. There followed a daughter, Agnes ('Nan'), Hardie's most devoted helpmate in later life and, in some ways, his political heir. A second son, Duncan, was born in 1887: he was to die tragically in 1920, burnt to death in an accident at an electrical works. Somehow, Hardie, now an unemployed miner and widely suspect as an agitator, had to clothe and feed his family. He gained a little income for a time by keeping a small grocer's store at Cumnock. He also took on such part-time posts as that of a local agent for the City of London Fire Insurance company. His major lifeline, however, proved to be journalism. Entirely self-taught, he had made himself more than a competent writer. Earnestness and passion compensated for any lack of polish. He obtained a post at £1 a week as a reporter for the *Cumnock News*, a local Liberal newspaper. Then he found a more permanent assignment with the *Ardrossan and Saltcoats Herald*, a weekly. From April 1882 to December 1887 he contributed a regular column, usually headed 'Black Diamonds or Mining Notes worth Minding'. His pseudonym was 'Trapper' which recalled his early boyhood ventures down the mine; many of his contributions were heavily autobiographical. For the next few years, as he passed relatively placidly through his late twenties, he had a regular means of subsistence through the grace of a sympathetic and tolerant editor. It was also at this time that his political and social outlook took on a more permanent shape.

It is clear from Hardie's voluminous writings in the press in the years up to 1886 that his outlook was not fundamentally altered by his experiences during the miners' strikes of 1879–81. He entered and left the industrial struggles of these years as the apostle of self-help and the other imperatives of the Lib-Lab creed. He drafted the rules of the Ayrshire Miners' Association in March 1881 in strictly class collaborationist terms.[25] He rebutted the view that the organization of a trade union implied a state of industrial conflict. On the contrary, he looked forward to a time 'when the war hatchet will be buried for ever, and when Capital and Labour shall meet together under a roof tree, to smoke the pipe of peace, and as the smoke slowly ascends it shall carry with it into oblivion all the feelings of discord that ever existed between those twin brothers whose best interests are inseparable'. The Miners' Association did put forward a series of interventionist demands for state action, notably the eight-hour day for miners. But it assumed also that the regulation of wages could be accomplished through 'some amicable and equitable arrangements' with the employers. Samuel Smiles could not have asked for more.

Hardie continued in this vein for many years more. At least down to mid-1886 his newspaper columns and speeches were a hymn to self-improvement and moral reform. He wrote pungently, and with acute personal knowledge, of the realities of distress in the Scottish coalfields. But he urged that 'the temperance and the co-operative movements are destined to be the forces which will eventually elevate the working classes of this country into a position of high social comfort and independence'.[26] While he was unsparing in his attacks on individual employers who neglected safety precautions in the pits, he was effusive in his praise of coalowners such as Galloway of Trabboch who improved working conditions and provided decent holidays. At the dawn of 1883 he reflected cheerfully that 'a better time seems to be setting in when employers and employed will recognize that their interests are identical'.[27] He remained generally optimistic in his diagnosis of the economic prospects for the coal industry. The trade depression he attributed to over-speculation or, alternatively, to under-consumption, the fashionable radical nostrum of the time which he had picked up in his reading. Throughout 1883 and 1884 he constantly urged the miners to adhere to the restriction of output as the means of securing a stable level of wages; he deplored the failure of other Lanarkshire miners to support the Larkhall men in this policy. By the summer of 1885, a sharper note appeared in his columns. He was now a fierce critic of the 'conscienceless iron companies' who imposed wage reductions and laid off miners. He commented ironically in August

1885 that a kindly action by a mineowner was now sufficiently unusual to merit comment.[28] Even so, there can be no doubt that even in the early months of 1886, Hardie was still convinced that social progress was perfectly possible within the existing capitalist framework, and that, given temperance, discipline and dedication by the working men a new and hopeful era could be brought about, even in the depressing poverty of the western Scottish coalfield.

Hardie was in no sense drawn to socialism in these first thirty years of his life. He read, with mild interest and little sympathy, of the lecture tours in Scotland of the land reformer, Henry George, the advocate of the single tax on land. Hardie later claimed that George's *Progress and Poverty* 'unlocked many of the industrial and economic difficulties' of the nation for him, but nothing in Hardie's later career gives this view any substance.[29] Nor did Hardie play any part in the early ventures in Scotland of young apostles of the Social Democratic Federation, such as J. Bruce Glasier. Hardie did meet James Patrick, an SDF evangelist, at Cumnock in 1885, without being drawn towards his creed. He also began to read *Justice*, the journal of the SDF launched by H.M. Hyndman in 1884. *Justice* added to Hardie's rhetoric a few derivative phrases about labour being the sole creator of wealth (in no sense a distinctively socialist belief). But his intellectual horizon was still firmly bounded by ideas that had dominated his mind since the late 1870s – temperance, self-improvement, moral regeneration of the individual. His public activity was still partly channelled into the total abstinence movement. He regarded modest social improvement as the antidote to extremist agitators propounding 'crude ideas'.[30] He also had some inclination for political activity, but was pessimistic of his ability to fulfil it. 'I belong to that class of men who do not and cannot push themselves forward, nor seek for favour by currying', he wrote in his diary.[31] He became known as a speaker in the Cumnock Junior Liberal Association from 1884 onwards, and frequently spoke on Liberal platforms. In the general elections of November 1885 and July 1886 he took a vehement line in his newspaper columns on behalf of radical Liberal candidates like Eugene Wason in South Ayrshire. He urged the miners to endorse the Liberal Party after its support for such measures of reform as the Mines and Employers' Liability Acts.[32] Indeed the Liberal Party as a whole seemed to Hardie to be moving in the right direction in the earlier

1880s – increasingly radical, increasingly responsive to its popular mass support in working-class areas and in the Celtic countries. In Scotland, particularly, the cry for land reform was uniting the rural radicalism of the crofting areas of the highlands, still oppressed by the 'clearances', with urban dissenters in Glasgow and the west of Scotland. Hardie warmly welcomed the schism of the Whigs from Gladstone's Liberal Party during the Irish home rule crisis of May–June 1886. It would make the Gladstonians all the more faithful mirrors of the mass democracy of self-respecting, self-improving, working-class electors.

In the late summer of 1886 Hardie's career underwent a change. All students and biographers of Hardie agree that this period, and the winter of 1886–7, form a watershed in his emergence as a political and industrial leader. What is much more open to dispute is how fundamental a breach this implied from his previous position as a Gladstonian Lib-Lab of a remarkably orthodox kind. In circumstances which remain hard to determine, Hardie re-emerged as a leader of organized labour in August 1886. He gave up his assignment with the *Cumnock News*, and accepted the secretaryship of the newly-formed Ayrshire Miners Union at a salary of £75 a year. Its programme, as drafted by Hardie, followed largely traditional lines – the enforcement of all laws relating to the mining industry, a sliding scale for wages, a court of arbitration to settle labour disputes and the agreed regulation of output according to the requirements of the market.[33] These were familiar enough demands, although the inclusion of the more basic issue of an eight-hour day underground was a notable extension of them. Further, the preamble of the new union's objectives, drafted by Hardie in October 1886, contained a striking set passage on labour as the sole creator of wealth. Its tone suggests a sharpening of Hardie's philosophy. 'Those who own land and capital are the masters of those who toil. Thus Capital, which ought to be the servant of Labour and which is created by Labour, has become the master of its creator.' It was the declared aim of a disciplined and organized trade union to restore the natural order of things. He was soon caught up in a fierce struggle to build up the Ayrshire Miners' Union and to promote his favoured scheme for the restriction of output on a voluntary basis. Elsewhere in Scotland the miners were taking up a more militant policy. Miners' unions in Lanarkshire, Ayrshire, Fifeshire and the

Forth and Clyde valleys sought to create a combined Scottish union to promote a co-ordinated approach. A new Scottish Miners' National Federation was set up in October, with Hardie again as its secretary: the eight-hours bill was its central objective. It boasted a membership of twenty-five thousand.

At this time moreover, Hardie began to form contacts with other militant miners' leaders, most of them also young men, some far to the left of himself. He struck up an alliance with William Small, the general secretary of the Lanarkshire miners since 1882 and a forceful propagandist of the socialist cause.[34] It may have been through Small that Hardie was briefly introduced to Friedrich Engels in 1887, although neither was over-impressed by the encounter. Hardie also formed the beginning of a life-long association with Robert Smillie, another young and aggressive Lanarkshire miners' leader, born in Belfast in 1857, with whom Hardie had been associated during the 1880 'tattie strike' and also on the cricket field.[35] Another colleague at this time was R. Chisholm Robertson, the highly controversial miners' leader from Stirling and a fierce hammer of the Lib-Labs, with whom Hardie's relations were to go through many vicissitudes. Yet another ally, but one with a very different outlook, was John Weir, the thirty-four-year old secretary of the Fifeshire and Kinross miners. Weir was a dedicated 'Lib-Lab' who often clashed fiercely with Chisholm Robertson. On the other hand, the Fifeshire men, who worked in a coalfield where much coal went for export, were the most powerful element in Scottish mining trade unionism; back in 1870 they had become the first miners' union in Europe to win the eight-hour day, a short-lived but significant triumph. Weir's views were thus listened to with respect. Scotland had long been a weak link in the trade union movement, particularly among the miners. Only about two thousand Scottish miners were members of unions at the start of 1884. Now something of a generational change was occurring. Hardie tirelessly propagated the Scottish miners' unions' demands, in the *Ardrossan and Saltcoats Herald*, and in missionary campaigns throughout western Scotland. In particular, he pressed for the adoption of the programme of the Scottish Miners' Federation, drafted at Glasgow in November 1886 by a committee which included Hardie, Small, Smillie and Chisholm Robertson. An eight-hour bill and a uniform policy of output restriction throughout the Scottish coalfield were fiercely proclaimed and an end demanded to the unplanned anarchy of *laissez-faire*.

Even at this stage, however, Hardie remained within the Liberal fold, perhaps a trifle uncomfortably. He cited John Stuart Mill and other Liberal authorities as sources to justify the growth of trade unionism. He remained optimistic about the industrial and commercial outlook: it was very possible that capitalism might reform itself. 'The good days are upon us, men, be faithful and prosperity is assured', he wrote in October 1886.[36] He was still an admirer, though with growing qualifications, of national 'Lib-Lab' miners' leaders like Burt, Pickard and 'Mabon'. Hardie himself was no more than an advanced radical, anxious to persuade local Liberal Associations to adopt more working men as candidates. It was known throughout early 1887 that he was actively seeking the Liberal nomination for North Ayrshire. In January of that year he had founded a new monthly journal, *The Miner: a Journal for Underground Workers*.[37] It was a caustic and belligerent advocate of mining trade unionism and of the programme of the Scottish Miners' Federation. Even so, its demands were at first entirely compatible with evolutionary advanced radicalism, as espoused by the Gladstonian Liberals since the Irish home rule schism in 1886. Indeed the first issue of *The Miner* contained a welcoming article by Thomas Burt MP on the entirely reassuring theme of 'Self-Help'.

It was not a commitment to doctrine, but rather a response to a changing industrial situation, especially to the employers' savage reaction to the Miners' Federation, that drove Hardie away from Lib-Lab orthodoxy and into a political no-man's-land that he was to occupy uneasily for at least the next five years. The coalowners, and even more the ironmasters, of Lanarkshire, were quick to respond to strike action by the Lanarkshire miners with a naked show of force. Blacklegs were despatched into the coalfield from Glasgow – an inevitable provocation. At Blantyre on 7–8 February 1887, there were bloody clashes between strikers and the police and widespread rioting.[38] Hussars were sent into the coalfield from Glasgow to preserve order. Despite assistance from Weir's Fifeshire miners, the Lanarkshire men were forced back to work on terms of total surrender. Hardie's dreams of industrial conciliation had been totally shattered, although he urged the Ayrshire miners to press on with their own demands for an eight-hour day and five-day week. In a leader in *The Miner* in May 1887, he admitted that social change now required a far more sweeping impetus than would be provided by such palliatives as temperance reform. 'The capitalist has done good service in the past by developing trade and commerce. His day is nearly past.'[39] But Hardie remained an optimist. A national system of work, an eight-hour day, total reform of the land system would 'transform this land of ours into a paradise for the toiling millions'. The first echoes of the transition from *fin-de-siècle* radicalism towards social democracy are clearly to be heard.

Hardie was grievously disappointed at the failure of the Scottish Miners to co-ordinate their policy in an effective manner. Individual unions and coalfields continued to pursue their own parochial demands. Hardie was even more despairing at the failure of miners elsewhere in Britain to provide assistance for their Scottish comrades. A national miners' conference at Birmingham in January 1887 showed the Scottish delegates, Hardie, Weir and Robertson, how isolated they were in their demands for a restriction of output. The militant collectivism advocated by the Scots was rejected outright and the Scots concluded that they must fight their own battles henceforth.[40] *The Miner* now became increasingly severe in its comments on Burt, Pickard, Mabon, and other national miners' spokesmen, all Liberals to a man. The 'good fellowship' which Hardie had noted as prevailing as late as the miners' conference in December 1886, was evaporating fast. New generational and sectional rifts were opening up within the mining unions across the nation.

Throughout the year 1887 the dismal consequences of industrial defeat unfolded for the Lanarkshire and Ayrshire men. By the late summer the Scottish Miners' Federation itself was largely in ruins. Scottish mining unionism generally was as fragmented and disorganized as ever. Even so, the crisis in the Scottish coalfield had made Hardie, at the age of thirty, a labour leader known throughout Scotland for the first time. Now he was about to emerge on the wider British industrial scene. He had visited London for the first time early in 1887 and led his companions, Robertson and Smillie, hopelessly astray on a sightseeing tour by bus. 'Experience will prove the best teacher,' Hardie laconically observed.[41] Later in the year, he was sent to the twentieth annual Trades Union Congress, held at Swansea in September. He was representing here the Ayrshire Miners' Union, one of the smallest of the affiliated bodies with 1,600 members. Here his resentment at betrayal of the Ayrshire and Lanarkshire men by their fellow miners at the TUC, and by the Liberals in parliament, boiled over in dramatic fashion.[42] Many events had conspired to push Hardie over the brink. Poverty and distress in the western Scottish coalfields were increasingly severe. An already inflamed situation was made worse by yet another appalling mining tragedy, this time at Udston colliery in Lanarkshire. Here again, the neglect of elementary safety and inspection procedures by the mineowners was the clear root cause of the disaster. Hardie had hurled himself into full-time organizing work for the unions for many months past and the strain was beginning to tell. Already he looked older than his thirty years. He was often away from home for long periods on lengthy rail journeys to London, Birmingham and elsewhere, fitting in his journalistic commitments as best he could. He told his readers in the *Ardrossan Herald* in June 1887 that he had enjoyed a mere six hours of sleep that week. Already his stocky figure, broad head, luxurious beard, emphatic gestures and earnest Lowlands accent were symbols of industrial protest throughout Scotland. At the Swansea TUC they first became familiar to a wider public. Hardie chose to train his fire on Henry Broadhurst, the secretary of the Parliamentary Committee of the TUC, the very model of conformism, class collaboration and the Liberal alliance. On several issues the little-known Hardie and the domineering Broadhurst clashed violently. Hardie, supported by some other Scottish delegates, tried to move a motion which condemned Broadhurst's opposition to a miners' eight-hours bill; but only fifteen voted for it, with eighty in opposition. Hardie also tried in vain to add some amendments to the draft for an employers' liability bill. Most significantly, he moved a motion on behalf of greater working-class representation in parliament, with a new 'labour party' to push it forward. There was implied condemnation of the parliamentary representatives that the workers already had. To Broadhurst, the most devoted of Gladstonians, this was anathema, and his fury erupted. 'These intolerable, un-English and lecturing attacks by Mr Hardie were a new feature of the Congress. He was surprised at a man coming here for the first time and showing such bad taste (hear, hear).' The Tory press would, he claimed, exploit Hardie's speech: he flayed 'the high priest and prophet

from Ayrshire' with bitter rhetoric. At the Swansea congress, inevitably, Hardie's attacks were brushed aside, while their *ad hominem*
flavour alienated delegates and diminished their appeal. Even so, there
was a new atmosphere apparent at the Swansea TUC in 1887. In the
next four years, Hardie's initiative was to help lead to a major transformation in the policy and outlook of the British trade union movement. Two years before the London dock strike, which captured the
headlines in 1889, the 'new unionism' was in the making.

By the end of 1887, Hardie was apparently inexorably set on a course
of industrial militancy. He was inexhaustible in his activity in the press
and on the platform on behalf of the Ayrshire miners and in pressing
for an agreed wages and output policy. He upheld a wide range of collectivist reforms, including an eight-hour day, an amended Employers'
Liability Act, the establishment of a national superannuation and
insurance fund and even perhaps the nationalization of mining
royalties and the railways. At the end of December 1887 he bade fare-
well to the readers of the *Ardrossan and Saltcoats Herald*, where his
fierce diatribes of late had been at variance with editorial policy, for
all the known tolerance of that journal. In a speech at Irvine, in 'a
torrent of eloquence' as the press recorded, he defended his attacks on
Broadhurst at Swansea. Hardie claimed that the Liberal alliance was
becoming outdated; indeed, the two parties were largely indistinguishable in their attitude to labour. 'A party pledged to the interests of
labour alone' was the best available instrument of social advance.[43] As
for Broadhurst, his association with capitalist employers like Brunner
and Mond, in whose firm he was a small share-holder, belied his
claim to represent the ranks of labour, the sole creators of wealth.
Hardie was never one to spurn populist-type assaults on 'the money
power' or to fail to point out that capitalism, like charity, began at
home.

Even so, it would be a major error to see Hardie's outlook as totally
transformed as a result of the events of 1887.[44] Despite his call for a
new 'party' to promote the cause of labour, he still felt himself to be
within the Liberal tabernacle. It was a Labour pressure-group, not an
independent party, for which he was contending. He sang the praises
of Gladstone in May 1887 – 'God bless him! May he be spared to
accomplish the great work to which he has put his hand.'[45] In the
Miner in October, he extolled the labours of Stephen Mason, the

Liberal member for Mid-Lanark, on behalf of the Scottish miners. Mason, Hardie claimed, would become Chancellor of the Exchequer when Scotland gained a parliament of her own. Hardie's Liberal credentials, then, remained largely intact. Far from having accepted an overtly socialistic position, he still believed that, with compromise and good sense, backed up by relentless pressure from the unions, reform was possible even within the harsh system of industrial relations that prevailed in the Scottish coalfields. He attacked those coalowners who introduced Polish blackleg labour: 'conduct like this is playing directly into the hands of the Socialists and the extreme men generally.' The *Miner* at the end of 1887 was still proclaiming the political economy familiar to advanced radicals for over a decade. Overproduction was the root cause of low wages and the stagnation of the market. Purchasing power must be restored to stimulate consumption. The essential means to this was the restriction of exports and a growing dependence on the home market.[46] The species of collectivism that Hardie espoused was entirely compatible with the principles of advanced Scottish Liberals such as Eugene Wason and Stephen Mason, and of enlightened Conservatives such as Lord Randolph Churchill. The one pre-condition was for the miners to unite. The political programme advanced in the *Miner* in July 1887 contained sixteen items.[47] Most of them were agreed Liberal policy – adult suffrage, triennial parliaments, graduated income tax, free education and the like. Industrial items such as the eight-hour day were already advocated by many Liberals of moderate views, quite apart from maverick freelances like R.B. Cunninghame-Graham and Dr G.B. Clark. Even now, Hardie retained contact with his early years of struggle and self-improvement in the 1870s. Sobriety, self-education and education were the keys to progress. Unionization meant in essence the combining by workers who exemplified these qualities and who pooled them in a common cause.

Hardie, while something of a collectivist, was far from being a thoroughgoing socialist. Marxism was still virtually unknown to him. He had no vision of industrial society beyond the limited world of the Scottish miners. It was noticeable that at Swansea he concentrated on mining issues solely; he did not proclaim the eight-hour principle more generally. He still retained that distrust of socio-economic doctrine which marked his entire career. Socialists were acceptable allies, but they needed the practicality and experience of real working men to make their dogmas relevant and not mere philosophical abstractions. Hardie remained a gradualist, despite his readings of Carlyle. He retained most of the assumptions of a self-improving labour aristocrat throughout his life. 'It is the intelligent well-off artisan in Great Britain who responds to the Socialist appeal, and it is the slum vote which the Socialist candidate fears most', he was to write in 1907.[48] Class discipline, not the class war, was his objective. The indiscriminate use of strikes as a weapon should be avoided. Hardie's turning to political and industrial agitation in 1887 did not, then, lead to a total transformation of his philosophy. His continuing involvement with such movements as the Good Templars was testimony to this. There was no Damascus-like conversion in the summer of 1887 to doctrines of class conflict and of total social change. Still less is it true that Hardie henceforth was to be a consistent, if covert, Marxist. It was the religious conversion of 1878 rather than the industrial conversion of 1887 that remained the dominant experience of his life to date. On the eve of his entry into national political prominence at Mid-Lanark it was self-reliance rather than socialism that drove Hardie on, and made him the dominant agitator and prophet for his class. As for Carlyle in *Sartor Resartus*, which had fired his youthful imagination, it was personal regeneration that would herald the dawning of that social progress that Hardie sensed would surely arise for the folk whence he had sprung.

II Mid-Lanark and After (1888–90)

For years past, Hardie had been fascinated by politics. Now into his early thirties, he sought an outlet for his talents and energies more satisfying than Scottish trade union organization, or part-time journalism. He had been active in the Liberal cause in Ayrshire constituencies since at least 1883. His columns in the local press kept him well in the public eye. The transformation of the Liberal Party in Scotland, after the crofters' disturbances and the schism over Irish home rule, with the new opportunities apparently opening up for working-class candidates, sharpened his appetite for a parliamentary career. In early 1887 it was made known that Hardie was being canvassed as Liberal candidate for North Ayrshire. His main sponsor was R.B. Cunninghame Graham, a flamboyant radical MP who had seen active service on the Argentine pampas. Graham eloquently told a miners' demonstration at Kirkintilloch that 'Mr Hardie was not going to stand as a Liberal, a Conservative or a Unionist. He was going forward as a representative of working men, as a working man who had worked in the pit, who had starved and sweated.' Chisholm Robertson added the further endorsement that in the past twelve years no man had suffered more acutely in the miners' cause than had Hardie.[1] Even so, there was scant prospect of the North Ayrshire Liberals adopting so radical a candidate, and in November the Whiggish barrister, Sir William Wedderburn, was selected instead.[2] Hardie's record of persistent and dispiriting failure seemed amply confirmed.

In reality, the prospects for independent working-class intervention in politics were brighter than for many years past. This was in large measure the result of the enterprise of H.H. Champion, an eccentric Tory socialist invalided out from the Indian army, who had been an active propagandist for the Social Democratic Federation since 1884.[3] Champion's aim was the destruction of the Liberal coalition. His violently fluctuating relations with Hardie between 1888 and 1895 played a considerable, though now largely forgotten, role in determining the pattern of working-class politics. Their tensions and quarrels were faithfully recorded in Corvo's *Hadrian the Seventh*, where Jerry Sant's assassination of the Pope mirrors Hardie's character assassination of Champion, as Corvo, himself briefly active amongst the Aberdeen socialists, regarded it.[4] Champion had revitalized the Labour Electoral Association set up by the TUC in 1886 to promote working-class candidatures, and had given it a much more aggressive strategy. Known socialists like Tom Mann were enlisted to promote the cause of the LEA. The Association made it known that it would run independent working-class candidates if the other parties did not provide satisfactory guarantees for their attitude towards labour questions. Such a candidate was run at Dulwich in December 1887. At Deptford in January, Champion's own candidature was forestalled only by a vague conciliatory statement about the desirability of working men as candidates by Arnold Morley, the Liberal Chief Whip.[5] A more hopeful omen still appeared in West Glamorgan, or Gower, in March 1888, when David Randell, a candidate sponsored by local miners and tinplate workers, captured the nomination from a Whiggish barrister from London.[6] The fact that Randell soon proved to be the most loyal adherent of Welsh Liberalism in its more nationalistic vein did not diminish the hopes of Champion and the LEA that the Gower constituency was a portent that the local caucus could be defeated, and that working-class candidatures were now possible.

Scotland, with its increasingly clear evidence of class tension, in mining areas and the crofting districts alike, had long been viewed by Champion as favourable territory for a confrontation with the Liberals. So it was that the LEA came into contact with Hardie, with fateful results for his subsequent career. It was well-known that he was looking out for a constituency; in March 1888 he found one. Stephen Mason, the popular left-wing Liberal who sat for Mid-Lanark, announced his retirement on grounds of ill-health. At once, Hardie's name was pushed forward by his mining supporters in such areas as Larkhall.[7] Hardie himself, more cautiously, advanced his cause in the columns of the *Miner*. Mid-Lanark seemed an ideal scene for a challenge to the local caucus, he wrote. On the other hand, he stated carefully that he intended no final breach with Liberalism. 'Better split the party now, if there is to be a split, than at a general election.'[8] On 15 March he wrote to Baillie Burt, the chairman of the Mid-Lanark Liberal Association, offering himself as a candidate. He described himself as 'a Radical of a somewhat advanced type' and a loyal supporter of Gladstone's Irish home rule proposals, who had been a member of the Liberal Party all his adult life. He pledged his support for temperance reform, electoral reform and Scottish home rule – all staple radical fare – as well as for a range of proposals for the mining industry, including an eight-hour day. His campaign address to the miners of Mid-Lanark claimed that a vote for Hardie would be 'a vote for Gladstone, Parnell and YOU'.[9]

It was clear, however, that Hardie was more than a conventional advanced radical. His candidature injected something new into Scottish politics. His essential platform, underlying all other issues, was the right of the workers to have their own direct representation in parliament. In pursuit of this, he would stand against an 'official' Liberal if the need arose. His professions of loyalty to the local Liberal Association were largely a matter of form. He never had any serious expectation that it would nominate him as a candidate, in view of his controversial reputation as a labour agitator since the 'tattie strike' eight years earlier. While he remained close to the Liberal position on general issues, he had determined to stand for Mid-Lanark whatever the cost. His independent candidature and his challenge to the Mid-Lanark caucus, dominated by the middle-class 'shopocracy' was fore-ordained.

Hardie's appearance at Mid-Lanark first brought his name before the wider British public. It was of far more than parochial interest, as the Liberal press recognized, since the likelihood of either Hardie or the Mid-Lanark Liberal Association giving way was remote indeed. Further, Hardie's candidature was one supplied with teeth. He had already an array of backers, including the Glasgow Trades Council. He also informed the miners that a mysterious 'well-known Labour sympathiser' had donated £100 for election expenses.[10] This benefactor was almost certainly Miss Margaret Harkness, a philanthropic Glasgow lady of social standing, but it inevitably aroused the alarm of 'Tory gold' which had caused so much dismay in Liberal circles in 1885. The irregular nature of Hardie's campaign finance continued to dog him throughout the by-election. But his main support came clearly from Champion and the LEA. On 16 March Champion wrote to Hardie in euphoric terms, urging him to stand.[11] Success, Champion believed, was certain, especially since Hardie had reassured him that the mining and the Irish vote in Mid-Lanark amounted to 3,500, half the electorate, and felt assured of both. Champion had already been in contact with the Liberal whips and hoped to terrify the local Liberals as effectively as David Randell had done in Gower. The main priorities, he wrote to Hardie, were first to impress on the Mid-Lanark Liberals his absolute determination to stand there, whatever the consequences, and secondly to organize the labour voters in such a way as to lend impetus to the cause. 'It would be fatal for a man in your position to run as a third candidate, and only get a few votes. It would damage you and me, and give the Liberals in all constituencies near and far excuse for not having any more labour candidates. . . . Remember if we can triumph in your case, after Deptford and Glamorgan, we are bound to win all along the line. We shall have proved our capacity and earned our success. You are for the moment the standard bearer and the fate of thousands literally hangs on your coolness, judgement, boldness and hard work.' He made an immediate promise of £250 towards campaign expenses.

In the next few days Champion bombarded Hardie with advice, money and enthusiastic intentions. He forwarded money to the total of £300, including £250 for expenses which mysteriously came from his own funds; this was probably remitted by Maltman Barry, the purveyor of 'Tory gold' in 1885, who had promised Hardie financial assistance during the TUC conference at Swansea.[12] Champion continued to put pressure on the Liberal whips. He threatened them with the probable loss of West Ham South, Central Finsbury and other Liberal seats in London unless they gave Hardie a free run in Mid-Lanark. Champion also approached Parnell, threatening him with a possible Labour-Unionist alliance on behalf of social reform if the Irish vote were cast against Hardie. Finally, Champion provided Hardie's election agents, first of all the Social Democrat, J.L.Mahon, who proved to be inadequate and was dismissed, and then the much more formidable figure of Tom Mann, from London.[13] It was not surprising that Liberals, who had endured taunts from Hardie that he was the truly Scottish and local candidate, now pointed out that it was he, with money, organizers and publicity arranged in London, who was truly the carpet-bagger.

Hardie himself, in a somewhat erratic way, had also been broadening his base in Mid-Lanark on his own account. He continued to underline his credentials as a party regular for the benefit of localLiberals. His election leaflets welcomed the Liberal party programme as laid down at Nottingham in 1887. 'On questions of general politics,' his address stated, 'I would vote with Liberal Party, to which I have all my life belonged.' He also made his own appeal to the Irish vote, which numbered at least 1,000 and was an uncertain element in the contest. He gained the support of the Home Government Branch of the Irish National League, a maverick branch of the Nationalist Party based in Glasgow. Its leading figure was John Ferguson, a friend of Michael Davitt and of Cunninghame Graham, a Liberal by persuasion with an attachment to the dream of an Irish-Labour alliance. The Home Government branch had long been unorthodox and soon found itself locked in conflict with Lanarkshire-based branches of the Irish National League. But it did give some substance to Hardie's claim to appeal to the Irish Catholic vote.[14] Just as he appealed to Irish nationalism, so Scottish separatism also was enlisted on Hardie's behalf. He received support from the London branch of the Scottish Home Rule Association, which had been founded on 6 March with the unknown Ramsay MacDonald as its secretary. This body unanimously recorded its support for Hardie as an indigenous Scottish candidate, who favoured local self-government and who should be endorsed by all patriotic Scotsmen, free from pressure by the party whips in London. The Highland Land League also joined Hardie's variegated army of supporters, with its cry for land restoration and for a single land tax as prescribed by Henry George. 'Don't withdraw but fight for independence', wrote Galloway Weir, an executive member, to Hardie.[15] Finally, there was the prospect of some assistance for Hardie from working-class organization in England and Wales. T.R. Threlfall, the founder of the LEA in 1886, wrote to him endorsing his candidature and urging him to form a LEA in Mid-Lanark without heeding the dictates of the local Liberal Association or its Irish acolytes. Edward Harford sent Hardie £300 via the Clydesdale Bank on behalf of the 'National Labour Party'.[16] John Wilson, the secretary of the Durham miners, also lent Hardie ardent support. Wilson pointed out that 'Hardie's programme proclaims him a Liberal. He adopts the Nottingham programme in its entirety. What more could the Liberals require if they had a middle-class representative selected for the constituency?'[17]

Despite all these hopeful omens, there was never any prospect whatsoever of the local Liberals adopting Hardie, or, therefore, of his success at the polls. Champion and the LEA had conducted no systematic survey of the electorate at Mid-Lanark. By 19 March it was evident that the Association, through its agent, J.T.T. Brown, was going to follow its traditional policy of having delegate conferences convened in the different areas of the constituency. This doomed any hope that Hardie might have an unopposed nomination.[18] Other Liberal candidates, inevitably, were nominated throughout the constituency, with Captain Sinclair and S. Macliver receiving some support. Neither of these, however, was overwhelmingly popular. Instead, there was imported J. Wynford Philipps (later created Viscount St David's), a Welsh barrister resident in Wiltshire who, oddly enough, persistently confessed to being 'an Englishman'. Hardie promptly withdrew his candidature from before the Liberal Association. A plea for a postcard ballot of all Liberal constituents was predictably rejected and on 9 April Philipps was nominated as Liberal candidate by 70 votes to 22.[19] Hardie dourly repeated that he meant 'to keep the field'. His speeches became more and more belligerent, his meetings more and more disorderly. The Liberals, he told an audience at Rutherglen, were the right party on general politics. 'But on the rights which affected the wages of the people they were, if anything, worse than the Conservatives.'[20] Indeed, the Unionist candidate, Captain W.R. Bousfield, adopted a remarkably progressive labour programme during the campaign, including a compulsory eight-hour day for miners, an accident insurance fund and poor law reform. Even now, however, there were indications that Hardie still adhered to the Liberal alliance as a long-term aim. 'Unless you admit our claims, and give us every manner of justice, we will work tooth and nail to give your opponents a majority, in order that you may find it worth your while to purchase our support when the next election comes.'[21]

As the campaign went on, until polling day on 27 April, Hardie's plight became more and more desperate. One popular explanation for this, after the result was declared, was the failure to win over the Irish vote. It soon became clear that Ferguson and the Home Government branch carried little weight in Lanarkshire. Local branches of the Irish National League, with the powerful support of the *Glasgow*

Observer, the leading Catholic organ in western Scotland, denounced those Irishmen who contemplated a breach with the Liberals. They were especially severe in their condemnation of John Ferguson.[22] In fact, Ferguson himself was now making conciliatory approaches to the Liberals. He tried to persuade Hardie that Wynford Philipps was favourable to labour's demands and might even retire at the next election in Hardie's favour.[23] But it was far more than the loss of the Irish vote (which only amounted to perhaps one-sixth of the electorate) which undermined Hardie's hopes. Most miners in the constituency remained loyal to Gladstone. In working-class areas like Wishaw, Hardie met with severe heckling.[24] Time and again, hostile questions were posed about his campaign funds. On this, he gave a variety of replies, none wholly satisfying. A London newspaper commented, 'Behind Mr Hardie is Mr Champion, and probably behind Mr Champion is Mr Maltman Barry, and who is behind Mr Maltman Barry is a mystery.'[25] Nor was Hardie's campaign well run. With a stage army of land leaguers, maverick Glasgow Irishmen, London socialists and Scottish home rulers behind him, all under the erratic generalship of Tom Mann, Hardie's campaign was a *pot-pourri* of late Victorian radicalism at its most variegated. He himself also left something to be desired as a candidate. He had courage and energy in abundance. He withstood with equanimity the disheartening evidence that his chances were being steadily whittled away and that the Liberal big battalions were too well armed. But he was also truculent and unconciliatory, all too prone to indulge in unprofitable and gratuitous attacks on the clergy or the royal family or to get side-tracked by angry exchanges with hecklers. He also showed other characteristics which often harmed his appeal as a candidate throughout his career – a weakness for being distracted by libel actions against newspapers,[26] a casualness about his schedules as a speaker and a comparative neglect of constituency organization. His campaign seemed destined to totter peacefully towards final oblivion. John Kane, one of his party workers, confided in his diary, 'I am afraid we are going to be badly defeated.'

By the middle of April, however, Hardie's challenge to the Liberal caucus had attracted nation-wide attention. He had acquired widespread notoriety as 'an interesting person', according to the Liberal Unionist newspaper, *The Scotsman*. He seemed to typify the strains of social division and Scottish separatism inherent in the Gladstonian ranks in Scotland and perhaps the wider, ultimate disintegration of the party in Britain as a whole.[27] It was the threat which he posed to the Liberal Party that provoked the episode which finally called the attention of the national press to Mid-Lanark. On 20 April, F.A. Schnadhorst, the secretary of the National Liberal Federation, travelled up to Scotland at the invitation of Sir G.O. Trevelyan and met Hardie briefly in Glasgow.[28] Schnadhorst was later understandably evasive about what had occurred. The purpose of his visit, however, it later emerged, was to offer Hardie a Liberal seat at the next general election, if he would retire from the fray at Mid-Lanark. Hardie later claimed that he was tempted with a salary of £300 which enabled him to add this to the list of 'bribes I have been offered'.[29] Schnadhorst's proposals were rejected by Hardie out of hand. He was too proud and too committed to back down at this late stage. But this left him more isolated and beleaguered than ever. Threlfall of the Labour Electoral Association rapidly withdrew his involvement in the contest and offered little more than brief advice about local organization and his pious good wishes.[30] C.A.V.Conybeare MP, another early Lib-Lab sympathiser, also backed out after the rejection of Schnadhorst's mediation. He cited the familiar bogey of Hardie's campaign finance as his major excuse. He deprecated the attempt to force a labour candidate on the constituency against its will.[31]

In the last few days of the contest the independent labour candidature, which had begun with such fanfares, more or less subsided. Cunninghame Graham, Ferguson and Champion were severely heckled. Only in Larkhall and surrounding areas did Hardie continue to pick up much support. He had to content himself with uttering home truths to Irish electors who failed to see that labour and Scotland had grievances of equal magnitude, too.[32] The treatment of his campaign by the local press became increasingly distorted. Dr Charles Cameron, a radical MP, pursued Hardie with virulent hostility in the *North British Daily Mail*. So, too, did the *Scottish Leader*, a 'Gladstonian hack', according to Hardie's aggressive solicitor, T. McNaught.[33] On 27 April the inevitable outcome unfolded. Wynford Philipps, with 3,847 votes, defeated Captain Bousfield (Unionist), 2,917 votes, with some ease. Hardie ended up with 617 (8·3 per cent of the poll), garnered, it was believed, mainly in the Wishaw area. All he could do was to offer defiant gratitude to the 'gallant six hundred' who had voted for him.[34] His association with Champion and Mann petered out, with a rather undignified wrangle about campaign payments.

Too much can be made of the Mid-Lanark contest. It was a severe defeat for Hardie, even taking into account all the financial and political disadvantages from which he laboured. Champion's handling of the campaign was criticized by one Scottish socialist, James Mavor. There was something in the complaint, too, that Hardie had brought in 'too many foreigners' during his campaign and that this had cost him support among the clannish voters of Lanarkshire.[35] The Mid-Lanark contest was soon forgotten as the Liberal-Irish coalition re-formed in the defence of Parnell against his detractors in *The Times* and in preparation for a general election. Even so, Mid-Lanark does merit more attention than just another forlorn Labour candidature in a remote constituency. It riveted national attention on the theme of working-class representation as no previous contest had quite done. It created a mood of apprehension in middle-class Liberal Associations throughout Britain which lingered on for a generation; it was still vivid in the minds of Merthyr Liberals, for instance, on the eve of the first world war. Mid-Lanark illustrated with crystal clarity the illusory and insulated nature of local party democracy, so prized by Gladstonian Liberals. It served to make labour representation the focus for the wider realization of working-class objectives. It generated an anxious dialogue between Liberal party organizers and labour spokesmen that eventually resulted in the MacDonald–Herbert Gladstone *entente* of 1903. Most of all, it focussed national attention on Hardie himself. Even as the desperate leader of a forlorn cause, he had gained new stature as the symbol of working-class revolt. He had anticipated a rebuff at the hands of the Mid-Lanark Liberal Association and its refusal to accept a test ballot of electors as he demanded. Nevertheless, the contemptuous nature of that rebuff, the cynical way in which a rich outsider was imported from southern England in preference to a known Scottish miners' leader like Hardie who had been before the constituency for several months – all this sharpened Hardie's political outlook. Even after Mid-Lanark, his political creed did not fundamentally change. His uncertain lurch towards socialism was, to the end, shot through with hesitations and contradictions. His ideas evolved erratically. At times in the future, he would revert to radical-

ism of the pre-Mid-Lanark era, before advancing on towards, apparently, an uninhibited socialism of the most class-conscious kind. His
Liberal heritage never left him. What Mid-Lanark ultimately kindled
in him, though, was a deep distrust of the Liberal Party as a political
instrument. The Liberal alliance was becoming for him, and for growing legions of working men, enfranchised and unenfranchised alike,
the strategy of the last resort. However decent and enlightened
individual radical segments of the party might be, it was, Hardie
believed, rotten at the heart. He was by temperament and upbringing
an outsider and an individualist. His experience at Mid-Lanark
strengthened his view that the only sure route for the working class, as
well as for himself, was the path of independence.

Labour sympathizers offered a variety of verdicts on the outcome of
the Mid-Lanark by-election. The journal of the quasi-anarchist
Socialist League, *The Commonweal*, predictably took the line that
parliamentary candidatures were premature. Socialism, it held, was
more suitable as a subject for education and enlightenment than for
party conflict. Bruce Glasier, then a struggling artist, writing of a man
with whom his own career was to be so closely intertwined in the
future, praised Hardie as 'a straightforward and honest working man'.
But the socialist revolution, he declared, would be achieved by
idealistic endeavour, not by 'the personal ambition, subterfuge,
insincerity and compromise inherent in party politics'.[36] It was hardly
a programme relevant for this world. By contrast, many of those
involved with the actual by-election campaign felt convinced that the
initiative taken up at Mid-Lanark must be followed up. Champion
called euphorically for a crusade to ensure victory for Hardie there at
the next general election. Even Threlfall, who had backed away from
total involvement in the by-election as failure became apparent, urged
Hardie to agitate, to organize and to form Labour Electoral Associations in other Scottish seats. He proposed Dunbartonshire, Elgin, East
Fife, Forfar, Kirkcudbright, Govan, South Lanarkshire, Peebles, and
Perth as Scottish seats where the Liberals were vulnerable. A threat of
Labour candidatures there might yield concessions from the Liberal
party whips in other constituencies.[37] But Threlfall's strategy was still
confined to bartering terms from within the Liberal fold. His letter
was prompted by the need to influence the forthcoming meeting of the
Scottish Liberal Federation. Hardie himself was leaving this position

behind. During the campaign he had declared that the Liberals' rejection of working men as candidates would lead to social conflict between the classes and the masses, and that the Liberal Party would be its victim. 'The day would come when Liberalism would be dead and buried in Great Britain, and only the Labour Party existed.'[38] This was a rhetorical flourish. Hardie's vision of a Labour Party seemed at this stage little more than a call to mobilize the working-class vote so as to achieve greater parliamentary representation. His Labour Party, if it ever existed, would not be confined to workers alone, let alone socialists. Even so, he had concluded, long before the poll at Mid-Lanark, that a new independent organization must be created to promote those industrial and political reforms for which democracy craved, but which the Liberal Party managers would inevitably suppress.

The outcome was the formation of a new Scottish Labour Party.[39] It was a direct result of the popular coalition forged at Mid-Lanark and Hardie was the central figure in its formation. But it was very far from being a working-class body. Its two major constituents were some elements in the Scottish trade union movement, represented by Hardie and Shaw Maxwell, and the Highland Land League, led by John Murdoch and by the Liberal MP for Caithness, Dr G.B. Clark. A Good Templar, a delegate to the First Socialist International and a highly individual radical freelance, Clark was a dominant figure in the new party. Land reform, however variously defined, was the common theme that held the different sections together. The Labour Electoral Association in London gave the new party its blessing, although Threlfall made it clear to Hardie that he still regarded it as an instrument for putting pressure on Scottish Liberalism and nothing more. John Ferguson of the Home Government Branch, one of Hardie's key allies at Mid-Lanark, also viewed the new organization from a strictly Lib-Lab viewpoint. 'My opinion', he wrote to Hardie on 17 May, 'is still it shd. enter the Liberal Association and work through it. There is certainly an element of danger in two political organizations holding the same principles coming into collision. In one organization the labour and trading classes wd. have to have a common interest, but divided all the bitterness that Louis Blanc points out as existing between the "bourgeois" and "proletaire" in France will arise here. . . . You must only ask what must be granted if the foundation of our social edifice is not to be destroyed.'[40] Under these mixed auspices, a founding meeting was convened at the Waterloo Rooms in Glasgow, on 19 May. [41] Twenty-seven were present, under the chairmanship of the crofters' leader, John Murdoch. Cunninghame Graham ventilated a wide range of demands including Scottish home rule, the abolition of the royal family and the House of Lords, as well as improvements in the living conditions of the people and increased working-class representation in parliament. But it was Hardie who struck the most challenging note. He declared that he had severed his connections with the official Liberal Party that day by taking on the secretaryship of the new Scottish Labour Party. On the other hand, he left an escape route. 'If the Liberal Party desired to prevent the Labour Party from splitting in twain, it was an easy way out of the difficulty to adopt the programme the Labour Party had laid down, and it would find the working men heart and soul with it, as good Liberals as they had been hitherto.' Even in Hardie's case this was something well short of a clarion call for a revolt *à outrance* against Liberalism.

This ambivalence surrounding the Scottish Labour Party was shown again at its formal inaugural meeting at Glasgow on 25 August.[42] Cunninghame Graham again presided. He struck a note of defiant isolationism. Working men, he declared, were more interested in questions of wages and work than 'in questions of who should rule in Japan or whether we should annex islands in the Pacific'. Dr Clark and John Ferguson, representing the Highland Land League and the Home Government Branch respectively, were elected vice-presidents; Hardie became secretary. The programme was largely a mirror image of 'advanced radicalism' as currently understood; there was little that was specifically socialist. There was outlined an array of political reforms, including adult suffrage, triennial parliaments, the payment of members, the second ballot and 'home rule all round'. There were other standard left-wing demands such as disestablishment of the church, civil service reform, graduated income tax, the direct veto on the liquor traffic and free public education. Labour and industrial proposals included the eight-hour day, national insurance, wage arbitration courts and homestead legislation. More striking were the land proposals which showed an advance from the meeting of 19 May. Then, the delegates' demands had spanned almost every known species of land proposal – reform of the laws on primogeniture and entail, the fixity of tenure for occupiers, the taxing of ground values, and a state rent of four shillings in the pound on current income. They ran the gamut from the Highland Land League to the Henry Georgites: only currency inflation, among the panaceas currently canvassed on both sides of the Atlantic, was left out. By 25 August, these had been subsumed into the proposal for land nationalization, a victory for Dr Clark in particular. This was associated with the most obviously collectivistic proposals of all – the nationalization of the railways, the banks and mineral rights. The Scottish Labour Party was distinctly closer to the socialist position than had been Hardie's platform at Mid-Lanark. Nevertheless the new party was manifestly the product of compromise. Even with Hardie as its organizing secretary, its purpose and future were obscure. He himself hoped to spread the net wide enough to catch a shoal of protest groups, socialist and non-socialist alike. Outside bodies like trades councils, Radical Associations and Single Taxers were allowed to affiliate. The danger was that some of the more extreme constituent elements in the Scottish Labour Party might deter would-be sympathizers. Already in September there were signs that this might happen. Severe criticism was voiced at the Edinburgh Trades Council of the objectives of the new party. Like the trades council of Dundee, it refused to affiliate. Again, at the annual conference of the Scottish Home Rule Association at Glasgow on 18 September, Hardie was criticized by those like Charles Waddie who had supported him at Mid-Lanark.[43] Hardie's poor performance at the polls was the subject of much deprecating comment.

The Scottish Labour Party lingered on for six years. It finally merged with the Independent Labour Party in 1894. From the outset, it made little direct impact on the Scottish scene. Its first venture in the Ayr Burghs by-election in June 1888 was a failure; no candidate could be found, despite Hardie's efforts. *The Miner* trained its fire on Threlfall who had openly urged the Ayr voters to support the Liberal, Captain Sinclair.[44] He was one of Hardie's opponents at Mid-Lanark with whom Hardie had had unsuccessful secret discussions during the campaign. Further attempts in 1889 to run Labour candidates at Govan, West Fife and Dundee also floundered. At least, however, the Scottish Labour Party could point to the strong labour programme adopted by Wilson, the Liberal candidate at Govan, who endorsed an eight-hour day for miners, anti-sweating legislation and even land nationalization. Hardie had tried to persuade John Burns, then associated with the SDF, to run at Dundee, but he retreated to a safe haven at Battersea. In addition to these electoral difficulties, the Scottish Labour Party was being undermined by internal dissensions. Many of its officials shied away from more than a verbal declaration of independence from Liberalism. John Ferguson, for instance, began to flirt with support of Liberal candidates who were known opponents of some labour demands. Eventually he was expelled from the Scottish Labour Party. More damaging was the first evidence of a split between Hardie and Champion. They had never really been of like mind. Champion was fundamentally a Tory collectivist; Hardie was still attached to his Liberal roots. Early in 1889 they apparently became closer when Hardie's *Miner* closed down as an independent journal and merged into Champion's new weekly, *The Labour Elector*. Hardie himself served as its Scottish editor for a time.[45] Even so, clashes of personality made relations between him and Champion increasingly difficult. This ultimately became a major embarrassment for the Scottish Labour Party at the time of the 1892 general election. While Hardie retained his appeal in the Lowlands and the mining areas of western Scotland, Aberdeen (for which Champion had been adopted as prospective Labour candidate) became a stronghold of Champion's supporters. The Aberdeen Trades Council became increasingly hostile towards Hardie; John Gerrie, one of Champion's friends, bitterly attacked Hardie's 'anarchist leaven'. All this added to the disarray within the Scottish Labour Party. Hardie's first secretarial report to the Party in 1889 was an optimistic survey of its first year of activity. It had made, he claimed, striking progress. It had spread a growing awareness of the need 'to free men from the bondage of the commercial system'. In fact its members were aware that after twelve months of electoral failure and internal conflict the Scottish Labour Party had made scant impact on Scottish, let alone British, politics.

Hardie's political tactics at this time continued to show many shifts and turns. It is, indeed, a period of his life that is singularly difficult to document. William Stewart, Emrys Hughes and other biographers provide only a scanty discussion of it. Hardie's links with Liberalism were still far from being severed. A new approach to him was made by Edward Marjoribanks, the Liberal deputy whip, in January 1890.[46] He met Hardie, Cunninghame Graham and Shaw Maxwell, representing the Scottish Labour Party, at Glasgow. Here, Marjoribanks offered them 'labour' candidates at Greenock and two other Scottish seats, if acceptable men could be found. The Labour Party showed interest, for all its previous declarations of independence. But, as at Mid-Lanark, the pact foundered on the hostility of the local Liberal Associations. Greenock Liberal Association turned down Cunninghame Graham's candidature,[47] while local Liberals blamed the association with the Labour Party for the loss of seats at by-elections at Partick and again at Ayr Burghs. As a result Hardie's resistance to official Liberalism again hardened. But this did not lead him to abandon the hope of enlisting the support of the major parties. In December 1889 he wrote on behalf of the Ayrshire Miners' Union to Lord Randolph Churchill, inviting him to address them on labour topics.[48] 'We are not party politicians in any sense of the word', Hardie assured him. 'As working men we are prepared to give support to any candidate for parliamentary honours who will, when returned, support measures for the shortening of the hours of labour & the general social elevation of the masses.' Churchill was warned that 'such controversial topics as Home Rule must be rigidly excluded from your speeches. .... You are I believe the first Conservative member of Parliament ever invited to take part in a miners' meeting in Scotland & if only to show that the social question is not the exclusive property of any political party, I trust you will strain a point to come down. ....' Hardie's original draft letter included a reference to 'the absurd prejudice which exists towards the Conservative Party'. The invitation bore no fruit and perhaps reinforced the distrust felt towards Hardie in orthodox Lib-Lab circles. He had already strained to breaking-point his relations with the Labour Electoral Association since Mid-Lanark. At its annual congress in Sheffield in October 1888, Hardie's proposal that two-thirds of the LEA committee should consist of bona fide working men or trade union representatives met with little support. His attempt to win election to the executive committee gained a mere nine votes.[49] He was still outside the mainstream of labour politics.

Hardie's energies were still partly consumed by industrial activity on behalf of the Ayrshire Miners Union and the Scottish miners generally. As a delegate at the Bradford Trades Union Congress in September 1888 he resumed his duel with Henry Broadhurst.[50] Again, however, his attack misfired. Hardie, speaking in support of

John Hodge's amendment in favour of greater working-class representation in parliament, diverted attention by another vigorous personal attack on Broadhurst. Again he denounced Broadhurst's connection with the firm of Brunner, Mond and his support at election times for known sweaters of labour like James Hill and Sir John Brunner. The whole debate was sterile, with Hardie's attack provoking, in return, similarly unprofitable abuse from Pickard and Broadhurst. Hodge's amendment was defeated by 82 votes to 18.

In 1889 the TUC met at Dundee and yet again Hardie led an onslaught on Broadhurst.[51] The outcome was even less satisfactory. Chisholm Robertson, one of Hardie's old allies in the Scottish miners' movement, counter-attacked in vigorous style. He claimed that Hardie's attacks on a local Dundee newspaper, the *Weekly News*, were inspired by personal gain, since Hardie had received an offer to write for a rival journal. He also alleged that Hardie's election literature at Mid-Lanark was printed by a notorious 'rat-shop' in Glasgow, which employed sweated labour. Other delegates then intervened for or against Hardie. Finally Broadhurst rose in full majesty to pour scorn on 'the great sage of Ayrshire'. He also picked up Hardie's references to his own youth and replied with derisive comments on Hardie's loss of hair and the decision (a very temporary one) to shave off his beard. In this welter of petty personal recrimination, Hardie's censure motion on Broadhurst was lost by 177 votes to 11. Nor were Hardie's interventions in other debates more successful. When he spoke on behalf of greater labour representation in parliament he was again the target of a scorching attack by Chisholm Robertson who claimed that Hardie had contributed to the disorganization of the labour movement in Scotland. Charles Fenwick, in a famous phrase, compared Hardie's unsuccessful career with the withering of Jonah's gourd. Hardie's motion to instruct the TUC Parliamentary Committee to work for an eight-hour day and the abolition of child and female labour won more support than before, but was still defeated by 88 votes to 63. Broadhurst received a flood of support for again beating off the attacks of Hardie and his other critics – 'these ugly badgers, these stinking foxes, these devouring otters, these hares, these wolves, these anything but men' in the excited opinion of Charles Brown of the Typographical Association. A Burslem Liberal congratulated Broadhurst on frustrating 'the knavish tricks' of 'these interest Hirelings', Tory agents in disguise.[52] Even so, the tide of opinion in the trade union world was turning against Broadhurst's conservatism and in favour of the eight-hour day principle.[53] The unemployment agitation in London since 1886, the nation-wide impact of the Bryant and May match-girls' strike in 1888 and above all the London dock strike of the following year had powerfully influenced working-class (and indeed middle-class) opinion in favour of the limitation of hours and more collectivist policies by the central government. Nevertheless, Hardie's contribution to the nation-wide debate on the eight-hours issue seemed a negative and destructive one. His credentials as a voice for organized labour were open to doubt. Indeed, questions were asked at the TUC Parliamentary Committee as to whether Hardie represented a bona fide union at all: an inspection of the balance-sheet of the Ayrshire Miners' Union was demanded.[54] As yet, Hardie's industrial record was as littered with setbacks and frustrated opportunities as was his career as a politician.

During this period Hardie began significantly to widen his horizon, far beyond his familiar world at Cumnock. He showed a growing concern to place the British working-class movement in an inter-national setting. His newspaper contributions in the Scottish press had throughout shown a noticeable preoccupation with industrial con-ditions overseas. Such themes as the call for emigration as a remedy for unemployment in Britain, had turned his attention increasingly to the progress of trade and industry in the United States, France and other countries. Hardie argued forcefully that the prospect of emigration in the hope of finding more stable employment, more tranquil industrial relations or greater prosperity overseas was a delusion. From 1888 onwards he was actively concerned with promoting closer relations with mining unions abroad. He attended the International Trades Congress in London in November of that year and took a prominent part in its debates.[55] He proposed that the unions of one trade in any one country should combine in the electing of an executive central body; that the central bodies of the different trades elect a general council; and that an international congress be held at least every three years. Hardie, the eternal freelance, for once was a committed advocate of centralization. He was in frequent contact with French miners' leaders and in May 1890 attended the international Miners' Congress at Jolinant in Belgium. All this added an important new dimension to his career. Even in his relatively brief period as a trade union leader, he was an instinctive internationalist, a natural choice as 'fraternal delegate' to conferences overseas. As a political leader later on, he was foremost amongst those who sought to wrench the British movement out of a purely insular context and to give practical expression to the fraternalism of the workers of the world.

An even more important venture into internationalism came in July 1889 when Hardie attended the conference in Paris which launched the Second Socialist International. He was one of twenty delegates from England.[56] Nine of them (including William Morris) represented the quasi-anarchist Socialist League, but they also included Edward Aveling (delegate for East Finsbury Radical Club) and Cunninghame Graham (for the Labour Electoral Association). Hardie was present as delegate both for the Ayrshire Miners and for the Scottish Labour Party. Characteristically, he chose to attend both the conferences which were held at Paris, the Marxist and the non-Marxist (or 'possibilist') meetings. Of all the variegated British delegates present at Paris, it was Hardie who perhaps provided the most reliable exposition of the realities of the labour world in his own country, in contrast to the euphoric excesses of the British Marxists present. As he told Engels prior to the Paris International, 'We are a solid people, very practical and not given to chasing bubbles. . . . We are not opposed to ideals & recognize to the full the need for them & their power in inspiring men, but we are more concerned in the realization of the ideal than in dreaming of it. This may account for the low ebb of the SDF in Scotland.'[57] At Paris Hardie went out of his way 'to declare that no person in England believed in other than peaceful methods to achieve the amelioration of conditions'.[58] All this aroused the predictable anger of Morris and the Socialist Leaguers, as well as of the German Social Democrats present. They all preferred to emphasize the revolutionary potential of the British labour movement; Hardie's pacific pragmatism was very much a minority view amongst the delegates. Nevertheless, he undoubtedly gained a new stature through his interventions at Paris, as a voice for moderation and for statesmanship, qualities he had not always displayed at home. From the start he took the Second International more seriously than did most British radicals or socialists. He saw it as a valuable forum for the debate of principles and tactics by working-class representatives. It provided him with important contacts with socialist movements abroad and offered the prospect of practical collaboration. It enabled Marxists and non-Marxists to work together on behalf of realizable objectives and to make common cause. As always in domestic politics, Hardie sought to work from below, to find limited areas of common ground where the 'labour alliance' could be made a reality and to leave ideology to look after itself. On this basis, he struck up enduring friendships with socialists of international stature such as Liebknecht and Bebel from Germany, and Viktor Adler of the Austrian Social Democrats.

At the same time the International afforded Hardie examples of what to avoid as well as what to adopt. He noted the doctrinaire rigidity of the German Social Democrats; this helped to convince him that the strategy at home should be to create an outward-looking alliance, not an introspective sect.[59] Finally, the Second International undoubtedly helped Hardie towards a more precise definition of his political position. Until 1889 he was essentially the advocate of a labour pressure-group, heavily influenced by the specific needs of the mining community. Thereafter he was concerned, however imprecisely, with changing the structure of political and economic power. While he retained to the end of his days important vestiges of his earlier radical upbringing, his ideas henceforth were ineradicably permeated with elements of socialism. Thus, he urged Engels to send him details of state enterprises at work, such as the publicly-owned coal mines at Saarbrucken, to show that nationalization of the means of production was a practical proposition.[60] Hardie's internationalism, then, was a central theme in his emergence as a labour leader. If he contributed to the labour alliance at home essentially the pragmatic talents of the organizer and the tactician, he was to become a major inspiration in the socialist world internationally. He attained a stature abroad that he never knew at home and he retained it, even in the disillusioning years that followed the formation of the British Labour Party.

At the start of 1890, Hardie, now aged thirty-three, was still an agitator in search of a satisfying role. He was now familiar, or notorious, throughout Britain as a pioneer of independent action by labouring men. His passionate Scottish rhetoric gushed forth from scores of platforms throughout Scotland and, increasingly, England. He was a powerful propagandist by means of the printed word. In February 1889 he had started up a new journal as successor to *The*

Miner. This was christened the *Labour Leader*, ultimately to become a major vehicle for spreading Hardie's version of the socialist faith. It was shot through with Hardie's familiar evangelical style; the first issue was headed with a poem by Tennyson on the theme of 'the Christ that is to be'. In addition, as has been seen, Hardie was gaining some celebrity as a figure in the international socialist world. Since 1887 he had struck up a relationship with Engels, to whom he had been re-introduced by Eleanor Marx. Time soon showed that there was a world of difference between the ideologue of 'scientific socialism' and the romantic individualist whom Engels dubbed 'that super-cunning Scot'.[61] Even so, the contacts built up between Engels and Hardie, through the spread of socialist literature and in consultations over the strategy for the Scottish Labour Party, emphasized the new authority Hardie was acquiring in British and international left-wing politics.

But what gave unity of purpose to this many-sided public activity on Hardie's part was still unclear. His career in practical terms had so far been a failure. He had shown ability and energy in working on behalf of the Ayrshire Miners' Union; the *Labour Elector* reminded its readers that Hardie had won them a wages advance of sixty-seven per cent in thirteen months.[62] On the other hand, his union was still a small and struggling one. Further, Scottish mining unionism as a whole was still fragmented and parochial. Apart from the Fifeshire union, only a tenth of the 70,000 Scottish miners were organized at all and they were dispersed throughout eight unions. In the British trade union world more generally Hardie's savage personal onslaught on Broadhurst had done little to promote causes such as an eight-hour day. The British trade union movement was undergoing fundamental transformation in 1889–90. The London Dock strike heralded a massive, if largely temporary, unionization of the unskilled, which commentators such as the Webbs were to dub the 'new unionism'. Hardie's contribution to all this was minimal. Indeed, he appeared to lack the patience and single-mindedness to make a successful union leader. His ventures into politics were equally unpromising so far. As yet he had still to be elected to any significant public office. He had stood for the new county council elections in Auchinleck in late 1889, but again failure attended his efforts. His parliamentary candidature at Mid-Lanark had been so far of no more than symbolic importance and had alienated such potential allies as the Labour Electoral Association. The efforts of the Scottish Labour Party to 'stimulate and strengthen the workers' had made little headway and there was scant prospect of successful candidatures in any Scottish constituency.[63] The Party at the end of 1890 presented a sorry spectacle of self-indulgent sectarianism. Hardie had already demonstrated the talents of the prophet and the agitator. He had still to show that he possessed the more mundane but more enduring skills of the politician. Indeed, the kind of political role that he visualized for himself was still most unclear, as his friendships oscillated from John Ferguson to Engels. There seemed little indication that he might not follow the apostles of the Socialist League into slow oblivion. Like Jonah's gourd, in Charles Fenwick's derisive phrase at the TUC, Hardie might simply 'spring up and wither in a night'.

III   The Emergence of the Cloth Cap (1890–2)

In the early months of 1890 Hardie's career underwent a major transformation. He was unexpectedly nominated for the London East End constituency of West Ham South. This arose under curious circumstances. The local Liberal Party had until recently been split between two rival candidates, J. Spencer Curwen and Hume Webster. A bitter conflict then ensued, which resulted in Curwen's finally withdrawing in January 1890.[1] Ostensibly, he did so to preserve party unity; in reality, Hume Webster's largesse and patronage were too much for him to counteract. But this only made the rifts dividing the West Ham Liberals far more profound. For West Ham, with its large vote of dockers, gasworkers and Irishmen, all of them much influenced by the 'new unionism' and the recent dock strike, was a constituency with a strong labour tradition. After all, even the 'labour aristocrats' of the dockyards and the Royal Arsenal in Woolwich across the river had become far more militant in the past few years; this new militancy was even more pronounced in West Ham. A 'Lib-Lab' candidate had been returned in West Ham South in 1885. Since then there had been striking Labour gains in local elections, on the municipal council, the School Board and the Board of Guardians. By 1892 there were seven 'labour' candidates on the municipal council, including the formidable Will Thorne of the Gasworkers, a prominent figure in the SDF.[2] Hume Webster was not generally popular in working-class circles and had in any event a dubious record in company speculation; he could never serve as a focus for party unity in West Ham South. Those radicals, headed by Dr John Moir, who had originally backed Curwen now sought a new 'labour' candidate and sections of the Radical Association consorted with the West Ham Trades Council to this end. A natural candidate might have been Will Thorne, in view of the branches of the SDF active in West Ham, in such areas as Silvertown and Tidal Basin. In fact, however, Moir and his friends through the mediation of Cunninghame Graham, an omnipresent figure in labour politics at this period, made an approach to Hardie, who still retained some of the charisma gained in the contest at Mid-Lanark. At the end of February Hardie visited the constituency for the first time, in the course of a visit to London with a miners' delegation which was interviewing the Home Secretary. He made several declarations in favour of the eight-hour day. At the end of March it was announced that he was in the field as candidate for West Ham South, to challenge the sitting Unionist member, Major Banes and the Liberal Association as well, if need be.[3]

Despite the progress achieved by labour and socialist bodies in West Ham South since 1885, however, the omens were not wholly encouraging for Hardie's hopes. After all, his career to date had been spent almost wholly in the distant labyrinths of Scottish politics and he had had virtually no connection with London. He lived in Ayrshire; he and his family had recently moved into 'Lochnorris', a solid stone house they had built in Old Cumnock, with money loaned to them by Adam Birkmyre, a wealthy Glasgow businessman who later emigrated to South Africa. Hardie's visits to the constituency of West Ham, then, could only be intermittent. But it was clear that his horizon was extending far beyond his native Scotland; his instincts were naturally outward-looking, in contrast to John Maclean and the later generation of Glasgow socialists after 1917 who conceived their socialism firmly within a Celtic context.

Hardie was not short of contacts with London politics. He had, for instance, developed a somewhat uneasy, though initially useful, relationship with John Burns since 1889. Through Aveling and Eleanor Marx he had been in communication with London branches of the SDF, although he was never among their members. More important, he had struck up a close friendship with Frank Smith, perhaps the person closest to him and most attuned to his changing moods for the rest of his life.[4] Smith was a manqué Salvationist who had left the Salvation Army after a bitter dispute with General Booth over the latter's approach to poverty and social welfare. Smith was active in administering city workshops and farm colonies in the Essex marshes, as a cure for urban unemployment; he also founded a new Christian socialist journal, *The Worker's Cry*. He embraced socialism of a peculiarly intense and unworldly kind. It owed almost everything to ethical judgement, virtually nothing to economic analysis. He was an idealist of the most dedicated type; Hardie nicknamed him 'St Francis'. Smith's socialism throughout was heavily permeated with a quasi-religious personal mysticism; he found an outlet for it in spiritualist seances. It was highly significant that he appealed at once to Hardie as a kindred spirit. Their careers were henceforth intimately interwoven. Hardie used him as a roving election agent in every campaign from 1892 onwards; Smith also acted as a part-time secretary during Hardie's many absences abroad. In addition, Hardie felt deeply drawn towards Smith's withdrawn, mystical personality. Like Smith, he believed in an incarnation prior to birth and yet another after death. They shared seances and other psychical experiences together and jointly consulted horoscopes and experts in palmistry. They pledged each other to communicate from the outer world when one or other of them died: Smith claimed that Hardie kept his pledge after his death. Hardie's friendship with Smith takes us near to the core of his personality. Ultimately, his vision of the socialist society was romantic, utopian, supra-rational. It was the product of a poetic as much as of a political outlook. Hardie was very far from being the typical working man, despite his long years at the pitface and as a union organizer. He was driven on ultimately by a blinding vision of a new society, in which man would be purified and re-incarnated and mundane human relationships superseded. To this strain of Hardie's character Frank Smith had an irresistible appeal. He powerfully influenced Hardie's political philosophy and notably reinforced his instinct for political isolation. In the short run, as an eventual member of the London County Council and a journalist, Smith also brought Hardie valuable contacts with London's radical politics, on which the prospective candidate for West Ham South was steadily to build.

Throughout 1891, Hardie made intermittent visits to West Ham. But it was generally assumed that his candidature was still obstructed by the presence of Hume Webster, who had won over such local labour leaders as Alderman Harry Phillips. Then, on 25 January 1892, Webster was removed from the scene in sensational fashion. He was found in woods near his Croydon estate, shot through the head.[5] The verdict was suicide, apparently the result of business worries. The failure of a deal to buy a South American racehorse was the explanation popularly cited for the mystery. This left Hardie alone in the field. Even though a dissident element of the West Ham South Liberal and Radical Association now spent its energies in trying to produce an alternative to Hardie, his chances of being nominated for West Ham and therefore of being elected to parliament, were now excellent, particularly in view of the declared sympathy of Marjoribanks, the Liberal chief whip, for working-class Liberal candidates. Even the nomination on 1 April of Joseph Leicester, the former Liberal member for the constituency and a former furnace worker who boasted of his proletarian credentials, seemed to offer little threat. A few months earlier, Hardie had resigned his secretaryship of the struggling Ayrshire Miners' Union, probably with relief, to show the voters of West Ham the serious intent of his candidature.

Until he came to West Ham, Hardie's main theme had been the eight-hour day, together with the other panoply of measures demanded by the Scottish miners. This emphasis on working and living conditions was perfectly compatible with the objectives of advanced radicals in London such as Dr Moir: it had won a warm response from the West Ham dockers who had long suffered the brutalizing consequences of the 'call on' for labour at the dock gates. Equally popular, and equally familiar, were Hardie's proposals for a graduated income tax on incomes of over £1,000 a year, with the increased revenue to be spent on Old Age Pensions. His ideas for 'land restoration', a euphemism for land nationalization, had been echoed by rural and urban radicals in Scotland and England since Henry George's lecture tours almost a decade earlier. What was strikingly new about Hardie's speeches now was his whole-hearted embracing of the theme of unemployment. As Dr José Harris has most convincingly explained in a comprehensive recent study,[6] the concept of unemployment as a permanent social phenomenon had gained widespread currency since the demonstrations in Trafalgar Square in 1886–7. It had inspired new welfare proposals by voluntary agencies like the Charity Organization Society and the Settlement Houses. It had encouraged new experiments with farm colonies, such as those begun by Frank Smith, and aroused widespread concern among 'Progressives' on the London County Council. Most important of all, it had lent massive momentum to the agitation in the trade union movement for an eight-hour day, the most popular current remedy for unemployment. A Royal Commission on Labour had

begun its enquiries in early 1892, with Tom Mann amongst
its members. Hardie came somewhat late to the broader aspects of the
unemployment agitation; yet he soon became more closely identified
with it in the popular mind than any other politician of the day.
Beginning with his addresses to the West Ham electors in such areas
as Plaistow and Silvertown in 1891 and early 1892, he eventually
became the leading voice of working-class concern with structural
unemployment. His experience at West Ham gave him concrete
evidence of the distress amongst those out of work. The 'member for
the unemployed' was emerging.

Hardie's statistics were inevitably erratic and impressionistic. He
extrapolated, from an alleged figure of 40,000 unemployed men in
London, that there were up to five millions out of work throughout
Britain as a whole.[7] He was quite unable to prove this – but then
neither was the crude statistical equipment at the disposal of the Board
of Trade any more reliable. Hardie's solutions for the problem of unemployment were equally open to criticism. His usual remedy was
the setting up of 'home colonies' in south-east England to deal with
the acute problems of distress in London. These would support the
unemployed in self-sufficient crafts, or in allotments or other agricultural work. Ten such colonies, Hardie claimed, would cost only
£120,000 and would pay for themselves. More cogently and less
speculatively, Hardie advocated the setting up of a register for the unemployed, the overhaul of the machinery of local distress committees,
and the encouragement of local public works, housing in particular,
by municipal authorities. The employment of 'direct labour' by the
Works Department of the London County Council was a precedent
for what Hardie had in mind. His proposals were largely derived from
radical theories already current. In particular, he was much influenced
by the writings of a Unitarian minister, the Reverend Herbert Mills
who had propounded under-consumptionist economics and the idea of
self-sufficient co-operative estates in a book, *Poverty and the State*,
published in 1886. Hardie cited Mills as an authority on structural
unemployment and trade recession, when giving evidence before the
Royal Commission on Labour.[8] In time, Mills's colonies bore little
fruit, and tended to be a refuge for the unemployable rather than for
those genuinely in need of productive work. Hardie's diagnoses,
inevitably, were inadequate; his remedies for distress were vague and

over-optimistic. Nevertheless, he directed attention, as no politician had done before, towards a fundamental social evil in the late Victorian economy. Unemployment became, and long remained, a social and political theme of primary concern, despite the political impotence of the unemployed, almost all of whom were unenfranchised or un-registered. For this Hardie deserves much of the credit. In addition, his involvement in the unemployment agitation served to reinforce the crystallization of his socialist instincts, by underlining the fundamental social decay inherent in Britain's capitalist economy. Hardie was an optimistic 'labour aristocrat' no longer.

He was, of course, much more than simply the candidate for West Ham South. As secretary still of the Scottish Labour Party and as an emerging voice for socialist demands (he temporarily joined the Fabian Society in 1890) he had a wider, national audience. He was still heavily involved in trying to make sense of labour's relations with the Liberal Party. Writing to John Burns on 23 May 1891, he still wrote in terms of a labour pressure-group, independent of, but with permanent lifelines to, the Liberal central organization:[9]

Desperate efforts are being made just now by Schnadhorst to entrap every man worth having. . . . Should the Liberals get into power at the next election, their neglect of the Labour question will compel some plain talking, and the fewer ghosts of former utterances there are to rise in judgement against us, the better will it be. Like yourself, I believe we have more hope from that party than from the other, but this applies to the rank & file only & not to all the leaders, & to prevent possible misunderstanding, the less said about this 'hope' the better.

Hardie welcomed Gladstone's partial, highly guarded acceptance of the principle of the eight-hour day. He told the West Ham electors in February 1892 that he supported the Newcastle Programme of the Liberal Party in its entirety. 'But the social condition of the people was of ten thousand times more consequence than their political condition.'[10]

The only area where Hardie and the Liberal whips came into direct contact was in Scotland. Here, any arrangements arrived at between Marjoribanks and the Scottish Labour Party were rapidly breaking down. At Glasgow (Camlachie), for instance, Cunninghame Graham had been most reluctantly adopted by the local Liberal Association. When he began to launch attacks on the Liberal party leadership, the

Association decided to run an official Liberal against him in revenge. Hardie enlisted John Burns's support on Graham's behalf, but it was apparent that Graham would face certain Liberal opposition at the polls. The same thing happened at Perth, where James Woolen of the Labour Party failed to force the sitting Liberal, C.S. Parker, into resigning his seat.[11] Marjoribanks was powerless to intervene, and the pleas of the Labour Party for a test ballot of Liberal voters went unheeded. In the event, the Scottish Labour Party could put up only five candidates in Scotland in the 1892 election – in the Tradeston, College, and Camlachie divisions of Glasgow (the last a two-member constituency), and in Perth. They stood under a bewildering variety of banners, and since each faced Liberal as well as Unionist opposition, they were all clearly forlorn hopes.

In addition, the internal dissension within the Scottish Labour Party continued. Champion returned from a controversial visit to Australia in 1891 and at once disagreement flared up between him and Hardie. There was a fierce dispute over the terms on which Champion would finance Scottish Labour Party candidates – even though it had been agreed that Champion would donate money to several Labour candidates in London, including Hardie in West Ham South. Hardie advised the Scottish Labour Party to steer well clear of Champion; the spectre of 'Tory gold' again stalked the land. In the event, Champion himself was nominated for Aberdeen, while Chisholm Robertson, Hardie's other enemy, stood for Stirlingshire, both of them outside the auspices of the Labour Party. With the mysterious Maltman Barry standing in Banffshire as a 'Tory Democrat', the fragmentation of the Scottish Labour world seemed complete.

In June 1892 parliament was dissolved, and Hardie bent his energies to his campaign at West Ham. From the start, he was aware that his return depended on his amassing the largest possible Liberal vote and inducing supporters of Joseph Leicester to throw their weight behind his candidature. Hardie emphasized repeatedly his agreement with the broad outlines of Liberal policy as laid down at Newcastle. He upheld franchise reform and Irish home rule. He stressed his long career as a temperance reformer: he pointed out that he was a Junior Chief Templar in the Grand Lodge of Good Templars. He bid hard for the nonconformist vote, parading local ministers like the Reverend Thomas Warren of the Methodist New Connexion (popularly nicknamed

'Hardie's chaplain') on his platform. 'He would support the Liberal programme in its entirety', Hardie declared to applause from a Plaistow audience, 'but at the same time would use his best endeavours to call attention to the social questions of the day'.[12] Hardie certainly underlined his appeal to labour; he addressed a steady stream of trade union demonstrations, dock gates meetings and other informal assemblies. But his appeal was sufficiently flexible to be entirely compatible with that of the Liberal Party. The question of socialism (apart from some incidental references to land nationalization, which many Liberals also supported) never intruded.

Hardie's broad-based radical appeal turned the tide in his favour. It was known that the vast majority of local Liberal and Radical Associations were now lined up behind him. Alderman Worland, alone of local Liberal chieftains, favoured Leicester's candidature which appeared increasingly unreal. It was little surprise when it was announced formally on 2 July, a little before polling day, that Leicester had withdrawn, 'after serious consideration and consultation with Mr Schnadhorst' as the press reported.[13] Leicester's erstwhile supporters were urged by the whips to give their vote to Keir Hardie.

It now remained only to defeat the somnolent sitting Unionist member, Major Banes. He was no Rupert of debate. On the contrary, he had had to explain away his long silence in the Commons since 1886 by denouncing the excessive time taken up by Opposition speakers. His campaign was a singularly passive one, compared with Hardie's frenzied activity. Six separate meetings were addressed by Hardie on 27 June alone.[14] On polling day, 4 July, the contest between 'the Major and the Miner', as the press dubbed it, came to a peaceful close. Hardie defeated Banes comfortably, by 5,268 votes to 4,036. Labour and socialist circles hailed his triumph, like that of Burns in Battersea, as a portent of the political awakening of the working class. There was great rejoicing in the SDF stronghold of Silvertown, with powerful effect on a young socialist enthusiast like Jack Jones. In fact, Hardie owed his return less to the faithful support of the dockers and other unskilled workers than to Liberal votes, carefully enlisted by a 'Lib-Lab' programme.

Immediately he was elected, however, he took an active part in contests elsewhere: in the period before 1918, elections did not all take place on the same day but were spread out over a fortnight. He now trained his fire on any Liberal candidates who had opposed the eight-hour day. This was eminently reasonable for a 'labour' candidate. What was a disastrous error was Hardie's recommendation that Liberal voters in these constituencies should actually vote for the Unionist. To take this step, immediately after his election largely on Liberal votes at West Ham, was widely taken as a sign of opportunism and cynicism. Bernard Shaw was not alone in telling Burns that it made Hardie look like a 'Unionist catspaw'. Shaw added that 'it looks like a formidable Unionist intrigue, with Champion at the wires. Keir Hardie or who-ever is pulling his strings, seems to be calculating that the situation is such that whatever man takes the initiative, the others must follow him. That however is a game two can play at. . . .'[15] Marxists were equally critical of Hardie's tactics: Engels's extreme distaste for Hardie as a shifty politician dates precisely from his tactics in the 1892 election.

The incident that aroused particular fury was Hardie's decision to work for the defeat of John Morley at Newcastle-on-Tyne. 'The old school of Liberalism had done its work and must give place to the new,' Hardie informed the Newcastle electors.[16] He denounced the rising tide of unemployment, which he now estimated at 1,250,000, and claimed that a shortening of working hours was the only im-mediate remedy. Morley's opposition to the eight-hour day was, therefore, unforgivable. It illustrated his inhumane, ivory-tower approach towards the workers; the conclusion now drawn was that working-class voters in Newcastle-on-Tyne should vote for Morley's Unionist opponent. The sharp drop in Morley's poll that resulted (the Conservative relegated him to second place) was widely attributed to Hardie's intervention. Unabashed, Hardie again urged the labour vote to be cast against Morley in the by-election that followed in the autumn when Morley was appointed Chief Secretary for Ireland. He recommended support for the Unionist, Ralli, whom Hardie dubiously claimed was sounder on labour questions. Hardie's antagonism towards Morley was entirely predictable. Morley had been a consistent and doctrinaire opponent of state intervention on social and economic ques-tions since his entry into national politics nine years earlier. He made public his alarm at the more collectivist aspects of the Newcastle Pro-gramme, even though they were vague enough. Clearly, he had little to commend himself to working-class voters. Hardie's attitude towards Morley, then, was completely logical – and the natural consequence of his deep suspicion of the Liberal party leadership since Mid-Lanark. Even so, the decision to urge the Newcastle voters to vote Unionist was surely a mistaken one. Logic had supplanted common sense. It made any co-operation between Hardie and backbench Liberals on such questions as an eight-hour day or unemployment polices a difficult cause. Hardie's record in parliament between 1892 and 1895, however inspiring in terms of propaganda, was a relative failure in terms of practical results. He was to prove less effective than, for instance, Burns, who diligently mended his fences with the Liberals. Hardie's role in the 1892 election confirmed the view that he was an incorrigible outsider. It went some way towards ensuring that he would represent West Ham in the Commons for one parliament only. If it served as a symbolic episode in the preliminary manoeuvres leading to a labour alliance, it alienated far too many potential Lib-Lab sympathizers. It ensured that for years to come Keir Hardie remained impotent in the wilderness.

His role in the new parliament was not easy to predict. He made conciliatory gestures towards Burns in the hope that they, with Havelock Wilson and other labour representatives, might co-operate in the new session. 'I have carefully avoided saying anything, either in speech or in writing, which by any possibility could be construed into a declaration of policy or action for the Labour party. I have made no definite announcement concerning what I personally intend doing in the House of Commons, & that does not go beyond where I intend to sit.'[17] This referred to his intention to sit permanently on the Opposition benches. Hardie and Burns agreed on the immediate policy of not taking part in debate until the House rose and Gladstone was confirmed as premier, and both sat with the Irish below the gangway on the Opposition side.

Still, Burns and the other 'labour' members could not view Hardie as an automatic or natural ally. Hardie had continued to pursue his role as critic at the Trades Union Congress, and was even more detested by the Lib-Lab establishment on the Parliamentary Committee. But now the tide of opinion was significantly changing. At the Liverpool TUC in September 1890 the congress voted in favour of the eight-hour principle for the first time.[18] As the unemployment campaign gained momentum, the arguments advanced by Tom Mann and other socialists on behalf of the limitation of working hours were now finding general support. At Newcastle in 1891, Hardie's amendment in favour of the eight-hour day on a compulsory basis, save where the workers balloted against it (a concession to groups such as the cotton spinners and the Durham and Northumberland miners), was carried by the large margin of 285 votes to 183.[19] Fortified by this, Hardie's aggressive campaign for the purge of the TUC Parliamentary Committee continued unabated. Broadhurst had retired as secretary in February 1890, giving ill-health as the reason. According to the *Miner*, he had long been suffering from 'an acute attack of the Labour Party, accentuated by an application of several of H.H. Champion's mustard plasters'.[20] Hardie continued his relentless assault on Pickard, Burt and the residue of the Lib-Lab old guard. It did not bode well for parliamentary collaboration with these men when Hardie arrived in the Commons.

One incident above all others influenced Hardie's parliamentary career from the start. It contributed more than any other episode to the legends that later surrounded his name. This was the mode of entry into parliament that he adopted on 3 August 1892.[21] His constituents in dockland had intended to give a rousing send-off for their new member. A two-horse brake was hired to transport him from West Ham to Westminster. A cornet-player in the box seat, in the absence of any agreed labour or socialist refrain, played the strains of the 'Marseillaise', presumably a hopeful portent of revolution. Hardie, however, had to alight when the police refused to let this unorthodox carriage proceed through the gates of the Palace of Westminster. What really provoked anxious comment, however, was Hardie's dress. In the words of an astonished London reporter, it was 'the ideal dress of a Labour member – yellow tweed trousers, serge jacket and vest, and soft tweed cap'.[22] A rosette was prominent in his button-hole. The contrast with the sartorial staidness of the other members could not have been more stark. George Lambert, a stupefied Liberal backbencher, in comparing John Burns with Hardie, commented: 'Here is a Labour man dressed like a gentleman, but look at that bugger.'[23] As luck would have it, Hardie's arrival coincided with that of Gladstone himself who reacted to this multi-hued bearded apparition from West Ham with ill-concealed amazement. 'The man in the cloth cap' had arrived.

Hardie's entry into parliament has generated a thousand legends. His

headgear in particular has become sanctified as the simple attire of a
rough Scottish miner, contrasted with the bourgeois conventionalism
of a frock-coated, top-hatted House of Commons. The cloth cap has
always been revered in Labour mythology as the touchstone of an
earlier, purer contact with the grass roots of working-class revolt. In
fact, Hardie's habitual style of headgear was a topic of some debate;
contemporaries provided a variety of descriptions of it. John Burns
saw him wearing 'an old deerstalker cap and knickers of check' in
1892.[24] While Hardie's election leaflets and posters invariably placed
a plain miner's cap on his head, he usually wore a Sherlock Holmes-
type deerstalker in the House thereafter. Sometimes a long purple
muffler added to the effect. Later after 1900 a slouch hat bought in
Philadelphia, backed up by a red cravat, crowned his glory.[25] Sometimes, in hot weather, he padded round the House stockingless in
sandals. Abroad, he sometimes favoured a kimono obtained in Japan.
These sartorial matters are of more than trivial importance. Neither
in headgear nor in any other respect was Hardie a conventional working man. His colourful attire on entering parliament in August 1892
was the last thing that a Scottish miner would wear. It revealed
Hardie rather as a bohemian, an eccentric, 'Queer Hardie' indeed, who
entered the labour movement as much for private, personal reasons as
for reasons of identity with the proletariat. Even in the working-class
world, he was an outsider; his dress, cap and all, only confirmed the
point. Mass movements were never congenial to him. The bodies he
was involved with – the Scottish Labour Party above all – were small
and schismatic. He was instinctively attracted to minorities. Hardie
even claimed that parliament itself was alien to him. 'He hated sitting
with the "gentlemen of England". He was not at home there. He
would like to be back home in the country with the birds and flowers.'[26]
It was in romantic moods like this that Hardie found Frank Smith a
congenial and responsive companion. It was worlds removed from the
tough, pragmatic approach of a parliamentary politician, let alone the
trade union organizer. Hardie's mode of entry into parliament was
evocative of the complex layers of one elusive personality, not of the
struggles of a class. The misunderstanding of the cloth cap of 1892 has
continued to mislead Labour militants down to the present time.

Hardie was at the cross-roads in his career in August 1892. His
industrial activities were now receding in importance; he was leaving

Cumnock behind. It was to his role as a political propagandist and organizer that his efforts were now being devoted. But his outlook as a politician seemed as contradictory as ever. He was foremost among those anxious to harmonize working-class and socialist organizations in Scotland, the West Riding, London's East End, and elsewhere, and forge them into a new alliance. Yet his political outlook was still ambiguous, no doubt deliberately so. He could still be located within the Liberal coalition. His election at West Ham was the outcome of Liberal sympathy with his cause, yet his challenge to John Morley at Newcastle largely threw it away. His relationship with the Liberal leadership seemed hard to determine. Ponsonby, her private secretary, told the Queen, 'Mr Keir Hardie – whom the Scotch would have nothing to do with – was elected for an East London district and presumed to be the mouthpiece of the "Labour Party". He says that party do not care for Home Rule but will support it in the hopes of getting Mr Gladstone to support their demands.'[27] Hardie proclaimed before his constituents the need for an independent Labour Party. But the strategy and philosophy of such a party remained obscure. Somehow in August 1892 he represented, vaguely enough, a policy on 'forward from Liberalism', and of bringing social questions such as the eight-hour day and unemployment, to the fore. His independence of outlook was dramatically confirmed when he handed over a cheque of £100 from Andrew Carnegie, the American millionaire steel tycoon who had so recently and so brutally suppressed American labour unions in the Homestead strike at Pittsburgh, to his own election committee at West Ham.[28] The same fate awaited a further £100 given towards his election expenses by Hudson, a soap-manufacturer sympathetic to socialism, which came through the enigmatic mediation of Maltman Barry.[29] Hardie could impose his own terms on gifts offered in the Greek manner by subtle capitalists. What his attitude would be towards Liberalism and indeed towards the parliamentary process in general, the new session would unfold. Only then would the implications of the 'cloth cap' be revealed. Until then, Keir Hardie would remain, as for long he had been, a political enigma.

IV Member for the Unemployed (1892–5)

In August 1892 Keir Hardie for the first time had a national platform. He was the first Labour member of parliament acknowledged to be independent; the charisma he acquired from this unique position would remain with him for the rest of his career. His entry into parliament also meant, naturally, a considerable upheaval in his private life. He had to find somewhere to live in London, and his income, now derived solely from journalism, was meagre. His eventual abode was Frank Smith's large house in Chelsea, which Hardie used as office and *pied à terre* throughout the 1892–5 parliament. Here Hardie and Smith communed on political and social questions of the day. Their interest in spiritualism and the supernatural was intensified; Hardie even attended a seance which was supposed to determine his vote on the 1893 Irish Home Rule Bill. (The outer world cast its vote in favour of Gladstone.)[1] For all that, Smith proved to be a generous and selfless friend. As Hardie wore himself out in ceaseless campaigning and speechmaking, in founding and building up the Independent Labour Party, in starting up a new weekly newspaper, and in crusading on behalf of the unemployed, Frank Smith's companionship and hospitality were indispensable.

Hardie, it may be surmised, found a calm release with Smith that he seldom found at home. Mrs Hardie played even less part in his public career following his election to Westminster. She stayed in the home at Old Cumnock, tending to the three children, and Hardie's visits there during the parliamentary session became more and more infrequent. His emotional resources were fully consumed in his public activities, in campaigning and propaganda on behalf of radical causes. Even so, his somewhat limited private life led to some frustration for so passionate and outward-going a man. He needed friendship, especially perhaps the balm of female companionship. He found these, in part, with Dr Richard Pankhurst, a wealthy barrister active in the socialist movement in Manchester, and with his handsome wife, Emmeline, already an ardent women's suffragist. Hardie's relationship with them was unquestionably political.

But he briefly struck up an acquaintance that was less Platonic. This was with Annie Hines, the pretty twenty-two year-old daughter of an Oxford chimney sweep who was prominent in the local branch of the Fabian Society. Between May and July 1893, Hardie's relationship with 'Sparks', as he affectionately nicknamed her, became highly involved, and he paid repeated visits to Oxford to see her. In the remote Buckinghamshire village of Botolph Claydon, close to the Verney estate much visited by Florence Nightingale, they had lengthy walks and discussions; their amorous character clearly emerges from what correspondence has been preserved.[2] To Annie, Hardie unburdened himself on the theme of marriage and on the male-female relationship:

Sympathy of the helpful kind is very largely sentiment or communion of spirit, and if the marriage tie, or rather the wedded life, degenerates into a business partnership, the development of a finer, higher feeling may be checked and no hypothetical gain will ever compensate for its loss. . . . With the wrong people, the relations can never be right, let the external arrangements be what they may.

By contrast, Hardie lamented the 'nine whole days yet before I see you. They will resemble nine ages or centuries'. He regaled Annie with sentimental accounts of the Knight Errant and the Lady Fair, who met at the imaginary city of Nodyalchplotob (in reverse). 'Her wondrous eyes spoke with a power which thrilled him through and through.' 'His cheek to hers he oft did lay and love was ever the tale he told.'[3] Hardie's relationship with Annie was brief but intense. He saw her both as a lover and as an indulged favourite daughter. As always, he emphasized his own advancing years, as though a man of thirty-seven was generations removed from a girl of twenty-two. Their correspondence is in many ways a pathetic one. In his letters to Annie, Hardie pours out some of the despair and sense of personal suffering which impelled him throughout his political career. The loneliness and sense of gloomy premonition that they reflect are the essential backcloth to the inspiring crusader and the inexhaustible organizer familiar to the press and the platform. They present a dimension of

Hardie, in some ways a tragic, unfulfilled personality, which the 'cloth cap' legends essentially miss.

Established in the House, he launched his efforts to make an impact on the Honourable Members. His first intervention came on 18 August during the address in reply to the Queen's Speech, a few days after Gladstone had taken office for the fourth time.[4] But Hardie's first appearance in debate was not an auspicious one. He had misunderstood a complex point of parliamentary procedure a few days earlier when he failed to rise to move an amendment calling for an autumn session to consider the plight of the unemployed. The Speaker informed Hardie, in patronizing tones, that since he failed to rise when his amendment was called, the discussion lapsed. As the new ministers had yet to take their seats, no questions about unemployment could be put to them. With MPs seething with anticipation about the new Irish Home Rule bill, Hardie was virtually brushed aside. Impatiently, he had to wait until the new session which met in February. On 7 February 1893 he made his maiden speech, a powerful declaration which drew attention to the industrial depression and the plight of the unemployed.[5] He claimed that four million of the working population and their families were now without means of subsistence. Pending a more comprehensive programme, he outlined some short-term proposals – an expansion of government labour in dockyards, factories and arsenals; an increase in the minimum wage for labourers to sixpence an hour; a forty-eight-hour week for all government employees; and, perhaps, some experiments with land colonies. It was a forceful speech, which met with a predictably negative response from the government. The division followed party lines, since his 111 supporters included 101 Conservatives. For the rest of the session, Hardie emerged in discussion usually as a persistent and fiery questioner of ministers such as H.H. Fowler, President of the Local Government Board. Hardie often raised the role of local authorities in combating local distress of the kind with which he was so familiar at West Ham. He also spoke on the operation of the Factory Acts, and on the use of troops to preserve order during a prolonged dock strike at Hull. In general, he kept to labour and social issues. He adopted a wider, and more radical, theme on 14 July when he tried to move a motion which deplored the congratulations being offered to the Duke of York on his marriage.[6] At a time of widespread poverty and distress, 'there is nothing in connection with the recent Royal Marriage which called for special notice by this House'. This, too, was brushed aside, and Hardie's republicanism aroused little comment.

When the House rose in July he could point to a prolonged series of interrogations on behalf of the labouring poor. No back-bencher had been more persistent in ventilating the issue of unemployment, and in exposing the crude repression used in putting down workers' demonstrations. It was a tense summer of industrial confrontations. There was a bloody hauliers' strike in the Welsh mining valleys: Hardie sought to move the adjournment of the House on this. In Featherstone in Yorkshire during the month of August, troops opened fire on demonstrating miners and two men were killed. The Home Secretary, Asquith, took a remarkably casual view of the incident, and 'Featherstone' was to take its place alongside 'Tonypandy' in working-class martyrology and oral tradition. Hardie was among the very few backbenchers courageous enough to expose repressive behaviour of this kind, at a time when local government reform, the Welsh church and the eternal morass of Irish home rule absorbed much of popular attention. His persistent emphasis on the supreme problem of structural unemployment helped to spur on discussion of social issues generally neglected. Even so, there is little doubt that he was a less effective member of parliament than he later became. His speeches, scribbled hurriedly in railway carriages on the way to public meetings or in midnight sessions in Frank Smith's Chelsea home, were too often rambling, his statistics too often impressionistic, even romantic. Further, he conveyed the clear impression that he viewed the proceedings of the Commons with disdain and found parliamentary debate to be a meaningless charade. Indeed, the time he spent at the House was strictly limited. He took part in fewer than half the divisions in the 1892–5 parliament, as was unfailingly pointed out by his opponents. Hardie unblushingly told his West Ham constituents that he found the conventions of the House distasteful and boring. MPs were consumed with 'pettifogging questions' like Welsh disestablishment or licensing reform.[7] He freely admitted that he spent much of his time travelling round the country agitating on behalf of labour and radical causes. In return, he was freely accused of neglecting his constituency, of concentrating on 'mankind' at the expense of men, of forgetting the dying bird of mundane, grass-roots issues. Many local radicals who had supported Hardie at West Ham in 1892 now complained that they had landed themselves with an irresponsible socialistic agitator instead. At the next election they would gain revenge.

Hardie's strategy at Westminster did not add to his effectiveness. In the *New Review* he renewed the call for political independence by the labour movement.[8] In practice, this meant an immediate conflict with the Liberals because 'they are the rival claimants for the support of the Democracy'. The major parties, he claimed, were indistinguishable when they were in office. They wasted time on trivialities like registration and Church schools, while millions of their fellow men were starving. 'The business of the new party [the ILP] is to do battle with Toryism. . . . The chief impediment is the Liberal Party.' The workers, he argued, needed the control of the land and the instruments of production to give them 'the full fruits of their labour'. He warned against local pacts with the Liberals in two-member seats, and advocated an independent stand by labour in politics as complete as that adopted by the Irish Nationalists. In parliamentary terms this made Hardie's role little more than a symbolic one. There were many pressure-groups agitating against the Liberal leadership in the 1892 parliament – radicals anxious to frustrate a 'forward' policy by Rosebery and Grey in East Africa; the Welsh Party demanding clearer guarantees on the future of Welsh disestablishment and 'home rule all round'; other lobbies involved with land reform, temperance and 'one man, one vote'. But all these factions, aware as they were that the government's majority had fallen to a little over twenty after by-election defeats and that any majority depended on the loyalty of the Irish, were still included within the Liberal coalition. Basically, in an ultimate test of confidence in Gladstone's government, they remained loyal to the party whips. This remained true even after Rosebery succeeded Gladstone as premier in March 1894 in circumstances which cast the fragmented parliamentary Liberal Party into further disarray. Hardie was an exception to this rule. He sought an independent role; indeed, as has been seen, he viewed the Liberals as the immediate enemy, even though he distinguished between aspects of Liberalism as a creed and the central Liberal Party machine. This made day-to-day co-operation with backbench radicals almost inconceivable. At the outset, Hardie had written to the Liberal back bencher, L. Atherley-Jones, 'I have the feeling that in the end the advanced men in the Radical Party and ourselves [the labour members] will get together somehow.' He suggested the appointment of a Radical whip.[9] Certainly, his demands for an eight-hour day, for state pensions, for the abolition of child labour and for an end to indirect taxation meant that there was much common ground between him and many radicals of the Dilke type. But, in practice, his refusal to moderate his opposition to the government deprived him of much more than nuisance value on most issues. The prospect of any collaboration with other labour members such as John Burns and Havelock Wilson disappeared. Burns complained about Hardie's habit of making spectacular gestures in the House 'without consulting with those who should have been asked upon the matter'. The Lib-Lab members, mainly miners, regarded Hardie as a wrecker, after his aggressive tactics at the TUC and his vitriolic personal attacks on Broadhurst and others. The result was that Hardie was a lone and ineffective figure in the House in 1892–4, exotic in appearance, frustrated and unproductive in action.[10]

Hardie saw his role in the House as basically prophetic, an index of the coming capture of power by the mass democracy. He was an agitator incongruously sitting on the backbenches, who addressed the voiceless masses outside the House in the slums and backstreets, rather than the over-fed, well-heeled members reclining on the green benches. He described with puritanical contempt the lavish menus provided in the House of Commons' restaurant and the anxiety of members to suspend parliamentary business for the sake of Derby day. His main enterprise was trying to create an independent labour party outside the House. This eventually came into being with the formation of the ILP at the Bradford Labour Institute on 13 January 1893. This new movement was the product of many influences, of which Hardie was but one. A new initiative had been taken in the summer of 1892 by Joseph Burgess, editor of the *Workmen's Times*. A body called 'the National Independent Labour Party', had been founded on 13 June at the Democratic Club in London, just off the Strand. Hardie was present here and he also presided over a further meeting convened during the TUC held at Glasgow the following September.[11] Here it was decided to create an independent labour party on a nationwide basis. For the first time, Hardie was closely associated with such 'new union' activists as Pete Curran of the Gasworkers in forming a new political organization. Its birthplace was easily determined. Bradford, in the West Riding woollen region of Yorkshire, was the home of over twenty labour clubs, together with Labour Churches and a militant Trades Council. There were two Labour councillors on the municipal council, one being Fred Jowett, a lifelong disciple of Hardie (whose private papers have been destroyed). Bradford, then, was the natural venue for inaugurating a revolution in British labour politics. Hardie himself took the opportunity to address the congress of the Congregational Union of England and Wales held there in October, and to flay the churches for their neglect of the issue of unemployment.[12] He declared:

> Christianity today lay buried, bound up in the cerements of a dead and lifeless theology. It awaited decent burial, and they in the Labour movement had come to resuscitate the Christianity of Christ, to go back to the time when the poor should have the Gospel preached to them, and the Gospel should be good news of joy and happiness in life. . . . Ring out the darkness of the land, Ring in the Christ that is to be.

Hardie's speech caused an uproar amongst the Congregationalists, and he was rapidly shepherded away. But to socialists and advanced radicals, he seemed the messiah of a new faith destined to regenerate mankind.

The delegates at Bradford in January, over a hundred and twenty in number, were predominantly northern in origin.[13] Over a third came from the West Riding woollen area. Nevertheless, from the outset the new body took a national stance. Hardie was throughout its dominant personality, showing how the impact of his entry into parliament had permeated far beyond West Ham. He was elected conference chairman by a majority of fifty-four to twenty-seven, over a local Bradfordian, W.H. Drew. John Lister, a landowner of eccentric personality from Shibden Hall, was elected treasurer. Hardie's chairman's address struck the keynote. He demanded an independent party drawn from the ranks of labour. Its object should be 'economic freedom – the natural outcome of political enfranchisement'. A socialist plank calling for the collective ownership of the means of production, distribution and exchange was adopted almost unanimously. On the other hand, bridges were left open to radical Liberals and to trade unionists. The overwhelming majority of the items on the new party programme were part and parcel of the standard advanced radicalism of the day.

Social policies such as the eight-hour day and the abolition of piece-work, sweating and child labour; political programmes such as the payment of members, shorter parliaments, adult suffrage and the referendum; fiscal demands such as a graduated income tax and the abolition of indirect taxation – these did not divide the Bradford delegates from radicals elsewhere. Much of this was the result of Hardie's flexibility. Indeed, his own pet theme of temperance reform also emerged strongly, an echo of earlier crusading in western Scotland. 'The Public house was the strongest ally on the side of the usurer, the sweater and the landlord,' Hardie cried, amidst loud cheering. The landlord and the capitalist were to be the main targets, but the inclusion of time-honoured radical demands dating from the Cobden-Bright era, with an ancestry that went back to Tom Paine or even the Levellers, showed that this was socialism of a singularly wide-ranging, insular kind. Indeed, the delegates received the warm congratulation of the German 'revisionist', Eduard Bernstein, who contrasted their flexibility with the rigid dogma favoured by most of his Social Democrat colleagues at home.

On all the key decisions of the conference Hardie's influence was decisive. He took the lead in demanding that affiliation should be adopted as the basis for branch organization – this would allow a wide range of local bodies, trades councils, radical clubs and other groups to be embraced within the ILP. Branch autonomy and weak central executive direction were the essential features of the new party at its inception. Hardie also argued successfully against the demands made by Manchester socialists, headed by his friend Dr Richard Pankhurst, in favour of the 'Fourth Clause'. This would have prevented ILP members from voting for sympathetic radical (or, conceivably, Tory) candidates in local elections. Hardie sought a flexibility of tactics for the ILP that he seldom displayed himself in the House. His political genius showed itself above all in the agreement that the party be called the Independent Labour Party, instead of 'The Socialist Labour Party' as Scottish delegates demanded. Hardie's intuitive awareness of the deterrent effect of dogmatic titles was a shrewd appreciation of the English working-class mind – one which, incidentally, carried him still further away from the labour movement in his native Scotland. The new party, in fact, left many options open. It could build on its claim for the support of Lib-Lab trade unionists. It could reinforce the growing tide of opinion within the TUC in favour of independent working-class representation. It could provide a haven for isolated groups of socialists, especially those weaned in the revivalist comradeship of the nonconformist chapels. At the same time, it provided a common denominator of co-operation for those advanced radicals who sought more modest changes in the control of the economy, but who also sensed the urgent need for social regeneration. It enabled working-class and middle-class reformers to make common cause. The ILP provided, in short, a platform for growth. This was confirmed by the fact that within a year four hundred branches existed, mainly in Yorkshire, Lancashire and Cheshire, with an estimated membership of 50,000. The contrast between the rapid early expansion of the ILP, attuned as it was to British political attitudes, and the sluggish growth of the Marxist SDF was widely noted.

Hardie at first turned down the presidency of the new party. However, when its executive, the so-called National Administrative Council (NAC) was chosen at the second annual conference at Manchester in February 1894, he was elected chairman by a massive majority.[14] He remained chairman for the next six years. From the start the new party was regarded as his personal creation. He was its symbol and its prophet. The party included several other formidable figures, notably Tom Mann of the Engineers who was elected party secretary in 1894 and to whose 'mercurial temperament' Hardie regarded himself as a counter-weight.[15] Nevertheless, Hardie dominated the new body from the outset. It was viewed in a special sense as a personal instrument – a fact which caused much political difficulty after 1900 as the party began to branch away from the forces which had originally created it and when younger men like Ramsay MacDonald and Philip Snowden came to the fore. Hardie's claim to be the only true begetter of the ILP could be challenged. As has been seen, it grew largely from spontaneous local movements in the West Riding; it was always centrifugal in character, despite the authority of the NAC. Without doubt, however, in parliament, in the press and on the platform, he was its ascendant personality, its major organizer, tactician and inspiration. In so far as the ILP provided the lynch-pin of the labour alliance that came into being after 1900, Hardie's contribution to its growth and to the revolutionizing of British politics, was of crucial importance.

Throughout the summer and autumn of 1893, he spent his energies in ceaseless campaigning up and down the country. One, not untypical, week was outlined to his readers in the *Labour Leader* – Tuesday, open-air meetings at Canning Town and Whitechapel in his constituency; Wednesday, at the Commons; Thursday, office work and a night journey by train to Scotland; Friday, socialist agitation in Scotland; Saturday, a speech to a labour demonstration at Dundee and an overnight journey to Leeds; Sunday, speeches at Leeds, Keighley and Halifax; Monday, further speeches at Halifax, Bradford and Bolton; Tuesday, back to London for more office work and renewed appearances in the Commons.[16] In these years, the legend of Keir Hardie was born. From these years also derived the intense physical and emotional strain that led to his premature death. The deep furrows on his brow, his greying hair showed the toll that was being taken. In addition, his life acquired at this time a wholly new dimension. For years he had been a tireless propagandist through the printed word. *The Miner* had given way to the *Labour Leader*, produced in Glasgow. Eventually, Hardie managed to amass the share capital to fulfil one of his ambitions – a London-based independent labour weekly newspaper. On 31 March 1894, the weekly *Labour Leader* appeared for the first time.

From the beginning, the *Labour Leader* bore the imprint of its first editor. It lacked the earthy humanism and the good humour of Robert Blatchford's *Clarion*. It was far more earnest, without being dogmatic. Hardie himself supplied much of the copy, some of the management expertise and some of the equipment (which later led to a fierce altercation in the courts with the Labour Literature Society of Glasgow). The much-harassed David Lowe ran the office. Hardie wrote all the editorial comment and also at times the women's column under the pseudonym of 'Lily Bell'. The children's column by 'Daddy Time', with its sentimental references to pit ponies and to the countryside ('Mother Earth in her spring dress') was signed in every line. Hardie gaily introduced his staff as if they were a family – Bob (Smillie), Sam (Hobson), Bruce (Glasier) and Fred (Brocklehurst). 'The floor slopes, the walls bulge but the flues draw. The bulges on the wall have been flattened and the office furniture specially designed to harmonise with the slope of the floor. If you are under 17 stone, call the first day you are in London.'[17] From the start, the *Labour Leader* was more than simply an organ proclaiming labour representation. It was uniquely identified with the ILP. There was no attempt to build bridges towards the SDF at this time of optimistic growth. The *Leader* was a unique fund of information about local ILP branches and divisional activities. On the other hand, it also reflected a private culture, an inner world, a wide-ranging critique of the values of late Victorian society. To a contributor like Bruce Glasier (who looked after the Scottish edition), its appeal was essentially aesthetic, a protest against the philistinism and squalor of *fin-de-siècle* imperial Britain.[18] In this sense the *Labour Leader* was far more than simply the organizational journal of the ILP, preaching to the converted. It was an evangelist proclaiming a secular religion. Its style was often dull and pedestrian. It compared badly with Blatchford's *Clarion* in humour and read-ability. Its connection with Hardie could cause difficulty and eventually was to lead to the ILP taking over complete control of the paper and in effect deposing Hardie as editor-manager, in 1903–4. Still, it rapidly became the most effective, because the most authoritative, vehicle for the social democratic cause. Its circulation mounted steadily, reaching an alleged 50,000 by mid-1894.[19] For thousands of working people, and for radical middle-class sympathizers, it became the most influential vehicle for their discontent with social conditions. It reflected the emerging strains within Gladstonian Liberalism, while retaining an evangelical, crusading tone which appealed to non-conformist radicals. And its unique identification with Hardie added force to his claim to be the supreme tribune of the voiceless and the dispossessed.

There were exciting events for the *Labour Leader* to describe in 1894–5. The Rosebery government frequently seemed on the point of imminent collapse, the flight of working-class voters towards the emergent ILP already well under way. The by-election performances of the new party were distinctly encouraging. Lister, its candidate at Halifax in March 1893, captured over a quarter of the poll. Hardie in the *Labour Leader* drew the moral later that any electoral arrange-ment with the Liberals should henceforth be scrapped. He himself seemed positively to welcome the prospect of Liberal opposition in the next election at West Ham South. The success of ILP recruiting drives in areas well removed from the original strongholds in the West Riding augured well: Hardie himself visited South Wales in March

1894 and described the formation of new branches at Neath, Briton Ferry and Cardiff among other places.[21] One disagreeable setback was renewed failure at Mid-Lanark. In a by-election there in April 1894, after Wynford Philipps's resignation, Bob Smillie polled only 1,221 votes, no great improvement on Hardie's performance six years earlier. An appeal by Hardie to John Burns to help Smillie in the campaign had met with no response, and £90 had to be spent from *Labour Leader* funds. Still, Hardie could again attribute this defeat to the defection of the Irish and could claim that it was not typical of the country as a whole.[22] Elsewhere, there were excellent ILP polls at by-elections at Sheffield (Attercliffe), Leicester and Bristol East. The result at Attercliffe brought Hardie particular satisfaction since the candidate here was Frank Smith, a last-minute import after the local Liberal Association had rejected Charles Hobson, a trades unionist. Smith's poll of over 1,000 in an improvised campaign convinced Hardie that the mass defection of working men from Gladstonian Liberalism was near at hand.[23] By the beginning of 1895 there were twenty-two ILP candidates nominated for the forthcoming general election and the party's leaders confidently spurned all overtures from the Liberal whips about collaboration in two-member constituencies. Also, significant recruits were being won for the party. Among them was the twenty-eight-year-old Ramsay MacDonald, who announced after the Attercliffe contest that he had finally broken with Liberalism and had joined the ILP. 'Liberalism and more particularly local Liberal Associations', he wrote to Hardie, 'have definitely declared against Labour, and so I must accept the facts of the situation and candidly admit that the prophecies of the ILP relating to Liberalism have been amply justified.'[24] So began the long-drawn-out tragi-comedy of the partnership between Hardie and MacDonald, which, with many shifts and turns and at the cost of much personal feuding, transformed the ILP from an inchoate pressure-group into the core of a nation-wide party.

If the ILP was making news, so emphatically was Hardie. He continued his many-sided campaign for the labour cause. He was encouraged by the new working-class support enlisted for the ILP by the 'new unionism' in unskilled trades and the rapid expansion of skilled unions such as the Engineers and the Railway Servants. He still attended the TUC annually and joined with other militants in pushing it decisively to the left. After the ratification of the eight-hour day as an official TUC objective in 1891, the Glasgow congress in 1892 carried by one vote an ambiguous motion on behalf of a 'Trade Union Labour Party'. At the Norwich TUC in 1894 a much more advanced programme was approved, including the passage, by 219 votes to 61, of Hardie's motion on behalf of the nationalization of the means of production, distribution and of exchange, and also of the land.[25] Under the pressure of growing trade recession and unemployment, and of mounting class conflict in the mines and the docks, the unions were moving decisively towards collectivism; Hardie was a significant figure in this process. On the other hand, he had never been a major figure in the union world and his role at the TUC was rapidly coming to its close. In 1895 the revision of the conference's standing orders effectively excluded Hardie, who was no longer a full-time union organizer.[26] He never attended the TUC again. This seems to have caused him little anguish, for, despite his frequent protestations to the contrary, it was clear that for him it was in parliament that the real struggle for power had to be waged.

Hardie had also made an appearance (February 1892) before the Royal Commission inquiring into labour conditions. He claimed to be representing the Ayrshire Miners as president; he had surrendered their secretaryship some months before. He used the occasion to renew his advocacy of the eight-hour day and also of state insurance. His emergent socialism also came out much more forcibly than before, as he urged the nationalization of the mines, although on the basis of local rather than of central control. He rejected the description of 'Anarchist' but, somewhat reluctantly, accepted that of 'State Socialist'. Asked whether 'you would be prepared to risk the dislocation of every industry to establish a new system of government', Hardie gave a passionate affirmative.[27] In fact, his entire career made a mockery of an emotional response of this kind. But in the circumstances, with propaganda as the immediate objective, his reply was manifestly the right one to give.

It was, however, through his activities as a parliamentarian that Hardie most powerfully established himself as the champion of labour. As the autumn session of 1893 petered out, with the final collapse of Gladstone's second Home Rule Bill for Ireland, Hardie continued his role as persistent critic of the ministers. As always, his most effective theme was that of unemployment. On 12 December 1893, he moved a motion on the adjournment for an inquiry into the deaths and suicides that resulted from unemployment and starvation.[28] He gave his estimate of the extent of the problem – 100,000 wholly out of work in London, another 50,000 casually employed, thousands more jobless in Birmingham, Hull, Sheffield, Liverpool and Barrow-in-Furness. 'It should not pass the wit of the House to devise means to prevent one man being killed by overtime while another was starving through lack of work.' He finished with a surging peroration. 'Within sight, almost within sound of this House, the moans of the wretched and the groans of the dying might be heard, and he trusted the outcome of this discussion would be to sweep away the disgrace which attached to this assembly to do anything to meeting the claims of from 1,000,000 to 1,500,000 of British workmen.' In reply, Sir Walter Foster, the minister responsible at the Local Government Board, questioned Hardie's statistics, but promised no action. It all confirmed Hardie's view, often expressed in print, that 'the workers are coming to see that Liberalism, not Toryism, is the foe they have most to fear'. In the following session he followed up with several cogent statements on behalf of the miners' eight-hour day, on employment conditions at government workshops such as the Woolwich Arsenal (until recently the very citadel of the respectable labour aristocracy), and on sweating in small industrial firms. Even the most hallowed of Liberal shibboleths did not pass unchallenged. Hardie observed (19 February 1895) that 'no-one who supported Trade Unionism could claim to be a consistent Free Trader. Free Trade was a good thing as long as there were equal conditions; but the Trade Unionists of this country had no intention of allowing the sweaters of the under-paid worker of continental nations to enter into competition with them.'[29] On the other hand, he denied that protection, as advocated by Champion amongst others, could be a basic cure for unemployment, for this was rooted in the malfunctioning of privately-run capitalism.

Hardie's activities in the House could well have modified the original impression he had created of being just an irresponsible firebrand. True, his parliamentary appearances did not meet with universal praise in the notoriously schismatic socialist world. Members of the Social Democratic Federation thought them exhibitionist. Hardie's unparliamentary dress – 'a peak cloth cap with braid round it; a dark blue pilot coat and a pair of brown trousers . . . the mere Sunday best of the ordinary navvy' – seemed to Blatchford in the *Clarion* the product not of revolutionary zeal but of simple vanity.[30] Other socialists disputed not so much Hardie's style as his strategy. Engels and the Marxist element within the ILP bitterly denounced Hardie as a crypto-Tory. Engels had now lost all his earlier admiration for him. 'Since his election,' he wrote to August Bebel, 'Keir Hardie has pushed himself in front in a partly ridiculous, partly disgraceful manner. . . . The success has gone to his head.' Writing to Sorge, Engels developed these attacks further. Hardie was 'an over-cunning Scot whose demagogic artfulness one cannot trust'. Money for the *Labour Leader*, he alleged, came from Tory and anti-Home Rule sources. Hardie appeared in parliament 'only at demagogic occasions to make himself important by speeches about the unemployed without achieving anything'. Engels looked forward with grim pleasure to Hardie's defeat at the polls.[31] But these opinions, which reflected the evolutionary gradualist theory of class consciousness which Engels elaborated after Marx's death, were not typical. Most members of the ILP regarded parliament as the forum of the nation and Hardie as their major political asset.

Hardie's career in the House, however, was marked by one episode which endured in the memory long after his constructive questioning on behalf of the unemployed had been forgotten. This followed a pit disaster at Cilfynydd in an area of east Glamorgan which Hardie had recently visited. In the Albion colliery 251 men and boys were killed in a terrifying explosion; indeed, over a thousand miners had been lost in explosions during the past three years alone. As events turned out, this mining disaster in a Welsh valley coincided with apparently more newsworthy events – the assassination of President Carnot in France, and above all the birth of a royal baby, the son of the Duke of York, later destined to be made King Edward VIII. Hardie's genuine anguish at this fatal pit disaster was turned into fury by the press celebration of the royal birth at a moment of such human tragedy. In his newspaper, his anger gushed forth. 'The life of one Welsh miner is of greater commercial and moral value to the British nation than the whole Royal Crowd put together, from the Royal Great Grand-Mama down to this puling Royal Great-Grand-child.'[32] It was hard to determine whether compassion or republicanism played the more dominant role in Hardie's onslaught. However, he could write what he liked in the *Labour Leader* for the benefit of ILP supporters. It was his decision to carry his protest on to the floor of the House of Commons that caused the outcry.

On 28 June Hardie rose during a conventional motion which sought to congratulate the Duchess of York on the birth of her son.[33] From the start, he was fiercely interrupted as his disgust with the royal charade poured forth torrentially. 'It is a matter of small concern to me whether the future ruler of the nation be the genuine article or a spurious imitation.' He weighed in with fierce muck-raking attacks on the royal family individually. The Duke of Cornwall, the Prince of Wales in another guise, owned property in London 'which is made up of some of the vilest slums', and from which he drew £60,000 a year. Hardie added, for good measure, that 'the fierce white light' which beat upon the Prince's private life 'reveal things in his career it would be better to keep covered'. The new royal child was not spared either (as the Duke of Windsor recalled in his memoirs years later). 'From his childhood onwards, this boy will be surrounded by sycophants and flatterers by the score (cries of "Oh", "Oh").' The government, which could waste time in discussing so trivial an event, could not find time for a vote of condolence for the relatives of 'those who are lying stiff and stark in a Welsh valley'. Hardie's passion was genuine and his point entirely just. The unconcern with which mining tragedies and industrial strikes were dismissed by parliament as almost everyday events, needed to be voiced. The callous indifference of the Welsh coalowners towards pit safety, then and later, was notorious, even if the Welsh members of parliament, so eloquent in discussing chapel leases or the historical origins of tithe, were silent on the point. The scandalized shock with which Harcourt and an Ulster Unionist rallied to Hardie's angry onslaught made the point better than Hardie could himself.

Even so, his methods on this occasion were almost certainly a mistake. The effect of his intervention (reinforced, of course, by distorted reporting in the press) was to link it in the public mind with an attack on royalty first and foremost; the tragedy of Cilfynydd receded in attention. It would have been preferable if Hardie had confined himself to the pit disaster, and left the issue of monarchy, a low political priority for most radicals since the decline of Dilke's republican movement twenty years earlier, on one side. The speech largely nullified the effect of Hardie's constructive labours in the House without any positive compensation. On his later career, this passionate intervention had a lasting effect, one which damaged him. It confirmed the view of him as an irresponsible fanatic. To that extent, it made him a less influential force in the parliament which he hoped ultimately to capture. His patience, tactical flexibility and gradualism after 1895, as he sought to win over echelons of trade unions to the ideal of an alliance with the socialist societies, had to be set against the impression of extremism he left behind him in his first parliament. Hardie detested the very idea of monarchy. It offended not only his sense of democracy and of social equality; its vulgar ostentation offended his puritan ethic as well. The linking of monarchy with imperial grandeur, with military expansion in southern Africa and elsewhere seemed to him a sign of the corrupting effects of the jingo spirit throughout the land. Troops used in Matabeleland led to troops being used in Featherstone; militarism was one and indivisible. In each case, imperial patriotism was its squalid justification. Hardie never shed his pre-occupation with monarchy. His assault on Edward VII's visit to the Czar in 1908 and his open letter to George V on the future of the Dowlais iron works in 1912 showed that it lingered on to the end. The fact remained that republicanism was a distraction, and certainly not a vote-winner. It deflected public attention away from the real social and economic causes championed by the ILP and made its parliamentary spokesman appear a whirling, irresponsible demagogue. Hardie for once misjudged the national mood. On 28 June 1894 his passions took control over his political instincts. A period of comparative impotence was the indirect result.

The furore over the speech on the royal baby continued to reverberate throughout the press columns for the rest of Hardie's time in parliament. It led to severe criticism even amongst the Liberals of West Ham. It partly overshadowed what was Hardie's supreme achievement in this session – indeed, perhaps his greatest single service to the cause of the workers prior to the formation of a Labour Party – the forcing to the front of the issue of unemployment. Throughout 1894 the trade depression deepened. Nowhere was it more widely publicized than in Hardie's own West Ham. Here, in a decaying dockland area, sprawling between the East End of London and the Essex marshes, there were in an unusual degree the problems of casual working and of urban overcrowding. The relief afforded by the Metropolitan Common Poor Fund was negligible; the policies of the central government had scant effect. A fund set up by the Mayor of West Ham led to relief work being afforded to over two thousand men on a piece-work basis. Nevertheless, all surveys showed that these measures together tackled only a small fraction of the problem. Hardie himself was much involved in action on behalf of the local unemployed. He urged the local Boards of Guardians to pool their resources and to use the legal powers at their disposal to the full. He collaborated with the Liberal member for West Ham North, Archibald Grove, in putting pressure on the local authorities.[34] When the Prime Minister, Rosebery, visited the area in December 1894, Hardie confronted the unbelieving premier with the statistic that the country contained over a million unemployed. Over seven per cent of skilled artisans were receiving out-of-work pay from their trade unions. The total of un-skilled workmen who were out of work was almost incalculable. At a meeting at Canning Town, soon after his meeting with the Prime Minister, Hardie openly drew what seemed to him to be the inevitable moral to be drawn – the need for the ILP to emulate the Irish and to break away from Liberal tutelage on an entirely independent basis.[35]

In the winter of 1894–5 the situation in East London became critical. The weather was appallingly cold, with the Thames frozen over. Some unemployed men used to sweep the ice for the benefit of skaters.[36] Consequently, it was announced on 13 February that a twenty-five-man Select Committee had been set up to consider 'distress from want of employment', under the chairmanship of Sir Henry Campbell-Bannerman. There would be twelve members each from the Unionists and Liberals; in addition, Keir Hardie would serve as the Labour member.[37] For the first time, then, Hardie was in a position directly to influence the course of government policy; it was a great tribute to his lone campaign in the House and the nation over the previous years. Early on during the committee sessions, on 22 February, he himself gave evidence. He called for a central relief committee to be set up in every town. The central government could grant an equal sum to back money raised locally and by charitable agencies. He suggested £100,000 as the possible amount of such a treasury grant. He accepted that an extra penny rate would yield a greater sum. But 'localities without some special encouragement do not respond so freely as they ought to', while Boards of Guardians could not grant parochial aid without depriving the recipients of their vote. He estimated that there were about 1,750,000 unemployed in Britain and provided detailed figures for Leeds supplied to him by Tom Maguire of the Bradford ILP. He admitted that a grant of £100,000 would be only a temporary palliative, but at least it would feed some of the suffering until work could be found and trade revived.

Hardie's evidence before the committee was the fullest explanation he had yet given of the possible extension and supplementation of relief programmes for the unemployed. S.G. Hobson's malicious version that all Hardie could suggest for the unemployed was 'feed them' is a complete fiction. He concentrated on the narrow issue of short-term relief and the administrative mechanics of its distribution. Wider policies such as land colonies and national workshops he left on one side. It was by far the most radical scheme set before the committee and, inevitably, Hardie came under fire. He admitted, in the face of interrogation by a sympathetic Liberal, A.H.D. Acland, that his proposal of £100,000 would go nowhere towards meeting the problem, if it really was the case that the unemployed and their dependants amounted to six millions, as he claimed. The most significant clash, however, came when Hardie was questioned by John Burns, also a member of the Committee. Burns had already been infuriated by Hardie's freelance tactics in the House, and kept aloof from the nascent ILP. In embryo, the social policies he was so rigidly and so disastrously to pursue at the Local Government Board from 1905 onwards were foreshadowed in the tone of his questions. Burns placed the emphasis entirely on local relief. £10,000 'spent quietly' in West Ham would do far more good than an imperial grant from the exchequer which would only lead to an influx of 'vagrants and casuals' into the area. He gained from Hardie the significant admission that he had no first-hand knowledge of the administering of relief. Hardie replied characteristically that he never sat on relief boards 'on principle', because there was much more urgent work to be done elsewhere. He also agreed that, if there were no franchise disqualification for recipients of poor relief, the money might be spent more effectively by local guardians. Throughout the interrogations, the dialogue between Burns and Hardie assumed a significantly sharper tone. The contest for the political allegiance of the working-class mind between 1900 and 1914 was already foreshadowed.[38]

The affairs of West Ham remained well to the fore during the Committee's deliberation. Percy Alden, a radical Liberal who had worked for Hardie in 1892 and who was warden of the Mansfield University Settlement there, as well as secretary of the West Ham relief fund, warmly endorsed Hardie's proposals. He also pushed the idea of land colonies set up by local guardians for the unemployed, a scheme which he was to advocate as a Liberal MP after 1905. Arnold Hills, the chairman of the Shipbuilding Company in West Ham which had offered money to the council for relief on a piece-work basis on the Wanstead Flats (thus running into conflict with the local Trades Council) made some concessions about the administration of a relief grant by the central government. However, he reiterated his hostility towards 'promiscuous charity'.[39] Hardie was also very pleased by the evidence of the Vicar of Pontypool on 30 March, although 'the lawyers & other harpies are making notes with a view to minimizing the effect of what he is saying. We will go on & on till the end of the session ... & next winter the unemployed agitation will begin again.'[40]

Despite these partly hopeful omens, the Select Committee was a grave disappointment. This was to some extent the result of the chairmanship of Campbell-Bannerman who lacked commitment or urgency over the issue of unemployment and was to prove apathetic towards social reform for the rest of his life.[41] The interim report the committee issued on 11 March made some modest proposals, including a register of the unemployed in each locality, an emergency fund for local relief works and a grant from the Local Government Board to back up local relief funds. These were mere palliatives. The nearest the committee came to forming a view on Hardie's proposal for an imperial grant came with a motion on 11 March to endorse a grant of £50,000 from the Local Government Board, backed up by £50,000 from the rates and a further £50,000 from voluntary contributions. This was defeated by seventeen votes to four, Hardie being supported only by two Liberals, David Randell and J.H. Whiteley, and by the Unionist and amateur social psychologist, Henry Bousfield.[42] Thereafter, the Select Committee crept on towards its demise. Hardie himself ceased to sit at its meetings after 10 May owing to the illness of his wife. In any case he rapidly lost interest in the committee. Perhaps the truth was that, with so many commitments, with editing the *Labour Leader*, campaigning for the ILP and trying to look after his constituents at West Ham, his involvement in any one single activity was bound to suffer. His many-sided interests were both a major source of his mass appeal and also of his frequent ineffectiveness.

Hardie's performance on the Committee later on came under fire from fellow-socialists such as Blatchford and Hobson. He recalled then his schemes for temporary relief, but admitted that personal and political pressures had prevented him from outlining his plans for the more fundamental cure of unemployment in a capitalist society.[43] Somehow, apart from general statements that socialism would provide a final solution for the maladjustments of the economic system, he never managed to do so, however plausible his specific plans for short-term relief, and however well-founded his criticisms of the existing machinery of local government. The Committee carried little conviction towards the end. There was discussion of such broad themes as the financial responsibility for the relief of local distress and of various methods of dealing more generally with unemployment. There was debate also on settling the unemployed on the land in small holdings and allotments. But the overriding factor determining the Committee's fortunes was that the course of party politics was making it irrelevant. The main question now was how long Rosebery's tottering government could survive. Its majority (only forty in 1892) had been more than halved by by-election losses. On the committee stage of the Welsh Disestablishment Bill in May–June 1895 its majority fell to single-figure margins on several occasions, even to as low as two votes.[44] Finally on 21 June the snap vote on the cordite supplies (an issue affecting Campbell-Bannerman, the Secretary of State for War) led to the government's unexpected defeat. Rosebery and Harcourt, in agreement for once, at once resigned, and faced inevitable retribution at the polls. The Select Committee for the Unemployed met for the last time on 26 June and carried, by Campbell-Bannerman's casting vote, a motion that it was unable to prepare a report owing to the dissolution of parliament. It was suggested that another committee be set up in the new session. A series of statistical tables was published to accompany the final report, with the bland comment that 'there does not appear to be any evidence of widespread trade depression'.[45] It seemed an appropriately inconclusive finale to Hardie's long crusade on behalf of the unemployed.

After 1895 the issue of unemployment receded in importance. Trade revived, a building boom absorbed surplus labour in the cities. Another Committee on Distress under T.W. Russell's chairmanship in December 1895 made only tentative proposals. Any suggestion of assistance from the treasury to assist with relief was held to be degrading to the unemployed themselves. Armed with this comforting palliative to the self-respect of the distressed poor, the Committee wound up its deliberations at the end of 1896. Years of agitation and inquiry had led to virtually nothing. Not until renewed trade recession, at the height of Joseph Chamberlain's tariff reform campaign in 1903–5, did unemployment re-emerge as a major political theme. Even so, it occupied henceforth a clear place in debates on social policy and Hardie deserves much of the credit. More than any other figure in parliament, he had aired the general plight of the unemployed and the specific problems of West Ham. A vital new dimension was being added to that 'New Liberalism' now emerging through middle-class discussion groups such as the Rainbow Circle, and of which men like Percy Alden were to be the spokesmen. Indeed, one ultimate result of Hardie's campaign was to throw into question his diagnosis that the Liberal Party was incapable of adjusting its individualistic creed and of embracing a more collectivist social policy.[46] Publicists like Chiozza Money and J.A. Hobson were to help revise Hardie's claim that the Labour and the Liberal Party were totally incompatible; they launched a new search for a broad-based progressive alliance of the left. More important, Hardie helped generate a national inquiry into the machinery for dealing with the casualties of a free-market economy. It was an inquiry which gained new momentum when the rival claims of free trade and of tariff reform were debated after 1903, and which led ultimately to the Royal Commission on the Poor Law being appointed in 1905. Even if Hardie's solutions for unemployment were optimistic, even if his costing of land colonies and the like was haphazard, yet his instinctive hunch that counter-cyclical activity could be generated by central government, survived. It broadened into the 'right to work' campaign a decade later. In more personal terms, Hardie had temporarily touched the conscience of the nation. For the rest of his career, he was honourably identified as 'the member for the unemployed'. It was one glorious legacy from an otherwise frustrating and disappointing first parliament as an independent labour member.

Hardie's immediate future, however, depended on whether he could hang on to his seat at West Ham South. Throughout 1895, in the press and parliament, he trained his fire on the Liberals for their failure to take action on the social front. In May 1894 the NAC of the Independent Labour Party voted to 'steer clear of any alliance with either party'; it resolved to fight the Liberals on a broad front at the next general election.[47] Eventually, the party put up twenty-eight candidates, fewer than hoped, but enough to substantiate the ILP claim to be independent. Twenty-four of these candidates faced Liberal as well as Conservative opposition. It seemed almost inevitable that Hardie himself would face a Liberal opponent at West Ham. *The Speaker*, a Gladstonian journal, declared that his 'wild socialism' was incompatible with Liberal beliefs.[48] Local Liberals complained that Hardie had acted at Westminster quite at variance with his pledges in 1892 and had been in effect an opposition member. In December 1894 a West Ham Liberal, Thomas Barker, toured the constituency and was spoken of as a possible candidate.[49] There were rumours also of a possible Irish opponent to Hardie, perhaps even Michael Davitt himself. But when the house dissolved at the end of June, the local Liberals were still in total disarray. Even the *Daily Chronicle*, stung by Hardie's statement to the effect that 'the Liberals are the real stumbling-block to progress', was forced to advise West Ham voters to support the anti-Tory candidate.[50] Since there was likely to be at most only the Tory ex-member, Major Banes, defeated in 1892, as an opponent, it seemed that despite his incorrigible freelance tactics on almost all issues, Hardie would again be returned as the erratic representative of the Liberal alliance.

The July 1895 general election in West Ham South was by any standards a most curious contest. Major Banes, the Unionist, was a popular local figure, a wharfinger and bonded warehouse keeper who employed much local labour. He allowed these qualities to speak for themselves, since he held no election meetings and delivered no speeches. He preferred instead, according to the local press, to tend his flowers in his back garden.[51] This taciturnity was well in accord with Banes's previous political record, but it proved to be a wise, if accidental, strategy. The opposition simply destroyed themselves.

Labour representation had declined in strength on the West Ham
Council since 1892. Will Thorne alone was re-elected in the 1894
elections, while there had been friction over municipal candidatures
between SDF, ILP and Christian Socialist groups. Despite this,
Hardie began the campaign in militant, over-confident vein. He dismissed such issues as Church disestablishment and temperance reform
as incidental. He would give a pledge on no question save unemployment which must remain the first priority. To Irish electors, he
inquired provocatively, 'Do you say that it is a case of Home Rule first?
I can understand an Irishman in Connemara saying that but here in
West Ham it is Labour first.' He even told the voters that he had no
great wish to be elected at all; he would prefer being 'at home in the
country with the birds and flowers and amongst the children'.[52] He
also spent an undue amount of time helping ILP candidates in other
parts of the country.

It soon became clear that this confidence was misplaced. Radical
party organization and registration were severely run down, as they had
been since Hume Webster's departure from the scene. Nonconformists
in West Ham made it clear that they were reluctant to work for Hardie
in view of his inability to make temperance a first priority and also his
unsound views on the Gothenburg system of municipalizing the drink
traffic. Irish voters were more openly hostile. Father Dooley informed
them that Hardie could not be considered sound on Home Rule in
view of his opposition to John Morley at Newcastle. Hardie, another
priest declared, was 'a bigger enemy to Ireland than Major Banes'.
Indeed, the latter, though a Unionist, at least had a Roman Catholic
son. Another local Catholic stated that in view of the socialist policy of
land nationalization, 'they as Catholics would have no safety for their
schools and churches'. Far away in Edinburgh, the *Labour Chronicle*,
edited by the young James Connolly, urged Irish electors in vain to
take the contrary view and to fuse nationalism and socialism.[53] Nevertheless, the Irish vote, supposed to number about 600, appeared
destined to go to the Unionist, Banes. Several local Liberals, who, not
surprisingly, took seriously Hardie's declarations of eternal hostility to
Liberalism and all its works, also worked covertly for the Unionist;
they were urged on by the *Daily Chronicle* which was now fiercely
hostile to Hardie. He declared bitterly after the poll that he faced an
unholy alliance of 'teetotallers and publicans, trades unionists and free

labour men, Liberals and Tories, Home Rulers and Coercionists'.[54] As a result, he was defeated by 775 votes. Banes, with 4,750 votes, increased his poll by over 700, compared with 1892, while Hardie, with 3,975, had lost well over 1,000. 'Put not your trust in canvassing books,' he wrote wryly to an ILP supporter. Since there was a lower poll the presumption must be that many Liberals stayed away rather than vote for Hardie, quite apart from registration difficulties. The result caused rejoicing in many and varied quarters. Engels wrote to Lafargue expressing his delight. Beatrice Webb, who thought the ILP emotional and unscientific, and Hardie a poseur, wrote in charac-teristic fashion, 'Hardie has probably lost for good any chance of posturing as an MP and will sink into the old place of a discredited Labour leader'. The *Daily Chronicle* commented that it was no sur-prise that 'South West Ham had closed its doors to one who has so misused his opportunities'.[55]

Out of parliament himself, Hardie spent the rest of the campaign in a bitter anti-Liberal crusade of revenge that helped drag down the rest of the ILP candidates as well. In the *Daily Chronicle* of 19 July, he came out with a ringing statement of hostility to official Liberalism that doomed ILP men all over the country. As compensation, Hardie's renewed appearance at Newcastle had the satisfaction of helping defeat John Morley, the dedicated opponent of the eight-hour day. Fred Hamill, the ILP candidate, polled 2,302 and Morley was defeated by 308 votes. For the rest, the results were generally dismal for the ILP. All their 28 candidates were defeated, most of them heavily. They fared especially badly in Glasgow, where Hardie had called for the defeat of every Liberal candidate. With the four SDF candidates thrown in, the total socialist vote amounted to 44,000.[56] It was far from being a derisory total, as Bernard Shaw pointed out, but was a grave disappointment after the euphoric hopes of two years earlier. The results threw the whole Hardie strategy of adopting an attitude of all-out belligerence towards the Liberals into question. Indeed, Hardie, and to a lesser extent Tom Mann, became the scapegoats for the party's defeats and poor organization. The disorganization of the party machinery in West Ham was notorious. Hardie himself drew the correct moral that much more needed to be done to win over trade unionists and co-operators. He also appealed to radical Liberals to free themselves from their thraldom to capitalist monopolists and to work with Labour.[57] Nevertheless, it was clear that basic questions needed to be asked about the purpose of the ILP. Several options were open – socialist unity with the SDF (whose electoral performance was even worse than that of the ILP), strict independence, or renewed approaches towards radical Liberals. Even at its period of greatest despair, the ILP seemed as protean and many-sided as its chairman.

His first parliament and the defeat that followed it marked a great divide in Hardie's career. It was in many ways a disillusioning period. Despite his association with the unemployment agitation in West Ham, it was not a natural constituency for him, even though he remained nominal Labour candidate until 1899. He was by temperament a provincial, like his party. The ILP had slender roots in London. West Ham itself was largely dominated by the SDF and many of its members resented Hardie's former attacks on their party and on Champion. Will Thorne of the Gasworkers was a local councillor and a powerful figure in his own right, and this led to personality clashes with the sitting member. Hardie's role in the Commons had brought much publicity, but, apart from the abortive Select Committee on Unemployment, few tangible results. He had deliberately chosen isolation; in a sense, he had gloried in his ineffectiveness. The failure to win results showed how class-ridden and privilege-conscious the House of Commons really was. Hardie's parliamentary record was indeed a mixed advertisement for a party aiming at the democratic capture of power.

On the other hand, the possibilities for Hardie in the House of Commons as it existed in 1892 were strictly limited. His performance there had its positive aspects, especially in connection with unemployment. There were hopeful portents in the growing disunity of the Liberal Party. Internal divisions over imperial policy were symbolized by the struggles between the 'imperialist' and 'little England' wings, championed by Rosebery and Harcourt respectively. There still might be unattached radicals attracted to a Labour alliance – men of the Channing or Lloyd George type. Outside the House, the basis had been laid for a viable independent party, even though on a patchy and highly localized basis. The main apparent weakness was the lack of mass working-class support, but the growing prominence of ILP members as key officials in major trade unions such as the Engineers could redress this in time. Through the ILP, the *Labour Leader* and the various campaigns with which he was associated, Hardie had become the identifiable symbol of working-class protest in a way true of no-one else in public life. The main effect of his parliamentary defeat in 1895 was to turn his thoughts away from London and the hothouse world of Westminster manoeuvres, away to the populist grass roots, to party organization, to negotiation with trade unionists on their own ground, and to try to forge a labour alliance on a local basis. After the 1895 defeat Hardie gradually regrouped his shattered forces and learnt from his mistakes. The period of propaganda was substantially ending. The period of constructive achievement was about to be launched.

V Towards the Labour Alliance (1895–9)

Many of Hardie's critics in the labour and socialist movements thought that his career as a credible working-class leader was now largely over, after his defeat at West Ham. The ILP had been shown to be, so far, only a divided and impecunious splinter-group. Hardie had frequently to appeal for funds through the columns of the *Labour Leader*. His own financial position was also acute; he had to ask publicly for the payment of expenses of up to three guineas for any speaking engagement outside London.[1] Indeed, his entire reputation in money matters was somewhat suspect at this period. He had often landed in difficulties over finance in the past, at least since his quarrel about union funds with Alexander McDonald in 1880. Now he found himself in a singularly squalid dispute with the Glasgow-based Labour Literature Society which had until recently printed the *Labour Leader* on machines loaned by Hardie. The quarrel was a complex one.[2] Hardie claimed that £195 of the funds of the Scottish Labour Party had been loaned to the Society and should be returned. In return, the Society made a counter-claim of £150 on their trading account with Hardie. There were further disputes over the use of Hardie's printing machines and over the *Leader*'s premises in Brunswick Street, into which Hardie had invited the Society in 1894. He had finally given the Society notice to quit in February 1895; the case then went to the sheriff's court. By June, he had begun legal proceedings (which finally petered out inconclusively) and had also set up his own rival printing establishment in Glasgow. The episode did not add to Hardie's prestige at a critical time in his fortunes. It made him appear competitive and capitalistic. 'A crime against his comrades in Glasgow and a grave blunder as leader of the party,' was Glasier's view.[3] The way in which he ran the *Leader* offices under strict personal supervision underlined Hardie's reluctance to brook any rival to his domination of the ILP.

The affair ended in August 1896 with the Labour Literature Society broken and bankrupt. Especially in Scotland, it added to the controversies that surrounded his reputation at a time when he sorely needed friends.

In the first instance, he found release from the stresses of the 1895 election through his first sustained experience of overseas travel. In the company of the faithful Frank Smith, he sailed to the United States in the steamer *Campania* and stayed there fifteen weeks, from early September until mid-December. The original purpose of the visit was to address the Labour Congress at Chicago on 2 September, at the invitation of the Illinois Populist-radical, Henry Demarest Lloyd, but Hardie took the opportunity to travel widely throughout the breadth of the United States.[4] It was a time of intense social and political turmoil there. For almost three years American society had been undergoing an acute crisis. The economy had been on the point of collapse in 1894 when a massive run on the gold reserves closed most of the nation's banks. Rising unemployment led to violent labour troubles; they culminated in the Pullman strike of 1894 which led to the imprisonment of the railwaymen's leader, Eugene V. Debs. Elsewhere, there was the march of Coxey's 'army' of the unemployed on Washington; while the rise of radical Populism in the south and in normally quiescent areas of the Mid-West such as Kansas seemed to presage a terrifying sectional explosion, as profound as the civil war thirty years earlier. Populist demagogues like 'Pitchfork' Ben Tillman in South Carolina and 'Sockless' Jerry Simpson in Kansas threatened the financial centres of the north-east with an explosive conflict between the debtor regions of the south and west and the money power of the eastern seaboard. The issue focussed on the Populist demand for 'free silver', coined at the ratio of sixteen to one, to reverse the slump in farm prices and to provide ready credit. When the Democrats adopted a 'free silver' advocate, William Jennings Bryan, as their candidate in the presidential election of 1896, in opposition to the Republican 'goldbug' McKinley, the lines seemed to be drawn up for a sectional upheaval that would paralyze the nation.[5]

Hardie arrived in America when the political campaign was in full swing and from the first was a keen observer of it. From the start, his visit was controversial. Even on the ship crossing the Atlantic, he took the opportunity to harangue his middle-class fellow-passengers on

the evils of a competitive society.[6] He and Smith made contact with
the various segments of the American labour movement – with Daniel
de Leon of the Socialist Labor Party, with labour union leaders in New
York City, with Eugene Debs himself, languishing in Woodstock
gaol. Hardie and Debs, together with Thomas Morgan, a Chicago
socialist, discussed socialism there for an entire day. They drew up a
scheme (which Debs disavowed later) for an International Bureau of
Correspondence and Agitation, to work for an industrial commonwealth. Debs' main recollection of Hardie's visit was of one characteristic episode, when Hardie spent some time transferring a locust
trapped in a bottle to a matchbox filled with grass. 'I conclude that a
man who had solicitude about the comfort of an insect could be safely
trusted not to wantonly injure his fellow men', Debs wrote.[7] Hardie's
address to the American Labor Congress at Chicago on Labor Day
passed by successfully: it was an index of the international stature he
had already won as a political champion of labour. He and Smith then
pushed on across the great plains and into the Rocky Mountains,
where they received instruction in the mysteries of bimetallism and
free silver. At Butte, Montana, funds ran out. Four hundred dollars
were required for hotel bills, and Hardie and Smith were bailed out
by the fortuitous appearance of some Scottish pipers whose playing
brought financial relief. Smith himself went on to investigate the congenial community of the Mormons at Salt Lake City, Utah, and duly
marvelled at the Tabernacle there. Finally in California came the oft-
quoted attempt by Dick Smith, the 'Silver King', the Mayor of San
Francisco, to buy off Hardie with 100,000 dollars, if only the ILP in
Britain would declare for bimetallism. This was cheerfully added by
Hardie to the long list of 'bribes I have been offered'.[8] His lengthy
reports of his journeys made excellent reading in the *Labour Leader*.
They had plenty of local colour on such issues as the public ban on
smoking in restaurants, on the poverty in evidence on the Bowery and
other slum areas of American cities, on the role of ethnic minorities
such as the Germans, Jews, Chinese and Negroes. Hardie's assessment
of the United States was remarkably shrewd. He sensed the revolutionary potential in a land truly 'born free', the instability in its
economy, the growth of trusts, the rapid rise of labour unions and
socialist bodies. At the same time, he also noted the wide gulf that
already existed between the American Federation of Labor (the

Broadhursts of the new world) and Socialists such as Debs and de Leon. In America, even more than in Britain, there was an urgent need for working-class unity. Hardie was also struck by the jingoism manifested by Americans during the Venezuela crisis with Britain. 'The gold in Venezuela and the gold in the Transvaal are giving us a lively time,' Adam Birkmyre wrote to him a few months later.[9] Meanwhile the comfortable victory of McKinley in the presidential election, with most of the urban workers voting Republican rather than ally with debtor farmers, silver-mining capitalists or advocates of 'funny money', revealed again how immense was the task confronting American socialists in trying to convert the industrial workers.

Back in Britain, Hardie found enough problems of disunity and disorganization of his own. Much against his will, the ILP had launched moves during his absence to investigate the prospects for fusion with the SDF. Of all the options open to the party this was the one least congenial to Hardie. He saw the SDF as sectarian and doctrinaire, its dogmatic creed alien to the temper of the working-class mind. An upper-class Marxist like H.M. Hyndman aroused his instant suspicion. However Tom Mann, the secretary of the ILP, was more sympathetic to 'socialist unity' and put out feelers to the Social Democrats. To Hardie's relief, the latter turned down the proposal flat. Hardie's relations with the SDF at this time were particularly sour, especially in Scotland. The feud with Champion and his supporters had had wide repercussions and had helped reduce the polls of ILP candidates at the general election. An SDF candidate run in a by-election at Southampton caused more bad blood. Hardie himself experienced the backwash of it in May 1896 when a seat became vacant at North Aberdeen. In this citadel of Champion's supporters the local ILP turned down Hardie as a candidate. Instead, Tom Mann was nominated and received open SDF backing during the campaign. In disgust, Hardie seriously thought of resigning his party chairmanship. Mann's dramatic improvement of the ILP poll, with 2,479 votes on a clear 'socialist unity' platform, was an ironic commentary on the affair.[10]

During 1896 and 1897 the theme of socialist collaboration continued to foster tension between Hardie and many of the ILP rank-and-file. He himself was the target of bitter attacks from SDF sympathizers in Scotland. John Gerrie of Aberdeen (actually an ILP-er) was a particularly violent opponent. Writing to Ramsay MacDonald, who had himself been considered for the ILP candidature in North Aberdeen, Gerrie complained that Hardie preferred to mouth generalities about socialism instead of working for practical reforms such as the eight-hour day. 'It is an easier thing for a weak man like Hardie to advocate socialism than to run the Eight Hours Day. The employing class know quite well that Socialism won't touch *their* pockets, but are deeply conscious that the Eight Hours would.' The 'Hardie element' in the ILP should be purged. Gerrie urged MacDonald, in vain, to see himself as the Brutus who would purge the Caesarism inherent in Hardie's cherished party.[11] Apart from this personal antagonism from Champion's admirers, Hardie also found himself embroiled in doctrinal disputes with the Social Democrats. At the International Socialist Congress which met in London in August 1896, he and Mann took an outspoken part in disputes over whether the Anarchists should be allowed to attend. Hardie's basic argument was the one of tolerance. He claimed that the socialist movement took a variety of forms in different societies. Less wisely, he attempted to argue that the Social Democrats, the ILP and the Anarchists shared common objectives, and differed only about methods. Hardie distinguished himself from 'the State Socialists of the German type'. His objective was a socialist commonwealth not a juggernaut of bureaucratic, centralized power. He felt that he could make common cause with what he termed the 'Free Communists' of the type of the Dutch co-operator, Domela Nieuwenhuis.[12] Hardie's political theory was sketchy in the extreme; it aroused the predictable fury of the SDF and its organ, *Justice*. It also won scant gratitude from *Liberty*, the organ of British Anarchists. The SDF argued, not unreasonably, that the Anarchists' aversion to any kind of political organization and their preference for small-scale private property distinguished them radically from socialists of any kind.[13] John Gerrie thought the episode merely confirmed that Hardie was at heart an Anarchist himself. Conversely, Hardie had to ask the Austrian, Viktor Adler, to rebut criticism that he was a covert Tory agent.[14] The affair caused further strain between the SDF and the ILP. Hardie's hopeful account of the 'fraternizing' between the delegates from the British socialist world at the international congress seemed the more ironic.[15] In the *Clarion*, Nunquam's (Blatchford's) sarcastic reporting helped widen the breach and led to several violent altercations with the *Labour Leader*.

Despite this tension, pressure from ILP delegates for a new overture to the SDF went on. At the 1896 ILP annual conference at Nottingham a motion was carried, despite Hardie's opposition, which demanded new negotiations with the Social Democrats. In vain did Hardie remind his followers of the SDF failure to give him adequate support at West Ham and the consequences of this at the polls. More attractive to him was an alternative proposal for a joint conference of the socialist societies with the Parliamentary Committee of the TUC, which the latter predictably rejected. The pressure for socialist unity was renewed at the ILP annual conference in 1897; indeed, it went further and recommended the early fusion of the two major socialist bodies. Hardie, Mann, MacDonald and Russell Smart, for the ILP, met with Hyndman, Quelch, Lee, Lansbury and Barwick of the SDF to consider proposals for amalgamation.[16] At the very least, joint committees could be set up to promote individual socialist parliamentary candidatures. Complete fusion was not ruled out. Despite Hardie's reluctance, the ILP members were balloted at the end of 1897 about the possibility of fusion. The NAC managed to get the issue postponed until the 1898 annual conference at Birmingham.[17] Here, fusion was successfully side-stepped, amidst powerful denunciations, by Bruce Glasier amongst others, of the 'doctrinaire, Calvinistic and sectarian' nature of the SDF Marxists. Instead, the idea of 'federation' was floated and local ILP branches balloted on this issue also. The whole affair petered out with discussions as to whether a unified socialist party should or should not be called a Socialist Labour Party. By the end of 1898 fusion was a dead issue. *Justice* drew consolation from the thought that the ILP was anyway merely an independent labour body, 'with socialistic tendencies'. Hardie took refuge in the extent of local branch opposition within his own party to the very notion of fusion – an opposition which in all probability he greatly exaggerated.[18]

Hardie's determined hostility towards any kind of union or even joint meetings with the SDF is apparent throughout. Indeed, the Social Democrats were the more conciliatory throughout the negotiations. Hardie was fully sustained in his view by all the leading members of the NAC, particularly by Ramsay MacDonald who was first elected to the committee in 1896 and was at this time a close ally of the chairman. The only major dissentient was Tom Mann. In fact, he resigned the party secretaryship at the end of 1897, amidst grave accusations of drunkenness and sexual incontinence which caused Hardie much distress; eventually Mann sailed to Australia.[19] Hardie's instincts throughout were sound enough. He sensed that partnership with so isolated and self-contained a movement as the SDF would doom any real possibility of a successful approach to the trade unions. He dismissed 'the feckless *Clarion* crowd who don't believe in organization etc.'[20] He had seen at West Ham the essential gulf between the ideology of the SDF and the flexible radicalism of his own party. He fully endorsed Glasier's attacks on the 'bigotry, brutality and conceit' of the SDF.[21] Socialist unity was a goal worth pursuing as long as it might help the political and industrial wings of the labour world to come together and to promote a labour alliance. As a long-term strategy for the ILP it was a blind alley. The subsequent impotence of the SDF, save only for a few trades councils, largely in London, confirmed the wisdom of Hardie's judgement.

But, if socialist unity were to be rejected, what was the alternative strategy? The ILP was in a far from flourishing condition after the 1895 election. Membership and affiliation fees were both falling away. Many local branches were skeleton organizations and only in a few new areas like South Wales was there a sign of new growth. The record of the ILP in by-elections (save, ironically enough, in North Aberdeen) was depressing. The humiliating defeat of Pete Curran, the ILP candidate, at Barnsley in a by-election in 1897 seemed the sign of a final disintegration. According to Hardie, Curran had only been adopted after a Swiss jeweller donated a £25 ring towards election expenses; the candidate had to endure abuse and even stoning from 'Lib-Lab' Yorkshire miners.[22] Neither was there evidence that the trade unions were paying serious attention to the message of working-class unity that Hardie proclaimed. Indeed, the outstanding feature of party politics in these years was the dramatic revival of the Liberals, who showed every sign of recapturing their *élan vital* in a series of by-election triumphs. In his journal, Hardie had continued to wage unremitting warfare against the Liberal Party.. 'Liberalism represented Commercialism just as Toryism represented Landlordism.' Private monopoly of land and of capital, with the corollary of production for profit were the hallmarks of the commercial society. The common ownership of land and of capital, based on production for use, were the hall mark of socialism. Between the two there could be no compromise.

To be 'Liberal-Labour' was to endorse the existing social and economic order, with all its injustices. The true socialist had to be independent.[23]

But Hardie retained sufficient realism to acknowledge that Liberalism in Britain could still claim hundreds of thousands of votes denied to the ILP. To strike a posture of independence without trying to build bridges to the radical left, was futile. In this connection, Hardie's unexpected intervention in a by-election at Bradford East in October 1896 is an instructive episode. Precisely why he stood for this constituency is a mystery, unless it was the general assumption that any section of the town which had witnessed the birth of the ILP must be worth fighting for. He thought his chances there were 'favourable'.[24] In fact, Bradford East was the least hopeful of the Bradford divisions: the previous member had been a Unionist Churchman, Byron Reed. It contained a large, prosperous suburban fringe, although the Bowring iron works did employ a considerable body of working-class electors. Hardie was adopted as ILP candidate for the constituency on 12 October; Frank Smith and Alderman Fred Jowett served as his election organizers. The local press commented on how worn out Hardie appeared and how the pressures of the last few years had told on him. He described himself as 'a shattered and aged man', even though he had just passed his fortieth year.[25]

His campaign at Bradford East was in marked contrast to the schemes for 'socialist unity' currently being canvassed; it was 'radical unity' that Hardie embodied at Bradford East. He appealed to Liberals in the constituency to consider whether 'there could not be a fusion of advanced forces' in the new situation created by Rosebery's resignation as Liberal leader and the succession of Harcourt.[26] Hardie, as before, laid most emphasis on the question of unemployment. The passage of the eight-hour day bill, the cultivation of vacant land and similar policies were again aired. At the same time his attitude towards the Liberals was markedly moderate. He returned to the theme, last heard from him on the hustings at West Ham in 1892, that he was an impeccable radical. He re-asserted his ardent support for Irish Home Rule. He urged the reform of the educational system on a secular basis: he had effectively championed this theme at the International Socialist Congress in August when he pushed a motion in favour of the public maintenance of all schoolchildren without regard to ability or examination success.[27] He strongly attacked the 'military system of Europe' and bid hard for the votes of 'little England' Liberals.[28] Indeed, Hardie increasingly turned his attention to overseas affairs, perhaps in response to his American travels and his recent experience of the Second International. In the 1892–5 parliament he had ignored foreign and imperial affairs lest they should deflect attention away from the condition of the masses at home. Now he derided the occupation of Egypt to satisfy the rapacious demands of foreign bond-holders. 'In every county of merry England there was a real demand for British goods without going beyond the seas.' He also denounced the idea of a war against Turkey on behalf of the Armenians, as the aged Gladstone was demanding. That policy had already cost at Khartoum the life of General Gordon, 'the most Christ-like man this country had ever seen'.[29] On all fronts, Hardie refurbished his radical credentials. He declared again his support for church disestablishment; he strongly endorsed temperance reform and reminded the voters of his Good Templar background; he called for land reform and for taxation of those who benefited from inflated land values in Bradford. He claimed to be the best Liberal candidate available and appealed through a campaign newspaper, _Hardie's Herald_, for the support of Liberal and Irish voters. 'Hardie spoke all through the contest in the most converting and beautiful style', wrote Glasier.[30]

But the hope of avoiding Liberal opposition was a vain one. Alfred Billson, a former Liberal member, was adopted and this ruined Hardie's prospects. As a result, in the last two weeks of the campaign, his strategy markedly changed. His campaign literature now laid emphasis on his socialism. 'In politics, I am a Democrat; in trade matters, a Trade Unionist; in economics, a Socialist.'[31] The object of the ILP was the 'socialization of land and capital'. The by-election, he declared, was as much a contest between the employers and the workers as was a strike or a lock-out. At the same time, he continued to speak on a wide range of domestic and international issues. The Sultan of Turkey, Hardie informed the breathless Bradfordians, was praying for his defeat.[32] The Sultan's prayers, if any, met with their appropriate response. Hardie's campaign lost momentum and received less and less newspaper coverage. He finished well at the bottom of the poll, with 1,963 votes as against 4,921 for the victorious Unionist, Captain Greville, and 4,526 for the Liberal, Alfred Billson. 'A real disappointment,' wrote Glasier.[33] Hardie, exhausted by a strenuous series of speaking engagements, wound up at the Bradford Labour Church after the poll in characteristic vein. His 'prophetic instinct,' he told the congregation, had informed him that he would be defeated. But, peering far into the future, he forecast that the year 1953 would see 'the introduction of socialism and the overthrow of the commercial system'.[34] The rift between Labour and Liberalism seemed as wide as ever, and Hardie himself one of the major victims of it. Immediately after the poll, he strongly opposed T.D. Benson's proposal of an electoral arrangement with the Liberals at Manchester and Salford.[35]

Even so, the advances he made to radical elements in the Liberal Party were more than just a by-election tactic. He continued to affirm that the crisis undergone by Liberalism in Britain, as in Germany and elsewhere, opened up new vistas of a radical re-alignment. A short-term collaboration with Liberals on specific issues he never ruled out. Indeed, when Frank Smith was elected to the London County Council in 1898, Hardie wrote warmly in praise of his association with Progressive councillors on behalf of radical social policies.[36] The official ILP line now was to fight as many constituencies as possible on a broad front at the next election; Hardie himself often endorsed this view. In practice, the NAC modified this severely. The party's parliamentary committee (Hardie, MacDonald and Brocklehurst) recommended in July 1898 that only twenty-five candidates at the maximum be adopted next time and that only areas of the greatest potential be given preference. Only eight constituencies were marked down definitely for ILP candidates – West Bradford, Dundee, Manchester (Gorton), Halifax, Leicester, South West Manchester, Southampton, and South West Ham, where Hardie was still in theory the prospective candidate. Covert negotiations took place with the Liberals in the hope that ILP candidates might be given a free run in these eight constituencies in return for some understanding about support for a future Liberal government.[37] The Liberal chief whip, the Welshman Tom Ellis, was also anxious for a new understanding with Labour.[38] An article in January 1899 in the *Nineteenth Century*, bearing the signatures of Hardie and MacDonald, took this pragmatism still further.[39] It declared that the ILP expressed the 'evolutionary and experimental character of British socialism' and that it differed from the older Liberalism mainly in the 'haphazard and circumstantial' nature of the latter's programme. But independence for the ILP did not mean isolation. The ILP 'could now afford' to consider a series of specific issues on which collaboration with radicals and anti-imperialists was feasible – an attack on the House of Lords, a legal eight-hour day, the taxing of ground rents, democratic reform of the suffrage, local government and educational reform. The NAC believed that the co-operation of socialists and radicals, as had already taken place in France through the agency of Jean Jaurès, was not inconceivable in Britain also. The *Nineteenth Century* article (which swelled party funds by £25)[40] was essentially the work of MacDonald; its renunciation of Marxist dogma in favour of a vague quasi-biological evolutionism bore his unmistakable imprint. Even so, Hardie's recent experiences, especially in view of the hopeless impasse reached over 'socialist unity', made him equally sympathetic to the views expressed. The rise of an imperialist and jingo spirit in the later nineties, the new tension in international relations, made a common front on the left increasingly urgent. Hardie detected, through the columns of his newspaper, the upsurge of the military spirit in areas as far removed as Cuba and the Sudan.[41] An outward-looking socialism should seek assistance from wherever it derived.

Hardie's long-term ambition was now clearly the formation of a broad-based Labour alliance. Bring the socialists and the trade unions together in the promotion of labour causes, and dogma could take care of itself. But in the frustrating years 1896–8 nothing seemed less likely to emerge. In retrospect, Hardie and his followers tended to give an aura of inevitability to the coalition that was eventually forged with the formation of the LRC in 1900. Many historians have followed this view and given a spurious consistency to Hardie's political gyrations after 1895. In fact, the idea of a labour alliance made only halting progress until the end of 1898 and Hardie's erratic efforts to promote one made slight impact. He himself was now almost wholly detached from the trade union world. He was pleasantly surprised when he saw an authentic workman reading the *Leader* on Preston railway station.[42] He had forsaken the life of an active union organizer for good when he resigned from the secretaryship of the Ayrshire Miners in 1891. He had not attended the TUC for many years, since the revision of Standing Orders at the Cardiff congress in 1895 effectively excluded him. He himself was suspect in some trade union circles; after all, as manager of the *Labour Leader* he was something of a capitalist employer himself. Even James Sexton of the Dockers' Union attacked him as an enemy of trades unionism, while Hardie had quarrelled with Ben Tillett, 'that dirty little hypocrite'.[43] This pressure had finally told against Hardie in West Ham. The local trades council, with its powerful SDF leavening, had been running a campaign against Hardie as a 'carpet-bagger' whose record as member in 1892–5 was a patchy one. Labour successes in West Ham in the 1897 and 1898 municipal elections, when four, and then eight, seats were gained, strengthened the hold of the SDF on the borough. The SDF continued to boost the claims of Will Thorne, a powerful figure locally and nationally, a member of the West Ham council for several years and the general secretary of the Gasworkers and General Labourers' Union. In distinctly uncomradely terms, the candidacy for West Ham rumbled on in the columns of the *Labour Leader* and *Justice*. Finally in April 1899 it was announced that Hardie had withdrawn as candidate in view of the powerful claims of Thorne. He wrote a letter to Thorne in which he acknowledged the Gasworkers' leader's powerful local appeal. The NAC reluctantly endorsed his decision. 'The Council recognized that the circumstances under which the retirement took place exist only as long as a local Trade Union official like Will Thorne, supported by a special vote of his Union is the candidate, and in the event of any failure on Thorne's part to proceed to the election, the council claims for the ILP priority in a further selection.' In practical terms, the episode confirmed Hardie's difficulty in appealing to local working-class opinion, whatever his towering national reputation.[44]

If Hardie was isolated at this time, so in many ways was the ILP itself. Nothing is further from the truth than to see a dramatic recognition amongst trade unionists that the ILP could provide the essential cement to bind together the fragmented sections of the labour world. The ILP was now five years old. Some of the revolutionary passion of its formative years was distinctly waning. It was somewhat losing its capacity to reflect working-class opinion, despite the growth of ILP representation amongst unions such as the Railway Servants and the Boot and Shoe Operatives.[45] The outstanding figures on the NAC now were all distinctly non-proletarian figures – Bruce Glasier, an unsuccessful pre-Raphaelite artist and designer; Philip Snowden, once a minor civil servant; Ramsay MacDonald, who had begun work as a chemist. All were basically journalists; none of them was in a union.

With the departure of Tom Mann, some of the proletarian *élan* had departed from the ILP. It was now more effective as a vehicle for the conscience of the middle-class idealist rather than for the working-class activist. Its membership was in decline, its newspaper in financial trouble and its funds meagre. Dr Henry Pelling traces a fall in its membership from 10,720 in 1895 to 6,084 in 1900.[46] Its by-election record was disappointing. Such moves as the party had so far promoted for discussions with the trade unions, for instance the joint conference proposed to, and rejected by, the TUC Parliamentary Committee in 1897, had been tainted with the flavour of 'socialist unity', although through no fault of Hardie's. With Hardie himself veering between renewed approaches to the unions and offering encouragement to left-wing Liberals, there seemed no clear direction to follow.

Hardie himself continued to plead the cause of working-class representation in parliament. He announced his dogged determination 'to go on', whatever the cost. He seized what opportunities came to sharpen the class awareness of trade unionists. He gained valuable publicity by a meeting at Boggart Hole Clough in Manchester in 1896 which the authorities tried to prohibit. After this, Hardie, Bruce Glasier and Dr Pankhurst were unsuccessfully prosecuted. Hardie used the simple strategy of threatening to call every one of the thousands attending the meeting, including the lord mayor of Manchester, as a witness.[47] He also vigorously exposed the exploitation and evils of private capitalism at the expense of Lord Overtoun, a philanthropic Scots Presbyterian, prominent in the Sunday Observance Society. Overtoun had worked his men at the Shawfield chemical works a seven-day week at a wage of barely threepence an hour and at grave cost to their health. 'The Overtoun horrors' roused widespread excitement. Hardie's brilliantly effective series of tracts on Overtoun, entitled 'White Slaves', stirred up the same passions as did W.T. Stead's more lurid Babylonish exposures, or the 'muckraking' journalists in the American magazine press.[48] They reinforced the growing critique, broadening through the 1890s, of late-Victorian society. But they had little effect on the creation of a Labour alliance.

What provided the key to the new political transformation and suddenly lent relevance to Hardie's tireless crusading, was the embittered industrial climate of the later 1890s. After a period of prosperity and of relative social harmony after the 1895 election, there erupted a series of violent labour disputes which totally reversed the pragmatic strategy of the TUC. Even the Parliamentary Committee felt itself to be on the defensive in a new way. In 1897 there was a prolonged strike by the Amalgamated Society of Engineers, which resulted in their utter defeat. The *Leader* took pains to give sympathetic treatment to its secretary, George Barnes, and to improve on a photograph of him. In the same year, the Penrhyn quarry strike in North Wales ranged a tyrannical feudal proprietor against a small local community of slate quarrymen; it attracted widespread sympathy, and financial support from the TUC. Hardie took a close interest in this dispute. 'The main question,' he wrote, 'is the right of Lord Penrhyn to do as he pleases with his own, the rights of one man against the rights and liberties of 4,000.'[49] In the following March, a six months' stoppage began in the South Wales coalfield. A hundred thousand men were thrown out of work; soup kitchens were set up to relieve starvation in the mining valleys. Hardie himself visited the Welsh coalfield at this time and conducted 'a kind of royal procession'.[50] He held stirring ILP meetings at Penydarren and elsewhere (notwithstanding the armed constables lying in ambush in case of trouble) and donated £10 from the *Leader* to the Relief Fund. The Welsh miners returned to work in September, crushed and humiliated. Even 'Mabon's Day', the monthly holiday named after the Welsh miners' exceptionally moderate leader, was abolished.[51] New ILP branches sprang up in the valleys as a result. Throughout the trade union world, there were renewed fears of an employers' counter-attack, somewhat on the lines of the confrontations being forced by trusts and combines in the United States. In addition, a growing trade depression, which affected iron and steel workers amongst others, a consequence of the impact of competition from the USA, Germany and elsewhere, generated a new sense of economic insecurity. One result was the emergence of more and more ILP men as union organizers. George Barnes in the Engineers, G.J. Wardle in the Amalgamated Society of Railway Servants, showed that the respectable 'Labourist', new model unions of skilled artisans of the mid-Victorian heyday were gradually being transformed.

Hardie's call for labour unity now seemed to have a new meaning. Like MacDonald and others on the ILP executive, he urged a concentration on the simple issue of labour representation in parliament, on the basis of sectional self-interest rather than of class conflict, still less of social revolution. He pointed out that trade unions and socialists had already co-operated in running joint candidates in local and parliamentary elections in Glasgow, Leicester, West Ham and other constituencies.[52] 'Programmes are matters of no moment,' he wrote characteristically. 'It is labour representation which needs keeping to the front.' He proclaimed that democracy would survive only if working men actively used the political power that had been accorded to them. In the new atmosphere of the later 1890s, Hardie's dramatic call for change was reflected in a motion carried on a card vote in the 1898 TUC in favour of a liaison with 'the working-class Socialist parties'.

But the British TUC, even with its growing contingent of ILP delegates, was still a pretty formidable fortress to breach. The means to penetrate it lay tangentially through an organization with which Hardie had previously had little contact – the Scottish Trades Union Congress, formed as recently as March 1897. The chairman of its parliamentary committee was Bob Smillie, an old ally of Hardie's in Hamilton and the heir to the ILP candidature in Mid-Lanark. Its conference at Aberdeen in 1897 called for trade union support for 'the working-class socialist parties already in existence'. On 26 September 1898, Hardie and Bruce Glasier attended a special consultative meeting of the Scottish Parliamentary Committee and raised there the general issue of labour representation. It was then agreed to convene a special conference of Scottish socialists, trade unionists and co-operators, to which ILP branches could also send delegates, to consider the prospects for future joint parliamentary action.[53] At this meeting on 4 March 1899, Hardie, Glasier and William Stewart, representing the ILP, managed to force through a motion in support of united working-class action at the next election; Hardie threw in a sharp criticism of the cautious approach of the Scottish co-operators. Finally, at the third annual conference of the Scottish TUC, held at Dundee on 26–7 April, Hardie was amongst those present. He was allowed to give a ten-minute address on the theme of labour representation and a motion was then passed calling for a Scottish delegate conference the following January at which a permanent form of long-term association would be considered.[54]

This meeting of the Scottish TUC was a very odd affair. Without doubt it was most adroitly stage-managed by Hardie and his friends.

Loftily, he told the NAC later that 'the congress did not impress me very favourably, a lack of business capacity being painfully evident, a fact chiefly due to the chairman's lack of knowledge'. He added, however, that three-quarters of the delegates were members of the ILP and that a conference with the Scottish TUC was likely in a few months' time.[55] If the conference was somewhat disorganized, Hardie was able to capitalize on its failings. Miss Irwin, the lady secretary of the Scottish TUC, complained bitterly to MacDonald about Hardie's tactics:[56]

He was never off the platform all the time – got permission from the Standing Orders Committee to address the Congress, and even favoured us so far as to move thanks in the name of the Congress to our musicians and entertainers. . . . We find that his presence and the actions of some of his satellites in the Congress have been hotly resented by many of the Delegates and it is openly said that our Congress is being nobbled by Keir Hardie and will be run by him & wasted on the desert air. The immediate results were very apparent at the Congress itself. While some of the followers of Mr K.H. were vapouring all day long in the foreground, the representatives of the big societies like the Iron Moulders, Steel Workers, Typographical and others silent and sulking in their tents in the back of the hall. Since I have come home, I have heard that not only will the ASE have nothing to do with us now, but it is just a toss up whether the Societies above named including the Railway Servants & sections of the Miners, who are highly disgusted, will also not formally withdraw.

She also complained that Hardie was trying to undermine her own moderating influence in the Congress by 'playing on class prejudice'. Obviously he had won a major triumph over advocates of a non-political labour 'interest' like Miss Irwin. For the first time, he had won the clear commitment of a representative working-class organization on behalf of united political action. For the first time, he had gained a clear decision from organized trade unionists to pursue parliamentary representation on an independent basis. It was a crucial breakthrough, one which compensated for long years of disappointment. It was almost Hardie's last major involvement with the labour world of his native Scotland, but it was by far the most fruitful and decisive.

It now remained to permeate the British TUC with the same enthusiasm for political involvement. There was little direct pressure

that either Hardie or the ILP could bring to bear here. Resolutions
passed by the NAC in favour of direct action by the TUC Parliamentary Committee carried no weight. Even so, there were many
hopeful straws in the wind. In July 1899, the by-election at Oldham
in which James Mawdsley of the Cotton Spinners was defeated as a
Conservative candidate opposed by local Lib-Lab trade unionists, drew
attention to the need for a common political front. The crucial motion
at the TUC at Plymouth in September came from the Amalgamated
Society of Railway Servants. Dr Pelling has shown that it was drafted
by Thomas Steels, an ILP member of the union in Doncaster.[57] There
is no direct evidence to link Hardie or the ILP with the formulation of
this motion; but Philip Snowden and others claimed confidently that
Hardie and MacDonald actually drew it up.[58] Certainly it conveyed
the essential point (in highly familiar language) for which the ILP was
contending – the need for a common denominator which could unite
trade unionists and socialists along agreed minimal lines. It was the
policy of flexibility and empiricism – yet it also had the sanction of
Marx's advice on how the workers in a parliamentary system ought to
allow their class-consciousness to develop, as Hardie took pride in
explaining. In a tense debate at the TUC the Railway Servants' motion
was attacked by the major unions – coal and cotton. On the other hand,
a growing army of smaller unions and of unskilled workers emphasized
the need for political power as the essential basis for securing legislation
on behalf of labour. Even a conservative union like the Cotton
Spinners was qualified in its opposition to the motion. The result was a
decisive one – 546,000 for the motion, 434,000 against. The
jubilation with which ILP delegates greeted the news underlined its
significance. The wording of the motion was discreet enough. It called
for the co-operators, trade unions, socialists and other working-class
bodies to convene a special congress 'to devise ways and means for
securing the return of an increased number of labour members to the
next Parliament'. The object was 'securing a better representation of the
interests of labour in the House of Commons'. There was no mention
of any specific programme, let alone of a separate party. Nevertheless,
the momentous breach with 'labourism' and Gladstonianism, with the
class collaboration of the Lib-Lab alliance, was clearly foreshadowed.
Hardie and MacDonald, on behalf of the ILP, conducted somewhat
delicate negotiations with the TUC Parliamentary Committee (rep-

resented by Bowerman, Thorne, Steadman and Woods), with the SDF delegates (Quelch and Taylor) and the Fabian delegates (Shaw and Pease). After some dispute as to whether the terms of reference for the conference had been materially altered by the TUC, it was agreed to hold it at the Memorial Hall, Farringdon Street, London, on 27–8 February 1900. The stage was set for the creation of a broad-based, mass-support Labour Party.

The later stages of the negotiations leading to the Memorial Hall conference owed much to fortuitous outside factors. The depressed state of the economy in the face of closed markets overseas and the threat of an employers' counter-offensive continued to propel trade unionists towards the idea of independent political action. The outbreak of the war in South Africa in October encouraged further, as will be seen, the mood of unity in the face of the common dangers arising from an imperially-directed capitalism. At the same time Hardie's directing role was clearly a crucial one. Without the unique combination he showed of personal charisma and close-quarters flexibility, it is difficult to see the link between the trade unions and the socialist societies being so easily established. He and the ILP were the decisive instruments in the forging of a common front.

Hardie's strategy had shown many gyrations since 1895. His initial reaction to his electoral defeat at West Ham had been a fierce denunciation of the Liberals and uncompromising assertion of his socialist faith. But the later years in the wilderness led to major shifts of outlook. He revived again the hope that left-wing radicals could be won over from a declining Liberal Party. The bridges he tried to build at Bradford East remained in existence for the rest of his career. Hardie's radicalism, far more than his socialism, enabled him to appeal successfully to middle-class sympathizers, as against the Fabian advocates of 'permeation'. MacDonald, who consorted with advanced Liberals of the Hobson-Masterman type in such journals as the *Progressive Review*, reinforced Hardie's arguments.[59] Conversely, the futile exercise of 'socialist unity' with the SDF confirmed Hardie's long-held view that an outward-looking, non-socialist policy must be followed. The socialist bodies would have to approach the trade unions on terms largely dictated by the latter, since the optimistic hopes of a vast explosive growth of the ILP entertained in 1893–4 had so frequently been dashed. Socialism, Hardie saw, was a fragile basis for any new party. There was, indeed, much dispute as to what it meant. The doctrinal variations between the Marxism of the SDF, the 'possibilist' radical-socialism of the ILP and the 'free Communism' of the Anarchists had been sharply underlined in the confused negotiations with the other socialist bodies in 1896–8. By mid-1899 *Justice* was again pouring contempt on the opportunism of the ILP and concluding that the detailed negotiations of the past few years were but a charade.[60]

Hardie's own inclinations towards a flexible, loosely-defined approach to the trade unions were fully shared by all his closest associates. Ramsay MacDonald, now emerging as the most formidable personality in the ILP after Hardie himself, was the very personification of evolutionary gradualism and the parliamentary method. Bruce Glasier, for some years a member of the SDF and an apostle of William Morris, had sharply reacted against the inward-looking sectarianism of his former party. Socialism to Glasier was essentially ethical, not materialist, in its basis. 'All the means of life should be socialized – science, art, health, leisure and human sympathy.'[61] The harsh asperities of Hyndman's class war dogmas were as alien to Glasier's romantic temperament as (he rightly suspected) they were to the British workers as a whole. MacDonald, Glasier and Hardie were an awkward trio. Each viewed the others with uncomradely suspicion. MacDonald, with his personal links with Fabian intellectuals, the London Progressives and the parlour radicals of the Rainbow Circle, was temperamentally removed from Hardie, who always felt most at home in mass evangelizing. The sex scandal of the Dora Montefiori case added to the tension between them.[62] Hardie viewed it as his major ambition to rouse a working-class passion for socialism as intense as that kindled by the England–Scotland football international at Birmingham which he attended with MacDonald in 1898.[63] The football crowds, not the Fleet Street patricians, were his target. Glasier, by contrast, found Hardie aloof by temperament, unpredictable, often vain. He quarrelled violently with Hardie over a hostile review of Katherine Glasier in the *Leader* in March 1897. There was little enough romance in Glasier's experience of Hardie's personality: not until 1902 did Glasier detect a genial reference to himself in the columns of the *Labour Leader*.[64] On the other hand, Glasier's diary fully reveals how petulant and angular he himself could be. Philip Snowden, the other rising star of the NAC in these years, was also a prickly personality, although perhaps closer to Hardie at this time with their common zeal for the causes of evangelicalism and temperance. There was little that was fraternal or comradely about these suspicious, proud, vulnerable chieftains who dominated the ILP during its early years. What they had in common was a shared instinct for progressive evolution towards minimum goals and this determined the strategy of the party at a crucial time in its history. They also sensed Hardie's unique mass appeal. As Glasier noted after hearing Hardie deliver a powerful speech at Birmingham, 'There is no other man in our party who can speak with such sturdiness, such wisdom of range and such tact as he at his best'.[65]

Hardie's own attitude towards a possible Labour Party was as ambivalent as ever. As always, a shrewd sense of tactical possibilities contended inside him with a utopian urge for personal liberation and release from the squalor of industrial conflict. The poet and the pragmatist were always at odds with each other. Hardie told Glasier at the end of 1899:

There are times when I have seriously and sanely discussed with myself the wisdom of getting out of the position into which circumstances not of my seeking have driven me by taking a plunge into the void as the best possible service I could render the movement. Ambitions I have none, and qualifications few.[66]

Even on the brink of attaining his life's political ambition, he was never the ruthless, committed professional. Months of devoted pressure on behalf of one single-minded objective would be followed by periods of indirection which Hardie's romanticism would take command, to the despair of his friends. His unique detachment from conventional politics, the vague yearning for spiritual release from his mortal coils – these were at once Hardie's greatest strength and greatest weakness as a labour leader. The cloth cap disguised a myriad of conflicting inner tensions. They were to assume strange and unexpected forms in the new political era heralded by the momentous meeting at the Memorial Hall.

VI   Boer War and Khaki Election (1899–1901)

The preparations for the labour conference in London were far from being of dominating interest even within the socialist world. In October 1899 war suddenly erupted in South Africa. Years of tension following the fiasco of the Jameson Raid in 1896 culminated in the rejection by the two Boer Republics, Transvaal and the Orange Free State, of the ultimatum presented to them by the British High Commissioner, Milner. By the second week of October Britain had plunged into its first major war since the Crimean, a crisis of empire that was to generate far-reaching changes in domestic politics and the course of social policy, as well as radically affecting Britain's international position. Hardie, whose attention had been riveted by the negotiations with the trade unions for many months past, became passionately absorbed by the Boer War. Although he had socialist friends there, he knew nothing of South Africa at first hand. Some socialists who did, for instance some of the Fabians (and, for a brief moment, even Bruce Glasier), warmly endorsed the British position. They supported war with the Boer republics as a means of achieving 'national efficiency' at home and a secure imperial relationship overseas. Furthermore, it could be claimed that the war was being fought on behalf of liberal democratic principles, since the ostensible *casus belli* was the denial of the franchise to those Uitlanders on the Rand who had migrated to the Transvaal to work in the gold and diamond fields.

Hardie's reaction, like that of almost all his ILP colleagues, was immediate and unequivocal.[1] It was for him a capitalists' war, the product of the exploitation of the native South African, white and black, by British investors, mineowners and speculators, a last desperate struggle for survival by a decaying class. Hardie denounced the war from every aspect. It was in itself immoral, a crude attempt to coerce the Boer people. Hardie depicted the latter as a society of independent rural freeholders, in revolt against tyranny. 'Try to imagine what the free Yeomen of England were like two hundred years ago and you have some idea of Boer life.' 'Their Republican form of government bespeaks freedom . . . while their methods of production for use are much nearer to our ideal than any form of exploitation for profit,' he assured his fellow socialists.[2] The grievances of the Uitlanders were negligible by comparison with those of miners in Britain itself. To political bondage the British imperialists added economic slavery, since contract labour had been imposed on the workers of all races in the diamond mines. In addition, the war would be ruinous for the British economy, even if lucrative for a few. Hardie brushed aside arguments that it would lead to an increasing demand for British goods and raw materials. The cost of maintaining troops in South Africa, the diverting of shipping to military purposes and away from the international carrying trade, the dislocation of British overseas trade, the rising burden of direct and indirect taxation – all these would lead to financial disaster. He pointed to a decline of exports of £5,500,000 in the first six months of 1901, according to the Board of Trade returns. Finally, he feared for the consequences of war for British society. The erosion of civil liberties, the emergence of a new militarism already revealed in labour disputes, the corrupting effects of the psychology of racism and ultra-nationalism – all threatened to undermine democracy itself.

Hardie's onslaughts on the war continued without abating from the outbreak of fighting in October 1899 down to the peace of Vereeniging in May 1902. Throughout, his courage and consistency were never seen to better advantage. At least until the 'khaki' election of October 1900, the critics of the war were a distinct minority and ready targets for abuse and persecution. The offices of the *Labour Leader* and of several local ILP branches were attacked or stoned. In the later stages of the war as the 'methods of barbarism' employed by Kitchener in concentration camps on the Rand, with immense loss of life amongst Boer women and children, caused widespread disgust, the anti-war critics gained a new respectability. But in the first year of the war men like Hardie, with their associates in the labour world and a few, isolated Liberal critics like Channing, Stanhope and Lloyd George, had to struggle hard for survival.

Hardie's attacks on the war frequently used the concepts and terminology of Marxism. The word 'capitalism' invariably appeared in his diagnoses of the causes of the war. He seemed to depict the war as the last gasp of an economic system in crisis, the result of years of monopolistic expansion in the form of cartels, of diminished outlets for investment at home, of the relentless struggle for markets abroad by all of the imperial powers. Yet a careful study of Hardie's analysis of the war makes it clear that his criticism of it rested basically on traditional radical arguments. It differed very little in kind from Bright and Cobden's denunciation of the Crimean War almost fifty years earlier – with which Hardie, indeed, drew frequent comparisons. His diagnosis of the war was basically populist rather than socialist. It arose, he argued, from the machinations and ambitions of specific capitalist conspirators on the Rand, rather than from the inevitable decay of monopoly capitalism (about which he was ultimately optimistic). Contrary to his own version a few years later, he was making war on a class, not on a system. His attack on the gold speculators was remarkably similar in style to the rhetoric of the Populist silver advocates in the United States at the same period, when they inveighed against the conspiracies of the 'gold bugs' in Wall Street. Like them, Hardie beheld the 'cross of gold' being constructed in South Africa and saw the British democracy crucified upon it. His diagnosis of the origin of the war was essentially political, not economic. It echoed the arguments used at the same period by J.A. Hobson – though without his anti-semitic nuances. The war was the ugly fruit of a democracy gone astray, perverted by class rule and by under-consumption, but still capable of redemption by right-thinking radicals. Precisely because Hardie did not view the Boer War in the simplistic terms of the Marxists or explain it away through a crude economic determinism, his criticisms of it were all the more compelling. It lent his appeal a political flexibility. It enabled the ILP to stay within the main stream of a revived British radicalism, and gave Hardie himself a new authority right across the political spectrum.

The political consequence of Hardie's stand against the Boer War was to renew, even while the Labour Representation Committee was in the making, demands for collaboration between labour men and anti-war Liberals. 'Class against class' gave way to the idea of a Popular Front. Even in the first few days of the war, Hardie speculated in the *Labour Leader* on the prospects of a new alliance of socialists, trade unionists and radicals.[3] He made new overtures to the anti-war Liberals, convinced that the dominance of the imperialist wing of the party condemned it to disruption and decline. His years of fierce denunciation of Liberals of all shades as the symbols of a corrupting commercialism were now forgotten in the face of this new crisis which threatened to undermine British society at its foundations. Old enemies were instantly forgiven. John Burns, also a caustic critic of the war, now found himself subjected to warm eulogies in the ILP press. Welsh and Scottish radicals like Lloyd George and Bryce, often attacked in the past for failing to display a consistent view on social and economic issues, were now hailed as popular tribunes. Most ironically of all, even John Morley, Hardie's particular *bête noire* over the years, was clasped to labour's breast. A powerful anti-war speech by Morley at Oxford in June 1900 was hailed by Hardie in terms that, in retrospect, seem not a little absurd. Morley was invited to link the tyranny imposed on the Boers by capitalists in South Africa with the similar bondage inflicted on the workers in Britain itself. 'Those of us who are Socialists are so because we are Altruistic individuals, that is, believers in freedom for the individual as long as it is consistent with equal freedom,' Hardie declared. 'The principles of freedom expounded by Bentham and enlarged and systematized by Mill lead logically to Socialism.' Would Morley, he wondered, now 'cross the Rubicon' and serve as the new inspiration and leader of the new socially-conscious radicalism?[4] It was all a very far cry from the general elections of 1892 and 1895 when Hardie had travelled up to Newcastle and successfully urged the workers there to vote Tory as a punishment for Morley's blinkered dogmatism on the eight-hours issue. Morley's predictable refusal to respond to this unlikely invitation (and his preference for writing the *Life* of Gladstone) did not diminish the warmth of his reception in ILP circles for the remainder of the war. For many months the *Labour Leader* trumpeted the need for labour-radical collaboration and for pacts at the forthcoming general election. Where, some socialists wondered, was Hardie's much vaunted labour independence now?

Again, just as the 'little England' Liberals and their advocates in the press like H.W. Massingham and A.G. Gardiner, kindled new enthusiasm in ILP circles, so, too, did the Irish. For Redmond's newly-reunited Irish Nationalists were as zealous in their sympathy for the Boer case as was Hardie himself. Like him, they wanted the Boers to remain undefeated. They attacked the very basis of the war, not merely the 'barbarous' methods by which it was being fought. Hardie now tried to forge new links with the Nationalists, with whom his relations had been sorely strained since the Irish vote at Mid-Lanark, West Ham (in 1895) and East Bradford had been cast against him. He renewed his old ties with Michael Davitt; he sang the praises of the reunion of the Parnellite and anti-Parnellite factions. He negotiated with Redmond over sharing out the Misses Kippens' bequest. All this was some way removed from Hardie's earlier outlook. For the Irish Nationalists, radical on imperial and Irish questions, were notoriously conservative on the home front, with little sympathy for the trade unions. The young Scots-Irish Social Democrat, James Connolly of Edinburgh, was amongst those who pointed out the inconsistency of Hardie's position. Until the war Hardie had been his idol. Connolly had served as the Glasgow agent for the *Labour Leader* and had received £50 from Hardie to launch a new journal, the *Workers' Republic*. When Hardie now lavished praise on Redmond and Dillon and finally toured Ireland in September 1901 under the personal guidance of the member for Kerry, John Murphy, it seemed the final token of his erratic 'opportunism'. Connolly instead fiercely championed the cause of the Irish Socialist Republicans, a fusion of Marxists and ultra-nationalists.[5] For Hardie, his feelings were never the same again: the glory and the dream had passed away.

Apart from a few individuals like Connolly, however, there is little doubt that Hardie's new approach, accompanied by similar overtures to the radicals by MacDonald and Glasier, greatly enhanced his political stature. He was frequently associated with radical Liberals on joint platforms in condemnation of the war in South Africa. The writings of J.A. Hobson, full of the corrupt machinations of the Beits and Barnatos in South Africa, in full pursuit of the corrupt investment of their surplus capital, lent Hardie and the radicals such as Lloyd George a common ideology and rhetoric. Even the Oxford Union provided Hardie with an unexpected forum for winning converts to the radical front – preceded by an agitated correspondence with the president of the Union, R.C.K. Ensor, on whether a dinner jacket could be dispensed with before that assembly.[6] The growing tide of 'new Liberalism', fired by the revelations such as those of Seebohm Rowntree's inquiry into poverty in the city of York, added momentum and depth to Hardie's campaigns. A new 'progressive alliance' was in the making and Hardie was a part of it.

These developments somewhat overshadowed the formation of the Labour Representation Committee on 27–8 February 1900. Even so, the creation of something that resembled an independent labour party was a vital phase in Hardie's strategy. In the progressive alliance it would give the workers a reinforced bargaining position, perhaps in time a dominating one. In fact, the forming of what was eventually to prove a new British party did not arouse immense interest at the time. Even Hardie himself in the *Labour Leader* was more preoccupied with praise of Hobson's diagnosis of the war in South Africa.[7] Nevertheless, the conference was a total success in every respect. As Hardie later explained its secret: 'The object of the conference was not to discuss first principles but to endeavour to ascertain whether organizations representing different ideals could find an immediate and practical common ground.'[8] Areas of collaboration would be found between the trade unions and 'the movement based on socialism', but each would operate, financially and organizationally, on a strictly independent basis. The principles would look after themselves.

It was in this flexible, pragmatic mood that the 129 delegates had assembled at the Memorial Hall.[9] They included representatives of over half a million trade unionists, including such major unions as the Gasworkers and the Railway Servants. The chairman was a trade unionist Liberal MP, W.C. Steadman. But it was Hardie and the ILP who dominated proceedings, displaying tactical acumen of a high order. It was Hardie personally who determined the major strategic decisions reached. Any attempt to restrict labour candidatures to working men or to socialists or to advocates of the class war was voted down. So, by contrast, were proposed working agreements with the Liberals similar to those operated by many Lib-Lab MPs. The enemies of the Labour alliance, both the SDF Marxists and the Lib-Lab possibilists, were outmanoeuvred. Instead, Hardie carried the vital amendment that there should be set up 'a distinct Labour group in Parliament, who shall have their own whips, and agree upon their policy, which must embrace a readiness to co-operate with any party which for the time being may be engaged in promoting legislation in the direct interests of labour'. This agreed formula, which provided the maximum area of manoeuvre for enlisting the support of trade unionists without any implications for long-term objectives, set the tone for the Labour Party as it was to evolve during the first eighteen years of its history. All the major questions about relations with the Liberals, about electoral tactics, party discipline, financial control and a host of other issues, were set aside for future deliberation. The very concept of socialism never intruded itself on any of the new 'Labour Representation Committees' platforms. Even John Burns, present as a delegate of the Engineers, felt compelled to give reluctant support to Hardie's amendment, although he was constrained to add that men like himself and Sam Woods, 'who had not worn trilby hats and red ties', had been doing all the real spadework for labour representation since 1895. Hardie's motion was carried unanimously. But if socialism was seldom prominent at the Memorial Hall, individual socialists were. The ILP delegates carried another crucial amendment which would reduce the committee of the Labour Representation Committee to a mere twelve, of which five would be drawn from the socialist societies, a remarkably high proportion for their numbers. Two of these five would be from the ILP – James Parker, and, inevitably, Hardie, were those selected. The Fabians, whose influence Hardie distrusted, were left only one executive place, filled by Edward Pease. Finally, the first secretary of the new LRC was also drawn from the ILP, Ramsay MacDonald, who retained this crucial post until 1911. Since he was known to be close to many Liberals through his *Progressive Review* and Rainbow Circle connections, the atmosphere of conciliation and of flexibility was again maintained.

In this free-ranging manner, the LRC came quietly into being. Candidatures would be promoted by local political and trades bodies as before. Finance was set aside for future discussion. The degree of trade union commitment was still hard to predict, since most of the major unions – the miners, cotton workers and engineers conspicuously – still held aloof. Even so, Hardie knew that the vital breakthrough had been made. A working alliance had been forged with the unions and indissoluble links created with his own ILP. He wrote to Ensor on 2 March: 'The Conference here was most successful and promises well for future work. One thing struck me very forcibly – the determination of nine-tenths of the Trade Unionists present to have a strictly independent party.'[10] What he and the ILP had still to work out was the precise character of that independence in the light of the new political situation created by the Boer War.

Hardie by this time was restless for a new political base. His association with the ILP underwent something of a change at about this time. Many of the party rank-and-file felt that a new chairman was desirable in view of the party's desperate struggles since 1895. Hardie, by contrast, was reluctant to go, even though Glasier tried tactfully to persuade him to do so. 'Any procedure that would seem to display a desire either on your part or ours of the NAC to maintain you in the chair – even on the plea of urgency of your occupying that position for the party's welfare – might in view of last year's resolution and statements then made, be misunderstood by a section.' Since no-one of the stature of Mann or George Barnes was available as a replacement, Glasier hoped (or so he claimed) that the local branches might be approached to reconsider Hardie's resignation.[11] Privately, he was disturbed at Hardie's possessive attitude towards the ILP as his own creation. In particular, he resented Hardie's attempts to win the party secretaryship for the faithful Frank Smith, in place of John Penny. 'This is one of Hardie's strangely disquieting moves. Smith has absolutely no claims and the party does not trust him.'[12] Fortunately for the state of the party's administration, Penny was persuaded to stay on as secretary for the immediate future. When the ILP annual conference met at Glasgow on 16–17 April, Hardie departed quietly and Glasier himself was unanimously selected as the successor. It was a sign of a cyclical shift in the brief history of the Independent Labour Party, the end of its first pioneering phase. Glasier noted in his diary: 'Hardie seems pleased I am elected. Miss McMillan and many others say it will do good, by showing that the movement is not merely a Hardie one, and that many who never have taken to Hardie will join.' In public, Glasier adopted a more charitable attitude. He paid warm tribute to Hardie's labours for the party, despite the 'wear and tear' it had brought for his health and constitution. Throughout the years Hardie 'had remained faithful to the class to which he belonged'. After the conference Glasier wrote to Hardie in more realistic vein:

Neither I nor any one who loves our movement can wish for anything that would withdraw you from the very front of our fighting line where you have always been. Though you have retired from the chair, you are still 'by divine right' leader of the party, and although I shall try to do my duty in your seat,

I shall look and the party will look to you for guidance and as commander-in-chief as of yore.[13]

Still, Hardie's retirement from the ILP chairmanship made his political position much more fluid. Ultimately, without doubt, he sought a speedy return to parliament; but the mechanics for securing this were unclear. As has been seen, he was no longer candidate for West Ham South and his links with any specific constituency were tenuous in the extreme. In any case, his successful adoption for any hopeful seat would depend in practice on the kind of working arrangement with the Liberal whips which he had enjoyed in West Ham in 1892 and which had been responsible for his election there, however much the NAC might continue to declare its sea-green, incorruptible hostility to any such arrangement.

Throughout the spring and summer of 1900, as the crisis of the Boer War reached a new depth of popular hysteria during the aftermath of the relief of Mafeking, the search went on for a suitable seat for Hardie. From March onwards two were under active consideration, Merthyr Tydfil in South Wales and Preston in Lancashire. Merthyr seemed from the outset the more likely of the two.[14] It had an old radical, Chartist tradition; it had returned the Welsh pacifist, Henry Richard, in the momentous election of 1868. It boasted a vigorous Trades Council in Merthyr itself and also in Aberdare, in which committed socialists like C.B. Stanton, the Aberdare miners' agent, and Edmund Stonelake, were prominent. It had been deeply stirred by the six-months' coal stoppage in 1898. Hardie himself had toured the area for several weeks then, and had written compassionate articles on the Welsh valleys in the *Labour Leader*. The ILP subsequently launched a missionary drive in the area and *Clarion* vans toured the coalfield. Hardie urged that 'a Welsh-speaking Welshman' should fight Merthyr for the ILP.[15] A network of local socialists in the Merthyr area, notably Dai Davies, an ILP official from Pant, and the famous radical barber, Llew Francis, provided a vital range of contacts for Hardie, on which he could build. On the other hand, there had never been a Labour candidate for the constituency before – unless the claims of one of the sitting Liberals, the gold speculator, W. Pritchard Morgan, to have been elected as a 'labour' man back in 1888 were admitted. The ILP executive after surveying the constituency declared that organization there was at a low ebb, depending heavily as it did on the local Trades Councils. 'Reports from [Merthyr Tydfil] were vague and unsatisfactory.'[16] Hardie himself continued to hanker after Merthyr as a likely seat. He told Glasier on 21 July, 'I am not the least bit drawn towards Preston. I wish someone could go to Merthyr and spend a few days making inquiry. My own preference is for that, altho' probably Preston wd. be safer thing for a good vote....'[17] Personally, as a Scot, he had a sentimental attachment for Welshmen: 'like all Celts, they are socialists by instinct'.[18] He wrote lyrically in his journal of the moving experience it had been to hear Welsh miners singing the hymn 'Aberystwyth'. 'What more wonderful than that the language of the little nation who thrice repelled the hosts of Rome two thousand years ago, who endured conquest after conquest, and even had their language penalized, should be heard at all in this distant day.'[19] Nevertheless on 28 July the NAC announced that despite great pressure by the Merthyr men, Hardie would be nominated for Preston instead, thus following Glasier's advice.[20]

Why exactly he chose to fight so unpromising a seat as Preston is a mystery. To Sam Hobson, later to move from the ILP into the British Socialist Party and to write for A.R. Orage's *New Age*, this choice of constituency convinced him that 'Hardie had not the least political judgement'.[21] It appears to have been John Penny, re-elected the secretary of the ILP and himself a Preston man, who was a key figure. Far from being a stronghold of socialism or even of advanced radicalism as Merthyr Tydfil was, Preston, as a local labour man, Thomas Charteris, wrote to Ramsay MacDonald in May, was 'a very slow, old Conservative town, and anything like a move goes badly with our co-operators'.[22] The Conservatives had held both seats there since 1885. Although Hardie was mooted as a candidate in the spring, by September nothing positive had been done to build up local LRC organization. The only hopeful augury for him was that this two-member constituency was unlikely to put up a Liberal at the polls and that he might hope for some Liberal support in fighting the two sitting Unionists, R.W. Hanbury and W.E.M. Tomlinson. Hardie himself told the Preston electors,

I was at first adverse to becoming a candidate at all, but my colleagues in the movement pressed me to stand. I have had the refusal of four constituencies in the country, one in Wales [Merthyr], one in Scotland, and one in the north of England [probably Chester-le-Street, Durham]. My personal preference would have been for the mining constituency in Wales, and I should have gone there but for the fact that during the coal strike some 4,000 miners became disfranchised.[23]

It was hardly a cordial gesture towards an alien Lancashire constituency. An additional complication was that in Preston the tension between Orange and Catholic voters was specially acute as a result of the exceptionally large Irish population there together with an indigenous Catholic population. At least one third of the population was Roman Catholic. Hardie observed that 'the church may play a part in the campaign, the Orangemen being savage with the sitting member for not supporting some bill'. But, he concluded cheerfully, 'As I am void of offence – & conscience – on matters theological, I will if I can encourage these upholders of Church & State in their revolt. The trouble is that the Catholics want a university for Ireland – of which demand I am a supporter – & will vote for no candidate who doesn't support it, while the Orangemen will vote for no candidate who does.'[24] Still he remained distrusted in Catholic circles, while the Anglican vote was overwhelmingly thrown behind the Unionist cause. By contrast, Preston nonconformists were less numerous, barely one-sixth of the population. Nevertheless despite the sketchy nature of the information he received about Preston and his own ignorance of the constituency, Hardie moved steadily nearer to becoming the candidate. The only issue still uncertain was whether he would retain his connection with Merthyr in the event of a defeat at Preston.

In mid-September the issue was put to the test. The Salisbury government dissolved parliament and appealed to the country on a 'khaki' ticket. The jingo mood was at its height. The war still commanded mass popular enthusiasm and anti-war radicals of all shades, from Leonard Courtney in the Unionist ranks through men like Lloyd George and Burns to the ILP on the far left, faced a severe challenge. Hardie faced the added problem of divided loyalties. On 22 September 1900, at a somewhat unorthodox joint meeting of the Merthyr and Aberdare Trades Council, he had been nominated as LRC candidate for the Merthyr Boroughs.[25] There was angry resentment at this from the supporters of local Welsh miners' leaders, many of whom favoured William Brace, the notoriously Lib-Lab vice-president of the South Wales Miners' Federation. Brace's supporters finally left the meeting, alleging, not without justification, that the ILP had rigged it. Hardie was then nominated, in preference to Tom Richards, another Welsh miners' leader and treasurer of the South Wales Miners' Federation, by thirty-two votes to seven. Still, in Merthyr it was a case of Hamlet in the avoidable absence of the Prince, as Hardie remained in Preston. Here his speeches certainly had their socialist ring, as he called for public ownership of the mines, minerals and railways. But the main tenor of his campaign from the outset was an unmistakable bid for Liberal support. It was a social reform rather than a socialist platform that he set before the voters. 'Social reform and militarism were incompatible', Hardie declared, before going on to a fierce attack on the war in South Africa. The gold of the Transvaal should 'not be handed over to a gang of international swindlers'.[26] On 25 September he explained why he had decided to serve as candidate for two constituencies in widely different parts of the country.

His earlier life had been that of a working collier and colliers did not learn much anent the requirements of textile operatives. . . . With the people of his own trade he had felt that he would be more in touch, but it had been thought by his friends in Preston that after the enthusiastic way in which the resolution at Monday night's meeting had been carried it would be tantamount to a breach of faith were he not to carry the campaign through to a finish. It was on that score that he accepted the invitation of the Preston ILP.[27]

Fortified by a £150 cheque from the cocoa magnate, George Cadbury, towards election expenses, he launched his campaign.

It was a forlorn hope from the start. Hardie's tactics were to train his fire on Tomlinson, the junior and more vulnerable Unionist, and hope thereby to pick up the maximum vote from dissident Unionists and from nonconformist Liberals. He had some success. The *Preston Guardian* (a Liberal newspaper) praised on 29 September 'the wonderful transformation' that had overtaken the attitude of Preston Liberals. Hardie was described as 'the actual, if not the nominal champion of Liberalism'. Hardie spent much time training his fire on such time-honoured Liberal targets as the liquor traffic, as well as making ferocious attacks on the government over the war. Joseph Chamberlain's irresponsibility and ambition he compared with the high standards set by 'the old leaders of the Conservative Party'.[28] But there was little hope of Hardie's making much impact. As has been seen, Preston was no citadel of radicalism; many of its Liberals, including the local

Lancashire Daily Post, were sympathetic to the war. Anti-Catholic prejudice helped imperialist sentiment to flourish. Above all, Hardie's divided obligations to Preston and to Merthyr told against him. One day, 27 September, he went to bed at 1 am in Preston, then caught the 6.30 am train to Merthyr, addressed five open-air meetings there, retired to bed at 2 am and finally on the early morning of the 29th returned by train to Preston where he held three further meetings that day.[29] Even for one of Hardie's iron will, it was an immense strain – and also a schedule that lent itself easily to ridicule. Hanbury, the senior Unionist at Preston, derided Hardie. 'He was in the field of politics a Bedouin of the desert, an Ishmael whose hand was against every man and every man's against him.' Changing the metaphor, Hanbury added that 'this gay Lothario was apparently desirous of becoming a political bigamist (renewed laughter). Fancy the absurd position of a man with his arms round the waists of two constituencies – with one eye on one and the other on the other, speaking to one in Welsh and the one in Lancashire.'[30] At the polls Hanbury headed the field with 8,944 votes, followed by Tomlinson with 8,067. Hardie lagged behind with only 4,834. He attributed his defeat partly to press antagonism but also drew the moral that radicals and socialists should make more effective common cause in the battle for the soul of humanity and for peace.[31]

His only hope now was to salvage his cause at Merthyr. Here the local ILP and Trades Council had been battling on without him. Indeed he later claimed that he spent only 'eleven waking hours' in the constituency before the poll.[32] It was apparently an uphill fight in Merthyr, too.[33] The valleys had prospered during the war years. Here, like other parts of Wales, imperialism was in full flood, as Lloyd George and other anti-war men found during the campaign. The junior member, Pritchard Morgan, was a fanatical advocate of the imperial cause. He was, later on, to trade in uninhibited red-baiting – 'Socialism means sedition, anarchy, no government, no King, no God – absolute, impenetrable darkness!' He added the gloss that Hardie was a Scottish carpet-bagger, totally ignorant of the needs of Wales. But other factors worked in Hardie's favour. If imperialism was rife in South Wales, so too to some degree was anti-imperialism. The pacifist traditions of Henry Richard were still a factor of substance in the constituency. Some Welsh journalists even claimed that there was a kinship between the Welsh and the Boers – also a small, predominantly pastoral, God-fearing people of Calvinist stock. The more specifically working-class traditions of Merthyr – traced down from the Merthyr riots and the execution of 'Dic Penderyn' in 1831 through Chartism, the 'great election' of 1868, Thomas Halliday's Amalgamated Association of Miners in 1871–4, down to the coal lock-out of 1898 and the rise of the ILP – all this created a distinctive working-class radical culture peculiar to Merthyr alone in South Wales. In no other Welsh constituency could a candidate so committed and anti-militarist as Hardie have made such an impact.

Even so, the course of the election makes it clear that Hardie could never have carried Merthyr on his own. It was still overwhelmingly a Liberal seat. The decisive fact was that the Merthyr Liberals were divided – and had been since the two sitting members, D.A. Thomas and Pritchard Morgan, had quarrelled fatally at the time of Morgan's return to parliament in 1888. During the Boer War, while Pritchard Morgan was an uninhibited imperialist of the crudest type, D.A. Thomas was with some qualifications hostile to the war.[34] Although a wealthy coalowner, he was not unsympathetic to social reform. He had himself urged an enlightened labour policy, a minimum wage and a planned, controlled approach to coal production in South Wales, instead of the primitive anarchy of *laissez-faire*. Thomas's willingness to experiment and his antagonism to Pritchard Morgan were such that he was even prepared to welcome a socialist outsider like Hardie, rather than endorse his detested Liberal colleague. Without this split in the Liberal camp, Hardie could never have been returned.

This factor turned the scale. Hardie's campaign owed little to the war. His few speeches in Merthyr concentrated largely on the local industrial situation and on efforts to prove that he was a proper representative for the Welsh radical tradition in such a constituency. After the poll he listed three main reasons for his success – a desire for independent labour representation after the 1898 stoppage; anti-war sentiment amongst 'better-class Liberals'; and a determination to get rid of Pritchard Morgan, 'the member for China', whose quest for gold had taken him as far afield as Korea. 'The moment Mr Pritchard Morgan declared himself a supporter of the war and an imperialist, his doom was sealed', amongst the erstwhile supporters of the Rev. Henry Richard, Wales's apostle of peace.[35] In the event, while Thomas com-

fortably headed the poll, Hardie received 5,745 votes to Pritchard
Morgan's 4,004. Of Hardie's votes, few were 'plumpers'; 4,437 were
shared with D.A. Thomas in this two-member seat.[36] Hardie was
returned as an unequivocal representative of the ILP and the LRC.
Nevertheless, without this clear evidence of Liberal endorsement and
the backing of Thomas's private machine, Hardie would have been as
disappointed at Merthyr as he had been at Preston.

At Merthyr he entered a world in many ways alien to him. His
acquaintance with Welsh affairs was slight. The upsurge of Welsh
political and national consciousness in the past twenty years, with men
like Tom Ellis and Lloyd George as its tribunes, was remote from his
experience. Nevertheless he soon adapted himself to this new environment. He joined at once the Welsh parliamentary party in the Commons. He later collaborated with his Welsh Liberal colleagues in
denouncing the 1902 Education Bill and the 1904 Licensing measure.
He was ardent for Welsh disestablishment and disendowment – the
latter on somewhat eccentric grounds, since he welcomed the expropriation of the funds of the established Church as the forerunner of a
general attack on all vested interests, those of capitalists and landlords
included.[37] He even learnt to sing the Welsh national anthem, *Yr Hen
Wlad fy Nhadau*, in a rich Scots baritone, to beguile or confuse his
listeners. He praised the national *eisteddfod*: it was a gathering, he
claimed, originally devised to protect the medieval Welsh bards against
literary blacklegs.[38] He claimed to be a Welsh home ruler. Indeed,
this chimed in well with his attacks on state socialism and on centralized
control. Self-government for Wales always appeared on his election
addresses in Merthyr as members of Plaid Cymru faithfully recalled in
the 1970s. He claimed that the ILP were the true Welsh nationalists,
since they alone wanted the land and the natural resources of Wales to
belong to its people. He poured scorn on the spurious nationalism of a
cosmopolite like Sir Alfred Mond, the advocate of 'Vales for the
Velsh'. 'The Nationalist Party I have in mind,' Hardie wrote, 'is this—
the people of Wales fighting to recover possession of the land in Wales
. . . that is the kind of Nationalism that will be emblazoned on the red
flag of Socialism.' *Y Ddraig Goch a'r Faner Goch* (the Red Dragon and
the *Red* Flag) was his watchword.[39] On this, highly individual, basis,
Hardie readily identified himself with the major progressive currents
of Welsh life.

In Wales, as in England, he was less the international socialist, much more the symbol of the local Progressive alliance. He readily identified himself with his new constituency. Indeed, some ministers of the local nonconformist chapels, formerly hostile to socialism but now increasingly influenced by the 'new theology' of the Rev. R.J. Campbell, found in Hardie an ideal spokesman for the 'social gospel' which they sought to extend to the slum-ridden backstreets of darkest London or darkest Merthyr. For the rest of his life Hardie was the prophet of radical-socialism in its highly-distinctive Merthyr form. Throughout his later career of intense nationwide campaigning, his many tours of foreign lands, his trip around the world in 1907–8, his links with his constituency were steadily reinforced. Merthyr was never entirely a safe seat. The Liberals continued to top the poll there for the rest of Hardie's parliamentary career. A determined attack on him by two Liberal candidates would probably have unseated him. In some parts of his scattered constituency, notably in Mountain Ash, LRC organization was weak and its support meagre. Hardie's towering personality to some extent masked his weakness at the grass roots. Even so, despite all these difficulties, he had now found the secure radical base from which he could resume his task of building up an independent labour movement. He summed up the local mood in writing to MacDonald after the poll. 'We have had most excellent meetings down Merthyr way and every one is in the best of spirits and good feeling obtains all round. How long it will last is another matter.' Of one thing, though, he was convinced – 'the advanced state of political thought in the Principality'.[40]

The LRC greeted Hardie's return to parliament with intense enthusiasm. Public meetings at Glasgow and elsewhere showed that his unique charisma had survived in full since 1895. Glasier echoed the prevailing mood: 'A great day. Hardie returned for Merthyr. I could hardly speak for joy. . . . It is a great event, the turning point in the poor ILP's career. My heart, too, is glad for Hardie. He has suffered and toiled so much.' He added, after hearing Hardie give a powerful address on the Boer War at the Free Trade Hall, Manchester, 'Never so struck with the greatness of Hardie. We have none like him.' The NAC was also lyrical in its congratulations.[41] A request from Hardie for campaign expenses after the election and some argument about the fees due to him for lecturing tours did nothing to sour the mood of rejoicing. In addition, Richard Bell, admittedly a well-known Lib-Lab, had been returned as LRC candidate for Derby. There had been other excellent Labour polls, including John Hodge's fine vote at Gower, or West Glamorgan, another Welsh constituency. Here he was only narrowly defeated by, in the free-wheeling terms adopted by the *Labour Leader*, 'a brewer, coalmaster, money-lender and employer of women dockers'.[42] Conversely, Hardie perhaps took private satisfaction from the failure of Will Thorne to capture West Ham South, despite (or perhaps because of) Major Banes's antagonism to the Boer War. Labour disorganization there was as pronounced as in 1895; the registration of voters remained chaotic. Elsewhere there was the positive satisfaction of the return of known anti-war Liberals like Channing, Labouchere, Burns, and, most significant of all, Lloyd George, despite the massive currents of jingoism which brought the Unionist government another crushing victory overall.

In December 1900, then, Hardie resumed his old seat in the House of Commons. Many wondered how the intervening years had affected his parliamentary style. The *ILP News*, in a friendly account of his return to the House, observed: 'Perhaps Keir Hardie has gained somewhat in grace of political manner by adversity . . . if only just a little of the "Old Adam" of positiveness has been strained out of him, he will still prove none the less formidable to his foes and lovable to his friends.'[43] Hardie's appearance was as exotic as ever. 'Queer Hardie' was still a flesh-and-blood reality, save that the old 'ninepenny cap' of 1892 had been exchanged for a strange new hat bought in Philadelphia during his American visit. He himself viewed the House with an ironical and quizzical eye. He regaled his readers with a sarcastic account of the ritual of Black Rod. Although the House was more comfortable than in 1895, with its new dining-room, smoking-room and baths, the Commons still needed an effort to convert 'its shame and frivolities into realities'.[44] He signalled his return to the House in 1901 with a renewal of his attacks on the royal family. He denounced the £20,000 granted the Duke and Duchess of York to visit the colonies. He condemned the expenditure on the Queen's funeral!: 'the dead body of England's Queen was being used as a recruiting sergeant'.[45] He also queried why the British royal family had to be paid so very much more than the American president. Even so, there is no doubt that Hardie approached his new period in the House in a less agitated frame of mind. He was more concerned to convince, less anxious to shock. He produced a series of cogent interventions on labour questions such as workers' compensation and the conduct of the strike in the Penrhyn slate quarries in north Wales – issues on which he could expect widespread Liberal support. He joined with Lloyd George and other radicals in fierce criticism of the methods used in coercing Boer families in South Africa in clear defiance of the Hague conventions. For the first time, he had a consistent, constructive role to exercise in the House of Commons. The press noted how he was cultivating a House of Commons manner, how he was more willing to debate and not merely to declaim. One journalist added: 'Much experience and pondering of the hard side of life have put furrows of suffering across his forehead and have given his face an immobility of seriousness that imparts a curious effectiveness to his speech.'[46] The years of parliamentary influence, perhaps, were at last about to begin.

The role that Hardie was to fulfil in public life henceforth was a highly complex and many-sided one. Until the formation of the LRC in February 1900 his career had been one of agitation, of digging rather than of building. Now that his chosen instrument of an independent labour party was in being, there was almost inevitably an air of anti-climax. The role for the LRC now was one of consolidation, of trying to wean more and more trade unionists away from the Liberal alliance. In fact, the fortuitous announcement of the Taff Vale verdict by the Law Lords in 1901 was doing the LRC's work for it. A decision given against the Amalgamated Society of Railway Servants in effect seemed to threaten with huge financial penalties every union which went on strike. The annual conferences of the LRC in 1901 and 1902 spoke of the huge increase in strength that Taff Vale had brought about. Trade union affiliated membership rose to 353,070 in 1901 and to 455,450 in 1902. Sixty-five unions and twenty-one trades councils were now attached to the Committee as affiliated organizations; and already those unions in the TUC who remained outside the LRC were a distinct minority. This laborious task of consolidation was less congenial to Hardie. The main initiative now lay with permanent party officials such as Ramsay MacDonald, the secretary of the LRC, a younger man by ten years whose influence could well eclipse Hardie's own. In the party organization, by contrast, Hardie was something of a detached figure, still secure in his

editorship of the *Labour Leader*, his private entourage of friends like
Frank Smith and Mrs Pankhurst, and a wider army of rank-and-file
admirers, but remote from day-to-day decisions. A national appeal for
funds initially brought him a steady income of over £160 a year, which
he could supplement with journalism and lecturing, and this helped
preserve his independence.[47] Still, amongst the grass-roots party
workers at the pitheads, amongst the blackened mills and blast furnaces
of industrial Britain, Hardie exercised a matchless and majestic authority. He could inspire devotion in a manner given to no other Labour
leader. His pamphlet, *Can a Man be a Christian on a Pound a Week?*
(1901) made a powerful appeal to the national conscience on behalf of
the under-paid and the over-worked. 'The outcast', he wrote, 'in his
lonely broodings and his fits of remorse will get nearer to the heart of
God than will those who observe all the rites of Christianity but are
strangers to its spirit.'[48]

Perhaps there was something autobiographical in this account of the
social outcast. Hardie himself appears more and more as a lonely figure
at this time, moving in and out of the main echelons of the working-
class movement in an evanescent, tantalizing way. His marriage, as
before, brought him little joy. He was additionally saddened by the ill-
health of his beloved mother. He was worried about money and
appealed for a further £50 a year to meet the various claims of travel,
constituency work and entertaining visitors in the House of Commons.[49]
He was also anxious about the future of the *Labour Leader*. Its
tone was less vigorous, its arguments less clearly focussed. It was in
serious financial trouble as advertising revenue fell away.[50] Above
all, Hardie was unhappy about how to make an impact in the
new House of Commons. He poured out his soul to Glasier in
August 1901:

> Our trouble is that we have been, and in the very nature of the case had
> to be, chiefly a propagandist organization, and even now there are serious
> pitfalls ahead if we attempt any other role. Had we half a dozen men in parlt.
> everything would be changed. At present we don't baulk largely in the public
> eye as a political force. One thing we might do, altho' it is very risky, is
> encourage candidatures in a great many constituencies.[51]

In addition to this outpouring, which the recipient briskly termed 'a
bit pathetic', Glasier had to try to mediate in another fierce quarrel

between the *Labour Leader* and the *Clarion*. Hardie and Blatchford were yet again locked in fierce doctrinal dispute. 'Indeed I like Blatchford and Hardie but have to forgive them many faults,' Glasier wrote. 'But Hardie's letter is the healthier and sweeter & he is the greater man.'[52]

Hardie's intermittent depression was heightened by his sense of despair at the crushing effects of the Boer War on the national spirit. He veered erratically between the idea of building up a powerful labour party on an independent basis and the vision of 'a really independent militant political party in substantial agreement on the more pressing needs of the hour, than on the proclamation of a dry, doctrinaire creed'. This party should include socialists, radicals and Irish members, he wrote in the *Woolwich Labour Journal*.[53] But in the House he had no allies to promote either of these policies. The other LRC representative, Richard Bell of Derby, was so transparently a Lib-Lab that any prospect of long-term collaboration between him and Hardie dissolved almost from the start. From John Burns, despite his fierce opposition to the war, Hardie continued to keep aloof, while he had little direct contact with any of the anti-war radicals on the Liberal side. Indeed, Lloyd George, on whom Hardie placed some hopes, disillusioned him by his unexpectedly friendly response to Lord Rosebery's speech at Chesterfield in December 1901 and by his acceptance of the annexation of the two Boer republics.[54] In parliament, then, Hardie was still isolated. He could hope to achieve more in the nationwide organization of the LRC where his task was to crystallize and to synthesize. He agitated successfully on its executive for the affiliation of local trades councils (with their known socialist membership), for approaches to the Scottish Labour Representation Committee and to the trade unions. But for a man of Hardie's poetic, intuitive temperament, this unheroic, constructive labour was not enough. Beyond day-to-day tactics there was a profound political, moral and emotional cause to be defined and fought for:

Looking out upon life from his ethical watchtower, the socialist sees the land that gave him birth, the land he loves, the motherland staggering to its ruin under the double burden of War and Mammon. Blind to the beauties of art and dead to the pleasures of literature, its conscience dulled by lust of power to that sense of justice which is the salt of national life, it reels towards its doom.[55]

With that overwhelming sense of almost Old Testament self-identification as a latter-day Moses which he so naturally adopted, Keir Hardie armed himself anew as the prophet and the saviour of post-war democracy.

VII   The New Progressivism (1902–6)

The later stages of the South African War, leading up to the peace at Vereeniging in May 1902, were a period of unusual personal strain. Hardie's beloved daughter, Agnes, fell desperately ill and for many months hovered between life and death. He wrote, half humorously, of his plight:

Mrs Hardie fortunately has been well in herself. A woman's powers of endurance are a marvel when love is the driving force. . . . I wonder what the respectable Liberals of Merthyr would say if they knew that their junior MP has been washing dishes, lighting fires, carrying up coals, and playing the part of the scullery maid of late.[1]

By the spring the crisis was over and Agnes restored to health. Then came another cruel blow. In April Hardie's mother and father both died, within an hour of each other. He was deeply moved, especially at the loss of his mother, who had been so dominant an influence in moulding his early career:

Closed for ever are the grey eyes which blazed resentment or shed scalding tears when hard, untrue things were spoken or written about me or my doings. . . . Stilled are the beatings of the warm, impulsive heart which throbbed with pride and joy unspeakable when any little success came her laddie's ait.[2]

In the *Leader* Hardie laid bare his soul. He wrote of 'a chastened form of suffering which somehow feels as if it were half a joy'. Glasier noted in his diary, 'Poor Hardie – what assaults he has to bear'.[3] It is not surprising that Hardie's own health began to deteriorate seriously under the private and public burdens he had to bear. He looked years older than forty-six, already a weary veteran in early middle age. He gloomily recalled that, back in 1893, an astrologer and a lady palmist had both warned him of serious illnesses between his forty-sixth and forty-eighth years.[4]

There were also problems of housing. With Frank Smith's 'prophet's chamber' no longer available due to family bereavement, Hardie sought and eventually found a flat in London, at 14 Nevills Court, Fetter Lane, near to the *Labour Leader* offices. It was a rambling Tudor building and Hardie was delighted with it. It consisted basically of one large room, divided into a sitting-room, bedroom and kitchen. There was also a garden, 'thirty inches wide and fifteen feet long', where Hardie, always a keen gardener, managed to grow Welsh leeks and a few primroses. His flat at Nevills Court, his office, home and refuge, became almost legendary in the socialist world. He himself described it for the delight of his readers:

From the top of the tea caddy in the middle shelf within the deep recesses of the ingle nook, the dual face of Ralph Waldo Emerson, fashioned by the skilful hands of Sydney J. Morse ... looks sternly philosophic from his right eye across at Walt Whitman ... whilst with his left eye the genial philosopher winks roguishly at Robert Burns in his solitary corner near to the window.[5]

The books and ornaments in this humble flat, where Hardie invariably lived alone, became familiar to his readers everywhere. For visiting miners from Wales and Scotland, for socialist exiles from India, Russia or Australia, his home became a place of pilgrimage, almost a shrine. When his travels around the world became more extensive, it almost resembled a kind of socialist museum, adorned proudly by such mementoes as the tattered Union Jack carried away from a stormy meeting at Johannesburg. In 1911 Hardie moved across the way to 10 Nevills Court. Here the accommodation was a little more spacious, with a sitting-room, small bedroom and a closet. This building, later occupied by Fenner Brockway and finally destroyed during the London blitz in 1941, was the nearest he came to having a home for the remainder of his tortured life.

It was a stern, spartan life that he led here – 'like a hermit's cell' was Glasier's description of his flat.[6] Out of an income of little more than £3 a week he had to find perhaps £1 for food, 15s for secretarial assistance and 6s 6d for the rent.[7] His attempts to boost his income through investment proved unsuccessful, while the addiction to gambling of his elder son, Jamie, added to his financial burdens. It is not therefore surprising that Hardie's natural caution about money matters and his suspicious attitude towards the financing of his newspaper enterprises became more pronounced during these years. Even so, he somehow managed to recapture his serenity, and address himself anew to the complex political situation confronting him in the parliamentary session of 1902. Typically also, he found some spare time for helping destitute people in Salvation Army shelters.

The immediate task that absorbed his attention was the need to make labour an effective and viable parliamentary force. As the Boer War came to an end, the temporary mood of unity amongst radical and Lib-Lab backbenchers drained away; Hardie found himself as isolated and apparently powerless as before. His only possible parliamentary allies were John Burns, Richard Bell, and, much more doubtfully, the Lib-Lab members of the Pickard–Burt–Woods-Abraham type. On all fronts, Hardie met with frustration and disappointment. He had occasional dealings with Burns, for instance in demanding an inquiry into labour conditions in the Woolwich arsenal. He withheld a parliamentary report to the LRC annual conference in 1901, lest he upset his currently friendly relations with Burns. In April 1903 Hardie found him 'in a specially gracious and amiable mood'.[8] But Burns's links were almost wholly with Liberals of the Lloyd George wing; he regarded Hardie as an intractable extremist. The brief reunion of the Boer War period soon disintegrated. With Richard Bell of the Railway Servants, Hardie's relations were briefly more cordial. Bell was even persuaded to second, formally, Hardie's motion on 23 April 1901 on behalf of a socialist commonwealth.[9] Bell was elected president of the Labour Representation Committee for 1902–3. But it rapidly became apparent that Bell saw the LRC as a pressure group and no more. He pugnaciously resisted the idea of an independent party and actively advocated open by-election pacts with the Liberals. By the start of 1903 he was urging working-class voters to support Liberal candidates at Newmarket and Liverpool (West Derby), which made a mockery of the objectives outlined at the Memorial Hall conference in 1900. Glasier placidly commented that Bell's tactics were playing into the hands of the LRC. 'Had he waited till he had half a dozen fellow delinquents with him the position would have been critical.'[10] Even so, Bell's open warfare against his LRC colleagues seriously threatened the appeal of the Committee to trade-union affiliated members. He soon fell out with Hardie. On 9 March 1903 he wrote to Hardie to attend a conference of radical and labour members to consider joint action and balloting on labour and other questions. Hardie replied in thunderous terms:

Who arranged the joint conference and when did the Labour members agree to attend? I understood that we decided two weeks ago to meet each Thursday to discuss our own business and I regard any joint meeting of the kind you refer to as a breach of that understanding, and as being contrary to the constitution of the Labour Representation Committee. In addition we have in my opinion everything to lose and nothing whatever to gain from such a gathering and so I will not be present and ask you not to again take the unwarrantable liberty of inviting me to any future meeting of the kind.[11]

At first, the LRC deferred action on Bell's freelance tactics, but worse was to follow. Bell continued to act in a way virtually indistinguishable from that of orthodox Liberals. In the Norwich by-election at the end of 1903 he refused to support the LRC candidate, G.H. Roberts, and ostentatiously sent a letter of congratulation to the successful Liberal candidate. Further, he refused to sign the LRC constitution devised at Newcastle. This led to a complete severance of relations with Hardie and a savage controversy then erupted, first in the *Labour Leader*, then in the columns of the *Merthyr Express*.[12] Throughout 1904, inconclusive discussions took place between the Railway Servants and the LRC about efforts to bring Bell to heel. The outcome was that he ceased to be recognized as an LRC candidate. Hardie's potential army of labour members had been still further diminished.

With the other Trade Union members, Hardie's relations were even more frigid. He viewed with the utmost suspicion attempts, inspired in part by Sir Charles Dilke, to achieve some common action between radical and trade-union backbenchers in securing legal redress from the Taff Vale verdict. This led to a furious dispute between Hardie and Sam Woods, the secretary of the Parliamentary Committee of the TUC and himself an MP. Woods wrote angrily to MacDonald, as secretary of the LRC, 'I regret to say that although I try to be as charitable as I can in reference to these repeated statements of Mr Keir Hardie that I am tempted to believe sometimes that there is in his mind some lurking spleen and vindictiveness against the work of the Parliamentary Committee'. The LRC defended Hardie against these 'uncalled for and unjustifiable' charges. He himself added that he and Bell had been deliberately ignored by the TUC in preparing deputations designed to reverse the Taff Vale decision. 'I am neither animated by spleen nor resentment against the Parliamentary Committee.' Hardie added,

I am however sincerely desirous that the status of Labour shall be raised to the point at which it will command the respect of politicians, and one method of securing this end is that the organized labour bodies when desirous of raising questions in Parliament should first of all approach and consult the Labour members there. If Mr Woods is content to have Labour dragged at the tail of a disunited and discordant faction such as the Liberal Party in Parliament is, I at least will be no party to aid him in his decision.[13]

This episode virtually eliminated all contact between Hardie and the Lib-Lab members in the House; it made co-operative action on such pressing themes as unemployment virtually impossible. It markedly increased tension between the ILP and the trade-union elements in the LRC. Further, it added to the distrust widely entertained about Hardie in many trade-union circles. His speeches, John Ward of the Navvies Union complained, had turned a homogeneous movement 'into a divided rabble'. Hardie was accused of wanting to turn trade unionists against 'anyone who does not shout the party Shibboleth'. Again he was left impotent in the wilderness. 'None of us seem to have the grit & go of former days,' he wrote gloomily. 'Would to God the Liberals were again in office. Then we could make things hum once more.'[14]

The only feasible way ahead was somehow to build up the parliamentary strength of the LRC group in the House of Commons. But this seemed to rest entirely on the patronizing goodwill of the local Liberal caucuses. Here the outlook was depressing. At North-East Lanark in September 1901, when Bob Smillie was selected as LRC candidate, the local Liberal Association insisted on putting up a wealthy Liberal Imperialist candidate against him, in the person of Cecil Harmsworth. Smillie, inevitably, finished up at the bottom of the poll. Two months later, in another by-election at Dewsbury, the Liberals again put up a candidate, this time the wealthy shipowner, Walter Runciman. The ILP were further embarrassed when the SDF decided to fight this election, which led to a fierce altercation between the *Labour Leader* and the *Clarion* yet again and reduced relations between Hardie and Blatchford to a new extreme of frigidity.[15]

The first major boost for the LRC came quite unexpectedly in July 1902. In an unopposed by-election David Shackleton of the Weavers' Union was returned, as an LRC-sponsored candidate with tacit Liberal support, for Clitheroe in Lancashire. Originally, Philip Snowden had been considered as an ILP candidate; but he withdrew in the light of Shackleton's declarations of strict party independence. Hardie publicly acclaimed Shackleton's return as a great victory for the LRC's strategic approach. However, his ILP colleagues had regarded Shackleton's candidature and return to parliament with much suspicion. Glasier wrote that 'it would be a great misfortune were Shackleton to prejudice the independent attitude; and I am wondering if we cannot in some perfectly frank and courteous way indicate that any Liberal compact business will alienate the ILP and resolute labour vote'. Snowden, he added, had withdrawn 'on the assumption that Shackleton would run true'.[16] Hardie urged MacDonald that Snowden and Glasier be instructed to put pressure on Shackleton to this effect. 'That gang which is working in the interest of Dilke is adding its pressure to the other to induce Shackleton to accept the Liberal whip. It would be a serious matter for the LRC if they succeeded.' Hardie correctly guessed that Shackleton would pay more attention to a letter from MacDonald than one from himself. In fact, A.B. Newall and the local labour officials in Clitheroe had gone to some lengths to keep Hardie away from the by-election lest he inflame local Liberal opinion. After Shackleton had entered the House, he proposed Burns and Bell, rather than Hardie, as his official sponsors. 'Keir Hardie has somehow got an impression abroad against him that would lead one to infer he has at some time been indiscreet in his references to the Liberal Party. But to us he is yet Keir Hardie.' Nevertheless, Hardie himself in the *Labour Leader* warmly welcomed the presence in the House of a man like Shackleton, an avowed lifelong trade unionist. Further, he was ardently committed to women's suffrage: indeed, he depended partly on the financial support of women members of the Weavers' Union. Shackleton was, Hardie maintained, a living vindication of the pragmatism of the ILP in contrast to the dogmatic postures being struck by the SDF.[17]

Still the fight for an independent labour position went on. Hardie professed to believe that, divided and disillusioned as the Liberals were under Campbell-Bannerman's leadership, a break-up of the party was possible. Indeed, Hardie even claimed to detect the dissolution of the party system itself, in favour of the election of groups on a basis of proportional representation as obtained in Switzerland. The Liberals, he wrote confidently, 'have no principle, no ideas, no programme'.[18] Labour, by comparison, had a full range of reforms on hand, including housing, pensions and public ownership. But it remained desperately difficult to make any headway at election time. Further by-elections at Bury and North Leeds produced Liberal victories, as the attack on the 1902 Education Act gave the party new unity and new heart. Hardie himself occupied a very detached position at this time. He was not a member of the official LRC committee which negotiated on local labour candidatures. On the other hand he had a unique stature in the labour and socialist movements and his private initiatives could carry much weight. He spent considerable time and energy on the Cleveland constituency in October 1902 when a vacancy came up there. He addressed local miners' demonstrations and met the representatives of local trade unions. However, he received little backing from MacDonald and the LRC in his attempts to get a labour candidate to stand, while ill-health curtailed his visits to the constituency. No Labour man stood at Cleveland; impotently, Glasier was left to fume at the insolence of the Liberal, Herbert Samuel, in calling himself a 'labour candidate'. He warned Hardie against the extreme policy of recommending the local working-class electors to vote Tory, but urged the publishing of an ILP manifesto which would repudiate the 'imperialism and pseudo-labour pretensions of Samuel'.[19] Cleveland provided further testimony to Labour's difficulties.

Hardie by this time was seriously ill from stomach trouble. 'Was touched to see how painfully he walks,' Glasier wrote.[20] Hardie had a brief period of convalescence in Belgium, during which, in a characteristic episode, he was temporarily arrested after an anarchist had tried to assassinate the King of the Belgians. Hardie, with his beard and exotic garb, was obviously everyman's idea of an anarchist. This illness temporarily removed him from some of the decisive manoeuvres at the time. They were to affect fundamentally the growth of the LRC, still a struggling organization and still on the fringe of political life. In

January 1903 Ramsay MacDonald began discussions over a secret pact with Herbert Gladstone, the Liberal chief whip. Under this, about thirty seats at the forthcoming general election would be earmarked for LRC candidates, without any Liberal opposition.[21] How far this agreement, which remained strictly secret for many years, compromised the independence of the LRC was open to doubt, although MacDonald forcefully argued that he took part in the talks with Gladstone on an entirely independent and unfettered basis. The only member of the LRC that he consulted, inevitably, was Hardie, and that after the negotiations were under way. In fact, Hardie, wearied by years of parliamentary frustration, had come to accept the necessity of some kind of global agreement with the Liberals, provided that no local entangling alliances or joint candidatures were involved. In the *Labour Leader* he had appealed to the Liberal whips not to run candidates in those Scottish seats where LRC men were already in the field. As an alternative policy he wrote an open letter to Lloyd George, who was now rising to new stature as an opponent of the Education Act in Wales. Hardie vainly appealed to Lloyd George to cut himself adrift from the Liberal leadership and head a new radical movement. Even John Burns found himself the recipient of a similar invitation.[22] The corollary of stern independence at the local level should be tactical alliance at, or near, the summit. For one of Hardie's impulsive temperament, it was a singularly difficult tightrope to walk.

From the time of the MacDonald-Gladstone *entente*, whether Hardie recognized it or not, the LRC was sucked into the new flood-tide of progressivism sweeping through Britain in the aftermath of the South African War. The new unity imposed on the warring Liberal ranks by Chamberlain's raising the banner of 'tariff reform' in May 1903 (a move that Hardie found 'mystifying')[23] made the new radicalism all the more irresistible. Campbell-Bannerman now gained a new authority as the left-of-centre leader of a revitalized Liberal coalition. Hardie's public stance continued to be that the Liberal Party as such was doomed, that its past record confirmed its inability to appeal to working-class voters or to fight for labour causes, that it was kept alive by appealing to dying causes such as 'one man, one vote' or church disestablishment. On the other hand he acknowledged that the immediate aims of Liberalism were largely those of labour also. He denounced Chamberlain's tariff reform campaign as a direct threat to the standard of living of the working man. The protection of home industries would not lead to the protection of the workers. He attacked also the effect of the coal export tax on the Welsh and Scottish coal industries, which depended so heavily on overseas markets.[24] Beyond this, there were more and more signs that, at least on the theoretical level, the assumption that Liberalism was incapable of coming to terms with collectivism and social reform was being disproved. The New Liberalism of social welfare was claiming increasing attention in Liberal journals and in newspapers such as Gardiner's *Daily News*. Writers like Samuel, Hobson, Masterman, Hobhouse and Chiozza Money were, in their different ways, turning to formulate a new 'constructive' programme which would combine the traditional Old Liberal assault on vested interests and privilege with a wider attack on poverty, malnutrition, unemployment and slum housing. Chamberlain's tariff reform campaign posed with new urgency fundamental questions about the health of British society under free trade. In this climate, men like MacDonald moved easily in the company of the Webbs and their Liberal allies. At least in terms of doctrine, Liberalism, if not yet the Liberal Party, was rapidly moving towards the position long held by the LRC. When the MacDonald-Gladstone agreement was finally concluded in September 1903, it seemed an appropriate political recognition of the radical alignment that was already taking place.

Hardie viewed these developments with less enthusiasm than did MacDonald. He wrote ironically on 'the offended deity . . . of the great Liberal Party'.[25] This prickly attitude had in part a personal basis. He was never at ease in the company of Liberal middle-class intellectuals. Especially did this apply to the Fabian 'Co-efficients', some of whom had been strongly pro-war in 1899 and who had an ill-concealed contempt for the ILP. He could never share MacDonald's liking for patrician reformers of the Haldane-Buxton type. H.W. Massingham chided him for lagging behind European socialists in co-operation with the radicals. Still, elementary realism alone impressed on Hardie the need for some kind of electoral accommodation with the Liberals. He himself was already on record as saying that the isolation and impotence of the Social Democrats should be avoided and that doctrine was a secondary consideration. 'We want socialism. But whether it comes to us under the name of Social Democracy, or Labour Party, or Municipalization, or Collectivism is to me a matter of supreme indifference.'[26] This was almost a Fabian Hardie speaking, Sidney Webb in a cloth cap, preaching the gospel of the permeation of the right-thinking in all parties. The crucial test to him, though, was still the preservation of the independence of the LRC; by this he meant in effect an independent bargaining position with the Liberals. He was the foremost advocate of the resolution passed at the annual conference of the LRC at Newcastle in February 1903, which laid down that labour should not identify itself with or assist 'any section of the Liberal or Conservative parties'. In addition, the decision was taken to set up a parliamentary fund for LRC candidates, to guarantee them a maximum salary of £200 a year.[27] The unexpected return of Will Crooks at Woolwich in a by-election in March, with wide support from many political shades of opinion, lent substance to Hardie's belief that an independent LRC had a hopeful future.

But how independent the LRC was, and indeed how independent Hardie was, remained hard to determine. After all, Crooks, in the by-election campaign at Woolwich, largely owed his return to the support of Liberals in the constituency. Nothing in his programme was incompatible with current Liberal policies and he associated exclusively with Liberals when he arrived at Westminster.[28] In another by-election at Preston in May it was significant that Hardie, even though he had been the candidate in the previous general election, was not invited to speak in the constituency by John Hodge, the LRC candidate. This was in spite of the fact that Hardie had warmly backed his candidature as 'our best card' after MacDonald had withdrawn. Glasier, who did speak for Hodge at Preston, was told by him that 'he had decided not to ask Hardie as Hardie, owing to his previous fight there, might prejudice Tory working men from voting for him'. Hodge noted that, despite the 'religious perversity of the Roman Catholic element, and all the forces of monopoly and capital' in Preston, 'that impregnable fortress of Conservatism', he had polled 6,490 straight Labour votes, compared with only 3,453 'plumpers' for Hardie in 1900.[29] Evidently Hodge's flexible appeal to the supporters of other parties was a stronger electoral asset there than was Hardie's apparent class-consciousness.

An even more delicate situation arose in July in Barnard Castle, in Durham. Here, in a complex series of manoeuvres, Arthur Henderson was adopted as LRC candidate with widespread Liberal support – this despite the fact that a local Liberal was also standing. Henderson came top of the poll by 47 votes in this three-cornered contest, with the Liberal a poor third. Again it was noticeable that Hardie was kept well away from the constituency by the local LRC. MacDonald wrote to Henderson that Hardie felt his exclusion very keenly. He added that the ILP might have to consider 'how far the party can support candidates who deliberately plan to reject its speakers'. Hardie himself noted that Henderson had agreed to have Snowden as a campaign speaker only with great reluctance. 'The comical part of the business is that he is depriving himself of the assistance which ILP speakers could give him, and yet has to bear the odium of being an ILP candidate.'[30] Despite all MacDonald's and Glasier's persuasion, Hardie was never summoned to Barnard Castle; at the time of the poll he was addressing a miners' demonstration at Maesteg in South Wales. Henderson's victory, gained with no help from Hardie, seemed to confirm that the latter was not necessarily regarded as an electoral asset by the LRC, let alone by the progressive front more generally.

In all these episodes, at Woolwich, Preston and Barnard Castle, it was evident that the image of Hardie differed sharply from the reality. The real Hardie was exceptionally flexible in his attitude to relations with the Liberals. He supported a nationwide electoral alliance through the whips or through individuals like Lloyd George, provided that it gave due recognition to the independent status of the LRC. He was equally pragmatic in his attitude towards the internal composition of the LRC, and was a consistent critic of the class postures struck by the SDF (which had led to their secession from the LRC at the end of 1901). He persistently advocated short-term agreements in pursuit of minimal reformist goals. Even his socialism was shot through with old-style radical-populist assumptions, as has been seen in his attitude towards a realignment of the political left during the South African War. To a man like Hyndman, Hardie was the very epitome of opportunism and of the doctrine of the short run.[31] And yet to Liberals and many Labour men throughout the land Hardie was still marked down as an irreconcilable and an extremist. A man like MacDonald was far more attuned to Liberal sensibilities and far more in contact with Liberal leaders. The private *tête-à-tête* that Hardie held with John Morley in April 1903 was a rare event indeed;[32] normally Labour's Achilles stayed in his tent. Hardie's reputation for intractability is still something that requires explanation. Of course, his fierce attacks on the

Liberal Party in the recent past were still fresh in the memory. Almost every week the *Labour Leader* included an insinuation that the party was moribund or disintegrating: the only issue remaining seemed to be how long the Liberal corpse would take to lie down. Hardie was notoriously reluctant to co-operate with Liberal MPs: in 1905 he was hesitant to write on behalf of women's suffrage in a publication to which leading Liberals were also contributing.[33] To the general public he was still generally viewed as a destructive critic, apparently hostile to orthodox or conventional opinions of all kinds. He did not appear to fit into the mainstream of opinion on any major question. He opposed the 1902 Education Act as a secularist, rather than as a nonconformist. He welcomed disestablishment of the Church as a preliminary to a general attack on vested interests, not on grounds of religious equality. He attacked tariff reform because to him free trade embodied a vision of international fraternalism which was essentially socialist. On all these questions he was a man apart. As W.T. Stead ruefully remarked, 'Like most prophets, he is somewhat difficult to get on with'.[34]

Hardie was also a fierce controversialist, constantly in the public eye in acrimonious disputes. In the autumn of 1903 he became embroiled in yet another, arising from Horatio Bottomley's setting up a 'Liberal Labour League' in South Hackney, a body which roped in Ben Tillett. The old public quarrel between Hardie and Tillett (reinforced by a dispute over Tillett's attempted candidature for Swansea District) again flared up violently. Tillett denounced the attacks made on him in the *Labour Leader* – ' a combination of menace and whine'. Hardie in turn referred to letters in his possession in which Tillett appeared to endorse Bottomley as a parliamentary candidate. There were rumours and counter-rumours of libel action. The LRC eventually backed up Hardie: Frederick Rogers defended him (July 1903) against 'the Bottomley masquerade'.[35] But it reinforced the surly, truculent image of Hardie that prevailed. The dominant impression against which he had to contend was that he was a man apart who deliberately sought his own counsel, an outcast by choice. To many LRC supporters this was a role that required heroic courage. George Barnes praised 'poor old Keir who has had to stand against the crowd of Simon Lappertits for so long'.[36] And yet it was noticeable that Hardie made almost no attempt to establish social contacts outside the narrow world of the ILP: very few trade unionists were numbered amongst his friends. He was an increasingly isolated figure even in the ILP, prone to commune in solitary fashion with Frank Smith and to take refuge in palmistry and spiritualism. There were many even in the ILP who would have echoed John Morley's charge of 'Ishmaelitism' against Hardie, 'setting Labour apart as a sort of scowling and sullen class'.[37] There were pressing personal reasons at this time which reinforced Hardie's penchant for self-imposed seclusion. He was in especially poor health at the latter months of 1903. Family problems added to his depression. Glasier noted Hardie's renewed concern about his son Jamie's addiction to gambling. 'He had to pay up to £45 for him before he went to sea a few weeks ago. He confessed that his wife's sullen temper greatly hurts him.' On the other hand, Hardie was deeply moved by his wife's dogged courage when he faced an operation. 'I don't think she ever quite realized what a terribly important body her man is in other folks' opinion. She is suffering most and I will be glad for her sake when it is over.'[38]

In October 1903 his health finally broke down; appendicitis was diagnosed. At the end of the month he wrote to Glasier, 'I am making a record recovery as far as the operation is concerned, but Sir T. (the surgeon) puts it that the shave was a close one and that I have sailed very close to the wind'. Hardie's spirits were raised by a letter of sympathy from King Edward VII, himself a recent sufferer from a near-fatal attack of appendicitis. 'What could be nicer', Hardie commented.[39] He was soon looking forward to a period of convalescence, *incognito* if at all possible, in one of the remoter parts of Cornwall. 'Mrs Hardie goes back to Cumnock on Monday. She has proved a wife indeed all through this business. It is the hour of trial which reveals qualities.' On 22 October he wrote cheerfully to Glasier:

I have been scraped with a razor, scrubbed, paraffined & perfumed in preparation for tomorrow until I was driven to think of myself as a sacrificial lamb, the sweet savour from which was to titivate the quivering nostrils of an offended deity. When the deity took on the form, in imagination of course, of the great Liberal Party, I brotched [?] with the fun of the thing. . . .

Soon Hardie was back in the fray, deeply immersed in the complex internal politics of the ILP. Even so, the impression of him as an isolated figure, with narrow sympathies and few close friends, remained imprinted on the public mind. His role as a reconciling and mediating figure in the labour world suffered as a result.

His main political platform through the years had been the ILP. Even after stepping down from the party chairmanship in 1900, he had remained the dominant figure in the party. He was its major strategist, its main link with the trade unions, its lifeline to socialist movements on the continent, its symbol and inspiration. He was a regular attender at meetings of the party's executive, the NAC. With Snowden, MacDonald and Glasier, he provided a powerful central axis which dominated the party's deliberations and controlled its central institutions. He felt especially attached to Glasier – 'more of a brother than a colleague'. The rise of younger men like Fred Jowett of Bradford had not seriously challenged the supremacy of this inner group. With MacDonald, Hardie laboured hard to try to restore the central position of the ILP within the LRC. He complained, with justice, that NAC members, apart from MacDonald and himself, were unable 'to rise to the occasion' at LRC annual conferences.[40] He regarded the emerging party of labour as essentially the creation of the ILP alone. It was, therefore, a shattering blow for him in late 1903 when his position within his own party was seriously disturbed.

Like many of the personal crises in his life, it arose from problems about money. The occasion was a change in the management of the *Labour Leader* of which Hardie had been editor, part-proprietor and sole shareholder since it first appeared as a weekly in 1894. For many years past, the *Leader* had been a unique voice for democratic socialism. If it lacked the sparkle and humour of the *Clarion*, it carried far more authority and inspired more trust. Hardie's own editorial control gave it a consistency and direction which enhanced its influence. Nevertheless, the *Leader* had recently been going through difficult times. It had severe financial problems, resulting in part from a drop in advertising revenue, in part from a fall in circulation (which amounted to only 13,000 by 1903). There were also staff disputes, such as that in 1901 which saw the departure as manager of David Lowe (an old Scottish Labour Party colleague of Hardie and later to serve as one of his earliest and best-informed biographers).[41] Above all there was growing concern about the function of the *Leader* as the organ of the ILP. In theory it was an official journal of the party, sharing that role with the *ILP News*. In reality, as Glasier wrote to Hardie (25 June 1902), 'It seemed to be a duplication of your voice and opinion'. The NAC had turned down Hardie's proposal in April 1898 that the *Leader* should carry official council reports. Through his editorial whim the ILP found itself embroiled in disputes with Blatchford, Hyndman, Tillett and others with whom it had no direct cause for quarrelling. Glasier added, with brutal frankness, 'I feel, too, that the movement desires to feel assured that the power and persuasion of your leadership is not created by your happening at present to hold a "monopoly" of the parliamentary representation and the press of the party'. He urged Hardie to think of giving up the editorship – adding, for good measure, that the *Leader* paid scant attention to the activities of local ILP branches (a charge which a modern historian finds it very hard to justify). Glasier added that the paper was padded out with many dull inserts and translations of unoriginal material. In his diary he expressed himself more pithily: 'The *Leader* has proved a fiasco; but for Hardie's own political articles it is but rubbish'.[42]

No other question could have caused Hardie so much pain as this attack on the *Leader*. It was more than just his own creation, the heir to the long series of journals he had personally sponsored since the *Miner* appeared back in 1887. The *Leader* was also Hardie's megaphone, through which he harangued, speculated, argued, communed before the mass democracy. More than any other institution, it was his essential channel of communication with the people. But Glasier's criticisms were becoming more widespread. It became known that MacDonald echoed them. 'The *Leader* is really getting pottering,' he wrote to Glasier. 'To its dullness I do not object but if it claims the right to be dull it ought to grant us the right of having accuracy and proportion for our money.' He was also alarmed that the *Leader* was obtaining private information from the central offices of the LRC.[43] On 22 May 1903, therefore, the NAC initiated a lengthy and delicate discussion about the party's acquiring the *Leader* as an official organ, through a newly-created Labour Press. A new bank account, in the names of Hardie, MacDonald and T.D. Benson, was to be opened in the name of the ILP. As a consolation prize, Hardie was to be given charge of a new party committee which would control ILP party literature.[44] In the early stages the discussions went surprisingly well, despite Hardie's obvious resentment of criticism of his editorial abilities. The talks coincided with a massive wave of public sympathy for Hardie during his recovery from his operation for appendicitis. The letters that flooded into Nevills Court, the public testimonial that was launched and over-subscribed to meet the costs of his hospital treatment and convalescence and to assist with Mrs Hardie's financial difficulties, all confirmed that Hardie could still touch the heart of the labour world in a manner unique in the working-class movement. On 11 November Benson reported that Hardie would be willing to be bought out for £1,500 for the *Leader*, with an immediate cash payment of £250. Glasier paid him £20 for his forthcoming holiday of convalescence.[45]

From then on things went from bad to worse. Hardie's temper rapidly deteriorated. On 22 December Glasier reported that Hardie was now asking Benson for £1,800, a sum of £300 more than originally agreed, on the grounds that certain sums agreed with Benson did not represent debentures but debts against Hardie himself. 'This is very disappointing & shows a looseness & callousity [*sic*] regarding money matters on Hardie's part which mars his otherwise sincere & sturdy character.'[46] The decision to put MacDonald in temporary charge of the *Leader* as 'supervisor' did not improve Hardie's temper. Eventually, on 25 January Hardie's brother David and W.M. Haddow, his financial representative, agreed that, with effect from the previous 1 January, the *Leader* should be taken over by the ILP and that Hardie should be paid £1,550, less debentures, less interest of £498 3s 8d and less loans of £194 17s 5d. The old company would remain responsible for all debts due up to 31 December 1903.[47] It was all very tense and unpleasant. Hardie, still recuperating at Cumnock from his operation, wrote in anguish to Glasier on 28 January:

Nothing that I can recall has ever depressed me so much. It seems another illustration of the truth of the adage that the simple man is the beggar's brother. . . . My mind goes back over the past 10 years of unpaid drudging on the paper, resisting the temptation and the promptings of friends to seek for success by being less loyal to the Party, and this is the result. It is cruel. What adds bitterness to the thought is my strong conviction that were the transaction to be carried through on strict business lines the price would be double that asked for. I have struggled and sacrificed, and paid everyone connected with the paper the full 20s in the pound, and now when it comes my turn to be paid I am asked to accept 17s. Nothing, I repeat, which I have ever experienced has raised the same feeling of heart-breaking resentment as this.

Glasier commented in his diary: 'I feared this would be so, but Hardie only looks at his own side. The fact that the *Leader* has been a constant loss for 12 years does not add to an increased claim for its purchase price. Have written a kind & I hope soothing letter.'[48] A week later final agreement was reached: Hardie received a further £750 for his shares. His explanation of the position won over MacDonald and Snowden 'who were chiefly hostile to any advance in the terms'. The balance of £500 would be paid after the next general election. Hardie would continue to serve as a regular columnist in the *Leader*, but the editorship would be taken over by Glasier. Hardie's last editorial contribution in the newspaper was a typical warning to labour men to preserve their independence from the Liberals and not to be too preoccupied in the defence of free trade to the exclusion of social questions.[49] Then he was gone. For the first time for over seventeen years, Hardie had no regular mouthpiece in the press.

The *Labour Leader* episode was patched up, or so it seemed. The journal continued to lavish praise on Hardie's editorial labours for it over the years. The financial terms agreed to in February proved generally acceptable and the new Labour Press flourished. Hardie resumed his role as a propagandist and produced a series of pungent pamphlets and tracts which denounced social and political abuses. Even so, the *Leader* affair continued to rankle. Glasier, it is true, continued to enjoy close relations with Hardie and to admire him to the point of adulation. He was rapturous in his praise for a speech of Hardie's at St Andrew's Hall. Although somewhat inhibited by the presence of the Countess of Warwick on the ILP platform, Hardie delivered 'a great speech – the most passionate I have heard from him . . . masterly and great'. Only Hardie's 'rough tweed knickers – very much out of taste' slightly marred the occasion in Glasier's fastidious view.[50] Nevertheless a new element of strain henceforth appears in the Hardie-Glasier relationship, previously so intimate. It could hardly fail to be otherwise with Glasier now installed in Hardie's old editorial chair at the *Leader* offices. Here Glasier had to exercise his editorial pen in censoring some of Hardie's contributions and this inevitably caused some resentment. 'They were not up to the mark and rather of the nature of self-advts.', Glasier commented. 'Still,' he added, 'I do not wish to hurt him, and must stretch a point on his behalf.'[51] Hardie could not fail to notice how the paper flourished, at first, under Glasier's direction: its readership climbed from a nadir of 13,000 to 24,000 by the start of 1906, although the changed political climate probably helped.

Hardie's relations also became more distant with other prominent figures of the ILP. After the *Leader* imbroglio, his friendship with Snowden lost something of its early intimacy. Less and less often did they stump the country together on missionary campaigns or share beds in remote hotels for Hardie to expound on socialism, reincarnation, astrology, or any other theme that caught his fancy.[52] Between Hardie and MacDonald, two supreme prima donnas, personal relations became the most difficult of all. Hardie continued to prime MacDonald with advice and assistance on local LRC candidatures, especially in South Wales and other mining areas. His influence was valuable behind the scenes in securing LRC backing for Tom Richards, the Welsh miners' leader and noted Lib-Lab, when he sought the representation in West Monmouthshire in succession to Harcourt in October 1904.[53] This was all the more remarkable since Richards was manifestly the candidate of the West Monmouth Liberal Association. Hardie continued to write to MacDonald in cordial tones. When MacDonald fell ill in his turn at the start of 1904, Hardie urged him, 'Haste ye well, but for God's sake be careful when you get on your legs again.' Even so, they could never establish a lasting relationship. A joint holiday of recuperation at Bordighera in Italy in 1904 (on which Hardie was armed with Buckle's *History of Civilization*) was not a success. Hardie complained:

Mac. is not an ideal travelling companion. In all the arrangements he discussed his own plans apparently without regard for my inclinations, and altho' he always at once and with the utmost readiness fell in with any suggestion of mine, that was not the same as thinking first of the weaker brother. He wanted to see everything not so much I think from any real interest as to be able afterwards to talk at dinner tables about what he had seen.[54]

The truth was that Hardie and MacDonald, both solitary brooders, were too alike in temperament. At a deeper level, Hardie's basic sense of identification with his own class clashed fundamentally with MacDonald's liking for middle-class political and journalistic society. The social chasm in the leadership of labour, ultimately to erupt in the division that led to the National government in August 1931, was already in the making.

In the ILP and in other circles, Hardie seemed to have lost some ground as a dominating figure in the labour world at this time. What raised him back to the pinnacle of public attention, even at the cost of some revived party bickering, was the re-emergence of the issue with which, more than any other figure in political life, he was identified – that of unemployment.[55] This question had receded from the forefront of debate after 1895 and the brief boom stimulated by the South African War. Hardie tried vainly to raise it anew in parliament; in December 1902 he attempted to persuade the Speaker to accept a motion which called for a £100,000 grant from imperial funds to the local authorities to cope with distress. He was particularly anxious that the SDF should not exploit the issue for their own benefit. He tried to steer leadership of the movement away from the London Trades Council, on which the SDF were strongly represented. A new broad-based National Committee was set up, including not only Hardie and MacDonald for the ILP, but cross-party figures like Shaw and Cunninghame Graham and advanced Liberals like Percy Alden. Hardie himself, refreshed by his convalescence, again took the initiative in parliament. On the motion for the address on 1 February 1904, he called for a far-reaching policy to deal with unemployment, including the creation of a Ministry of Labour to channel assistance for public works programmes to the local authorities. This motion, introduced after close consultation with MacDonald,[56] began a new phase in the parliamentary history of the unemployment question.

Hardie's approach to the problem in 1904–5 showed all his familiar characteristics of drive and of extreme individuality. Unemployment was now again particularly severe, especially in London. It was calculated that men out of work totalled over five per cent of the labour force at the end of 1903. Chamberlain's tariff reform campaign, which identified foreign dumping, the closing of overseas markets and the absence of a tariff preference for colonial imports as the major causes of the trade depression, underlined the gravity of the situation in a manner highly embarrassing for Balfour's Unionist government. Hardie certainly joined in the standard Liberal-Labour attacks on tariff reform. He argued that by restricting commerce tariffs would add to unemployment, not reduce it. He also claimed, more cogently, that labour conditions in such countries as the United States, which had immensely high tariffs, showed little improvement on the situation in Britain.[57] Indeed, tariffs, by encouraging the growth of trusts and other monopolies, made things far worse. But, as always, Hardie sought around for wider solutions for distress. One of the most striking came through the agency of Joseph Fels, an American-Jewish millionaire who specialized in the production of 'naptha' soap, and whom Hardie had visited in Philadelphia during his visit to the United States in 1895. Fels had set up the Philadelphia Vacant Land Cultivation Society to provide gardens for unemployed workers; then he came to Britain and bought up land at Laindon in Essex which he let at a nominal rent to the Poplar Board of Guardians through George Lansbury. Fels, as his widow later recorded, was deeply impressed by Hardie's 'devotion and courage' as a champion of the unemployed. He in turn fascinated Hardie. He powerfully influenced his mind anew in favour of 'farm colonies' on which the unemployed would be occupied in craft or agricultural work on a self-sufficient basis. Fels also introduced Hardie to Lansbury, a member of the SDF it was true, but a tireless crusader on behalf of work relief schemes in London's East End, and one whose political and social attitudes chimed in with Hardie's own.[58] Hardie's proposals for remedying unemployment were a mixture of old and new ideas. He strongly upheld the claims of the land as a prime source of relief. The land offered constant employment, Hardie claimed, whereas that provided by industrial firms was limited and irregular. Idle land should be cultivated, waste land reclaimed, foreshores cultivated as on the Zuyder Zee and Haarlem Lake in Holland, afforestation schemes implemented. On the other hand, he proposed several constructive reforms of the machinery of relief – new joint committees for towns to deal with distress; a more active public works policy, especially road making; house building and drainage by local councils; new technical and training centres for re-training the unemployed in new skills; and a new network of elective administrative councils throughout the land under the supervision of a Department of Labour.[59] Local authorities should be given 'unlimited powers to experiment including compulsory powers for the acquisition of land'. It was all an interesting fusion of Joseph Fels and Sidney Webb, of utopian agrarianism and Fabian 'constructivism'. Hardie held that socialism was the ultimate answer to unemployment and the irregular functioning of the trade cycle. But, until that far-off time when the socialist society was realized, several immediate palliatives were possible and Hardie was willing to collaborate with almost any social or political body to implement them. This would at least provide a practical test of how far the New Liberalism and the Social Imperialism, championed by middle-class social critics in the Liberal and Unionist parties, really went.

This soon led Hardie into political paths all his own. In October 1904 the President of the Board of Trade, Walter Long, made a modest proposal for locally-sponsored farm colonies and for new local district committees. Almost alone amongst the ILP leaders, Hardie welcomed these ideas as vital first steps. Here indeed he showed himself the least doctrinaire and most imaginative member of the party. In the *Labour Leader* he welcomed the money that trickled in from voluntary sources to support Long's appeal; £20,000 in the first month alone was subscribed.[60] When the government, through Long's successor, Gerald Balfour, introduced an Unemployed Workmen's Bill in April 1905, Hardie fiercely attacked aspects of it, particularly a provision that the payment of trade-union wage rates should not apply to relief work undertaken for local authorities. On the other hand, he saw positive merits in the measure. It affirmed that the community should provide work for all those thrown out of jobs through the vagaries of trade – 'the right to work'. It laid down also that this should be a charge on public funds and that (an issue much deliberated before the Select Committee in 1895) the receipt of relief should not involve any disfranchisement or less political eligibility. He saw Gerald Balfour privately and told him other Labour members sought to wreck the measure. 'K.H. alone in defence of Bill,' Burns noted after an unemployment conference in London.[61] Hardie, in support of his own view, promptly organized a series of demonstrations and marches in various provincial cities, in Manchester and elsewhere. He told them that he was strongly in favour of trade-union rates of pay being paid to unemployed workers on relief work, but that nevertheless the bill contained the seeds of wider reform and should not be rejected out of hand. These initiatives were taken by Hardie without consultation with his leading ILP colleagues. Glasier was taken back by Hardie's organized marches and the line he took in the *Leader*. 'All this is characteristic. There is genius and a touch of damned nonsense about it.' Henderson joined Glasier in deploring Hardie's showmanship. MacDonald, by contrast, was much more sympathetic, not least because Joseph Fels had guaranteed

£200 towards the agitation on the unemployment question. On 2 June the executive of the LRC formally endorsed Hardie's view.[62]

For the first time for many years, the ILP and its representatives in the House had a distinct cause of their own; as in the past, Hardie was its voice and symbol. He considered one of his Commons speeches on unemployment 'the best I have ever made'. In the previous session, Hardie had been warned of the dangers of the LRC members of parliament – notably Crooks, Henderson and Shackleton – showing 'a tendency to merge in the Liberals'.[63] Now all that was forgotten in the public outcry on unemployment. When the government introduced their new measure in July it met with a furious response from Hardie and his colleagues. The bill was to have only a temporary duration, it would not harness rate aid for the relief of unemployment and money would be drawn only from voluntary sources for the payment of wages. Hardie suspected that the government basically preferred to work through voluntary movements such as the Church settlements and the Salvation Army; but this was quite unacceptable. It was charity, not collectivism. When riots by unemployed men in Manchester followed, as a result of a police baton charge, Hardie sent his warm congratulations to them and evoked memories of the massacre of Peterloo a century earlier. He won the support of such varied members of parliament as Shackleton, Henderson and even Burns in resisting the new bill in the House.[64] This outcry clearly shook the Balfour government, already paralysed by internal dissension and fearful of a holocaust at the polls. The original bill was restored in August 1905. It was, Hardie wrote, still a poor thing. But at least it did leave poor law guardians and borough councils their previous powers to develop and systematize relief schemes. New forms of municipal undertaking could be experimented with. Farm colonies, such as those pioneered by Fels at Laindon, Hollesley Bay and Mayland in east London, were also possible; Fels himself had already promised financial support if the government provided £300,000 for 'home colonies'. The widest possible front must be mobilized, Hardie argued, to operate the new bill in the most expansive and progressive manner possible. In addition – a typical Hardie footnote – the unemployed of both sexes must be organized as one.[65] Finally, a new push must be made in the local elections in November to secure the return of Progressive and Labour members. A Right to Work Committee was set up in November, with George Barnes of the ILP as its chairman, Frank Smith as secretary and Hardie, amongst others, on its committee.

Throughout the autumn demonstrations continued in favour of a national policy on behalf of the unemployed. Hardie himself continued to point out several anomalies in the Act of 1905 that must be reformed. Destitution, not unemployment, was the general test applied in the determining of relief – reminiscent of the charity doled out by the Charity Organization Society. Unemployed men could be, and often were, used as blacklegs in a strike. Finally, the rates of pay offered to men on relief were a bad breach of faith, since they fell below those given to an unskilled labourer. Less eligibility still dominated the bureaucratic mind, at the local and the national level. Yet despite all these defects, Hardie still argued cogently that the government's bill should be given a chance. After years of neglect, it had served to make unemployment and the 'right to work' major priorities in political life.

Hardie was criticized by Glasier and Snowden for his tactics during the unemployment agitation in 1905. It was said that he was too easily satisfied by the government's good intentions and that he had been duped into giving a welcome, however qualified, to Long and Gerald Balfour's proposals. 'He has been Long's Bonnet, that and nothing more,' wrote John Burns.[66] It was also claimed that Hardie was going back on his earlier declarations by renewing contact with the Social Democrats. Lansbury was well known as a prominent member of the SDF executive, while the Right to Work Council included not merely him, but also Harry Quelch on its executive committee. The SDF shrewdly concentrated its strength on one or two candidates for the committee, while the ILP put up over a dozen. The errors of 'socialist unity' ten years earlier, which Hardie had then resisted so strenuously, now seemed likely to be repeated. Hardie's independence of approach was also attacked: MacDonald criticized his failure to consult him on the Central London Unemployment Committee in October 1905.[67] Even so, there is little doubt that it was Hardie who was the more far-sighted in the manner in which he raised the issue of unemployment. It wrenched the ILP and the LRC in a vigorous new direction. It helped erase the bitter memories of the *Labour Leader* dispute and other internal squabbles in pursuit of the overriding objective of social justice. It powerfully influenced government and particularly Board of Trade policy, as the Lloyd George and Churchill eras at the Board of Trade under the Liberal governments between 1905 and 1910 were to demonstrate. As Hardie had forecast, the new administration saw 'the state committed to the principle that part of its duty is to find work for all'.[68] He helped to bring unemployment again to the fore, as part of the wider arguments about trade, tariffs and industrial competition, and to make the Labour movement the major vehicle of protest. For Hardie himself, the unemployment issue powerfully refurbished his radical credentials and his powers of national leadership. It confirmed his reputation as a constructive reformer, not merely a declamatory agitator. It raised him up from the shadows and confirmed anew that he was without a peer in inspiring and guiding the labour and socialist movement, in offering it a cause to fight for and a faith to live for. No episode in his career more effectively illustrates his qualities of greatness, perhaps of genius, as a political leader.

By the time of the autumn demonstrations against unemployment, however, Hardie had wider themes to absorb his attention. On 4 December 1905 Balfour unexpectedly resigned, probably hoping to catch the Liberals off guard and to produce a rift between the supporters of Campbell-Bannerman and of Rosebery. In the event, Campbell-Bannerman showed unsuspected reserves of cunning and authority. Under his leadership, a powerful new Liberal team was assembled, with representatives of the whole spectrum of Liberal opinion, from an imperialist like Haldane to a 'pro-Boer' like Lloyd George; John Burns went to the Local Government Board. Hardie viewed the new administration with a sceptical eye. He noted the plethora of Whiggish peers in the government and found little cause for enthusing about it. Lloyd George he dismissed as 'a politician with no settled convictions on social questions' – a just enough conclusion at this time. Morley had retreated 'to a barren and sterile individualism'. If these two proposed leaders of a new radical alliance in 1900 and 1903 were given short shrift, Asquith and Haldane were dismissed as 'cold-blooded reactionaries of the most dangerous type' – shades of Featherstone.[69] Nevertheless, Hardie well knew – better than anyone except MacDonald – how utterly dependent the LRC was on Liberal goodwill and how it based its hopes on the Liberals faithfully observing the pact of 1903 and giving Labour a free run in its agreed quota of seats. In particular, such double-member seats as Merthyr, Leicester (where MacDonald was standing) and Blackburn (where Snowden stood for the LRC) were crucial to the arrangement. The main object was now to make sure that the LRC maintained a distinct position in the campaign. It had been enormously strengthened by the adhesion of trade unions in the aftermath of the Taff Vale verdict. Every major union save for the Miners' Federation of Great Britain was now affiliated to the LRC. Hardie himself observed the steady progress being made in the Welsh mining valleys by socialist advocates, which promised to tilt the balance of opinion within the MFGB in favour of affiliation. He himself took a keen interest in the situation in the constituencies. He urged, for instance, a massive LRC effort in Leeds, where 'the Irish vote in the city will be cast solid for LRC candidates as Redmond is bent on a war of extermination against Roseburyian candidates – a term which applies to every one of the sitting members for Leeds'. He was also appointed to an LRC 'sub-Committee for Emergencies set up in cases where candidates were in abeyance', a body that included Henderson, MacDonald, Curran and Pease in addition to himself.[70]

But Hardie's main contribution to the campaign, inevitably, was not as an organizer but as an evangelist. With his health and spirits now fully restored, he flung himself into an immense nation-wide speaking tour. In three days during the campaign in January 1906 he travelled 1,120 miles and addressed seven meetings. He was at Norwich on 5 January, Merthyr on the 6th and 7th, Blackburn on the 8th, York on the 9th, Sunderland on the 10th, Middlesbrough on the 11th, Jarrow and Newcastle on the 12th, and Birmingham and Stockport on the 13th. Further meetings followed at Dewsbury and Glasgow.[71] Without doubt, he was regarded as the LRC's main asset in this election; immense and generally enthusiastic crowds flocked to hear him proclaim the gospel of labour. Hardie followed a course all his own in one constituency when he spoke on behalf of George Lansbury at Middlesbrough, in defiance of the policy of the ILP which distrusted anyone with an SDF background. Mrs Coates Hansen, Lansbury's lady organizer in Middlesbrough, later commented, 'We all thought of Hardie. He is the only man of this decade who has perpetually associated himself with this movement.' She told Lansbury on another occasion, 'Only Hardie sticks by us through everything. We have been unable to get one other MP to speak at any of the demonstrations we are arranging.'[72]

As at West Ham in 1895, however, Hardie had somewhat mis-calculated through over-confidence. He had expected that he would run in tandem with D.A. Thomas at Merthyr, and that no second Liberal would enter the field. Very much at the last moment, Henry Radcliffe, a wealthy Cardiff shipowner and a prominent Methodist, was put up as a Liberal also, with much nonconformist support.[73] Hardie's campaign literature poured abuse on Radcliffe. He was 'the head of a shipping company which employs foreign seamen, whilst hundreds of our own Jack Tars are unemployed, and which has besides a reputation for paying the lowest wages in the shipping trade'. Radcliffe's supporters were condemned as 'a few blacklegs'. But it was again not surprising that some Merthyr Liberals took seriously Hardie's lengthy series of diatribes against their own party. Soon the faithful Frank Smith, who acted as agent in Merthyr while Hardie was on the stump in different parts of the country, had to appeal in desperation to the LRC executive for assistance. On 12 January he wired 'Hardie attacked by second Liberal. He cannot be here before Monday. Will you turn out all possible help.' On 15 January the tone was more panicky. 'Not a single elected member arrived, yet Keir risked all for them. Now gets excuses and good wishes in return. What does such conduct mean? Will spell disaster here.' Hardie himself asked for help from MacDonald or Snowden: 'Merthyr is a very big scattered con-stituency and we must have from four to six meetings.' MacDonald himself was less moved. 'The difficulty with Hardie is that his con-stituency is so far out of the way, and his chances of re-election are so good. If however he would really like us to send someone to help him you might do your best to do so.' Jim Middleton, the LRC's acting secretary, offered Smillie, Thorne (an odd suggestion) and perhaps MacDonald as aids to Hardie's campaign.[74]

In the later stages of the election Hardie found himself having to fight for his life in his own Welsh constituency. He appealed to the Merthyr electors on the widest radical front. His platform and election address included the abolition of the House of Lords, women's suffrage, old age pensions, a reduction of expenditure on armaments, Welsh disestablishment and home rule all round with priority for the Irish cause. To these items, all acceptable to left-wing radicals, he added a

brief declaration of the need to take basic industries into public ownership. His assisting speakers included such miscellaneous figures as
Michael Davitt, to appeal to the large Irish vote in Merthyr (almost
Davitt's last appearance in an election campaign), Annie Kenney of
the Women's Suffrage movement and various local nonconformists
such as the Rev. George Neighbour of Mountain Ash and the Rev.
Herbert Morgan, who saw in Hardie the very epitome of the 'new
theology' based on social justice and the Immanence of God.[75] To the
general relief, the poll saw Hardie safely home, even if D.A. Thomas
led the field with over 4,000 votes more than him. Hardie's poll of
10,187 gave him a clear margin over Radcliffe's 7,776, on a huge poll
of 85 per cent. The whole campaign confirmed that Merthyr was still
far from being a socialist stronghold. Indeed, the bulk of the mining
vote in such places as Aberdare and Mountain Ash went to the two
Liberals. A second Liberal candidate with the personal influence of
D.A. Thomas (who did nothing to help Radcliffe's campaign) could
well upset Hardie even in his own radical stronghold. 'Cymro' in the
Labour Leader pointed out the dangers of over-confidence. In future
Hardie's first duty must be to himself and his own constituency.[76]
Nevertheless, Hardie's return brought immense gratification. At last
he had a permanent foothold in the assembly which his class sought to
capture.

Hardie stood at the threshold of a new era in January 1906. For the
first time, there was a sizeable independent labour representation in the
House, twenty-nine in all, thanks to the pact with the Liberals. At
least eighteen of them were members of the ILP, including men like
MacDonald and Snowden from the ILP's list of sponsored candidates.
Glasier, alas, failed to join them, being defeated in the Bordesley division of Birmingham. Hardie, like the LRC, had pursued a most
circuitous course since his return to parliament in 1900. He had veered
between direct overtures to the radicals and the Irish, and a rigid policy
of party independence of all factions. His individualism had been seen
to most effect during the unemployment agitation, when his comparative sympathy for the government's policy put him in a category
of his own. His reputation within the ILP and the labour movement
had fluctuated a good deal; his relations with other leading figures
such as MacDonald and Glasier had remained erratic and sometimes
tense. In January 1906 Hardie was still a political outsider – but an

outsider whose integrity and independence had survived through all
the shifts of politics since the previous election and whose reputation
for constructive statesmanship had been enhanced. He was still a stub-
born, proud, isolated man, hard to get to grips with; yet this isolation
had bred strength and self-knowledge. Amongst his own people,
amongst the unemployed workers who held demonstrations in the
summer of 1905, amongst the masses who flocked to his meetings in
January 1906, Hardie still retained a matchless authority. The basic
questions that surrounded the LRC remained unanswered at the start
of the new session, with Campbell-Bannerman now returned to power
with a huge Liberal majority behind him. How much impact the
twenty-nine Labour members could make in the face of the serried
ranks of hundreds of Liberals remained to be seen. How realistic their
avowals of independence really were, how far the LRC was really a
distinct party at all and not merely an assorted pressure-group of trade
unionists and socialist activists – all these issues remained in doubt.
Nevertheless, there was a solid basis for the joy with which Hardie
greeted the election returns as the herald of a new dawn of social
emancipation and human liberty. How far these soaring hopes could
be translated into practical achievements would still in large measure
rest on the dominating authority of Keir Hardie himself.

VIII Leader of the Party (1906–7)

After the tension of the 1906 general election Hardie enjoyed a rare week's relaxation with a visit to Ireland in the company of George Barnes. It was not Hardie's first visit to that troubled island. He had addressed the Dublin Trades Council in November 1894; in 1901 he had been given a conducted tour by Murphy, the Nationalist member for Kerry. He well knew the effects of religious sectarianism in under-mining the class solidarity of the Irish workers. A difficult situation had arisen for the LRC in 1905 when William Walker, a leading member of the Belfast ILP, had paraded the term 'Unionist' when standing as a Labour candidate in a Belfast by-election. As usual, Hardie managed to help cover his travel expenses by journalism. He wrote perceptively on how the fabric of landlordism in southern Ireland was being transformed by the land purchase legislation of the past twenty years.[1] But his mind was set on some more fundamental issues – namely the role and future policy of the new Labour Party (as it was now christened after its electoral successes). In particular the leadership of the new party was a theme for acute controversy well before the new House of Commons assembled in mid-February. Most observers assumed that Hardie, by far the most influential figure in the labour movement for the past fifteen years, would be chosen, but this was far from being a foregone conclusion. Many trade union members of the Labour Party felt that the mass movement that they represented, with their thousands of affiliated members and their lavish provision towards party funds, demanded a chairman of the party drawn from the ranks of trade unionists. Even at the outset, then, the unity of the Labour coalition, with its potential stresses between its industrial and socialist elements, was being called into question.

Even before the election returns were complete, there were moves by ILP members trying to caucus to secure the election of one of their representatives, presumably Hardie. Fred Jowett, newly elected for Bradford, was active in these. On the other hand, Glasier urged Hardie to accept the chairmanship only if it were unanimously offered to him – and this was highly doubtful. Glasier wrote:

It is much more important – much more important indeed to our side of the movement that you should be *free to lead the Socialist policy*, than that you should be stuck in the official chairmanship where you would be bound for unity and decorum's sake to adopt a personal attitude acceptable to the moderates. You must not be tied down in any way whatever that would destroy your Socialist initiatives. I feel that this is vital to us. . . . If Henderson, Shackleton or even Barnes accepts the position, you will nevertheless be the fighting front.

Glasier added that to elect a trade unionist would help secure the unions' loyalty to the infant Labour Party. If Hardie declined the chairmanship, the way would be open for it to evolve into a socialist party within a very few years. 'In this Parliament we who are not in it depend on *you*.' Glasier's views were a classic statement of the traditional ILP fear of leadership and power as factors that would compromise the forceful expression of the socialist faith. They reflected also the instinctive socialist belief in inner party democracy rather than a hierarchical chain of command as exercised by the older, capitalist parties. Hardie's reactions to this letter are not known. It may be guessed that Glasier's appeal struck a welcoming chord in his heart. More than most politicians, he wanted to be unmuzzled, to speak out fearlessly and without compromise or equivocation on behalf of social justice and human equality. He had written to Cunninghame Graham just before the election, admitting that he was equipped to be a pioneer, not a party leader.[2] On the other hand, he cannot have viewed with much enthusiasm the prospect of the new party being directed at the outset by a moderate trade unionist, representative of the 'economism' of the industrial world. The idea of a non-socialist like Shackleton becoming chairman must have been particularly unappealing. And, of course, personal pride entered into it as well. Hardie felt that the Labour Party, like the ILP in the past, was in a special sense his own creation. Proudly independent as he was, he could hardly look forward with enthusiasm to taking a subordinate role to a junior figure like Barnes or Henderson. The new party needed him at the helm.

Thus he accepted the nomination of the ILP members to serve as chairman of the new party, at the meeting of 12 February. Typically, the Labour Party decided to have only an annual chairman elected at the start of each parliamentary session, and nothing resembling a permanent leader, with all the dictatorial overtones that that might imply. The choice of chairman was a tense affair. The two candidates nominated, Hardie and Shackleton, nicely represented the balance in the party between socialist activists and trade union affiliates. The vote taken, on a show of hands, produced an indecisive result. The first ballot produced another tie, fourteen votes being cast for each candidate. Another ballot saw Hardie narrowly home, fifteen to fourteen. The decisive vote here was apparently cast by MacDonald who abstained the first time. (Lord Elton's statement that MacDonald voted for Shackleton is not correct.) Writing to Glasier some months later, MacDonald admitted 'I voted for Hardie as chairman with much reluctance as I could not persuade myself that he could fill the place.'[3] MacDonald's hesitant support, to some extent the product of personal jealousy of Hardie, showed that even amongst the ranks of ILP-sponsored members, as well as amongst trade unionists, Hardie would have to struggle to command confidence. Nevertheless, the *Labour Leader* was surely right in arguing that he alone had the stature and prestige to serve as the founding chairman of the party. He was a working-class member, he had a unique record of dedicated service, and he was a socialist whose approach was sufficiently flexible to conciliate all sections of the party.[4] Hardie himself, who celebrated the news by appearing at the House adorned by a particularly brilliant red tie, appeared to accept his election, even by so close a margin, in confident mood. Contemporaries noted how he seemed far more relaxed in his work in the House as a result. Fred Jowett and G.H. Roberts (Norwich), both of the ILP, were appointed his parliamentary secretaries.

Hardie's year and a half as chairman of the parliamentary Labour Party has invariably met with severe criticism. Following Philip Snowden's version in his memoirs, Hardie has been accused of being unbusinesslike, unconciliatory and unreliable. Glasier wrote that the chairmanship proved to be 'a seat of misery' for him.[5] Without any doubt, Hardie himself gave up the chairmanship with the utmost relief. He would have resigned at the end of the 1907 session, even if ill-health had not forced the decision upon him. The entire period of his chairmanship seems to confirm the popularly-held view of him as essentially an impractical agitator rather than a constructive party leader.

This, however, is a partial picture. In its early months the parliamentary Labour Party made a significant impact. It generally aligned itself with the Liberal government and dutifully cast its votes on behalf of such major government legislation as the Education Bill introduced by Augustine Birrell. A measure such as this, designed to meet the grievances of nonconformists against Balfour's Education Act of 1902, was profoundly appealing to large sections of the Labour Party and there was little sense of strain for Hardie in endorsing the government's bill, despite his own preference for the 'secular solution'. He strongly supported an amendment to eliminate the teaching of sectarian creeds in publicly-supported schools during school hours.[6] When the Education Bill eventually came to grief in the House of Lords, Labour enthusiastically acclaimed the government's threat to undermine the powers of the upper house in dismantling government legislation.

At the same time, the Labour Party and Hardie himself managed to carve out a distinct position for themselves on several issues affecting the working class. The party was evidently more than just a left-wing appendage of the Liberal coalition. Hardie himself made several effective sorties on the familiar themes of unemployment. He launched a series of vigorous onslaughts on John Burns, who proved to be a particularly negative and obstinate departmental head at the Local Government Board. Hardie rebuked Burns for his failure to revise the 1905 Unemployed Workmen's Act, or to provide national aid for necessitous local authorities in the provision of relief. He accused Burns of being particularly complacent on the question of unemployment in London. Burns himself was enraged to distraction. 'K.H. is intoxicated with sense of newly acquired power,' he raged in April. In May, he recorded, 'K.H. dour and so intense in his desire to be the personal medium of Frank Smith's hatred of myself that he failed in his own purpose'. Burns's resentment became more vehement as Hardie's attacks continued. 'A pitiful sight to see this vain, wild dervish preaching his Jehad of hate', he confided to his diary in 1907.[7] The continuing running battle of the Labour Party with Burns merely drew public attention to the minister's inadequacy. Hardie served as the agent through whom unemployment retained its priority as a pressing social need, at a time when the Liberal government, from Campbell-Bannerman downwards, showed little concern for social reform.

On an even more momentous question, the Labour Party under Hardie's leadership scored a spectacular victory, one whose implications still continue to influence the pattern of British industrial legislation. This was the passage of the Trades Disputes Bill, which effectively reversed the effect of the Taff Vale decision and made trade unions immune from prosecution for financial loss incurred during strikes or lockouts. Hardie had referred to the urgent need to nullify the Taff Vale verdict in the course of an effective maiden speech as chairman during the debate on the address on 19 February 1906. 'If an officer offends against the law, punish the officer, but do not punish the whole of the members for his indiscretion or want of judgement.'[8] On this issue, the whole of the parliamentary Labour Party, from Shackleton to Jowett, was absolutely unanimous.

When the government's Trade Union Bill was introduced, it was seen to be totally inadequate. It left the financial immunity of trade unions still in doubt and fell far short of the complete enfranchisement for which Hardie had called. Instead, Labour promoted its own bill, sponsored by Shackleton in the first instance but signed by Hardie amongst others, which would give the trade unions complete immunity. Hardie pointed out in the House that since strikes had been long since legalized, it was natural justice to allow unions the means by which strikes, should they be necessary, could be conducted. Funds were the ammunition of the trade unions. Labour only called for working men to be allowed the same freedom to combine that already existed for employers. The Liberal government soon discovered that, for all its huge majority, it could not make progress with its own bill. A whole series of Liberal backbenchers, even men as right-wing as the Hon. Ivor Guest, rose and declared that they had given pledges to working-class electors in their constituencies during the general election that trade union funds would be accorded a complete legal immunity. Hardie provided leaflets to show that Walton, the Attorney-General, had endorsed this during his own campaign. Hardie had discreetly helped on this backbench protest through his new intimacy with Sir Charles Dilke, a kind of unofficial chairman of 'the social radicals' on the

Liberal side, who had consulted with Hardie and John Redmond, the Irish Nationalist leader, about collaboration on labour and radical issues. Joint balloting on labour measures was pushed forward. Faced with this powerful pressure, the government gave way. Campbell-Bannerman assured Shackleton in the House that Labour's bill would simply be taken over by the government as if it were its own and that the government bill would be buried. In December, after a comparatively straightforward passage through the Lords, Labour's Trades Disputes Bill became law. Hardie played a relatively minor role in the later debates on the bill in parliament. MacDonald even complained that Hardie's attacks on the government's law officers at the ILP annual conference had almost doomed the bill and that Hardie himself had played no part in the delicate discussions with the Attorney-General and the Liberal whips in rescuing it.[9] Shackleton was rightly given most of the credit. Even so, the way in which the government had been compelled to reverse its policies and pass one of the trade unions' cherished magna cartas was an immense triumph for the new party, and augured well for Hardie's leadership.

In other areas, also, Hardie displayed a new stature as party leader. As chairman of the Labour Party he served on two select committees in 1906. On one, a Select Committee on the Procedure of the House of Commons, Hardie played a comparatively minor part.[10] It was hardly the kind of topic that fired his imagination and he attended only ten out of its fifteen meetings. Nor did he play a prominent part in its discussions. Most time was spent on such details as the hours when the House met and rose; no opportunity was found by Hardie to ventilate such wider questions as governmental devolution, which might allow more extensive attention to the affairs of Scotland and Wales.

The Select Committee on the Income Tax, under the chairmanship of Sir Charles Dilke, Hardie found much more interesting and he was actively involved from the start.[11] He was no expert on public finance; even he was apt to be unduly impressed by civil servants such as Sir Henry Primrose of the Inland Revenue. He gave his support to Dilke's own report which proposed a graduated income tax and a differentiation between earned and unearned incomes, the latter to be taxed much more severely. However, only five of the committee's seventeen members supported Dilke. Hardie himself submitted a memorandum to the Committee, backed up by further evidence from Snowden, the

ILP's expert on finance, which urged the need to distinguish between the taxing of earned and unearned incomes. The latter (mainly from land and property investment) should be taxed heavily, whereas earned income, Hardie claimed, derived from the personal exertion of individuals. It showed how primitive Hardie's socialism really was in its economic aspects, how it often tended towards a populist animosity towards 'the rich' rather than to a socialist analysis of the redistribution of wealth. On other aspects, however, he had several cogent points to make. He argued for a super-tax on incomes above £5,000, for a graduated overall income tax and for a revision of death duties. He argued that an estate subject to a twelve per cent death duty should be subject to an equal impost during a man's life, in the form of higher income tax (equivalent to 1s 6d in the pound) on unearned income. His views played some part in the discussion of a reform of public finance: this led to Asquith's budget of 1907 which included a graduated income tax among its provisions. (It was left to Lloyd George to introduce a super-tax in 1909.) Furthermore, Hardie strengthened his alliance with Dilke and the radical backbenchers. W.C. Bridgeman, one of the Unionist members of the committee, sourly commented on how 'Dilke was intriguing all the time, generally with Keir-Hardie [*sic*], to whom he is playing up tremendously now (possibly with a view to leading a Labour government)'.[12] The committee helped to broaden the appeal of the new Labour Party and to give Hardie himself a platform for expounding the financial implications of the radical-socialism for which he stood.

By the summer, then, Hardie's first period as chairman of the Labour Party had several achievements to its credit. The Labour Party seemed to be effective and in good heart. And yet Hardie's chairmanship was already coming under severe fire. Perhaps this was inevitable in a new party of such varied composition and so well-stocked with prima donnas. Personal tensions within the party were becoming almost intolerable and Hardie was at the centre of them. He himself continued to feel a dualism between the parliamentary Labour Party and the ILP. He surged with enthusiasm to carry the socialist faith into new areas such as amongst the agricultural labourers of Norfolk and Suffolk, or the quarrymen of north-west Wales. By contrast, the day-to-day routine work of a party leader, in the arranging of business and the formulation of party strategy, failed to command his attention. To

MacDonald and others, he still seemed basically an agitator, a Prometheus only temporarily chained. Hardie was despondent that the party rejected his advice, for instance over when to force divisions, and that even an ILP man like Philip Snowden failed to back him up. By June he was even talking of resignation. Glasier's intended encouraging word that 'the party is but a symbol of the movement' was unhelpful to a parliamentary leader.[13] Significantly, it was ILP members who were most prominent in expressing their dissatisfaction with the chairman. Snowden, already emerging as a formidable parliamentarian, considered:

> Hardie's leadership of the party a hopeless failure. Hardie never speaks to me. He seems completely absorbed with the suffragettes. I can assure you there is intense dissatisfaction amongst the ILP members. I doubt if he would get two votes if the leadership were voted upon today.[14]

MacDonald, the most authoritative Labour figure in the country after Hardie himself, was more critical still. Hardie, he complained, failed to attend conferences with House of Commons officials or to consult parliamentary colleagues about the business of the House. 'He has work, I know, but we never know where to find him. The result is that we are getting into the objectionable habit of coming to decisions without consulting him. He feels it – and we feel it; and friction arises.' Over arrangements with foreign socialists also, Hardie kept his own counsel. MacDonald summed up, 'If Hardie will become a loyal co-operator with Henderson and Shackleton in the autumn session, working steadily in harness, our second year's work will be even better than that of our first.' Somewhat unconvincingly, MacDonald assured Glasier that the storms of the early months had passed by and that there was a basic harmony between the leading men in the party. No change in the chairmanship had ever been whispered, or thought of, least of all by himself. 'If Hardie only knew the desire to make his leadership a success, he would take some more pains to make that desire fruitful.' Glasier was inclined to dismiss much of this as the product of vanity on MacDonald's part. He defended Hardie against MacDonald's and Snowden's attacks. 'They have not the instinct of agitation,' he commented shrewdly on the latter, while their penchant, and that of Mrs Ethel Snowden, for going to 'rich parties' confirmed that they were succumbing to the aristocratic embrace in London.[15]

MacDonald showed this trait, long before he ever encountered Lady Londonderry.

Even so, a growing number of Labour members were inclined to criticize Hardie's methods of leadership, his waywardness, his inaccessibility, his frequent absences from the precincts of the House. By August, this criticism found a new focus in the failure of Bob Smillie, the Labour candidate in the Cockermouth by-election in Cumberland. 'Cockermouth was awful,' Arthur Henderson complained, with party organization at the constituency level virtually non-existent.[16] Since Henderson himself had to carry much of the burden of negotiations in the House with the Liberal, Irish and Unionist whips, his disaffection was yet another blow to Hardie's authority. Indeed in one sense the Cockermouth defeat was peculiarly associated with Hardie since his advice to the party there had shown a singular lack of direction. This arose from the failure of the Labour Party to forge an alliance with the suffragettes in the constituency – indeed, the eventual eve-of-the-poll advice from the Women's Social and Political Union to the Cockermouth electors was to vote Unionist. Since Hardie himself was so intimately involved with the suffragette leaders, and so often their champion on the platform, the odium for the suffragettes' decision fell upon him, however unfairly. Glasier met Hardie soon after the Cockermouth by-election and discreetly raised the question of the party leadership with him. 'Find that he does not realize how strong the move is against him.'[17]

Throughout the autumn and winter Labour Party morale steadily sagged. In the country, indeed, many of the portents were encouraging. The trend amongst the miners, led by the South Wales men, for affiliation to the Labour Party, suggested that the Miners' Federation, the only major union still holding aloof, would soon throw its massive weight behind the Labour Party. But all this was a promise of potential reinforcement in the future. The immediate reality was the repeated failure of Labour to add to the gains made at the general election in by-elections, and a disappointing record in the November 1906 local government elections. Amongst other disappointments, the Progressives lost control of the London County Council. Hardie, it was often alleged, was a cause of this decline. He was too independent in temperament, too aloof from his fellow-members, too prone to depart to distant ILP platforms in far-flung parts of Scotland or the north, or to socialist conferences on the continent (of which he attended several in 1906). The most severe criticism of all, however, and the one most persistently aired, was that he was failing to devote himself single-mindedly to the cause of labour. Other issues were claiming his attention to the detriment of the party in parliament. It was in this connection that the role of the suffragettes in Hardie's career became of crucial importance and a major factor in speeding on his departure from the party leadership.

From the start of his political career, Hardie had been an uncompromising supporter of women's rights. Votes for women had figured in his election addresses at Mid-Lanark and West Ham, and he had long established his reputation as one of the most determined and dependable advocates of the suffragettes' cause. His personal secretary, Mrs Margaret Travers Symons, the daughter of a wealthy Welsh architect, was a militant suffragette. Hardie claimed to link women's rights with socialism: 'the sex problem is at bottom the labour problem'.[18] But it is clear that his support for women's suffrage rested philosophically on the broad democratic argument – equally acceptable to socialists and to non-socialists – that there was no political or moral ground for discriminating between women and men. Hardie supported the liberation of women in all respects. He welcomed the growing security women enjoyed as owners of property, in the professions and in public life generally. He warmly championed the rights of women trades unionists, for instance in the 'sweated trades' like dressmaking and laundry work, of which, like Dilke, he was a fierce critic. He also condemned the low wages paid to women typists in government departments. Conversely, Hardie did not see why women should not own factories as well as work in them. He accepted that in most cases a woman's place should be in the home: his own wife was a conspicuous example of the modest role that a woman filled in late-nineteenth-century working-class life. At the same time, he argued that an educated, self-respecting woman with an intelligent interest in current affairs would be all the more able to contribute to the rearing of the children and to setting up a tranquil and culturally stimulating home. He looked forward to women's influence permeating the whole fabric of British society and culture. In all this, he was following what had become the conventional view of women's rights as advocated by a growing number of male sympathizers, outside and inside the House, since the days of John Stuart Mill. Apart from his special interest in women's trade unions, Hardie had no particular Labour or socialist slant to the arguments he adopted. Like almost all women's rights advocates at the time, he saw the granting of the franchise to all adult women, in parliamentary and in local elections, as the essential key to a wider emancipation. Without the right to share in the exercise of power, women would always remain a subordinate and subjected section of the community, without rights, status, or security.[19]

Hardie was, then, a persistent and courageous advocate of votes for women on basic liberal-democratic grounds. There were, he argued, no grounds for distinguishing against women in the granting of the franchise; the principle of sexual equality had already been accepted in other aspects of legislation. However, he also had some private motivations of his own. The role of women in public and private life was a theme that fascinated him in a wider sense. He was an ardent admirer of professional or politically-active women such as Eva Gore-Booth, Mrs Cobden-Sanderson or the Pankhursts. More, Hardie was a passionate man, and the challenges posed by sex absorbed him in some ways more completely than did problems associated with class. Years later, in 1912, he was deeply stirred by the Queenie Gerald affair, when it was alleged that Cabinet ministers were clients of a brothel in Piccadilly.[20] He was stimulated by reading some of the more erotic novels of George Sand and entered into emotional relationships with many young women he met in the socialist movement, from Annie Hines onwards. Hardie was well aware of the physical dimension of human relationships and a keen observer of the response to it shown by others. He wrote to Glasier of the reactions of Dr Stanton Coit, an eccentric American prominent in the ILP, to 'a Yank, the handsomest girl I have ever seen. . . . She was displaying a very full & well formed bust and C. was enthralled. . . . C.'s face was literally ablaze with the passion he cd. not conceal'.[21] Hardie's own reactions to a stimulus which must have taxed Dr Coit's ethical austerity to the full are not recorded. It is not demeaning Hardie's own courageous advocacy of the cause of women's rights to suggest that he was intrigued by sex as well as by sexual discrimination and that the wider aspects of sexual relationships added fire to his advocacy of the cause.

He had a first-hand reason for promoting the rights of women in 1906, namely his close friendship with the Pankhurst family. He had been in touch with them since Dr Pankhurst and his wife emerged as leading figures in the Manchester ILP and Board of Guardians in the early 1890s. Pankhurst, an ardent believer in nationalization, generally lined up behind Hardie in giving impetus to the more socialist aspects of the ILP's programmes. They took part together in the famous meeting at Boggart Hole Clough in 1896 and were defendants in the court case that resulted. When Dr Pankhurst died in 1898, Hardie wrote a warm tribute to him as the kind of wealthy professional man (Pankhurst was a barrister) whose idealism and intelligence the ILP hoped to enlist. With Pankhurst's wife, Emmeline, Hardie also established a warm friendship. She had, he wrote, 'placed the socialist movement on a higher level' in Manchester.[22] He was closely in touch with her when the Women's Social and Political Union was founded in 1903. He addressed the demonstration held at the Free Trade Hall, Manchester, that greeted Christabel Pankhurst and Annie Kenney on their release from Strangeways gaol in the autumn of 1905. Suffragettes such as Annie Kenney and Mrs Despard took part in his election campaigns at Merthyr. So when Hardie became chairman of the Labour Party, his association with Mrs Pankhurst was already well known. Occasionally, it gave rise to wry speculation: Mrs Pankhurst was, wrote Glasier in a particularly Delphic utterance, 'the Delilah who had cut our Sampson's locks'. Frank Smith had to write to MacDonald in April 1907 to explain that Mrs Pankhurst's presence on a train with Hardie at St Pancras was a pure coincidence. 'He had not the remotest idea she was anywhere near. . . . For various reasons he would like you to know this.' MacDonald himself had already commented ironically to Glasier that Hardie had left for the train with Mrs Pankhurst on one arm and Mrs Cobden-Sanderson on the other. But 'he wrote next day explaining that Mrs Pankhurst and he had not made a tryst'.[23] There seem no grounds for supposing that Hardie's attitude towards Mrs Pankhurst, handsome as she was, amounted to more than genuine admiration for a dominating public personality who exercised so commanding an authority over the women's movement.

Towards her daughter, Sylvia, Hardie developed a deeper attachment.[24] The young Sylvia was more involved with working-class people than was either her mother or sister. She was enthralled by her first sight of Hardie. 'Like a sturdy oak, with its huge trunk seamed and gnarled, and its garland of summer leaves, he seemed to carry with him the spirit of nature in the great open spaces. . . . His deep-set eyes were like sunshine.' She became a regular visitor to the flat at 14 Nevills Court. She noted such personal details as the skill with which Hardie made a fire. 'In a few moments, there would be a cheerful blaze. Then he would bring forth bread, butter and Scotch scones, the main staples of his diet, and tea.'[25] Hardie would read aloud to her extracts from Shelley, Byron, Scott, Shakespeare or Whitman. He would tell her of the suffering he endured in his childhood, and of his premonitions of another, happier existence. Sylvia responded to this admixture of socialism and spiritualism with total admiration. Hardie's romantic temperament chimed in with her own and soon she was supplying him with accounts of thought transference, of how telepathy would convey their feelings towards each other when they were apart. She painted Hardie's portrait on more than one occasion. Two were donated to the National Portrait Gallery in 1956: the overtones of emotion are immediately obvious. Hardie drew closer to Sylvia when she was imprisoned in Holloway gaol in 1907. He raised her case several times in the House. He also sent her books, notably *Noctus Ambrosiana*, 'which had a great vogue in Scotland fifty years ago', and found openings in the press for her journalistic efforts.[26]

Busy years of public life meant that Hardie and Sylvia saw each other only intermittently; yet by 1911 they were passionately involved in a relationship which clearly had its physical side. Hardie frequently entertained her alone in Nevills Court, and also took her out to dine in London restaurants and in the House of Commons. During a tour she undertook to the United States in 1911, Sylvia's affection for Hardie was ardent in the extreme. She penned several love poems which it would be maudlin to reproduce. Hardie, in return, variously addressed her as 'sweetie' and 'my little sweetheart' in letters which were as passionate as Sylvia's own. 'Don't you think the satisfaction which comes from the pressure of my arms round you must be the transference of something from one to the other?' he asked rhetorically and mystically.[27] In the years after 1911 they seem to have drifted apart; yet the relationship remained a close one to the end, especially as Sylvia devoted herself to social work in London's East End. She was one of the last visitors Hardie received at Caterham sanatorium in July 1915 just before his death. She wrote a passionate obituary of him in the *Woman's Dreadnought* – 'a child of nature . . . the greatest human being of our time'. Even after Sylvia left the ILP for the Communist Party, she continued to revere Hardie's memory. Her son she named Richard Keir Pethick Pankhurst; a daughter would have been named Keir. For the rest of her life, she was haunted by the memory of Hardie as a pure, brave, uncorrupted champion of human freedom and of women's rights. The significance of the affair between Hardie and Sylvia Pankhurst for the historian is clear enough. It lent a powerful personal dimension to Hardie's advocacy of women's suffrage. It massively reinforced the pressure that the women's movement was bringing to bear on the Labour Party, and on the mind, heart and soul of Keir Hardie himself.

At the outset of the 1906 session, it was natural enough that the Labour Party should champion the cause of women. The ILP had included several women amongst its prominent executive members, including Margaret Macmillan, Mrs Pankhurst, Margaret Bondfield and Mrs Katherine Glasier (herself a warm admirer of Hardie's integrity). The trade union movement also regarded itself as a champion of women's social rights; Shackleton, as member for Clitheroe, was heavily dependent on the subscriptions of women trade unionists. There was, therefore, no protest when Hardie championed the cause of the women in the House of Commons, nor when the Labour Party announced that it would introduce its own Women's Enfranchisement Bill in the 1907 session. Hardie spoke out strongly, with general approval in his party, about the treatment accorded to women's suffrage demonstrators in Trafalgar Square.[28] Theresa Billington and other women had been given the severe penalty of a £10 fine, or up to two months' imprisonment. Miss Billington chose the alternative of two months in Holloway prison. In succeeding months, Hardie effectively drew parliamentary attention to the rough justice meted out to Sylvia Pankhurst and other arrested women, to the perfunctory nature of the evidence offered against them, to the prejudiced nature of the trials at which they were convicted and to their subsequent harsh treatment in prison. The Labour Party echoed its applause as it was generally believed that the cause of the women and of the workers was one and the same.

But it was apparent by the summer of 1906 that a major cause of disaffection with Hardie's leadership of the Labour Party was his absorption, almost to the point of obsession, with the women's suffrage question. He seemed more accessible to officials of the Women's Social and Political Union than to his own parliamentary colleagues. Some Labour members were suspicious of the suffragettes as mainly rich professional or middle-class women who were socially cut off from the mass of the workers, and whose socialist credentials were doubtful in the extreme. No other Labour member championed the women's cause in so uninhibited and uncompromising a manner as did Hardie. Philip Snowden was the only other member so ardent in the cause and even he was soon to attack Hardie's preoccupation with the women's question. The potential division between Labour and the suffragettes came in the summer of 1906, and boiled over at the Cockermouth by-election. Instead of urging the voters to support Labour, the WSPU concentrated on a campaign to turn out Liberal candidates: in practice, that usually meant urging the electors to vote Unionist. The message from Mrs Pankhurst, like that from Hardie for the Labour Party, was one of strict independence, of avoiding any entangling alliance with any political party, even one as apparently sympathetic as the Labour Party. Indeed, the growing trend for the women's movement was to proceed beyond constitutional pressure, as that had led nowhere after thirty years of campaigning, and to go in for demonstrations, direct action and the search for public martyrdom.

With all this, the Labour Party was uncomfortable in the extreme. Its very existence was a denial of such tactics, and it stood to suffer at by-elections as a result. After Cockermouth pressure built up, therefore, for Hardie to devote himself more to leading the Labour Party and to minimize his contacts with the Pankhursts, mother and daughters. He appeared to accept, very reluctantly, that the Labour Party would have to cut itself adrift from the WSPU; but this had little effect on his personal position.[29] In November he spoke at a series of election meetings in Huddersfield; he addressed 2,500 at the local Hippodrome. 'He is a gem,' Glasier wrote admiringly. 'I fear, however, he is much too sympathetic towards the Women's Political Union (the Pankhursts etc.) who are holding great meetings advising the people to vote *against the Liberal* but are giving no help to our candidate.' In January 1907, Glasier passed on to Hardie criticisms voiced by Fred Jowett, his parliamentary secretary and one of Hardie's warmest supporters, that 'the women's suffragists have run away with him'. T.D. Benson added that 'the women have now ceased to be

Labour and are now under rich Tory control'. Hardie replied mildly that he believed Mrs Pankhurst wished the Labour Party to be dissociated from the Women's Union. 'Mrs Pankhurst – why should we care what Mrs P. wishes us to do?' Glasier exploded.[30] Several males in the parliamentary Labour Party, far more chauvinist than Glasier, echoed his impatience.

The irony was that, as on so many other occasions, Hardie looked like an extremist when his attitude was really a moderate one. In theory he appeared as a total advocate of votes for women, one who defended suffragette tactics through thick and thin, whatever the cost to his party or himself. In practice, he was trying to urge caution on the women's movement and to suggest to them that the more limited policy of attempting to win the franchise in the first instance on the restricted basis already enjoyed by men would be more immediately practicable than insisting that all women be granted the vote at once. The dualism in his position came out at the Labour Party's annual conference at Belfast in January 1907 when the tension between Hardie's roles as party leader and as a spokesman for women's rights came right out into the open.

It was a tense and difficult conference. The temper of the delegates was not improved by having to make the tedious journey by rail and sea to northern Ireland in cold January weather. Frustration about the party's performance inevitably boiled over. The first crisis came with the issue of the role of the conference itself.[31] A motion was introduced to try to force the parliamentary party to act as the mouthpiece for resolutions passed at the annual conference; it was a major stand for the principle of inner party democracy. Hardie, as leader, took a firm line, supported by Henderson and all the leading figures in the party. The parliamentary party should regard the resolutions passed by the conference as 'opinions only'. The time and method of implementing them should be left to the elected representatives, in association with the national executive. Hardie added some wise words on the composite nature of the Labour Party. 'It was composed of the socialist movement and of the trade union movement. There must be some freedom of action, some free play between the two sections. Otherwise, they were in for a spill.' This statesmanlike view, the only policy capable of welding the labour alliance into an effective unit, carried the day comfortably by 642,000 to 252,000. But it left a sour taste in the mouths of many delegates, especially those from the SDF, who were present in some force.

When the sensitive issue of the Women's Enfranchisement Bill, recently introduced by the Liberal member W.H. Dickinson, came up, Harry Quelch of the SDF carried a motion, against the executive's advice, to endorse the immediate and total enfranchisement of all women. Ben Tillett, another old enemy of Hardie's, supported him. Hardie's explanation that the Enfranchisement Bill would give the vote to two million women, mostly working-class, was brushed aside. His reaction to this caused a sensation. Sweeping to the rostrum, he declared that:

if the motion they had carried was intended to limit the action of the Party in the House of Commons, he should have seriously to consider whether he could remain a Member of the Parliamentary Party. He said this with great respect and feeling. The Party was largely his own child, and he would not sever himself lightly from what had been his life's work. But he could not be untrue to his principles, and he would have to do so in order to remove the stigma of women being accounted unfit for political citizenship.[32]

Hardie's argument was entirely consistent with his previous position – what became later handed down as 'the 1907 formula', that party conferences could not bind the party in parliament. Labour leaders from Ramsay MacDonald to Harold Wilson continued to treat conference decisions, often the product of unrealistic euphoria conceived in the heady atmosphere of delegates assembled for an annual safety-valve of oratory, as statements of opinion, but not as mandates. Harold Wilson (at least while in office), like Keir Hardie, viewed government by annual conference as incompatible with the working of a democratic system.

Still, Hardie's threat to resign from the parliamentary party caused an immense stir. Glasier was dumbfounded – 'he never hinted he might do this, and he leaves us all sprawling'. In the *Labour Leader* he took the line that the unity and strength of the party were proof against the damage wrought by personal differences of view. Privately, he felt that Hardie's attachment to the women's cause had led him into a major political error. So, too, did Pete Curran, also a major advocate of women's suffrage, who broke down in tears at Hardie's announcement.[33] Soon Hardie was having second thoughts about the wisdom of his action. He was duly re-elected party chairman for the 1907 session, his election being moved by Shackleton and seconded by Henderson. The national executive, on Henderson's initiative, tacitly supported his stand against dictation from a party conference. Hardie was allowed to vote according to his convictions on the women's question – the origin of Labour's 'conscience clause'. But the constitutional correctness of his position was secondary to the fact that his association with the women's cause had apparently thrown into question even his membership of his own beloved Labour Party. The doubts entertained about the nature of his leadership were the more fully confirmed.

On a wider basis, Hardie's involvement with the women's cause is instructive. It showed how easily he could attach himself to a wider radical movement that included many non-socialists. The cause might be anti-imperialism, women's rights, colonial nationalism or the peace movement. Whatever the issue, it showed how Hardie's political outlook remained shot through with the democratic radicalism of the late nineteenth century and how easily his unique concern with socialism could be set aside. In the long term, his ability to fuse radicalism with social democracy was a major contributing factor to the growth of the Labour Party. It enabled it to make common cause with radicals outside the party and often to absorb them within itself. But in the narrower perspective of 1906–7, Hardie's shifts of outlook caused immense perplexity. His dualism of vision seemed in many ways a source of weakness, an index of his waywardness in the pursuit of private crotchets, instead of a dogged, single-minded advance on behalf of the working class. His commitment to the women's movement, reinforced as it was by his personal relations with the Pankhursts, threw into question, as did no other aspect of his political activities, the depth of his identification with the party of which he was regarded as the founder.

In the 1907 session Hardie's chairmanship continued to generate friction, with MacDonald, Snowden and Henderson prominent in the disputes that ensued. How far Hardie himself could fairly be blamed is exceedingly debatable. The difficulties in imposing a coherent policy on the party in parliament, let alone the rank and file in the constituencies, were almost insuperable. The dilemma of trying to preserve Labour's independence and yet retain the substance of the Liberal alliance as it had endured since 1903, would have taxed the ingenuity and resources of a more diplomatic and more dishonest man than Hardie. Successive chairmen of the party after him – Henderson, Barnes, MacDonald – experienced many of the same difficulties and were scarcely more successful in overcoming them. The Labour Party was in desperate need of a national Campbell-Bannerman figure to reconcile its warring factions, as the Liberals had been reconciled after 1902. But (perhaps until Attlee emerged in 1935) none was to be found. Certainly Hardie himself, proudly independent by temperament, staying close to his own circle of friends – Frank Smith, Fels, the Pankhursts – and only occasionally venturing into the forefront of political debate, was incapable of fulfilling such a role. He could create a new party, but he could not consolidate. The patient self-abnegation required to build up a new movement from the base demanded a different kind of political genius from his own. In any case, he remained impenitent in the face of all criticism and even carried the offensive back against Snowden and other opponents. He urged Glasier in March to ensure that the Labour Party maintained its contacts with the women's movement and suggested that the *Labour Leader* should be better primed with local news of suffragette branches. 'The ILP women are as anxious as ever to retain their membership and work for the ILP and we should make a mistake if we did not do all in our power to return them.' Again, he took new heart from the ILP annual conference in 1907; always he found this a far more congenial assembly than the mass gatherings of the Labour Party. 'The conference was magnificent and the tone and spirit of the gathering far in advance of anything we have hitherto had.'[34] He began consultations with Lansbury about forming a London Labour Party. Soon Labour was to enjoy its first real taste of success since the general election: Pete Curran was returned in a by-election in Jarrow in June 1907, in a three-cornered contest, despite T.P. O'Connor's attempt to persuade Irish voters to vote Liberal, to Hardie's disgust. At last Labour seemed to be on the move again.

Nevertheless there was a profound sense in the party that all was not well. It had made little impact on parliament during the session. Party discipline was hard to maintain: over education, for example, a group of Catholic members opposed the party's policy of secularism in the schools. The government's own programme had run into the ground, largely through obstruction in the House of Lords, and only Lloyd George at the Board of Trade showed a consistent record of departmental achievement. On the social reform front, the government had been almost a total failure. In particular, nothing had been attempted or achieved on behalf of the unemployed, thanks in part to Burns at the Local Government Board. Yet Labour had failed to take the opportunity to push its causes forward. A measure like the Mines Eight Hours Bill had somehow lapsed, with no fight put up on its behalf. Hardie wrote to Glasier on 7 May:

> I am struck with the fact that the party in parliament is somehow dropping out of notice. When one is on the spot, one does not notice it just the same. The cartoonists seem to be forgetting us, and somehow we don't seem to bulk so large as we did in the eye of the public. . . . We cannot afford this kind of thing. It all comes of luncheons and confabbing with Cabinet Ministers.[35]

To the wider industrial struggle, the Labour Party seemed almost an irrelevance. In branches up and down the country there were accounts of apathy and declining organization. Even in Hardie's own Merthyr constituency, his secretary in Aberdare, the schoolmaster W.W. Price (a Labour zealot there until the 1960s) wrote, 'The LRC is really dead here. The question of putting new life into it has caused a great deal of anxiety to our comrade Hardie.'[36] Relations with the miners were especially difficult. The glowing hopes of January 1906 were still far from being fulfilled.

The reactions of Hardie himself were the more significant as he was now removed from the forefront of the stage. In April he had been complaining to Glasier of 'a strange numbness all down the left side'.[37] Shackleton temporarily took over his duties as party leader. By the end of the month Hardie had broken down completely and was sent off to a hydropathic centre in the highlands of Scotland (in whose therapeutic qualities he had a profound belief). The question of how long he could continue to serve as chairman of the party was posed with a new sharpness. Finally it was announced during May that he would shortly set forth for a trip around the world, the costs being met partly by the Salvation Army. It was anticipated that he would visit Canada, Australia, New Zealand and South Africa, and stay away, in this somewhat vigorous phase of trans-world convalescence, until the beginning of 1908. Quite suddenly, then, the question of his chairmanship of the Labour Party was resolved. It became clear that the Party would have to elect another chairman – probably Shackleton or

Henderson – for the new parliamentary session. Hardie himself, writing to Glasier in June, was full of his plans for the world tour. He turned down an offer of financial aid from the Labour Party because it might be tied to donations from other political parties as well; as usual, rigid independence was the watchword. 'I have decided to go to Australia, and possibly South Africa. The latter is a bit risky after the Zulu letter, but I shall call at the Cape either going or returning. This is my one remaining chance for seeing these places and I may as well take advantage.'[38] At least he would find release overseas from the interminable conflicts within the movement at home.

Even in the last few weeks of his time in Britain, however, Hardie found occasion to become embroiled in party controversy. This arose from the independent candidature in the Colne Valley by-election in July of a remarkably militant and articulate member of the ILP, still in his twenties – Victor Grayson. He was standing on behalf of the 'Colne Valley Labour League'. From the start, Grayson's candidature posed an immense quandary for the Labour Party, which had decided not to contest the seat against the Liberals. Even the ILP refused to approve Grayson's name as an officially-sponsored candidate. On 28 June the emergency sub-committee of the Labour Party National Executive passed a resolution that 'as Mr Grayson's candidature has not been promoted in accordance with our constitution and practice we can take no action'. The Fabian Edward Pease noted, 'A momentous decision'. It was also urged that no official of the national or of the parliamentary Labour Party should go to Colne Valley to assist Grayson.[39] This was, however, remarkably difficult to implement. In fact only four members had attended the sub-committee meeting – MacDonald, Shackleton, Hudson and Pease. The others were divided between trade unionists, who wanted a cast-iron motion that would prohibit any official of the party going to Colne Valley, and ILP men like MacDonald who wanted it left to the discretion of individuals. ILP men like J.R. Clynes, who had promised to help Grayson in his campaign, asked for definite instructions but received only a vague injunction that it was 'inadvisable' to take part. The NAC, however, did relent somewhat. Hardie and Snowden criticized it for indecisiveness and forced through a resolution which backed the Colne Valley branch of the ILP in their support for Grayson. Snowden was sent down to speak on his behalf.[40] Still, in general the Labour Party kept clear of Colne Valley, especially as Grayson's flamboyant personality led him into declarations of militant socialism of an embarrassingly revolutionary kind.

Hardie himself then intervened, just prior to his departure for his world tour. He agreed with Labour's national executive that 'Grayson's candidature was wrongly promoted and that we cannot expect the Labour Party to endorse it'. On the other hand, Hardie was very reluctant to refuse to help any grass-roots protest movement, even if the dictates of party discipline argued the other way. Each MP should be left to decide for himself whether he should help Grayson, he wrote to MacDonald on 11 July.[41] He himself always took a flexible line towards party directives, and expected others to do the same. He had helped Lansbury at Middlesbrough in the 1906 general election, despite pressure from the LRC not to do so. Now he sent a warm message of support to Grayson at Colne Valley, one that was widely used during the campaign.

The national executive reacted strongly and the question of Hardie's endorsement of Grayson was brought up at its meeting of 24 July. Hardie's move was given the more prominence because, in a spectacular performance, Grayson defeated both the Liberal and Unionist candidates. The question of whether he would be recognized as a Labour Party member when he came to Westminster was now acutely embarrassing. MacDonald, like others in the ILP, was inclined to support a tolerant policy.

Our policy in Parliament must be, I think to get Grayson to join us and that cannot be done by hectoring. . . . In parties like ours there will always be a rising and falling in tides which do not indicate general and settled tendencies, but which on occasion may go beyond the maximum which the Party can bear without a crisis.

When the day of Grayson's arrival at Westminster approached, however, MacDonald was less confident:

I shall also wait until I see Grayson before taking any steps to approach his Colne Valley committee regarding maintenance. My impression is that they feel so aggrieved with us, and so proud of their own achievements that they will tell us that they are going to look after him themselves.

When Grayson took his seat MacDonald further lamented, 'Grayson is making an utter fool of himself in the House and has put up the backs of our men very badly'.[42] Hardie's action, without doubt, was a great embarrassment to the authority of the national executive, including some of its socialist members. The affair continued to rumble on for almost a year, until on 20 May 1908 Hardie's letter about the Colne Valley by-election was finally deferred *sine die*.[43] In any case even before Grayson was able to take his seat Hardie was on the high seas to Canada, and thus escaped yet another internal crisis. The whole affair merely reinforced the waywardness and populist 'spontaneity' with which Hardie regarded party discipline. It confirmed his disturbing tendency, the more surprising for such a constant critic of 'socialist unity', as preached by the SDF, to endorse rebels whatever their credentials. As events turned out Hardie gained nothing but personal worry from his conciliatory moves towards Grayson. The dissident element that he represented in ILP branches throughout Britain continued to plague Hardie for the rest of his career.

The Colne Valley by-election, with all its quasi-comic overtones, as Grayson's erratic personality revealed itself, seemed to set the seal on a fairly disastrous period of party chairmanship as far as Hardie was concerned. It seemed to confirm the divisive and fragmented nature of the party as it had lurched erratically through its first two parliamentary sessions. Hardie himself viewed his resignation as chairman only with relief. It was the only official position he ever held in the sphere of national politics, the only occasion when he was in a position directly to influence the conduct of parliamentary business. It proved to be a trial and burden for him. He resumed his familiar role as rebel and outsider thereafter, and never made any further bid for a position of power in the party. Apart from his membership of the national executive of the ILP, he retained no official position at any level of the movement and was unmuzzled as never before. The overriding impression of his period of chairmanship, then, can only be to confirm the long-held view that he was unsuited for authority.

On the other hand, few who have put forward this conventional view have made it clear how ungovernable and notably unfraternal the Labour Party really was in 1906. More than most political parties, it was hard to weld into unity, especially since it lacked anything like a stable constituency organization and was at the mercy of local bodies of activists, Labour Representation Committees, trades councils and socialist organizations. Only at the parliamentary level did any kind of united outlook prevail, and even here the fragmentation of the party in the country was faithfully mirrored. Nor was the Labour Party in a confident mood in 1906–7. Nothing would have more astonished MacDonald, Henderson and the rest than to be told that politics were now polarizing on the basis of class, that Liberalism was doomed, that the Labour Party was the inevitable residuary legatee of this process, and that it was about to supplant the Liberals as the spokesmen of the British Left. Nothing that occurred in 1906–7 – not even Jarrow and Colne Valley – suggested that Liberal England was in the process of undergoing a 'strange death'. Hardie's own consistent prophecies that the Liberal Party was on the verge of total disintegration and that all right-thinking radicals from Lloyd George downwards would find their natural home in the Labour Party had a more and more wishful and wistful air, as though constant reiteration would somehow speed on the course of history. In fact, Hardie as a realist well knew how entrenched the Liberals were after their general election triumph, how the Liberals still attracted the bulk of the working-class vote (even in Merthyr), and how years of patient persuasion would be required to build up the Labour Party into a credible challenger for power.

The relative feebleness of the party in 1907 was not Hardie's fault. It was inherent in the party's insecure posture as a labour pressure-group, which somehow asked to be recognized as an independent party. It was the Labour Party which contained the real ambiguities in these years, not Hardie's interpretation of it. He had given it little enough leadership in the conventional sense, as chairman: arranging for parliamentary time-tables and dull minutiae of this kind were alien activities for him. What he had done, and was to continue to do, was to provide Labour with a unique fund of inspiration and a style of its own. As Glasier wrote in June 1907, 'he knows how to stir the pulse of the movement', and in the first instance it was the 'movement' as much as the party at Westminster which needed to be galvanized. In pushing on with labour issues such as unemployment, in extending the horizons of the party to wider themes such as the enfranchisement of women, Hardie gave it an ideological impulse and breadth of vision more important and more durable than the pedestrian details of party chairmanship and parliamentary procedure. As he set off on his world tour in July 1907, Hardie was to develop these aspects still further. He was about to add a new international dimension to the outlook of what was still a profoundly insular party, however much it might orate on May Day about the brotherhood of man. He was to help wrench the Labour Party away from its own internal, often parochial disputes, to direct its vision anew towards the links that bound it to the exploited workers and the oppressed colonial peoples of a wider world.

IX   The Internationalist

'Mr Hardie had in a larger measure than, perhaps, any other man I have known . . . the international heart and mind.'[1] Philip Snowden's judgement crystallizes one of the dominating themes of Hardie's public career, especially in its later phases. More than any other Labour leader of his day, more even than MacDonald, Hardie was associated with the idea of international fraternalism, of united action by the workers of the world. The originality of Hardie's views should not be underestimated. The political labour movement in Britain as it emerged in the later nineteenth century was almost entirely insular in outlook. The days when Chartists or members of the Reform League felt a sense of kinship and of ideological identity with radical movements in the United States belonged to the distant past.[2] The Labour Party in Britain grew up entirely as a result of class conflict and political change within Britain itself. Hardie himself, as has been seen, made no pronouncements at all on foreign or imperial affairs during his period as member for West Ham in 1892–5, lest he compromise his essential commitment to the cause of labour at home. Even the impact of the South African War did not seriously modify the outlook of LRC or trade union leaders in Britain towards world questions. The Labour Party manifesto in the 1906 general election dwelt almost entirely upon domestic social, political and economic issues. It contained just one statement on foreign affairs: 'Wars are fought to make the rich richer.' In general, the Labour Party inherited the tradition of radicals of the Cobden-Bright era of 'no foreign entanglements'. Diplomacy and international affairs were maintained to bolster the pretensions of a fading aristocracy and of industrial capitalists. The root cause of war lay in the aggressive and competitive nature of the private capitalist system. The basic key to a world at peace, therefore, was the implementation of social justice. After this was achieved, foreign policies would largely wither away.

This insularity, however, was never wholly true of Hardie even in his earliest phase. As has been seen, his columns in the Scottish press in the early 1880s contained a good deal of discussion of international questions, mainly in the form of inquiries into the state of trade and industrial growth in foreign lands and of discouragement of emigration by British workers. Hardie's conclusions were usually nationalist, even mercantilist. Outlets for British products could be found in abundance at home; the competition for markets overseas was unnecessary. Nevertheless he continued to show an unusual interest in his journalistic writings in comparative political and economic developments abroad. In particular, events in the United States in the 1890s – the economic slump, the growth of trusts, the rise of agrarian and urban radicalism, and the emergence of a new imperialism – exercised his attention. In a very real sense, Hardie's early belief in Christian brotherhood also impelled him towards a feeling of kinship with working-class movements overseas: the legacy of Burns, and of the simple democratic internationalism that Hardie had imbibed through his poetry as a child, was a powerful stimulus to him as he grew older. As Hardie moved towards socialism in the late 1880s, this outward-looking approach led him into an increasing involvement with the working-class movement in the European continent and beyond.

His internationalism was always hedged around by realism; it was never merely sentimental. During the controversy that arose over the admission of alien immigrants to Britain in the period 1900–5, Hardie admitted that there could come a time when there might have to be regulations, for example to exclude criminals or those carrying diseases.[3] But his approach to the Aliens Bill of 1905 was uncompromising and honourable. The vast bulk of immigrants were refugees from persecution in eastern Europe, especially in Czarist Russia, the most hateful of all despotisms. The majority of these refugees were Jews escaping from atrocious 'pogroms'. They had useful skills and were law-abiding members of the community. Hardie's generous and humane instincts rebelled against using the bogeys of immigration or racialism to stir up prejudice amongst working people, or to claim that immigration was the root cause of unemployment and trade depression. Christian charity alone compelled Britain to admit them. 'Are we to say to those poor creatures that England of all lands under the sun is no resting place for them from the conditions now prevailing in their own country.' At a time when right-wing politicians were busy exploiting racial prejudice in the east end of London and in other cities, Hardie's internationalism (which reaped no political dividends for him) was a civilized antidote.[4]

As has been seen above, Hardie attended the first Socialist International in Paris in 1889, being present at both the Marxist and the 'possibilist' congresses there. From the start he took the International seriously, not so much as an instrument for united working-class action, but rather as a great forum where socialists and trade unionists of diverse shades of opinion could meet and exchange views. The International was, for him, a kind of world-wide equivalent of the Labour Representation Committee at home, where different ideologies would be expressed, and reconciled gradually, through discussion, tolerance and pragmatic reform. Hardie attended the congresses at London in 1896, at Amsterdam in 1904, at Copenhagen in 1910 and at Basle in 1912. He became one of the most prominent and respected voices of the European socialist movement; he missed the Stuttgart congress in 1907 only because he was on his world tour at the time. Hardie was an advocate of moderation and of pragmatism in the early congresses. As has been seen, he even supported the admission of the Anarchists and of 'free communists' like the Dutchman, Domela Nieuwenhuis, at the London congress in 1896, much to the fury of the SDF and of strict Marxists.[5] At the Amsterdam congress in 1904, Hardie and MacDonald both intervened in the great debate over 'revisionism'. Here, the delegates debated the participation of the French socialist, Alexandre Millerand, in the bourgeois radical government of Waldeck-Rousseau (to be followed shortly afterwards by the election to ministerial office of other French socialists such as Briand and Viviani). Hardie argued in favour of a flexible policy; he rejected any dogmatic refusal to associate with the processes of government in a capitalist state. He supported the majority view which endorsed the 'revisionist' policy. He noted shrewdly that the Guesde-Bebel standpoint, which condemned Millerand and in effect argued for complete political passivity until the socialist revolution came, was supported by the Social Democrats mainly in countries like Italy and Russia which had notoriously weak and divided labour parties.[6] In a land like

Britain, with its broad-based Labour alliance, effective intervention in local and national government was both desirable and feasible in the interests of the class he represented.

As time went on, Hardie was to take a more expansive and optimistic view of the potential of the International as an instrument of action. He kept in close touch with its secretariat and was very friendly with its secretary, the Belgian, Camille Huysmans. The reason for Hardie's concern that the industrial labour movement should be united lay in his growing fear of militarism – a fear that mounted after the Anglo-German naval rivalry had escalated in 1909. To Hardie the fraternal links that bound the British Labour Party and the German Social Democrats were one last bulwark against the war fever, generated by a desperate, ailing, capitalist class. Thus it was that Hardie at the last came to sponsor, with the French socialist, Edouard Vaillant, the famous resolution on behalf of a general strike against war. He championed it at Copenhagen in 1910, at Basle in 1912, and most tragically of all at the emergency conference of the International's executive at Vienna and the International Socialist Bureau at Brussels in the days before world war broke out in August 1914. Hardie's endorsement of a general strike by the workers, especially those employed in arms factories, seemed to many quixotic, even anarchistic. It met with severe criticism from German Socialists whose scientific rigour militated against romantic, utopian gestures of this pre-Marxian kind. But Hardie really saw the general strike against war as an extreme measure to be adopted in the last resort; it was a supplement to normal political pressure through social democratic parties in different countries, not an alternative to it.[7] In its way, the theme of a general strike was a testimony to Hardie's deeply and sincerely-held international sympathy, his refusal to believe that the exploited workers of all countries could blindly follow the merchants of death along their path of nationalism and chauvinism. When the events of the first week of August 1914 dispelled this simple faith, his internationalism received a shattering blow, one from which neither it nor he ever recovered.

In addition to attending the International Hardie also kept closely in touch with the leading Social Democratic parties of the time. He became the warm friend of Jean Jaurès, whose union of socialist and trade union sections in France so closely echoed Hardie's own policy in the LRC, and whose amalgam of radicalism, patriotism and Marxism mirrored Hardie's own confused beliefs. August Bebel, the doyen and leading ideologue of the German Social Democrats, was another of Hardie's associates, even though Hardie's own writings tended to give support to Bernstein and the 'revisionist' critics of SPD Marxist orthodoxy, of which Bebel was the symbol. More than any other British Labour leader of his generation, Hardie kept in intimate touch with socialist movements on the continent. His travels were considerable, especially for an age of leisurely railway journeys. In a period of eighteen months in 1912–13, he visited at various times Lyons, the United States and Canada, Budapest, Zurich (for Bebel's funeral), Dublin and Jena. He became for the British Labour movement the very symbol of a dawning internationalism, the most natural man to choose as fraternal delegate at the congresses of other socialist parties abroad or to put in charge of the drafting of the international platforms of the Labour Party at home.

Hardie, without doubt, loved travel. His articles in the press testify to the excitement he felt at seeing strange places and customs; his writings when abroad often show a vigour and vitality which his discussions of domestic labour issues frequently lack. He had a keen eye for detail, for individuals he encountered, for local folk customs: his visit to India is particularly rich in its accounts of the cultural and religious diversity of the sub-continent. Hardie, as a Scotsman who represented a Welsh constituency, was easily stirred by national folk cultures, patiently treasured by the common people throughout centuries of oppression. Some of his accounts of the vigorous use of the Welsh language at *eisteddfodau* and miners' conferences in the South Wales coalfield show the sincerity of his reactions.[8] But Hardie travelled to socialist congresses overseas for reasons other than curiosity or personal sympathy. He also went there for instruction, to see how other socialist movements managed to cope with the kind of political and ideological dilemmas he encountered at home and to see what morals could be drawn from their experiences.

The German SPD he found particularly instructive. He admired its discipline, its party cohesion, its sense of being a distinct sub-culture detached from the militarist and imperialist classes that ruled Wilhelmine Germany. Bebel in particular he regarded with intense admiration, especially in the light of his courageous championing of the peace movement in Germany. (Indeed, had Hardie but known it, Bebel was actively sending private information about German war intentions to officials in the British Foreign Office from 1907 onwards.)[9] On the other hand, Hardie thought the German Socialists showed the dangers of rigid dogmatism: they were in some respects the SDF writ large. He appealed to them for tolerance towards the Revisionists. He felt that 'revisionism' and 'radicalism', the two philosophies championed by Bernstein and Kautsky respectively, 'are matters of little moment', as revisionism was in practice the effective creed of the German socialists. He lavished praise on Ludwig Franck, the leader of the Baden-Baden SPD, which was temporarily expelled from the national party for agreeing to support the Baden government's budget and thereby giving indirect support to a liberal but bourgeois government.[10] Hardie acknowledged that the restrictions on the franchise in Germany made a revolutionary stance inevitable for the SPD. Still, in general the party seemed to him to offer clear arguments in favour of the need to avoid Marxist rigidity or a time-worn anti-clericalism in its doctrines — views which Hardie himself had tried hard to combat in Britain's labour movement.

The French socialists interested Hardie in a different sense. He admired the way, especially during the Dreyfus affair, they identified themselves with the patriotic tradition of the Revolution and how Jaurès in particular tried to adapt Marxist socialism to a French setting. Hardie watched with interest the tensions that arose between the middle-class socialist groups, represented in the National Assembly, and the growing elements in the French trade unions, especially in the CGT, calling for industrial action and for a general strike. Although Hardie viewed with alarm the rise of syndicalist doctrines of workers' control and saw it as a form of industrial anarchy, he drew the moral that middle-class and working-class movements in France, as in Britain, should draw closer together and hammer out a common policy. 'The party here badly divided, the Guesdistes playing the part of the SDF at home,' he wrote to Glasier in 1902.[11] In Italy, by contrast, Hardie saw the dangers of having a socialist movement preponderantly under middle-class leadership. He deplored the middle-class exclusiveness of the Italian Social Democratic leaders and their isolation from rank-and-file workers. On the other hand he also attacked the dogmatic abstractions of the Italian syndicalists led by Labriola who called for workers' control of railways and factories.[12]

The class war rhetoric of the young Mussolini Hardie found even more rebarbative. In general he was fascinated by the varieties of socialism to be found in Europe. He was particularly absorbed by the problems of ethnic diversity that existed in Austria and Hungary, which he discussed at first-hand with the Austrian socialist leader, Viktor Adler. He enlisted Adler's help in rebutting accusations that he was a crypto-Tory.[13]

Hardie found in European socialist movements something to learn and something to avoid. Their political cohesion was instructive, as was their discipline in parliament. (Hardie drew wistful comparisons between the German SPD and the Labour Party he had led in 1906–7 in this respect.) They also made use of the press very effectively: there was no British Labour journal equal in authority to *L'Humanité* in France, *Vorwarts* in Germany or *Avanti!* in Italy. This spurred Hardie on to the discussions which concerned the attempted founding of the *Daily Citizen* in 1911. On the other hand many socialist parties abroad, even the massive German Social Democrats who formed the largest party in the Reichstag after the 1912 elections, were inward-looking sects rather than crusading movements. (Gibbon's distinction between the Jews and the Christians is instructive here.) A socialist party in Britain or elsewhere should be capable of a flexible and sympathetic approach to a wider radical culture. It should identify itself with the genius of the nation in which it grew up rather than impose an alien dogmatic canon of belief. Hardie, without doubt, viewed socialist movements abroad through a British perspective. Lenin roundly condemned him as a Liberal-Labour 'opportunist' who 'squirmed and wriggled' and who missed the essential point of the Marxist dialectic.[14] Hardie could never really outgrow his British, indeed Scottish, roots. But his range of inquiry, his willingness to look at socialist parties and labour unions abroad at first hand, gave to his outlook an unusually broad international vision, unique in the Labour Party in his own day and often forgotten by the party since his death.

Hardie's internationalism was far from being confined to Europe. As has been seen, he had already made his acquaintance with the United States in his trip with Frank Smith in 1895. He visited America twice more, in 1908 and 1912, observing the presidential elections on each occasion, and took a keen personal interest in the labour and socialist movements in that country. In Britain he had discussed problems of workers' education with the historian, Charles Beard, a temporary tutor at Ruskin Hall in Oxford in 1899–1901.[15] In addition, he had many contacts with American socialists and labour leaders across the Atlantic. In particular, he kept in touch with Eugene V. Debs, president of the American Railway Union and later leader (and perpetual presidential candidate) of the Socialist Party of America. Hardie had also met Daniel de Leon, the apostle of 'one big union', but his doctrinaire Marxism, which soon alienated Debs, made him repugnant to Hardie also. Nor did de Leon show much admiration for Hardie either. He considered Hardie's speech to a poorly-attended American Labor Congress at Chicago in September 1895 to be a failure. Frank Smith he dismissed as 'an ex-Salvation Army colonel, a very clever speaker, but wholly sentimental'.[16]

Another of Hardie's American contacts was Sam Gompers of the Cigar Makers' Union, the British-born founding president of the American Federation of Labor. Although Gompers had begun life as a socialist, he soon imposed on the AF of L a philosophy similar to that of the craft trade unionists Hardie had encountered at the British TUC in earlier years. Gompers believed that American labour should steer clear of political activity of any kind, let alone socialism and should concentrate instead on winning short-term economic gains. They should use methods as vigorous and unrestrained as those of the capitalist employers, instead of attempting to change society fundamentally. 'What does Labor want? More!' However, Gompers kept up a friendly personal relationship with Hardie.[17] More, after 1906 even Gompers and the AF of L found themselves forced to engage in political activity to lobby the Democratic and Republican parties and to put forward their *magna carta* of grievances. This arose from what appeared to be an employers' counter-offensive somewhat similar to that experienced in Britain in the Taff Vale period. American employers backed up by the courts used the injunction as a weapon against union boycotts, and undermined all attempts to improve working conditions. Not until the *Muller* v. *Oregon* case in 1908 did judicial decisions seem at last to be going the workers' way. More serious, the use of troops or private 'Pinkerton men' by Andrew Carnegie and other industrial tycoons, which led to violence and serious bloodshed in the Pullman strike in Pittsburgh, in the Coeur d'Alène miners' strike in Idaho and on many other occasions – all this appeared to herald a particularly brutal attempt to suppress the workers' rights of combination and expression. It made Gompers newly sympathetic to Hardie and the British Labour Party. He viewed with much interest the passage of the Trades Disputes Bill in 1906 and subsequent attempts to protect political activity by the TUC. It was mirrored in the United States by the recognition of collective bargaining in the Clayton anti-trust Act of 1914 (later largely nullified by the courts). Gompers and Hardie had an odd relationship. Their outlooks were in many ways worlds apart. Gompers was anti-socialist, he accepted the capitalist framework, he welcomed at first the growth of trusts, he supported the capitalistic 'new freedom' of Woodrow Wilson in 1912, he opposed the interference of the federal government in labour conditions as a restriction of the freedom of the labour unions and a possible avenue for encroachment by corrupt vested interests. On all these points Hardie of course took a totally different view. But he saw the force of Gompers's achievements, and the progress of the AF of L, despite all crises, in the period 1902–14 was a major factor in reinforcing Hardie's rapt interest in the United States.

His observations on the American scene were remarkably shrewd. After his 1908 visit he noted the 'marvellous change' that had taken place there since he was last over in 1895, particularly the growth of the socialist movement.[18] The Socialist Party of America, with Debs as its leader, now claimed forty thousand members and was making inroads both in the eastern cities and in rural areas of the south-west where Populism had been rampant fifteen years earlier. Hardie speculated on the durability of a farmer-labour alliance in Britain. Again, there were heartening signs of socialist successes in elections, notably in Wisconsin where a largely German Social Democratic movement was becoming powerful, where six socialists had been elected to the state legislature and where Victor Berger was shortly to be elected as the first socialist member of the House of Representatives. Socialism, Hardie noted, had become respectable. It was accepted in the circles of government, notably in La Follette's state of Wisconsin – a laboratory of social experiment – whereas earlier it had been crudely identified with anarchism or violence. On the other hand, Hardie noted how wide the gulf still remained between the socialist and trade union movements in the United States. In the 1908 presidential campaign,

Gompers decided to swing his support behind Bryan, the Democratic candidate, instead of behind Debs, even though Bryan's platform was, Hardie argued, weak on the anti-injunction issue. There was a long way to go before trade unions and socialists would make the kind of common front in America that they had forged in Britain in the Labour Party. Meanwhile the American trade unions faced disruption from within at the hands of their own Graysons. Hardie viewed with dismay the rise of the Industrial Workers of the World, the so-called 'Wobblies', strongest among the copper and silver miners of Montana, Idaho and Washington state, areas which he himself visited in 1895. Hardie regarded these developments as anarchic and militating against a disciplined trade union movement. Nor did they help on the cause of socialism, especially with the tendency of 'Big Bill' Haywood and other 'Wobbly' leaders to advocate open violence.

The vital need, as Hardie saw it, was for 'a good friendly alliance' between the socialists and the AF of L. Following the British analogy he thought the best way to obtain this was at the local level first, for instance among the far western miners in their isolated, mountainous districts. Socialism, he felt, could well make striking progress in America: he attributed Debs's small poll in the election to the tactics of Gompers in backing Bryan and to the impact of the 1907 trade depression which drove many voters into the arms of Taft, the Republican candidate who seemed to provide a guarantee of renewed prosperity. There was, he claimed, a real socialist mood in America, for instance in welfare agencies such as Jane Addams's settlement houses in Chicago and New York, and in the pressure for a community approach in dealing with poverty and slum housing in major cities. What was needed was to harness this socialist outlook to a mass working-class movement.

When Hardie visited America again in 1912 a good deal of progress appeared to have been achieved. The American Federation of Labor had expanded steadily until it now claimed 1,750,000 members from the working class. The reform movement was also exploding in all directions in the United States, with the triumphant achievements of Progressive reformers in city government, in welfare policies, in promoting women's suffrage and in undermining corruption. Debs polled almost a million votes in the 1912 election, and many looked forward to having a socialist president of the United States. On the other hand, Hardie sensed that all was not well.[19] The rise of labour unionism was not keeping pace with the growth of the working population. Nor was America as thriving as it appeared: he gave statistics to show a falling rate of wages in many trades. Unemployment was widespread and labour legislation held back by the courts. Above all, the employers' counter-offensive was in full swing, with blacklegs widely used, striking anthracite miners being shot down in the Pennsylvania coalfield and unionism violently suppressed. Amongst the large mass of American unskilled workers, trade unionism was virtually non-existent. Hardie was not over-impressed with Debs's high poll: much of it was concentrated in depressed rural regions such as Oklahoma, with their Populist traditions. The mass vote in the major cities appeared to go mainly to the 'Progressive' or 'Bull Moose' candidate, Theodore Roosevelt. Debs had a long haul before he could hope to capture power. Hardie saw also the contrast between the American and British workers. He realized that there were immense regional, ethnic and religious differences which prevented the formation of a unified working class. What he failed to stress sufficiently was the difficulty American workers had in seeing themselves as a class bound down by the wage system. Rather did they regard themselves as independent artisan producers, who could hope to rise up in their turn to become self-employed or prosperous entrepreneurs, as the American pioneering ethic dictated. Hardie was inclined to draw too ready a parallel between the British and the American workers, and to assume that a Labour Party of some kind was an inevitable consequence of the American social and political scene. Even so, he looked at the United States in a remarkably clear-eyed fashion. He perceived facets of its development, especially in the labour world, hidden to most observers. The United States in its turn added depth and subtlety to Hardie's international outlook.

His internationalism received its greatest boost, however, from his tour of the world, which lasted from July 1907 to April 1908. This tour, financed partly by the Salvation Army, partly by Joseph Fels, was in many ways the apotheosis of Hardie's outward-looking creed. His accounts of his adventures afford the historian of labour a valuable source for the working-class movement in the empire, as well as being illuminating for the historian of Hardie's own evolving ideas. He travelled across the Atlantic in the S.S. *Empress of Britain* with Joseph

Fels and was seen off from Liverpool to the strains of 'Auld Lang Syne' and 'The Red Flag'.[20]

Hardie first visited Canada, a new country to him, where he spent about three weeks, travelling the continent from Quebec to Vancouver. The freshness and vitality of the country appealed to him.[21] On the other hand, he was struck by the high cost of living, especially in the eastern provinces and the difficulties posed for the Canadian trade union movement by immigrant Chinese and Japanese labour. Above all, he was anxious to try to unite the Canadian socialist and trade union movements. He gave a major address on this theme at Winnipeg at the end of July 1907.[22] The occasion was a dramatic one. Winnipeg, the centre of Canada's wheat boom, was a stronghold of prairie populism of the Canadian variety. Arthur Puttee's newspaper, the *Voice*, had been preaching socialism there since 1894. Hardie's visit caused immense excitement, including a major reception at the local Congregationalist Church. He praised the development of self-government in Canada; he drew a contrast with Ireland and with India as he did so. He urged anew the need for a *modus vivendi* between the trade unions and the Canadian Socialist Party, which was strongly Marxist in some sections. But his message bore little immediate fruit.

He recognized this in a second visit to Canada, when he addressed the twenty-fourth convention of the Canadian Trades and Labor Congress at Halifax, Nova Scotia, on 25 September 1908.[23] Again he received an enthusiastic reception from all sides; his stay was marred only by the theft of a cap, waistcoat and tobacco pouch. The local press in Halifax, Conservative and Liberal, gave him a cordial greeting. 'In manner mild and gentle, in action keen and alert, in conversation crisp and concise, and showing a broad grasp of matters relating to the great world of labour. He has won everybody's hearts', wrote one local reporter.[24] The French-Canadian president of the Canadian Trades Congress, Alphonse Verville of Montreal, praised Hardie as a constructive moderate. Hardie in his speeches in Canada took a wide-ranging series of briefs. He spoke, 'not as theorist but one who, as a collier originally, had passed through every phase of the movement (loud applause)'. He spoke of the growing influence of the workers in Britain, of the success gained in forcing through social legislation and of the work that still needed to be done in relation to public ownership and state insurance. He urged the Canadian workers to go for 'absolute political independence' as he had done. Above all, he urged Canadian socialists to adopt an outward-looking policy and to drop their present 'Phariseeism'. 'The autocratic attempt to force their shibboleth upon the people did not tend to the uniting of the ranks of the workers.' Hardie's speech was greeted, according to the official report, with 'a volley of cheers'.[25] He was presented subsequently with a gold-headed walking-stick. His appeal for unity struck warm chords among the delegates, concerned as they were to find a common platform for English and French Canadians. But his attack on doctrinaire sectarianism was mainly effective for home consumption in Britain. Although a Social Democratic Party was formed at Vancouver in 1909 as a reaction against the revolutionary creed of the Socialist Party of Canada, most Canadian socialists remained in dogmatic isolation. Hardie was amused to note that they declined to attend the Copenhagen International in 1910 because the Socialist International was 'compromising with capitalism'.[26] Among sections of the Canadian labour world – among the miners of Nova Scotia, many of them of Scottish extraction, in whose affairs Hardie took a keen interest and amongst idealists like the social gospeller J.S. Woodsworth – Hardie's blend of social justice and pacifism had a lasting impact.[27] His visits to Canada – he made a third, brief one in 1912 – were landmarks in the history of the Canadian labour movement. But the vision of a united working-class and socialist organization in Canada remained elusive and was partially achieved only by the CCF in 1932, years after Hardie's death.

From Canada Hardie sailed on across the Pacific to Japan. He took the opportunity to plead the cause of some imprisoned Japanese socialists to Count Okuma, the prime minister. He went on through the Straits Settlements – modern Malaysia and Singapore. But the high point of his tour came when he visited India. Hardie's visit had long been awaited with apprehension. India in 1907 was seething with unrest and political conflict.[28] Long-dormant hostility towards the British Raj, focussed in the Congress movement, flared up violently with the partition of Bengal in October 1905 and the creation of a new province of Eastern Bengal and Assam. This was interpreted as a crude attempt by the British government, and by Curzon the Viceroy in particular, to divide the Bengalis along religious lines. With a six million Moslem majority in the new province, Hindus in particular regarded it as a policy of 'divide and rule'. Anti-partition sentiment lent momentum to the growing pressure for the boycott of goods, for *svadeshi* (the economic liberation of India) and for *swaraj* (home rule). The Indian movement was in reality polarized between the approaches of two formidable political leaders, S.K. Gokhale, who, with his disciple Gandhi, favoured constitutional, liberal evolution along the British pattern, and the more militant B.G. Tilak, who advocated national liberation and Hindu cultural self-sufficiency. Gokhale looked to a westernized India as a self-governing part of a commonwealth. Tilak sought the immediate elimination of British rule and the purging of all western influences. But in the fury of the anti-partition movement these different strains seemed to unite, and thus Hardie arrived in India at a particularly critical time.

He himself had long been associated with a small group of radicals in the House of Commons concerned with Indian affairs. Including Sir Henry Cotton, a Liberal, and the Labour member James O'Grady, they were a fierce group of critics of the Secretary for India, John Morley. Once again Hardie found himself locked in conflict with Morley with whom his relations had undergone so many violent shifts. Hardie had hitherto no first-hand experience of the Indian subcontinent; but the mystery of the 'mystic East' fascinated him as it did so many of his generation from Kipling downwards. India appealed, Snowden wrote, to 'the mystic and the seer' in him.[29] For one of Hardie's temperament the secret contemplative mystery enshrined in Indian, especially in Hindu, culture, was deeply absorbing. He rightly judged India to be the critical area in the growing debate about colonial self-government. It was the key to whether the African and Asian races should be accorded the same privileges of self-expression as were subject nationalities in Europe. In the House on 20 July 1906 Hardie had fiercely attacked conditions in India – the rising death rate, the almost total exclusion of native Indians from local government, the low wages that prevailed in Indian textile factories.[30] Long hours and depressed wages gave the Indian factory-owner an unfair advantage in competing with British textiles. The Labour Party argued that loyalty and peace would only be achieved in India if its teeming peoples were accorded justice and dignity. Eighty-nine Liberal and Labour members voted against the government.

Hardie's visit in 1907 had aroused white fears before he even arrived in India. They were amply confirmed. Hardie toured the new province of eastern Bengal under the guidance of B.G. Tilak and of J. Chowdhury, another leading advocate of *svadeshi*. Exactly what he said in his speeches there was the subject of fierce dispute; but there is little doubt that he gave every encouragement to the Congress movement's campaign for Indian home rule. Cries of 'Bande Mataram', the slogan of the militant Tilak supporters, punctuated his words. Hardie's general line, so it was reported, was that India was as fully entitled to self-government as was Canada.[31] He compared the deaths of Hindus in India to the atrocities committed years ago in Armenia. He also sent a wire to London stating that the people of India were 'at the mercy of the corruptest police in the world'. All this caused an immense stir in Britain. *The Times*'s leading article on Hardie's Indian tour was headed 'Fostering Indian Sedition'. Hardie was guilty, it asserted, of 'criminal ignorance and criminal recklessness' in encouraging Bengali agitators and terrorists. The outbreak of rioting in Calcutta was directly linked with Hardie's visit and there were many cries for Hardie to be deported.[32] Morley himself was much alarmed. He wrote to Minto, the Viceroy, on 8 October, that 'the line taken by Hardie will be likely to multiply the difficulties of management'.[33] Above all, Hardie might persuade the Congress movement, both the Gokhale and Tilak wings, that he and the radicals associated with him in the Commons were a significant body of opinion in Britain. Minto finally met Hardie on 16 October. He found him 'a warm-hearted enthusiast who had come to India with fixed ideas'.[34] Hardie openly denounced the character of British rule in India. He told Minto that the Ordinance Bill was oppressive and would injure moderate Indian opinion. English administrators, he claimed, showed no understanding of Indian sentiments. Shrewdly, he added that 'the Mahommedans have been systematically played off against the Hindus'.

The exact content of his public speeches in India aroused much controversy. Frank Smith and other ILP friends wrote to the *Daily News* denouncing press misrepresentation of Hardie's speeches, while Shackleton anxiously told MacDonald that it would be desirable for the LRC to obtain the exact text of what Hardie had actually been saying.[35] Hardie himself denied that he had asked for India to be granted self-government immediately; his references to Armenia referred to the treatment of the Hindus by the Moslems, not by the British Raj. Even so he continued on his tour with increasingly bitter controversy surrounding it. He went on to Delhi, then to Madras, accompanied by Surendra Nath Banerjee, another *svadeshi* leader. He wrote cheerfully to Glasier on 8 October, 'I honestly believe that I am being worshipped in certain quarters & have been twice decorated with flowers taken from the Temples, an honour reserved for the holiest people. At Madras crowds hung about or pressed to touch me. It appears that in two of the famine districts rain fell after my visit and *I get the credit*.'[36] Hardie's tendency to self-identification as a kind of Christ-like prophet was reinforced. Finally on 17 October he left India, without the necessity of deportation, to the immense relief of Morley and the British authorities.

Hardie's visit to India is a major episode in his career. The reaction in the press and in government circles was crude and simple. *Punch* depicted him as raging around India in a Scottish miner's suit of rough homespun, waving a firebrand that was labelled 'sedition'. Morley also was consumed with fury: Hardie described a talk with him after his return to Britain as 'a waste of time and temper'. Even more pungent was the predictable reaction of Edward VII who wrote to Minto on 17 August 1909: 'What can one expect if such a scoundrel as Keir Hardie who is also a member of the House of Commons, foments sedition in India and at home against our mode of Government? The harm he has done is incalculable – and makes one's blood boil.'[37] Hardie's enthusiasm for self-government in India was not universally shared in the Labour Party but he himself continued to crusade for the cause. He took a vigorous part in Indian budget debates thereafter, well-primed with information gleaned from Indian Congress friends.[38] He led onslaughts on the rates and taxes imposed on the Indian *ryots*. He also launched an unsuccessful campaign to free B.G. Tilak who was imprisoned by the Governor of Bombay in July 1908 for sedition. The jury, consisting of seven Europeans and two Parsees but with no Hindus, imprisoned him for six years; widespread rioting inevitably followed, with Gokhale himself driven to a much more militant position. Hardie pressed hard for Tilak's release. In August 1912 he approached Lord Crewe, now the secretary for India, suggesting that Tilak's release would 'go far towards pacifying his immediate friends and followers'. This approach received short shrift from F.H. Lucas, the civil servant concerned in the India Office. He commented, acidly, 'Keir Hardie might prefer a less formal reply even if unfavourable.

There is some advantage in treating him as a human being when possible. He has a perfect genius for making his case appear just a little better than it really is.' Crewe turned down Hardie's plea without further debate. Tilak was finally released in June 1914. Again, however he complained of police persecution and of restrictions on his liberty, for instance in the official refusal to allow the photographing of himself being garlanded with flowers. Hardie took up Tilak's case again in July and August 1914; but Crewe, after consultation with the Governor of Bombay, and finding that Tilak had made some patriotic pronouncements about supporting Britain now that world war had broken out, still decided that no action need be taken.[39] Tilak and Gokhale then resumed their conflict for the leadership of the Congress movement, with Gandhi taking over the leadership of the moderate wing when Gokhale died in February 1915.

More significant than his efforts on behalf of individuals like Tilak was Hardie's publication of his conclusions on the situation in India. This made a considerable impact and played a major role in educating British liberal opinion on Indian affairs. Lenin noted with satisfaction that 'the whole of the English bourgeois press raised a howl against the "rebel" '.[40] Hardie's conclusions had originally appeared in the *Labour Leader*. In 1909 they formed the basis of one of his few books, a slim volume entitled *India: Impressions and Suggestions*, published jointly by the ILP and the Home Rule for India League. It sold at a shilling, after the large number of proof corrections Hardie made: 3,500 copies were printed.[41] This highly personal account is a successful amalgam of descriptive passages and facts and figures on the political and economic conditions prevailing in India. Hardie noted the abject destitution prevalent there; the average income was well under £2 per head per annum. Seventy-five per cent of the revenue from harvests went to the payment of taxes. Hardie also described the wretched schooling he had seen, the need for the overhaul of the agrarian system, the prevalence of rampant disease and pestilence. Above all, his book contained a damning indictment of imperial rule – 'a huge military despotism tempered somewhat by a civil bureaucracy'.[42] In Eastern Bengal the average Hindu was 'at the mercy of the police'. There was little viable local self-government, the district and municipal boards were severely restricted, and the Viceroy's legislative council was a mockery. Any demands for extended self-government were dismissed as 'sedition'. Yet, as so often, Hardie's specific plans for reform were as measured as his denunciations were fierce and elaborate. He proposed the employment of more Indians in the civil service, more extended powers for village councils (for instance in the collection of revenue quotas), an improved educational system. The 'colour line' should be eliminated in government appointments. Hardie did not argue for the immediate withdrawal of the British from India, but only for a gradual extension of self-government as had recently been implemented in Australia and South Africa. Demonstrable errors such as the partition of Bengal should be rescinded, to avoid a religious conflagration.

In the course of time many of Hardie's well-documented and cogently presented criticisms became the common liberal coin. Certainly Morley's period at the India Office proved a huge disappointment, in view of his impeccable Gladstonian credentials, as did that of Crewe. Not until Edwin Montagu went to the India Office under Lloyd George from 1917 onwards was any perceptible progress made towards effective self-government in India. The years that ensued only confirmed the broad outlines of Hardie's criticisms of the Raj – while the Bangladesh crisis in 1971 emphasized anew the original folly of the division of Bengal. Hardie's tour of India brought out some of his less judicious qualities. He was only in India for a few weeks and was too prone to jump to pre-selected conclusions. His association with Tilak was probably harmful to the Congress movement, since it was the more gradualist, western-orientated approach of Gokhale and Gandhi which was far closer to Hardie's own ideals. Even so, Hardie's continuing involvement in the movement for Indian independence is one of the most distinguished episodes of his career. It notably broadened the vision of Labour and radical opinion with regard to conditions in India, usually regarded as the private speciality of a few Anglo-Indian experts and the 'ginger group' led by O'Grady. Ramsay MacDonald also visited the sub-continent in 1909 and published his findings in a book, *The Awakening of India*, the following year. It began the process of giving Labour a viable imperial and colonial policy, one which bore fruit in 1947. It built a bridge between the western and the eastern mind at a time when official government policy was encased in a mould of bigotry. For India, Hardie was indeed a liberator.

The final stages of his world tour took Hardie first to Australasia and then, climactically, to South Africa. In Australia he felt thoroughly at home.[43] It contained a powerful Labour party with strong trade union roots. It would probably be the first country in the world to have a government drawn from the working class and a widespread programme of nationalization was likely there. He met many old friends in Australia. He resumed contact with Tom Mann, now preaching the cause of syndicalism in the Australian Workers' Federation, and with H.H. Champion, his old opponent of the post-Mid Lanark years. There was also Andrew Fisher, a former Ayrshire collier, now the first Labour Prime Minister in the world, who was later to visit Hardie in his Merthyr constituency. Hardie enjoyed the earthy, democratic atmosphere of Australia. At Adelaide he took part in a cricket match; playing for the press against the parliament he noted with pride that he scored eight runs, including a boundary. On the other hand, he noted other features of a Labour-run Australia that were less happy – the growth of protection, the reluctance of arbitration courts to grant wage increases, the rise of a jingo and militaristic spirit amongst such Labour men as Billy Hughes. A working-class government was not necessarily a pacific one, as Hardie saw, and he viewed with suspicion Australian and Canadian demands to serve on the Committee of Imperial Defence. Nor was it necessarily one fired with a belief in racial equality. On the 'white Australia' policy, Hardie wrote cautiously, 'Time alone will tell'.

New Zealand attracted him also with its eight-hour day legislation, its wage-fixing by the courts, and old age pensions of 10s a week.[44] On the other hand the Labour movement there was in a flabby condition. Trade unionism was struggling, Labour politicians like R.J. Seddon were almost indistinguishable from the Liberals, while the Socialists were small in number and largely confined to Wellington. 'The movement here is uninspired and, alas, almost purely utilitarian.'[45] The mixed reception Hardie received from local trades unionists after his inflammatory tour in India was also indicative of the mood in New Zealand labour circles. In New Zealand, also, he almost met with personal disaster. He was thrown from a horse-drawn carriage and severely cut on the scalp. It was almost a fatal ending to his worldwide convalescence, but he soon recovered.

The tour ended, appropriately, in uproar. This came in a brief visit

Hardie paid to South Africa. He had long been a severe critic of conditions in that country, originally of course in his lyrical defence of the
Boers during the South African War. But, more rapidly than most
contemporaries, he sensed the refusal of the Boers whom he had supported to accord any political privileges to the coloured population. He
had championed the rights of native workers as early as March 1903.[46]
He spoke forcibly in the House in December 1906 on the suppression
of the native uprising in Natal. In discussing the constitutions to
be accorded to the Transvaal and Orange Free State after self-
government, he emphasized the 'native question' and the need for
allowing the black population to live on its own lands according to its
tribal laws.[47] He also drew attention to the political rights of the
coloured majority. All this was anathema to most white South
Africans and Hardie's visit was awaited with immense apprehension.
A Johannesburg socialist wrote to MacDonald on 17 October 1907
that 'our comrade Hardie' would have an 'awakening' if he but raised
the colour question. 'I would go much further than most people here
and ask equal rights for the native – but inter-marriage and residence
with whites never. They were created different races and must remain
so.' In the Transvaal, the same correspondent added, white workers
go hungry, while 'the native with his simple wants waxes rich on 1/6
per day'. He added: 'We have created a new race here during recent
years. Half Kaffir and Half Chinese.'[48] South Africans like these expected Hardie to create a stir and he did not disappoint them. His
initial speech at Durban, which proposed opening trade unions to
coloured men, was fiercely attacked. At Ladysmith windows were
broken in the hotel in which he was staying. Finally, in a meeting at
Johannesburg, the epicentre of Boer South Africa and the Dutch
Reform Church, he raised the native question in unambiguous form.
He attacked the system of 'Kaffir farming' in Natal under which
squatter Kaffir farming drove out the coloured population.[49] But he
was not able to deliver more than a few sentences. The meeting broke
up in uproar. Hardie narrowly escaped with his life, preserving only a
tattered Union Jack from the meeting as a souvenir, proudly displayed
in Nevills Court henceforth. A few days later he was on the high seas
back to England, leaving behind an infuriated South African Dutch
population. Only a talk with the liberal Olive Schreiner brought him
any satisfaction.

South Africa remained one of his special interests in the House henceforth. He intervened powerfully in debates on the Union of South Africa Bill. He was one of the very few to point out the complete failure of that measure, conventionally regarded as a triumph for British liberal sentiment, to make any provision for the coloured population. Later, in 1913 and 1914, he raised the question of the use of troops in suppressing strikers on the Rand, and the use also of proclamations and of martial law.[50] Hardie was not as well informed on South Africa as on India, but here again he was an effective voice for minority opinion. At the time, relations between the races in South Africa were virtually never discussed. The conventional wisdom was to praise the liberalism of old Boer commanders like Botha and Smuts. *Apartheid* existed through custom and prejudice, but had not received the sanction of legislation. Here again Hardie's internationalism led him into a vital new area of political inquiry. Here again he showed a far-sightedness which the future was relentlessly to confirm.

He came back from his world tour in April 1908 to a tumultuous reception, and a great public meeting at the Albert Hall organized by the Labour Party.[51] But this was very far from being the end of his involvement with overseas socialist movements. Thus in July 1909 he addressed the annual congress of the Young Egyptian Party in Geneva, where he offered them some sane and characteristic judgements. He urged them to be constitutional in their pressure for self-government in Egypt and to take advantage of such reforms as Cromer had provided. He called for a new union of students and peasants in a mass movement; any plans for secret conspiracies or for armed uprisings would be divisive and destructive. The constitutional path was always the one to follow: this could lead to a new understanding between East and West.[52] The Wafd party followed Hardie's advice in later years, while he himself continued to condemn Britain's occupation of Egypt, which had led to John Bright's resignation from the government back in 1882. In relation to Egypt, as to India, Canada, and elsewhere, Hardie's message was one of moderation and of constitutional progress. Yet his world tour and much of his involvement in international affairs seemed to contemporaries only to confirm him as an irresponsible fanatic, a seditious firebrand who would give succour to any nationalist uprising against British rule. Fred Lewisohn, writing to R.C.K. Ensor, poured scorn on Hardie's judgements on India. 'What value would there be if a Burman Buddhist visited Ireland for a couple of months, knowing nothing of English, and with the late Colonel Saunderson for his guide?' He added later that Hardie had fallen into the hands of Indians,

who are no doubt patriotic in their own way, but are as utterly without a practicable policy as they are also poles asunder from any views which could be termed socialist. On the whole, I am with those who regard K.H. as an incubus on the party, and I expect there will be much very justifiable relief when he retires from the stage.[53]

Many echoed this view of Hardie as an irresponsible and ill-informed purveyor of snap judgements. It cannot be entirely dismissed. Like other observers to foreign lands, Hardie saw what he wanted to see. His views were preconditioned and he could dogmatize freely, as he did throughout his world tour, on the basis of a limited few weeks' or even days' acquaintance with the country in question. His language was usually abrasive, sometimes inflammatory. Even so, Hardie's observations on the countries he visited were generally well illustrated with factual evidence, culled from blue books, secondary works and information gained on the spot. His speeches on India or the native question in South Africa in the House between 1908 and 1914 were very far from incoherent declamations, but were well sustained with statistics, documentary evidence and first-hand observation. Nor, as his comments on the United States illustrate, did he look at foreign situations with a totally uncritical eye, as though there was a standard model Labour Party which naturally ought to evolve in every mature democracy. Like Aneurin Bevan, Hardie had an instinctive feel for relativism. In almost every case his observations stand the test of later scrutiny remarkably well. On India and South Africa in particular his vision put him far ahead of his time, in a period when virtually no-one in the socialist camp (save for a few Indian experts like H.W. Nevinson) had any sensible views or informed knowledge of those countries. Hardie on his return drew the appropriate moral – the need for closer collaboration between the Labour movements in the mother country and in the colonies. On so many issues – wages, unemployment and women's rights above all – they shared common problems with Britain; fraternal co-operation could only be of mutual benefit. In relation to the Empire, as to Europe and the United States, he urged his colleagues to take a wider view of the struggle in which they were engaged. His success was severely limited by the insularity of the Labour Party then and later, but it is perhaps not too fanciful to see the beginnings of a Labour colonial policy dawning in the years after Hardie's return. A credible European policy was still in the making in 1974. For Hardie himself the world tour of 1907–8 with all its sensational incidents marked a notable divide in his career. He was to emerge henceforth less as a locally-based champion of the British working-class in a purely domestic context and more as an international statesman. His reputation grew steadily in the Socialist International, amongst European Socialists, and amongst colonial freedom movements in India and South Africa, as it somewhat diminished at home. Hardie after 1908 developed a new kind of political style, one that appealed to a world-wide audience. It placed fraternity securely alongside equality as a central tenet of the socialist faith.

X The Political Theorist

'Socialism is much more an affair of the heart than of the intellect.' So wrote Hardie in a euphoric article in the *Labour Leader* in March 1906.[1] In this, he went on to compare the vulgar philistine pleasures enjoyed by the rich with the natural happiness to be found in contemplating a clear spring bubbling down a hillside on a summer's day. This kind of writing, sentimental to a degree, has usually been taken to characterize Hardie's approach to the theory of socialism. Historians as sympathetic as G.D.H. Cole have generally regarded him as a woolly-minded romantic who contributed nothing to the intellectual content of the labour movement. His attempts to analyze the nature of his socialist beliefs have generally been held to be derisory. His contribution to the Labour Party, then, appears as practical and inspirational, but not in any sense intellectual. It is not to be compared, we are told, to the hard-headed realism provided by the Webbs or even to the quasi-Darwinian evolutionary mysticism offered by Ramsay MacDonald. Hardie himself modestly contributed to this general view. He frequently declared that he was no theorist, that his meagre educational background left him ill-equipped to pursue the paths of political philosophy. He himself freely offered tribute to the more powerful mental attributes of Ramsay MacDonald – 'the greatest intellectual asset in our movement' – whose *Socialism and Society* had gained widespread acclaim and who sometimes seemed to dominate Hardie's own ideas.[2]

Nevertheless it is clear that Hardie did conceive a political theory of what socialism and the working-class movement were. It might not have won much acceptance in the cynical atmosphere of a university seminar. It might not have been securely based in philosophy, economics or history. Still, it exercised a powerful effect on the working-class mind of Hardie's day and for that reason alone, if for no other, deserves to be examined. It proved to be attuned to the circumstances attending the birth of the Labour Party in a way that the intellectual sophistications of the Fabians, conceived in esoteric middle-class debating circles, simply were not. Socialists as intellectually formidable as Bernard Shaw treated Hardie's expositions of his socialist and radical beliefs with respect. They were, Shaw acknowledged, more than mere repetitious slogan-mongering, as so much socialist theorizing was in Britain at the time. Rather, they were an honest attempt, by a man with little formal education, to work out a personal position. They helped make Hardie, to some extent, a prestigious figure in the international socialist movement as a theorist, as well as an activist and an inspirational dynamo. Above all, his attempts to work out the essence of his socialist principles, stumbling though they were, did try to relate speculative theory to a specific British situation, instead of elaborating a disembodied a-historical socialist dogma in the fashion of latter-day schoolmen. Hardie's political ideas were a significant part of the evolution of the Labour coalition and its emergence as an effective political striking force. For that reason alone, they should be an essential concern of any of his biographers.

Hardie himself often claimed to be a disciple of Marx. He invariably included selections from Marx's writings in the bibliographical notes to his books and articles. 'Socialism does not create the class struggle, it does not even accentuate it, it only recognizes it. That is the broad generalization of Marx which pedants have distorted out of all recognition and elevated into sectarian dogma under the name of the Class War.'[3] He praised Marx's perception of class-consciousness, his account of the historical process as the record of class struggles, his provision of scientific, analytic tools by which to interpret the course of history, and thereby to change it. Marx he compared with Darwin: 'Marx explained Socialism as being the working of a natural law, just as a scientist might have done in any sphere of science.'[4] Like Darwin, Marx emphasized the urge for 'sympathetic association' in place of competition. But it was clear from everything that Hardie wrote on socialist theory that his interpretation of Marx was highly personal. Aspects of Marxism greatly appealed to him, especially the romantic vision of a classless society in which the economic and social structure would disappear and human brotherhood prevail. Hardie relished the prospect also of the capitalists destroying themselves by their own moral corruption. It had been, he wrote, the 'ill-gotten wealth and debauchery' that had undermined the Roman Empire, not the incursions of the Goths and the Huns. Time and again, Hardie called attention to the emphasis in Marx's later writings, later given further development by Engels after Marx's death, which traced the peaceful, evolutionary road to socialism.[5] Hardie denied that Marx was a revolutionary save in the most theoretical sense, or that he contemplated a violent assault on the citadel of capitalist power. Marx was basically an evolutionary theorist, who analyzed the growth of human society just as a biologist or botanist might examine animal or plant life. He further believed that Marx's vision of a socialist movement was precisely mirrored in the Independent Labour Party, a broad-based movement of workers and middle-class sympathizers, slowly and relentlessly advancing towards political power by the evolutionary, constitutional process. Anything that resembled a 'violent outbreak', as demanded by some anarchists, was, Hardie argued, harmful to the socialist message as laid down by Marx. Doctrines of class war were self-defeating: they drew the workers further away from socialism, as did rigid dogmas of any kind. The comparative history of the ILP and the SDF, the former in close touch with the trade union movement, the latter languishing in self-imposed doctrinaire isolation, made the point as Hardie saw it – and he claimed that it was Marx's point also. Marx's socialism 'made war upon a system not upon a class'.[6] Conflict was possible within classes as well as between them; class war rhetoric should therefore be avoided at all costs, as it would lead to chaos.

In this context, then, Hardie claimed to be a follower of Marx. But it was clearly a very British, very respectable Marx that he presented – one quite unrecognizable to Engels, for example, who viewed Hardie's exegesis of Marxism with hostility verging on contempt. Hardie never subjected any single one of Marx's writings to rigorous scrutiny. Herbert Spencer or John Stuart Mill figured far more frequently in his own works. When Hardie came across violent exhortation to arms in Marx, notably in the Communist Manifesto of 1848, he condemned it outright. In presenting this interpretation, very loosely culled from Marx's later writings (and one which left entirely out of account Marx's ferocious critique of the SPD Gotha Programme of 1875 as being too committed to the political and economic systems of capitalism), Hardie was creating a Marx (as he created a Christ) in his own image. There is scant evidence that he had much first-hand acquaintance with Marx's writings or that his library contained many of them.

His loose use of fragments of Marxist phraseology in an unrelated way does not support such a view. Large areas of Marx's writings Hardie ignored completely. He totally neglected the whole economic dimension of Marxism – the materialism, the iron law of the accumulation of capital, the theory of surplus value, the ratio between fixed and variable capital, the falling rate of profit as economic decay set in. Marx's doctrine of the growing immiseration of the poor as capitalism lurched on towards its final collapse was rejected outright. On the contrary, Hardie welcomed the economic advances made by the industrial workers throughout the nineteenth century. An enervated impoverished proletariat would subside into serfdom rather than improve its lot.[7] Whatever Hardie's socialism consisted of, therefore, it cannot, save in the most incidental sense, be termed Marxist. Whenever Hardie actually came across flesh-and-blood advocates of Marxism, Hyndman for instance, he usually found little in common with them. If British socialism be said to have owed more to Methodism than to Marx, Hardie's socialism owed relatively little to either.

His socialism was founded not on dogma, but on experience and on sensibility. It was born of his experience of the working-class struggle in the Scottish coalfields, with a heavy overlay of the evangelical Christianity to which he was converted in the 1870s. His ideas were an individual blend of realism and utopianism, of the pragmatic and the apocalyptic. They did not greatly change throughout his career. Their essence can be traced in his multifarious writings in the press, particularly in his columns in the *Labour Leader* up to 1904 and in the Merthyr *Pioneer* after 1911. In these Hardie kept up a kind of running debate with his readers and himself about the political, social and economic issues in the Britain of his day. Only very seldom did he try to set down his views in systematic form. Usually these attempts were inspired by particular crises and had a short-term polemical purpose. This is particularly evident in two important pamphlets, sixteen and fourteen pages respectively, *My Confession of Faith in the Labour Alliance* and *The I.L.P. and All About It*, both published in 1909; they were directed mainly at the dissident doctrinaire element in the ILP, associated particularly with Victor Grayson. Another important statement of faith, *The Red Dragon and the Red Flag*, based on a speech delivered at the Merthyr Drill Hall in October 1911, was intended as an appeal to the Welsh workers to give their backing to the nascent Labour Party which had subsumed the older Liberalism in Wales. It was a pamphlet directed as much against the syndicalists and the apostles of industrial action as it was against the Liberal middle class. Pamphlets like these afford valuable clues to the nature of Hardie's beliefs; but they were fundamentally polemical in intent, and never really transcended their origins. They were effective as destructive and critical tracts: for instance the spurious appeal to Welsh nationalism put forward by Liberals such as Sir Alfred Mond was most effectively demolished. But they do not amount to a coherent statement of a political philosophy by themselves.

Only in one slim volume did Hardie try to crystallize and define the nature of his socialist beliefs. This was in *From Serfdom to Socialism*, a volume published by George Allen Ltd in 1907 in its 'Labour Ideal' series, and written during his convalescence, shortly before Hardie set off on his world tour. It was intended as a contribution to the growing debate on the need for collectivism that had been launched by J.A. Hobson, L.T. Hobhouse and other critics of the traditional individualist Liberal ethic. More, it was designed as Hardie's personal commentary on the wider international debate raging through the socialist world, between the exponents of Marxist orthodoxy and the 'revisionists' of various shades. For many socialists, Hardie's book, however cloudy in exposition, was held to contain the essence of the British socialist case and to lay down the kind of relationship that the British labour movement enjoyed with doctrinal factions overseas. His exposition of his views in this book, therefore, is worth particularly intensive study.

As elsewhere, Hardie's approach was at the same time utopian and down-to-earth. It was the very antithesis of 'scientific socialism' as preached by Engels and his followers or by the adherents of the SDF. It was heavily laced with the 'new theology' propounded by his friend, the Rev. R.J. Campbell; it included also frequent excursions into classical and medieval history, of a free-wheeling kind. 'Socialism', Hardie declared at the outset, 'is much more than either a political creed or an economic dogma.'[8] It was fundamentally ethical, a vision of justice and equality born of a new society, with man freed from the constraints of a capitalist environment. 'Socialism is woven from the same loom as Isaiah – of the same texture as that Kingdom of God which the early Christians believed to be at hand.' Communism, he wrote elsewhere, was 'a form of Social Economy very closely akin to the principles set forth in the Sermon on the Mount'.[9] Hardie claimed that the early Christian martyrs with their denunciations of usury and peculation were expounding a socialist faith, as also were Wycliffe, John Huss, the Anabaptists and the Levellers. This primitive socialist vision had been lost sight of, with the growth of new instruments of economic oppression. Above all, the birth of modern capitalism (which Hardie, following the much-respected Liberal economic historian Thorold Rogers, dated precisely from the Protestant Reformation), had undermined the position of the medieval freeman and had pressed him down into a new servitude. The fifteenth century had been 'the golden age of the English worker', in which the individual worker felt himself to be a human being with dignity, self-respect and an enhanced standard of living. The growth of capitalism and of mass industry, the replacement of the guild system by production for profit and above all the growth of trusts and other forms of economic concentration in the recent past in Britain, America and other countries, had eroded the workers' liberty and created a new dehumanizing serfdom.

Earlier socialists in Britain had called for a revolution to overthrow this new system: in particular, Hardie cited William Morris, 'the greatest man whom the Socialist movement has yet claimed in this country'.[10] But for Hardie the key to the achievement of socialism lay in the capture of power within the state. The organized Labour movement was the inevitable consequence of universal suffrage, with the thrust for political power by the newly-enfranchised worker. 'The ballot is more effective than is the barricade.' Property was power; through political action the state should expropriate land, capital and the sources of production. This was already occurring at the local level. In a pamphlet, *The Common Good* (1910), Hardie wrote enthusiastically of current experiments in municipal reform – the ownership of transport and public utilities by local councils, and the new forms of municipal trading that captured the imagination of American Progressive reformers. More than most Labour men then or later, Hardie took local government very seriously. He praised the greater efficiency and the elimination of vested interests which municipal socialism brought about. In municipal undertakings, unlike private enterprise, the capital was being steadily redeemed, so that in a generation a concern like gas or electricity or tramway services would become 'the absolute property of the citizens'. This restored a sense of civic pride and of public involvement; according to Hardie it was also a return to the spirit of the medieval commune and trade guild. These reforms in the municipal sphere would lead in due course to public ownership at the national level as well, until all the resources of the community were under communal control.

Other forms of liberation would follow on as the inevitable by-products. The co-operative spirit would permeate society as a whole: the changed attitude of the churches to social questions was a leading example. The institution of equality between the sexes would be another consequence of the new society, through the coming economic independence of women. Equality between different races would also follow. The kind of society that would ultimately emerge after land and capital had been transferred from private to public ownership, Hardie found it hard to predict. 'It belongs to the future, and is a matter which posterity alone can decide.' There was no finite form of socialism. It was constantly evolving with the growing complexity and size of modern industrial society. Either state socialism or free, voluntary association might prove a viable system, although Hardie preferred the latter. Ultimately socialism did not rest on institutional forms at all. As he wrote elsewhere, 'I am a socialist because socialism means fraternity founded on justice, and the fact that in order to secure this it is necessary to transfer land and capital from private to public ownership is a mere incident in the crusade.'[11] The march towards the socialist utopia was an eternal one, with the socialist as the human agent in the quest for a terrestrial reflection of the 'divine life'. It would indeed be the Kingdom of God on earth, based on universal principles of beauty and perfection, with Hardie as its prophet and evangelist proclaiming the glory of the Christ that was to be.[12]

The gaps in Hardie's version of socialism (and his version of medieval history) are obvious to the most casual observer, socialist and non-socialist alike. The economic rationale of socialism as he expounded it was never explored. Indeed, he never had much interest in economic analysis. The main thrust of *From Serfdom to Socialism* is sociological not economic: it stressed the helplessness and dislocation of the working man in the face of corporate capitalism. The bibliography of the book included a bewildering miscellany of socialist and non-socialist writers, including Marx, William Morris, Jaurès, Blatchford, Hyndman,

Ruskin, Kropotkin, Carlyle, Sidney Webb, Ritchie, Hobhouse, Henry George and Ramsay MacDonald. None of these afforded Hardie a clear economic analysis of contemporary capitalism; he himself never attempted to supply one. Marx's name is cited in the text of Hardie's book just once – 'workers of the world unite!' Hardie's various other writings included versions of most of the economic theories popular in his day. He made much use of theories of under-consumption as expounded by J.A. Hobson, the Rev. H.V. Mills and others, to explain the prevalence of poverty. On the other hand, he did not accept the Marxist analysis of the relentless immiseration of the proletarian poor. Social reforms had improved the lot of the worker in Britain and other countries, and this had brought political as well as economic benefits in its train. Socialism could not thrive on the basis of mass pauperism: 'it is the slum vote which the socialist candidate fears most,' Hardie shrewdly remarked.[13] He also made effective use of the current fears of the growth of trusts and cartels, which he regarded as a cause and a symbol of capitalist desperation at home and an aggressive militarism overseas, in the search for cheap raw materials and new foreign markets and areas for investment. But to Hardie, capitalism was a phenomenon that transcended economic analysis, and the socialism he preached was largely independent of it. 'Socialism is not a system of economics.'[14]

Neither did his brand of socialism include any searching examination of the institutional forms that socialism might take. Although he wrote a good deal on contemporary experiments in municipal socialism, he never offered any blueprint, however tentative, of a nationally-organized socialist system. When Fenner Brockway asked him in 1912 to produce a booklet for the *Labour Leader* outlining the specifics of a socialist programme, Hardie failed to do so: he wrote that he preferred to discuss 'fundamentals'. He never put forward any detailed scheme for public ownership, its mechanics, its financing, its forms of administration, the extent to which it would be subjected to democratic or to workers' control. For Hardie, nationalization was a vision not a programme. Neither he nor his Labour colleagues felt it necessary to explain it in any detail. No socialist did until Herbert Morrison evolved his version of public-board corporate socialization in the early 1930s. Nor did Hardie offer explanations, save in the most general terms, of the specific benefits that public ownership would confer in terms of greater efficiency of management, better industrial relations, or an enhanced status and improved rewards for the individual worker, compared with the private ownership of land and industry.

Hardie was always weak on the institutional framework. He repeatedly claimed that he was no adherent of state socialism. He repeatedly criticized the bureaucratic rigidities of the programme conceived by the predominantly Marxist German Social Democrats. He hoped that a state-run system might somehow evolve into 'free Communism' based on the principle of 'from each according to his ability and to each according to his needs'. He claimed to support devolution, both in industry and in the Celtic countries of the United Kingdom, and to be opposed to centralization. Yet the kind of reforms that he advocated — a national programme of development on behalf of the 'right to work'; a new welfare state on behalf of the 'national minimum' and the living wage — would inevitably entail an immense expansion of collectivism, with the resultant expansion of the civil service and of governmental control. Hardie himself warmly welcomed such collectivist developments as had taken place since the 'Tory Democracy' of Disraeli's day, even though he continued to deny his own attachment to 'state socialism'. On the other hand, he was unsympathetic also to doctrines of syndicalism or of workers' control. He condemned this as 'the recrudescence of anarchism in modern form'.[15] In so far as syndicalism encouraged class-consciousness and fostered the growth of mass trade unions, it was beneficial. But if it led to demands for local industrial action as opposed to national political pressure, Hardie was against it. He denied that the state was, in its essence, capitalist or oppressive. In so far as it was capitalist, it was so because the workers refused to exercise the power that had been granted them by the franchise acts and had failed adequately to support the Labour Party. Blind and desperate policies of local strike action could never replace intelligently-conceived political organization. The remedy lay within the workers' own hands. They should use the state, not destroy it. They should seize the power at their disposal by working for the return of a Labour government, not ignore the realities of power by indulging in a series of impulsive gestures of despair. Workers should use the vote as well as the strike. Only thus could solidarity not only be achieved but also made practically effective. Only thus could the coherent class consciousness of which Marx himself had been the prophet be brought to fruition.

In these terms, then, Hardie's socialism was out of sympathy both with the German collectivists and the anarcho-syndicalists who emerged in the Welsh valleys at the time of the 1910 Cambrian strike. He could never really make common cause either with Hyndman or with Morris. Yet neither did he entirely reject them. On the contrary, he often argued that any manifestation of socialist or working-class consciousness was desirable in pushing the cause forward. Since there was no ultimate blueprint of socialism, no finite form that the socialist society might assume, all the varied approaches put forward within the British Labour movement – the gradualism of the Fabians, the Marxism of the SDF, the 'Free Communism' (as Hardie termed it) of the Socialist League, the syndicalism of the Plebs League, all had their value. They all played their part in rousing the worker from apathy or despair and in transforming the climate of political debate. All the varied programmes comprehended within the socialist world in Britain could make their contribution to the socialist commonwealth that would one day emerge.

In all these respects, Hardie's philosophy was imprecise and ill-formed. It was flexible, almost at times to the point of disintegration. He too often took refuge, when declaiming against the corruption and exploitation of modern capitalism, in sentimental accounts of pre-industrial man, of sunshine and of hillsides, of lambkins gambolling in the spring time as portents of the new Jerusalem. His socialism was shot through with utopianism, sometimes with mysticism. Socialism meant a time 'when all the people shall be employed as Comrades in providing for every human need and increasing the sum total of human happiness' (*The Red Dragon and the Red Flag*). Yet however unsatisfying to the cloistered academic, all this was very far from being meaningless. On the contrary several points emerged in the application of Hardie's ideas which serve to explain his powerful influence on the public mind during the Edwardian era.

First, Hardie was always insistent that socialism did not rule out, and was not superseded by, the advance of social reform. After all in Germany social reforms had been extensive, yet it was there that the socialist movement had made most headway. He reacted totally against the 'everlasting negative' preached by the majority of the German SPD who, because of their utter certainty that socialism would come in the fullness of time, chose to abstain from effective political activity in the here-and-now.[16] Hardie was always sympathetic to Bernstein, and the socialists in Southern Germany, notably Baden-Baden and Wurttemberg, in their interpretation of the socialist cause. In his politics, as in his religion, he was a Revisionist, a 'Morisonian' among socialists. He argued that doctrinal rigidity was appropriate only for a sect – Calvinist or Marxist as the case might be. For a mass movement which aimed to win growing support from working-class voters, revisionism was the only practical policy. It should persuade, propagandize and permeate – and it should also seize all practical opportunities of pushing on with socialist policies from wheresoever they derived. Thus Hardie was quite impenitent in supporting Gerald Balfour and the Unionist Government in their Unemployed Workmen's Bill of 1905, just as he never believed that a modest extension of the franchise to women ruled out the prospect of a wider reform. Progressive social reform directly advanced the cause of socialism, by affecting the climate of public debate and by opening up new issues previously neglected. The Unemployed Workmen's Bill had led, Hardie argued, to a wider examination of the principle of the right to work, and of a nation-wide attack on unemployment and short time in a systematic manner.[17] It had clearly demonstrated the inadequacies of charity and of voluntary effort. The fact that this had penetrated the mind of one so conservative as Walter Long was in itself a dramatic portent. Similarly the arguments over a minimum wage for the coalminers opened up discussions about wages policy generally. But an essential condition was that reforms of this kind should serve towards the liberation of the worker and not impose additional burdens on him. Hardie was, therefore, a fierce critic of Lloyd George's National Insurance Bill in 1911 which aimed to raise contributions through the poll tax method, against which the peasants had rebelled as long ago as 1381. But in general Hardie warmly endorsed the social reforms of the Edwardian era, especially those introduced by the Liberals after 1908. Despite his distrust of Lloyd George, he accepted his 'People's Budget' as partly socialist in intent.[18] He particularly welcomed its severe taxation of land values for which he himself had called during the Mid-Lanark by-election. Indeed, he argued that it was the very existence of the Labour Party which had brought issues like Old Age Pensions, National Development, labour exchanges and health and unemployment insurance to the forefront and made them acceptable. Hardie's socialism, then, was an outward-looking affair. The pursuit of maximum socialism did not rule out the acceptance of minimum socialism. In particular, the extension of socialism at the municipal level was the precursor of a national socialist policy. Such developments as municipal banking and local insurance services could serve as case studies for the appropriation of capital and credit by the community as a whole. Social reform was valuable in itself in alleviating the dismal lot of the industrial and agricultural worker. It also hastened on the socialist state which the Labour Party would bring about.

Just as Hardie was pragmatic in the policies he supported, so he was flexible in the allies he enlisted. In the Labour movement he believed the essential strength lay in the broad-ranging alliance which the LRC had originally created. It had now drawn in the vast mass of organized workers: the last major union still to affiliate, the Miners' Federation of Great Britain, finally agreed to join the Labour Party in 1908. Through this alliance social issues had been pushed steadily to the forefront. Yet this had been done in a tolerant, flexible manner. Trade unionists had been approached on their own terms, in working for specific practical reforms like an Eight Hour Day. The very exercise of working on behalf of common objectives would bring socialists and trade unionists closer together. The vital need was to keep the cause of the working class in the forefront: socialism would follow in the fullness of time. Attempts to produce a rigid structure at the local level, to exclude non-socialists for instance, as proposed in the new Socialist Representation Committees championed by the SDF in 1908, were doomed to failure. It was in tolerant alliance with free play existing between all its elements, that the British Labour movement would march forward. Alliance (*ralliement*) was equally the basis of the growth of the French socialists under Jaurès's wise leadership. The ILP itself was a coalition which contained an immense range of opinion. 'A broad, tolerant catholicity has always been a leading characteristic of the ILP. It has never had a hard and dry creed of membership.'[19] It had never expelled anyone. It was this catholicity that had enabled the ILP to play the central role it had done in the formation of the Labour Party. One major point, on which Hardie laid constant emphasis, was that the ILP existed for the working class, but was far from exclusively of the working class. On the contrary, one of its major sources of strength was that it enabled middle-class and working-class socialists to work together. The ILP sought to 'blend the classes into one human family'.[20] Even aristocratic eccentrics like the Countess of Warwick were enthusiastically hailed as recruits for the cause. A powerful middle-class element in the party would give its arguments intellectual force. It might have 'more of the spirit of rebellion in its bones' than would working men, who were too liable to get bogged down in petty details about wages and hours.[21] The labour movement would offer an arena for idealistic professionals or business men. It offered the rich man or woman (a Fels, a Cadbury or a Miss Kippen perhaps) an opportunity to expiate his or her acquisitiveness in the joy of useful service for his poorer neighbour. Hardie argued consistently, at Labour Party conferences, against imposing narrow class or dogmatic conditions upon Labour candidates. He saw the need for party discipline – Victor Grayson's behaviour in the Commons showed how party morale could be undermined by one erratic and unpredictable rebel. But, provided a candidate had risen up through one of the many affiliated organizations comprehended within the Labour Party, free play and tolerance should be the official attitude towards him. As time went on Hardie's appeal for a wide-ranging and broad-based Labour alliance came under fire. He was attacked in the years before the first world war for debasing the working-class character of the ILP: more and more, its executive members and leading representatives were drawn from journalism and similar professional backgrounds. On the other hand, Hardie's vision of the ILP enabled it to provide a unique vehicle for the middle-class radical. Men like R.C.K. Ensor, H.W. Nevinson, H.N. Brailsford and J.A. Hobson, like many other intellectuals of the period, eventually found activity in the ILP the only effective avenue open to them in pushing on socialist policies in a practical sense, and this lent dignity and intellectual force to the Labour Party as it met the Liberals in open challenge.

Hardie was, then, an apostle of the widest feasible range of working-class, socialist and radical collaboration – an advocate of unity. But he did not endorse a unity that was bought too dearly. The French socialists, he thought in 1912 were being wagged by the syndicalist tail and being forced away from the flexible radical-socialist creed which had made them a parliamentary force under Jaurès.[22] Unity with the broad mass of organized workers was essential for an effective socialist movement. Fusion with a doctrinaire, sectarian minority, 'philosophic, abstract and dogmatic', especially one committed to policies other than a gradualist capture of political power, should be eschewed at all costs. He fought relentlessly against the SDF concept of 'socialist unity'. He viewed the efforts by Hyndman's supporters (now re-christened as the British Socialist Party) to re-affiliate with the Labour Party in 1913–14 with a stern and sceptical eye. Hardie was prepared to address joint meetings with Hyndman or Quelch. But when the BSP finally entered the Labour Party briefly in 1916, after Hardie's death, it was on the basis of that flexible Labour alliance which the SDF had always rejected and of which Hardie himself had been the outstanding advocate.

Hardie's ultimate contribution to British socialist attitudes was to ensure that its tactics and its philosophy were such that it was always acceptable within a native British framework. He sought to make the ILP a gradualist movement, representative of the main streams of late nineteenth-century radical thought. Its programme in 1893 was in large measure an inheritance from advanced Liberalism over the previous forty years. Hardie himself traced its descent back to Bright and Cobden, to the radicals of the French revolutionary era, back to the liberty tree handed down and cherished since the civil upheavals of the seventeenth century.[23] The British labour movement to Hardie was rooted in a specific society at a specific period in its national development. The extent to which socialist or radical movements abroad could provide useful precepts or doctrines was limited, however much European or Imperial socialist parties might collaborate on behalf of pacifism, anti-colonialism or other particular themes. In Britain itself, the Labour alliance, as Hardie saw it, always left bridges open to radical and trade union sympathizers.[24] He warned against Labour alienating Liberal supporters by indulging in gratuitous anti-clericalism on the lines of socialists in France, Italy and elsewhere. He welcomed the practical association of the ILP with radical backbenchers in pushing for meals for school-children, the taxing of land values, the campaign for housing reform, the enfranchisement of women, the crusade against militarism. Socialism in the future, the abolition of all private property and the organization of industry on the basis of production for use rather than for profit – all these did not eliminate the necessity for fighting for a more just society here and now, and trying to modify and humanize capitalism as long as it existed. The Labour Party was independent, but independence did not mean isolation and the frustrated impotence that followed from it.

In this way Hardie's vision of the Labour Party enabled it to expand. While he preached socialism, its character was so ill-defined and its establishment placed so far in an indeterminate future, that it presented no serious obstacle to practical co-operation with radicals of other parties, and of none on behalf of day-to-day progressive reforms. Hardie did not see his version of socialism as being in a distinct ideological compartment of its own. It was not rigidly detached from the aspirations of Liberal collectivists of the Hobson/Hobhouse schools. It was part of a wider movement of reform which Hardie claimed to see as an inevitable process as capitalism slowly reached a point of crisis, in which the ethic of co-operation (most powerfully symbolized by the Labour Party) replaced that of competition. Hardie saw the same phenomenon in the United States, where the humanitarian reform of middle-class urban Progressives lent momentum to the growth of the Socialist Party under the leadership of Debs. In the same way, Hardie, abused as he so often was as a bigoted, doctrinaire extremist who rejected all ties with other parties and as an isolated outsider in public life, became himself a symbol of the Progressive alliance in Britain. Certainly he ran on this basis at Merthyr Tydfil and previously at West Ham, despite his scorching attacks on the Liberal party leadership. He attracted thousands of natural Liberal votes as a result. Hardie in practice found himself aligned on the left flank of a broad radical alliance ranged behind the social policies of the Liberal Cabinet against the special interests of privileged interest groups like the peers, the clerics, the brewers, the landlords and the protectionists. The natural consequence was the MacDonald-Gladstone *entente* of 1903 and the kind of unofficial local electoral arrangements from which Hardie himself, Snowden, MacDonald and most other Labour leaders benefited. When militant ILP radicals like Fred Jowett at the annual conference of the party at Merthyr in 1912 proposed a severely class-orientated policy, one which judged issues in terms of Marxist orthodoxy and of the classless society of the distant future instead of looking at the contemporary scene in a pragmatic manner, Hardie was amongst those who voted them down.[25]

Hardie's socialism was never hedged around by rigid dogma. It was compatible with almost all of the New Liberalism of Lloyd George,

Masterman and their supporters in the press. It was compatible equally with the Old Liberalism of the chapels and of the struggle for democracy and for civic and religious equality. Hardie's rhetoric of socialism had heavy populist overtones which made it the more acceptable to Liberals. It concentrated more on the operation and manipulation of power than on its economic base. It assailed the capitalists rather than the capitalist system, the imperialists rather than the structure of empire. Hardie, contrary to his own avowals, actually made war on a class rather than on a system. The capitalist oppressor always had a name and address. He could always be rooted out, as Hardie smoked out Lord Overtoun, the Dowlais stockholders and many others. All this fitted in well enough with the individualistic radicalism of a much older generation, from which Hardie himself had sprung. Hardie's own abiding attachment to themes such as temperance reform and Celtic nationalism showed how enduring were the links that bound him to the Liberalism of his twenties and thirties. His socialism was in reality a radical-socialism of a singularly malleable kind. Like the American Populists, he thought that the cure for capitalist democracy was social democracy: popular involvement would overcome 'the money power'. The people would prevail. Hardie's socialism was never dominated by the one overriding objective of the public ownership of the means of production, distribution and exchange. Indeed to Hardie, absorbed as he was with the thousands of cases of actual injustice that afflicted the workers and the women at home and colonized races overseas, the long-term objective of a socialist commonwealth receded in importance. It was a symbol of faith, but not much more. It was this flexibility that enabled him to appeal to radical reformers far beyond his base in the ILP, and which helped to build the Labour Party's foundations in a wide range of constituencies. In Lenin's eyes Hardie's outlook was contemptible, the very epitome of 'opportunism', more damaging even than the evasions of the Mensheviks. To many British radicals, however, Hardie's opportunism amounted to simple common-sense.

Hardie's radical-socialism, then, fitted naturally into ideas of a Progressive alliance and of class collaboration. But there was always the essential qualification that the Labour Party must be an independent entity within it. Hardie's socialist theory, in its more detailed applications, was always geared to building up the party in practical terms. The Labour Party was a secular church. Theology was unimportant: the first aim was to assemble a viable congregation and keep it intact. Hardie's vague vision of founding 'Christ's Kingdom on Earth' with Jesus, the working-class son of Joseph the Carpenter, as 'the elder brother and the Great Comrade', was inspirational.[26] It fired the imagination of thousands of working men of nonconformist background caught up in the economic depression and the class warfare of the late Victorian and Edwardian eras. But the vision was subordinate to the reality of creating a self-conscious party of the workers and their middle-class sympathizers. Hardie's theory of politics, unlike that of many socialist ideologues long since forgotten, was always devoted to immediate short-term objectives. This later won applause in unlikely quarters. In 1924 the Communist Party of Great Britain praised Hardie for his dismissal of the Marxist theoreticians of his day and his concentration on the practical realities of the working-class struggle.[27] Hardie's views contained a logical force more durable than the elaborate 'permeative' collectivism of the Fabians, totally detached as they were from the trade unions whose history they studied. At the LRC's inaugural meeting at the Memorial Hall in February 1900, Hardie's political theory, however crude, stood the test of a crisis in the forging of a Labour alliance, while the Fabians' prescriptions, however articulately expressed by their well-educated advocates, proved empty and unreal. Its justification came after 1918 when the Labour Party became the leading social democratic party in the world, whereas the more theoretical socialist movements of western and central Europe crumbled in the face of the Communist challenge. It was a proud vindication of Hardie's belief, conveyed to Bernard Shaw in 1912, that the power of statesmanship could just as easily be detected in the common sense of the common man, as it could in the academic subtleties of the educated classes.[28] Hardie's theories, however limited in their intellectual content, however erratically and intuitively expounded by the man himself, were sensitively attuned to the real problems confronting labour in early twentieth-century Britain. As Marx had prescribed, they recognized the force of historic necessity – in a way that the theories of British Marxists seldom did. For Hardie as for Edouard Bernstein the means superseded the end. The goal was nothing. The Labour movement was everything. In this and in the monuments he left behind him, Hardie's supreme vindication as a political theorist ultimately rests.

XI Freelance Radical (1908–11)

Hardie returned from his world tour on 5 April 1908 to a spectacular Labour reception on the quayside at Plymouth. A mass public meeting was convened at the Albert Hall: Shackleton and Henderson were foremost amongst the speakers welcoming home 'Labour's Grand Old Man' (actually aged fifty-one at this time). Hardie himself replied with stirring declarations on behalf of world-wide fraternity. He enlivened his speech with cries of 'Bande Mataram', the freedom chant of the Indian Congress movement, which was enthusiastically taken up by the audience.[1] But behind this public display of comradeship, the Labour Party was lapsing into its frequent state of indecision, deadlock and internecine warfare. There had been some reluctance to welcome Hardie back in so demonstrative fashion, now that he occupied no formal position of authority in the party. Frank Smith had written around to whip up support for a public reception for 'our Keir' after his international adventures and had secured the somewhat reluctant agreement of Glasier. He tried to get MacDonald to join him in the reception party at Plymouth. 'It would be appreciated both by Hardie & the movement, and would have a fine effect for unity and friendliness all round. You and I do not think much about receptions but we have not made all men in our own image.' MacDonald, however, was suspicious and envious. His own overseas tour two years earlier had not met with any similar rejoicing and he resented Hardie's flair for publicity. 'Frank Smith has become a kind of advance agent for a show, and Fels is supplying the cash for the circus business.' He also resented Hardie's appropriation, as his own creation, of his own memorandum on Labour colonial policy presented to the Party's national executive.[2] Hardie's departure for a further Canadian and American tour at the end of August, shortly after his return from the world tour, again with massive publicity trained on his doings, stirred bitter animosity in MacDonald's heart. 'The showman business is one of my most deep seated antipathies. Genuine recognition of work done is one thing – it is a sweetening thing. A secretary paid to arrange cheers is a damned different thing, and try as I may to laugh at it, one day I will sneer at it in public and then –.' Glasier replied sympathetically, and also condemned Hardie's fondness for 'the stage management business'. 'From the beginning Hardie's great weakness has lain there and long ago I had to make up my [mind] that I must accept him with his defects or not at all. I have to take him in the lump, and he is so great as an agitator that I take his vanity as a necessary by-product of his finer self.' Glasier added soothingly that he appreciated that Hardie had not been generous or just in 'sharing the honour of the work of the party with you and others'.[3] There was, obviously, a considerable element of personal rivalry between Hardie and MacDonald, who, as agitator and organizer-theorist respectively, symbolized different facets of the soul of British socialism. But the episode reflected Hardie's curiously detached position in the party, a combination of his historical stature in the movement and his new zeal for all-purpose populist propaganda which made him difficult to fit into the orthodox structure of a political party.

In any case, the Labour Party was now in one of its frequent moods of despondency and destructive self-criticism. During Hardie's absence the party's lack of fight, and difficulty in establishing a position distinct from that of the Liberals had become increasingly apparent. Hardie's return and the belligerent postures he so naturally struck on a variety of foreign and domestic issues, illustrated for many the lack of fire shown by the party since his resignation of the chairmanship. He had been replaced by Arthur Henderson, but this had not been a success. On the contrary, under Henderson's leadership the Labour Party seemed merely to offer mute encouragement from the wings to the increasingly radical policies being adopted by the Liberal government. This was especially marked after April 1908 when Asquith became Prime Minister and Lloyd George, a radical, dynamic Chancellor of the Exchequer of a new and unfamiliar kind. In these circumstances Henderson's lack of militancy became all the more obvious. 'Henderson is not popular. He is reckoned – perhaps quite unjustly – as playing the Liberal game. Were he to resign and the rupture end there, I have no doubt that the feeling in our movement would be one of relief.' Glasier, writing to MacDonald, went on to criticize Henderson's 'seeming camaraderie with the Liberals'. 'His eternal appearances on Temperance and Methodist platforms and the absence of a single proclamation from him of a leadership order gives countenance to those miserable hints and accusations in the *Dispatch* and elsewhere that the party is becoming merely a Liberal tail.'[4] Henderson's inability to inspire the parliamentary party was irksome for MacDonald himself, restless as he was for the leadership. The party's failure to influence the Trade Boards Bill of 1909 over minimum wage rates was severely criticized. Henderson eventually retired as party chairman for the 1910 session, in favour of George Barnes. Meanwhile Labour's failure to make any more headway in by-elections – indeed its virtual total refusal to contest seats against the Liberals anywhere, despite the encouragement afforded by Jarrow and (more dubiously) Colne Valley in 1907 – appeared to confirm that Hardie's fighting party of working-class activists had turned into Mr Asquith's poodle.

Hardie was especially critical of the Labour Party's lack of fight and independence. The affiliation of the miners seemed to him likely to reinforce the 'Lib-Lab' tendencies in the party. On his return from his world tour, therefore, he sought to inject new vigour into a party which Henderson and the others had apparently lulled into conformity and quiescence. He spoke frequently in the House; his speeches on India, South Africa and the peril of militarism lent a new spark of life to Labour's debating performance. 'More like the great Keir of ILP meetings than the House ever had an opportunity of seeing,' as J.H. Harley wrote in the *Labour Leader*.[5] He also tried to carve out new positions which might contrast the passivity of the 1907 and 1908 sessions with the new life which he hoped to instil into his colleagues. As before he was militant in raising the position of the suffragettes, despite the criticism that his attachment to the Pankhursts, mother and daughter, had received and continued to attract. He now upheld in the press the WSPU's tactics of demanding votes for women on the same terms as those enjoyed by men. He was also active behind the scenes in pressing for the release of Christabel Pankhurst, now lodged in Holloway prison, and in urging that reading matter be allowed in for her by the governor. In 1909 he joined a deputation to the Home Secretary, Herbert Gladstone, one which also included Liberals like C.P. Scott, Sir Arthur Ponsonby and Ellis Jones Griffith, and demanded an inquiry into the conditions of suffragettes detained in gaol.[6] The forcible feeding instituted under the 'Cat and Mouse Act' roused Hardie to a new fury on behalf of women's equality.

On the other hand he was realist enough to sense that women's rights were a double-edged weapon with which to revive the Labour Party, particularly in view of the disruptive political tactics of the WSPU itself. The Labour Party was deriving little direct benefit from its involvement with the suffragette cause. Episodes such as Winston Churchill's by-election defeat at North-West Manchester in April 1908 suggested that it was the Unionists who were reaping the dividends from the suffragettes' tactics of all-out war on the Liberal government. Hardie disputed the suffragettes' claim to have been the cause of Churchill's defeat. He argued that it was rather the transfer of five hundred Catholic votes to the Unionists, because of Catholic hostility to the Liberals over the church schools issue, that lay behind the government's electoral setback. But he was forced to deplore the 'lack of definite point' in the women's tactics. 'To the average elector, the cry "Keep the Liberals out" is meaningless.'[7] He still felt (or wrote) that 'Socialism gains largely from their work . . . and propaganda' and hoped for a continued close liaison between the Women's Union and the ILP. He and Snowden continued to agitate on behalf of the women's grievances in the House. Even so there can be detected a gradual withdrawal by Hardie from his prime involvement in the women's cause as shown in the 1906 session before his world tour. He now feared that Mrs Pankhurst's Ishmaelite tactics might lead to the WSPU becoming to the women's movement 'what the SDF has been to socialism' – a small, sectarian, disruptive rump. Indeed suffragettes like Mrs Despard and Emmeline Pethwick-Lawrence were becoming alienated by the WSPU's militancy. Hardie himself was much embarrassed in October 1908 by the action of his private secretary and virtual housekeeper, Mrs Margaret Travers Symons, the daughter of a Welsh architect whose husband was a sheep farmer in New Zealand. She used her position as the private secretary of an MP to interrupt the debate in the House with cries of 'Votes for Women'. The Speaker then took steps to exclude her from the House, and the ban lasted for almost two years.[8] This had dire results for Hardie's private correspondence, always haphazardly dealt with quite apart from crises of this kind. Mrs Symons retained her close connection with Hardie. She acted as his secretary at Nevills Court despite the ban imposed on her in the precincts of Westminster and was also active in the City of London branch of the ILP, which Hardie joined and which occasionally held meetings at his flat.[9] Even so, Mrs Symons's growing militancy was an embarrassment to him, especially when she was convicted, along with other suffragettes, for obstruction during a stone-throwing demonstration in December 1911. If Hardie was to revitalize the Labour Party, the women's cause was unlikely to be the way to do it.

A much better proposition was the revival of the agitation for the relief of unemployment in the autumn of 1908. The Labour Party had introduced its Right to Work Bill in 1907. It was largely based on Hardie's schemes as put forward since 1892, with a central co-ordinating committee and afforced local committees to promote local public works, land colonies and similar enterprises. As before, the financing of these schemes was left imprecise. Hardie, on his return from the United States in October 1908, threw himself into the fray with his accustomed belligerence. He resumed his public harassment of John Burns, still immovable at the Local Government board. 'K.H. bitter, wild and inaccurate' commented Burns in October 1908 after a debate in which a Labour amendment was heavily defeated.[10] Hardie wrote several forceful articles in which he urged the Labour Party to make unemployment, especially in London, its main target. This was socially desirable in itself: he argued in the Commons that the proportion of skilled artisans out of employment was at least fifteen per cent. In addition, the unemployment agitation would enable the ranks of labour to be closed and would help on the process of converting the affiliated trade union organizations to socialism.[11] As usual Hardie, with the inevitable assistance of Frank Smith, pursued a largely independent course. He took part again in joint activity with the suspect SDF. He served on a Joint London Right to Work Committee with a Social Democrat, E.C. Fairchild, as its chairman; he appeared once again as a symbol of the 'socialist unity' against which he had repeatedly argued. On 8 December 1908 he introduced a two-tier bill to amend the Unemployed Workmen's Act of 1905.[12] It would have enabled local authorities to pay wages from the rates – at trade union rates – and it would allow local distress committees to collect statistics on local employment and to set up labour bureaux.

All this was Hardie at his best in many ways – his genius for agitation lending momentum and force to his human compassion for the thousands of men made unemployed by the trade recession of 1907–8. Hardie's campaign reinforced the urgency with which Lloyd George and Churchill turned to framing new long-term schemes for national development, labour exchanges, and health and unemployment insurance in that dramatic winter of 1908–9. It gave the Labour Party spirit and a distinctive cause after a year of inertia. But not many of the Labour leaders responded to Hardie's stimulus in the spirit intended. MacDonald remained incurably suspicious. 'To make the suffering of these poor men and women the raw material for mere party coin seems to me to be the most harmful departure from good feeling that is possible.'[13] He continued to distrust Hardie's showmanship especially when it led him into the perilous policy of co-operation with the Social Democrats. Even Joseph Fels began to draw back from the more collectivist and confiscatory policies Hardie advocated and turned instead to promoting Henry George's old panacea of a single tax on land.[14] The whole affair seemed to confirm Hardie's role as an incorrigible individualist. It was a view that he himself shared. Writing to Glasier in melancholy mood at the end of the year (27 December 1908) he commented:

Of this I am quite certain, that I could be of more real service to the cause were I not in parliament. . . . I suppose that we are in for another year of Henderson's chairmanship, which means that reaction and timidity will be in the ascendancy with disastrous effects to our side of the movement in the country.

He took little pleasure in the recent affiliation of the miners to the Labour Party:

The annual conferences will be controlled by coal and cotton, and, unless we can stir up the miners a bit and get them to send Socialist delegates, that means more reaction. There are times when I confess to feeling sore at seeing the fruits of our years of toil being garnered by men who were never of us, and who even now would trick us out gin they daur.[15]

Even the resumed offensive over unemployment, then, failed to restore a sense of unity or of identity between Hardie and the struggling Labour Party.

His efforts to give the Labour Party a new lease of vitality were in any event rudely disturbed by another unpleasant crisis in the ILP at this time. In some ways this caused him as much personal pain as did the *Labour Leader* controversy five years earlier. There had been growing dissidence from rank-and-file members throughout 1907 and 1908, focussing on the lack of militancy shown by the NAC and its lack of apparent or immediate success in converting the Labour Party to a more socialist policy. Attempts by the NAC to tighten up the rules governing the selection of ILP parliamentary candidates, in order to conform more closely with the Labour Party constitution, made matters worse by making the central executive, headed by dominant figures like Hardie, MacDonald and Snowden, appear dictatorial in character. It was well known that the NAC had recommended running only a limited number of candidates in the next general election — perhaps only twenty or twenty-five if the committee's recommendation were observed by local branches. But at the grass-roots disaffection was widespread amongst socialist zealots. And at last, for the first time in the history of the party since it was founded at Bradford in 1893, the rebels had found a credible leader in Victor Grayson, the new popular hero after his spectacular by-election triumph at Colne Valley in 1907.[16] From the outset he had been an immensely difficult parliamentary colleague, as MacDonald repeatedly complained. A delicate meeting of MacDonald with the Colne Valley Labour League did not clear the air entirely. But the local party workers in Colne Valley were at least approachable. Grayson himself was intractable. He made it clear from his arrival in the House that he would follow his own course and ignore attempts by the Labour whips to impose discipline on him. He refused to sign the party constitution. He made his own unscheduled interruptions in debate against the orders of the party leaders: for instance, he made a violent attack on the Liberal government for wasting time with a Licensing Bill (Grayson himself was no friend of the temperance cause) at a time of mass unemployment. Outside the House he made repeated attacks on the Labour Party leaders as conformists and crypto-Liberals. He led the ILP grass-roots members in denouncing the Labour Party's refusal to fight for socialism and its subservience to the trade unions. At the ILP annual conference at Huddersfield in April 1908 a motion to refer the executive report back to the NAC, moved by Grayson's supporters, and sponsored by such respectable members of the party as R.C.K. Ensor, was narrowly defeated. It was followed by a demand by the York branch of the ILP that a special conference be convened to consider the ILP's policy at by-elections and to re-examine the wider question of the ILP's affiliation to the Labour Party. With the currents of revolt sweeping through the ILP, Hardie's cherished Labour alliance was under severe strain within the party which he himself had created.

Ironically, it was Hardie himself who provoked the final crisis with Grayson. As has been seen, he had defied the Labour Party's orders and sent a message of support to Grayson during the Colne Valley by-election. He also made conciliatory gestures towards Grayson during the 1908 ILP conference and successfully proposed that he join the parliamentary Labour Party without signing the party's constitution, a compromise which Grayson himself accepted. Even so, Grayson's style of socialism was basically repugnant to Hardie. Grayson seemed to symbolize the kind of free-floating middle-class philistine who most alienated the cautious, modest members of the trade unions. His wild rhetoric, his well-known penchant for high living, his contempt for the cause of temperance offended Hardie's nonconformist ethic. In addition, he distrusted Grayson's growing friendship with his enemy, Robert Blatchford, now engaged in whipping up a nationalist hysteria about the threat of the German navy at a time when Hardie himself was endeavouring to make the international peace movement the more effective. An alliance seemed to be developing between Blatchford, Hyndman and Grayson, espousing nationalist socialism of a dangerously militarist kind. Blatchford himself attacked Hardie's suspicion of Grayson. He wrote of Hardie at this time: 'He is of the old Cromwellian type: his opponents are always "malignants". He is incapable of imagining such a person as an honourable soldier, sailor, or Tory.'[17] The vehement anti-German phobia being whipped up in the *Clarion* and *Justice* reinforced Hardie's distaste for Grayson and his new allies. The climax came at an intended 'socialist unity' meeting at Holborn Town Hall in November 1908. Grayson refused to appear with Hardie at this demonstration and made a bitter attack on the *Labour Leader*.[18] For members of the ILP, whatever their reservations about Hardie, this caused a major crisis. Grayson seemed to personify youthful rebellion by middle-class militants against the old guard, represented by Hardie, MacDonald, Snowden and Glasier. A generational conflict

was under way which threatened to divide the ILP more fundamentally than ever in its history.

As the ILP annual conference at Edinburgh in April 1909
approached, there seemed every indication of a schism as a result of
Grayson's disruption. Whatever their other differences, Hardie,
MacDonald and Snowden were united in their determination to resist
Grayson and his followers. MacDonald felt that the 'movement is more
shaken at the moment, than it has been for a long time, and the trouble
is that it is an internal rent and not an external blow that is the source
of our weakness'. He turned gloomily to contemplate a head-on clash
with 'the sons and daughters of anarchy' at the annual conference,
although he did suggest reforms such as placing more responsibility on
local ILP federations and reducing the centralized control of the
NAC.[19] Glasier was persuaded to hang on to the editorship of the
Leader, about which there had been much criticism from Grayson
supporters. He joined in deploring Grayson's showmanship: it had led
the latter to take part in a demonstration against the procession to the
Lords at the opening of the 1909 session of parliament – a demonstration from which Hardie kept aloof.[20] Snowden, somewhat more
inclined to reserve his position than were the others, decided to stay on
the NAC to combat over-militant local branches. As for Hardie, he
was initially shaken and dispirited by his conflicts with the Grayson
element; nothing was closer to his heart than the ILP and internal
dissension was intensely depressing to him. Nevertheless he took the
fight to the opposition, as was his wont. He attacked the activities of
the Clarion Fellowship (through which Blatchford was promoting
Grayson's cause) and urged ILP members to hand back their membership badges.[21] He took every opportunity afforded by the ILP press to
justify the parliamentary policy of the Labour Party, lately evinced in
the pressure for a Right to Work measure and the Miners' Eight
Hours' Bill. He denounced Grayson and Blatchford's tactics as
anarchistic gestures of self-indulgence which did little to help the
working class in practical terms. The climax inevitably came at the
Edinburgh annual conference in April, hailed by Hardie in advance,
ironically enough, as 'our merry meeting'.[22] He won here a major
triumph over Grayson on the issue of whether the latter's parliamentary salary should be paid even though he had refused to sign the
Labour Party constitution. He bitterly denounced the self-importance

which had led Grayson to cut himself off from the mass of the working-class movement. This was carried overwhelmingly, by 332 to 64. But a separate amendment by Grayson that the reference to his refusal to attend the Holborn Town Hall meeting with Hardie be deleted was unexpectedly carried by 217 votes to 194, with delegates as diverse as Jim Larkin, the Irish syndicalist, and R.C.K. Ensor, the leader-writer on the *Manchester Guardian*, speaking in support. The Old Guard of the ILP had been humiliatingly rebuffed.

That evening MacDonald, Hardie and Glasier agreed to resign from the NAC on which they had served for so many years – Hardie, indeed, from the very inauguration of the party sixteen years earlier. Shortly afterwards Snowden agreed to join them and MacDonald announced their decision to a stunned conference the next day. Glasier wrote: 'We all feel that the ILP fails to grasp the position, and that a strong stand is needed': he also resigned from the editorship of the *Leader*.[23] In vain did Ensor pass a resolution, carried by 249 votes to 110, that the committee members who had resigned be reinstated. In an open letter in the *Labour Leader* the four ex-committee members showed that they were adamant.[24] They denounced Grayson for wishing to expel the trade unions from the Labour Party and for making damaging criticisms of the work of the party in the House of Commons. They powerfully vindicated the parliamentary method and the gradualist evolutionary route to socialism espoused by the ILP since its foundation. The ILP thus found itself bereft of its dominant personalities, and lesser figures such as Russell Smart and Ben Riley strove to repair the damage. The NAC soon found itself much embarrassed by its apparent indirect commitment to Grayson. The ILP's membership and subscriptions now declined: in 1909–11 over forty branches disappeared. By 30 September 1909 the NAC was sternly rebuking Grayson for a vicious personal attack on the Labour member for Stockport, G.H. Wardle. It also passed on to Grayson and the Colne Valley ILP critical comments on his poor attendance record at the House.[25] The Victor Grayson bubble, in fact, soon burst. In January 1910 he was defeated at the polls; thereafter, he cut his links with the Labour Party entirely. Rebuffed by the ILP, he joined with Blatchford in creating a new British Socialist Party, with a heavily nationalistic aura. It finally came into being in May 1912. Grayson explained that it would seek university-trained recruits as an 'aristocracy of intellect' and would steer clear of the trade unions.[26] Soon after he vanished from the British political scene, his youthful vigour already severely undermined by alcohol. He mysteriously disappeared and later migrated to Australia and New Zealand. His meteor died away as abruptly as it had emerged. But if Grayson disappeared, the rift he created lingered on. For Hardie, it was especially serious. Not for two more years did he consent to serve on the NAC: his links with the ILP were severely shaken. He did make a brief attendance in November 1909 at the NAC to explain the details of the bequest made by the Misses Kippen.[27] He remained the inevitable party choice as fraternal delegate at international congresses. He remained a member of the local City of London branch (which supported him during the Grayson crisis). Nevertheless the ILP, his basic platform for the propagation of socialism for the past fifteen years, was now tangential to his career. He was temporarily as detached from his own movement as he was from the Labour Party more generally. His pamphlet, *The I.L.P. and All About It*, included an angry attack on 'the small knot of malcontents' at the Edinburgh conference. More and more he appeared a disillusioned and prematurely ageing man. Glasier mused in July 1909 about the prospect of a MacDonald cabinet in the future, on the model of Briand, the new radical-socialist premier in France. 'I hardly think Hardie will live to see that day and if he does I doubt if he would be asked to form a Cabinet or, if asked, consent to do so. Yet Hardie like all of us now realizes that the road to Socialism is going to be a slow and matter of fact one.'[28]

In the 1909 session the relations of Labour to the Liberal Party reached a critical stage. Lloyd George's 'people's budget', which the Labour Party strongly endorsed under its new chairman, George Barnes, was thrown out by the Lords on 30 November. Asquith promptly dissolved parliament and a new general election was called for January. It was inevitable that the Labour Party should now appear simply as a left-wing appendage in a progressive alliance. The new orientation of government policy, heralded by Lloyd George's reforming policy as Chancellor, blurred still further the distinction between Liberal and Labour policies. In any case the Labour Party was even more dependent on Liberal goodwill since the judgement in the Osborne case in the high court in 1908 had thrown into question the legality of the political levy by which trade unions supported Labour candidates. Hardie himself was a trenchant critic of Justice Fletcher Moulton's verdict in the high court.[29] He pointed out that the political levy was merely the logical conclusion of the legalization of trade unions and that Lord James had exposed the unsoundness of the judicial verdict. Even so, elementary realism compelled Hardie to recognize that the Liberal alliance was still the inevitable course for Labour to follow. He took part in demonstrations on behalf of the land clauses of the budget. He himself dined with Lloyd George, to whom his attitude continued to be ambivalent, some time in July 1909. The Chancellor confided that he was dependent on Labour support for carrying through the budget. 'Hardie asks me', Glasier wrote (18 July 1909), 'if I would approve the Labour Party issuing a manifesto in support of Liberals where no Labour candidates were in the field, in the event of a dissolution. I assure him I would heartily support the proposal.'[30] Hardie was also involved in secret negotiations with some of his fellow Welsh members in November about possible electoral deals in South Wales. D.A. Thomas was to move to the Cardiff seat, Sir Samuel Evans to join Hardie at Merthyr, thus leaving Vernon Hartshorn, a miners' agent active in the Mid-Glamorgan ILP, free to win Mid-Glamorgan in succession to Evans. While Hardie refused to enter into any formal pact, he did acknowledge that 'this is so far as I'm concerned quite a satisfactory arrangement. If we just keep firm, quite respectful but firm, we shall gain all the time.'[31] As so often in the past, Hardie's postures of party independence were interwoven with delicate qualifications; indeed, it was far from being crystal-clear what distinguished his approach from the Lib-Labism of Shackleton or Henderson, which he so often condemned.

Hardie played his usual active role in the January 1910 general election: he was, in fact, chairman of the Labour Party for 1909–10. He served, with Snowden, Henderson, G.H. Stuart and Pease, on the party's election propaganda committee and also on the sub-committee on ILP candidatures.[32] His own contest at Merthyr he viewed in a sanguine frame of mind. 'The situation there looks fairly healthy, but I must not leave anything to chance as there is always that undercurrent of Welsh national feeling to be reckoned with especially in out of the way places where English is a foreign tongue.'[33] Hardie's relations with the local Liberals created much of the usual difficulty. The Merthyr Liberal Association, dormant for twenty years, had been re-formed in November 1909: its apparent purpose was to fight Labour, perhaps to run two official Liberal candidates again as in the past.[34] During the January 1910 campaign Hardie's relations with the Merthyr Liberals continued to generate much friction. Despite his behind-the-scenes discussions with the South Wales Liberals, he continued to take a severe attitude towards party independence. He rebuffed tentative overtures from the one official Liberal who ran against him, Edgar Jones. There was a Unionist candidate in the field, A.C. Fox-Davies. But the only real threat came from Pritchard Morgan, the former member Hardie had defeated in 1900 who now returned as an independent Liberal of a peculiarly flamboyant kind. He waded into Hardie with fierce onslaughts which alleged that the Labour candidate endorsed atheism and free love. He received considerable support from local nonconformist ministers and also from the local Liberal journal, the *Merthyr Express*.[35] On 17 January Glasier found Labour workers in the constituency to be 'in the dumps. They say the feeling is turning against Hardie & in favour of Pritchard Morgan. The pulpits yesterday together with the huge spread of anti-socialist literature has [sic] worked a change.' But Hardie's position was never seriously in danger. On the following day Glasier noted – 'Aha! We have turned the tide tonight.'[36] Hardie spent much more time in the constituency than hitherto. He brought in the usual exotic array of speakers from outside – Bernard Shaw and Mrs Cobden Sanderson amongst them, all wearing his campaign colours of red, green and white. He shrewdly told MacDonald that the polling date of 19 January avoided 'giving the Liberals the advantage of the chapel influence on the Sunday'. He took pains, however, to emphasize his devotion to local causes, especially to the overriding issue of Welsh disestablishment. Redmond had already urged Irish voters to cast a vote for Hardie as well as for Jones. It was also noticeable that many younger nonconformist ministers, men like the Rev. Rhondda Williams, the Rev. James Nicholas and the Rev. T.E. Nicholas, showed that the chapels were no longer universally hostile to socialism.[37] In the event, Hardie easily defeated Pritchard Morgan and increased his poll by over 3,000 votes compared with 1906. His hold over his Merthyr stronghold was confirmed. His triumph was celebrated by a reception and dance at Cyfarthfa castle, which Hardie graced with a rendering of 'Annie Laurie' in a rich Scots baritone.

Labour generally, however, made little progress in the January 1910 election. Its tally of forty-two members represented no advance compared with 1906: the increase came basically from the accretion of the miners' members, now affiliated to the Party. In parliament the party continued to cut a poor figure. After much debate, Barnes was selected party chairman for the 1910 session. It was evident that MacDonald was still anxious for the leadership, but Hardie successfully persuaded him not to stand as 'we are in for more criticism than ever in the new parliament'.[38] MacDonald himself was still deeply suspicious of Hardie's shifts and turns. A few months earlier he had fallen out with Hardie yet again over the latter's involvement in a hopeless by-election contest at Croydon. Here the unsuccessful Labour candidate happened to be Frank Smith, still as close to his hero as ever he had been.[39] MacDonald, saddened by the recent death of his mother, agreed reluctantly to have Barnes as a stop-gap chairman. At once, however, Barnes fell into trouble. He led an onslaught in the debate on the address over the Liberal government's pusillanimous tactics over the budget and the parliament bill. In particular he condemned the government's failure to secure a definite pledge to have peers created by the King so as to push a parliamentary bill through without recourse to a second general election. On 21 February Barnes had the humiliation of being repudiated by his own party.[40]

Hardie was also a force for discord in the 1910 session. On 11 March he wrote a censorious article in the *Leader* which deplored the tendency of the Labour Party to be caught up in the Lords crisis. He urged the party to emphasize its separate identity from the Liberals by taking part in three-cornered by-election contests. At the present time, 'the movement seems to be drifting without any settled policy and that is bad'. He had already expressed this view in his presidential address to the Labour Party's annual conference at Newport in February 1910 which contained a strongly socialist tone.[41] His advice was peculiarly unhelpful in the circumstances of financial difficulty in which the party found itself after the Osborne Judgement, and met with a public rejoinder from MacDonald. Hardie had backed Barnes up in an angry debate within the parliamentary Labour Party on 21 February. This brought him into sharp conflict with MacDonald and Snowden. 'Had Barnes resigned the chairmanship,' he wrote to T.D. Benson, 'I should have at once resigned from the party, and this latter is still the feeling uppermost in my mind. . . . What jars me to the quick is that it was our ILP men who sold the pass. Some of the Trades Unionists like Walsh, Twist of Wigan and Hodge showed themselves of far better grit than those from whom better things might have been expected.'[42] Hardie also wrote to Benson deploring the failure of the Labour Party to move a 'Right to Work' amendment to the King's speech, and calling for a special party conference to consider the general policy of Labour in the constitutional crisis. Glasier wrote back to Hardie urging him not to create a schism in the party. He noted privately in his diary (28 February), 'This necessity of "petting" Hardie is irksome; I never have to do it with MacDonald. . . . What I feel is that Hardie is restless (as always) when he is not the acknowledged leader & is working underhand to compel recognition of his power.'[43]

Throughout the rest of the 1910 session, as negotiations between the Lords and the Commons ground towards deadlock, and the inter-party conference (livened up by Lloyd George's proposal for a Liberal-Unionist coalition) failed to produce agreement, Hardie found himself constantly at odds with most of his colleagues. His independent, often erratic, viewpoint was constantly underlined. He was in vehemently anti-Liberal mood again now, after his flirtation with Lloyd George and the Liberals just before the January election. In South Wales especially, there was acute tension between Liberal and Labour supporters. It exploded finally in a bitter by-election at Mid-Glamorgan in March 1910 when Vernon Hartshorn was soundly defeated by an unknown Liberal. In this contest, antagonism between working-class and middle-class elements reached a new bitterness. In particular, Hartshorn was savagely assailed by nonconformist ministers and by new anti-socialist unions that toured the coalfield.[44] For Hardie, this seemed finally to underline the mockery of any viable alliance with the Liberal party organization. Throughout the summer he continued to point the contrast between the weak-kneed timidity of Henderson and MacDonald, and his own declarations of militancy. At the ILP annual conference he had roused the delegates who had rebuffed him during the Grayson affair the previous year, by declaring that the next general election must be fought on a labour platform, that unemployment not the House of Lords was the prime political issue of the day, and that the Labour Party should act to throw the government out if it did not make the right to work its leading measure in the 1911 session.[45] The effete ceremonial that attended the accession of George V in the summer afforded Hardie a further opportunity of striking a militant pose. He almost caused a fracas in a hotel when he refused to join members of a golf club dinner in the singing of a national anthem.[46] But Hardie was already in many ways a somewhat dated figure in the Labour Party, his pre-eminence being overtaken by younger men like MacDonald. A Unionist back-bencher commented, not unfairly, that by 1910 Hardie had lost the glamour of the novelty caused by his first appearance at Westminster: 'he failed to hold the House when he spoke'. Glasier found himself having to steer a difficult course between MacDonald's anxiety to be party leader and Hardie's calls for rebellion. 'Hardie evidently suspects me of leaning to MacDonald,' Glasier sadly commented.[47] In any case, he himself, hyper-sensitive as he was, had been deeply angered by Hardie's criticisms of the editorial policy of the *Leader*. Throughout the summer and autumn of 1910 the Labour Party continued to drift on in fratricidal strife, with Hardie largely alone.

Despite Hardie's warnings, Labour went into the December 1910 general election again clearly committed to supporting the Liberal government and its Parliament Bill proposals. Hardie this time fought in Merthyr very much on his own with his private army of socialists, suffragettes and 'new theologians' to back him up. Again he had cool relations with the Liberals and fought a strictly independent campaign. His only real opposition came from a self-styled Liberal Unionist, J.H. Watts, who received the support of many of those professional anti-socialists who had backed Pritchard Morgan in January 1910.[48] Edgar Jones, the Liberal, again came top of the poll, but Hardie defeated Watts with great ease. Somehow, this victory failed to excite the Labour movement as in the past: Glasier did not visit the constituency or even send a wire of congratulation. Overall, Labour again merely held its position, with forty members as against forty-two in January. The ambiguous strategy of the party was amply confirmed in the new session. When George Barnes's annual report as chairman denounced the 'timidity' shown by his colleagues, MacDonald and Henderson agreed that a change must now be made. 'I have only held the fort. . . . I shd. say it is yours any time,' wrote Barnes to MacDonald.[49] At last then, MacDonald succeeded as chairman of the party. The continuation of the policy of Liberal-Labourism seemed destined to continue in even more emphatic form.

The two general elections of 1910 heightened Hardie's disaffection with parliamentary manoeuvres. Less and less was he identified in the popular mind with interventions at Westminster; more and more he resumed his most natural role as the great agitator and propagandist of the secular faith of socialism. He sought an instrument through which he could appeal directly to the masses over the heads of the honourable members at Westminster. So there arose yet another difficult crisis in Hardie's relations with his Labour Party colleagues, the struggle for a national daily newspaper that would propound the socialist cause.

Hardie made a series of concrete proposals to the national executive of the Labour Party in the latter months of 1910 and the spring of 1911. He had from the outset of his career been firmly convinced of the power of the printed word in making converts to socialism. Journalism had been his point of entry into the working-class movement, even before he became a regular official for the Ayrshire Miners' Union. He had devoted immense energy to building up the *Labour Leader* as a unique source of personal authority over British socialists, distinct from the ILP organization. Ever since Hardie had lost control over the editorship and management of the *Leader* at the end of 1903 he had had no distinct platform from which to convince, coerce or cajole the mass working-class electorate. Now, with the Labour Party apparently sinking into flabby pragmatism of a particularly indeterminate kind, was the time to put forward one of his cherished ideals – that of a socialist daily newspaper. On 15 March 1911 he put forward his scheme in concrete terms to the NAC. He was approaching the ILP, he explained to Glasier (1 January 1911) because the Labour Party executive would never agree to sustaining a distinct ILP organ. He pointed out the need for such a journal: tactlessly he stressed the declining circulation of the *Labour Leader* and its steady loss of £5 10s a week. Hardie proposed a daily with two editions, one morning and one evening. Capital would be fixed at £25,000 and subscribers would have the newspaper delivered at their homes on payment of 3½d a week. He proposed a separate company to manage the newspaper, much on the lines of the National Labour Press in Manchester. The capital would be raised by ILP members paying 10s each. Shares could be paid for by instalments. The trade unions could be approached to help in such matters as advertising, but Hardie insisted that it should be a strictly ILP-run affair.[50]

These proposals were marked by much of Hardie's usual business shrewdness. Yet from the outset they were marred by personal difficulties. E. Whiteley, a sympathetic business man on the National Labour Press, had promised Hardie up to £5,000 to launch the newspaper, but only on the understanding that it was to be a joint venture controlled by the ILP in conjunction with the Labour Party executive.[51] This was also the view taken by the ILP sub-committee on the newspaper project, headed by Glasier, Ben Riley and W.C. Anderson, an up-and-coming figure in the party. Whiteley told Anderson that joint control was the only policy which made financial sense. 'His brother had refused to do anything because he thought the paper was going to be Hardie's show and thought Hardie hadn't the business knowledge to make a success of it.' Anderson himself added, 'It will be a thousand pities if Hardie begins to splash about [at] the present moment. It would probably destroy most of the good work that is being done and can be done, and bring on top again all the elements of suspicion and unrest.'[52] Hardie however remained implacably committed to the idea of a socialist, ILP-run newspaper, presumably with himself having a powerful or decisive editorial voice. He lobbied the ILP branches and had a motion carried in favour of an ILP daily at the annual conference of the party at Birmingham in 1911. He approached the Labour Party national executive, more hopefully, and also enlisted the support of the disillusioned Glasier. The decisive meeting was the NAC meeting which Hardie attended on 11 May. Now he somewhat modified his previous position and affirmed his willingness to consider a paper run in collaboration with the Labour Party. But he insisted that the chairman of the board should be nominated by the NAC: the committee agreed and tactfully proposed Hardie himself.[53] But the final proposals published by ILP head office on 25 May showed up the essential irreconcilability. The proposed newspaper would be run under the joint auspices of the Labour Party and the ILP. Its policy would be 'in accord with the alliance of Trade Unionists and Socialists as embodied in the Labour Party'. Of its nine directors, six would be elected at an annual joint meeting of Labour Party executive and the NAC, two would be elected annually by trade unions who invested capital in the new company, and one would be elected by shareholders with an investment of £100 and more. The nominal share capital would be £100,000 in £1 shares.[54]

These schemes, put forward by Anderson, Glasier and Riley for the
ILP and by Francis Johnson, its secretary, were quite at variance with
Hardie's plans. At once he resigned from any connection with proposals for a Labour newspaper. He refused to serve on the board of
management as an ILP director and never offered his services to the
new journal in any capacity. He wrote to the NAC on 26 June, 'What
I had in mind was a Socialist paper under the control of the ILP.' To
Glasier, he poured out his resentment at not being supported by his
colleagues: 'I feel quite disappointed with Hardie's egotism,' Glasier
wrote.[55] The effect was to cut Hardie off still further from most of his
ILP colleagues: his newspaper scheme was, even more than most of
Hardie's proposals, an independently-sponsored venture. His relations
towards Glasier, who sneered in the safety of his diary at Hardie's
'Socialist Daily self-advertisement scheme',[56] remained cool for at least
the next twelve months. Younger ILP men like Anderson were also
now distrustful of Hardie. T.D. Benson, the treasurer of the party, felt
that Hardie's unorthodoxy over money had led to his undoing. The
£150 which Hardie had received as contributions to his socialist daily
had been appropriated for his own use, Benson believed, and still
Hardie was in sore financial straits.[57] The new *Daily Citizen*, launched
with a fanfare of rejoicing in 1912, proved to be to be dull reading and
was destined to splutter out on the outbreak of war in 1914. It was a
venture with which Hardie had no connection. The result, then, was
to place further barriers between him and his ILP colleagues, let alone
other segments of the Labour alliance. The trade unions, in particular,
could hardly have viewed with favour his attempt to exclude them from
the new journal from the outset.

And yet there is something to be said on Hardie's behalf. However
badly handled by him on the personal side, the scheme for a socialist
daily did point to a real gap in the armoury of the Labour movement.
Nothing concrete had been done to promote the idea by the ILP over
the years, despite frequent prodding by Hardie himself. The *Leader* at
this time was manifestly uninspiring, and winning few converts to the
cause. It was little more than a parish journal for the faithful. Hardie's
energy in pushing the idea of a socialist daily encouraged the triumphantly successful production of the *Daily Herald*, largely run by George
Lansbury, whose uninhibited socialism was made abundantly plain
from the start. As a propagandist of genius, Hardie needed a platform

for himself also. In June 1911 he created one, in the unlikely location of his own constituency. Managed by a small board of management set up through the Merthyr and Aberdare ILP and the local trades councils, published by the Labour Pioneer Company set up with help from local capitalists in 1907, there appeared the Merthyr *Pioneer*. It appeared on a weekly basis with a regular contribution (or 'budget') by Hardie himself.[58] This also filled an immense gap in the socialist world – the need for a local journal to express the kind of unofficial but constitutionally-orientated militancy of which Hardie himself was the supreme symbol. It lent new momentum to the flagging ILP in the Welsh valleys: appropriately, its Welsh editor was the radical eisteddfodic bard, the Rev. T.E. Nicholas.[59] Beyond, it gave a new crusading ardour to the missionary work of the apostles of socialism, long after the undignified squabbling surrounding the socialist daily had been forgotten. As so frequently occurred, Hardie lost the battle but won the longer-term engagement.

Armed with this new weapon, Hardie renewed his task of trying to inject a more belligerent attitude into the Labour Party. He had at least one useful ally newly returned to the House, George Lansbury, the new member for Bow and Bromley. Lansbury was a product of the SDF but had collaborated with Hardie in the past in the Right to Work agitation and in the women's cause, of which he was also a vehement supporter. He shared to the full Hardie's political style, triumphant for decades in the party after Hardie's death until it met with its nemesis at the brutal hands of Ernest Bevin in the 1935 party conference.

At first, Hardie was sanguine about the state of the Labour Party in 1911, despite its being inevitably overshadowed by the Liberals in the battle for the Parliament Bill. He told Glasier:

You will be glad to learn that the new men are behaving splendidly – Lansbury in particular. They have brought quite a new spirit into the party and now that Mac. and Henderson are working together and that Shackleton is out of the way [he had been made a Board of Trade conciliator] the whole outlook is distinctly better and more encouraging. Lansbury in his bluff, genial out-spoken way promises to be a real influence on the right side and Richardson and Goldstone are both doing well. . . . Even Jowett has found inspiration and spoke quite vigorously the other evening. And so a new atmosphere is being developed in which it is possible to breathe freely once more.[60]

He also made approving comments on MacDonald's chairmanship, which bade fair to weld the parliamentary party into a unified force for the first time, despite MacDonald's well-known vanity and sense of infallibility. But soon the usual danger signs manifested themselves, as the distinction between Labour and the Liberals became harder and harder to draw. At the 1911 annual conference of the ILP, while he paid a graceful tribute to MacDonald, 'the biggest intellectual asset in the movement', Hardie criticized the Labour Party for 'thinking too much in the terms of Liberalism' and not pushing on with socialist measures such as a Right to Work Bill.[61] By the summer once again he was relegated to a lonely, detached position in the party, despite the prominent place he took in Commons debates and in national campaigns. T.D. Benson felt 'Hardie is drifting into a lonely furrow and is become centred solely in trying to keep his name before the public by acting on his own stage.'[62]

On one issue after another Hardie criticized Labour Party tactics during the session. He had the added reinforcement on his side that the party's quiescent tactics were leading to disastrous results at by-elections, with successive Labour candidates coming well down at the bottom of the poll in three-cornered contests. There was no sign of 'Liberal England' being done to death, at least at Labour hands. Hardie was even at odds with policies that were generally welcome to the vast mass of Labour members and supporters. For instance, he created a sensation at the Labour Party conference, held at MacDonald's base of Leicester in March 1911, by attacking the granting of the payment of members: this stupefied trade unionists. But he went on to a stirring defence of the voluntary principle of service. 'They were going to have payment of members and that would mean that men of a very undesirable type would want to enter the House of Commons under the auspices of all parties in order to get the salary attached to the job.'[63] This curiously naïve adoption of a standard Tory argument was heavily defeated. Hardie was also a critic of the Trade Union bill, designed to remedy the effects of the Osborne Judgement, on the grounds of the dangers involved in 'contracting out' with regard to the political levy.

On one issue above all, he found himself again at the head of a dissident militant minority, the National Insurance Bill introduced by Lloyd George in the summer of 1911. Hardie criticized it both in detail and in general principle. He argued that the burden of 4d a week

contribution was far too high for low-paid workers and that those earn-
ing less than twenty-four shillings a week should be exempted
altogether, with the state and employers footing the bill. More basically
he pointed out in the Merthyr *Pioneer* that the ILP had always
opposed the idea of a contributory system of insurance which would be
simply a poll tax upon the workers. The contributory principle had
already been abandoned with regard to Old Age Pensions, education
and public health. Why should so regressive a scheme be retained for
dealing with sickness and unemployment? On this occasion, Hardie
had allies, including Snowden, Lansbury, Jowett, O'Grady and Will
Thorne. Fierce discussions were held during meetings of the parliamentary Labour Party, in which MacDonald and Henderson clashed
with Hardie. Henderson argued that negotiations with the other
parties, such as had recently taken place over Labour's attitude to the
Insurance Bill and its acceptance of the payment of members in compensation, would be impossible if Hardie's freelance tactics were to
prevail.[64] Hardie unleashed a stream of criticisms against the National
Insurance Bill in committee: he made cogent interventions on arrears
of payment, workers' compensation, maternity benefits, proposals for
medical benefits and for unmarried mothers. The amendment of the
Bill under Lloyd George's adroit generalship, so that trade unions were
brought in as approved societies under the act, did not modify Hardie's
criticisms. In the event, nine members voted against the third reading,
including Snowden, Lansbury, Thorne, Jowett and O'Grady. Hardie
abstained, but joined them in signing a manifesto which was published
in the *Labour Leader* justifying their action. 'The poverty of the
workers can never be cured by taxing their poverty,' the signatories
declared.[65] To MacDonald, already facing the familiar trials of
previous Labour leaders in trying to impose unity on the unruly comrades, this final defiance by nine colleagues on the floor of the House
was final confirmation of the impotence and fragmentation of the
nascent Labour Party.

As the 1911 session came to a close, Hardie could only look back on
four years of unedifying frustration. On most issues he had taken a lone
stance, and had emerged as an unpredictable rebel. It left him saddened
and disillusioned, and prone to 'introspective brooding'. Writing to
Glasier he deplored the effects of MacDonald's chairmanship, backed
up by Henderson's secretaryship and with Anderson behind them.

There could only be a serious clash when 'the revolutionary spirit of the working class asserts itself'. Hardie went on, 'I do not feel that I can justify the present trend of things any more than you. . . . Damn their payment of members and their offices, I thought. . . . During the past twelve months I have been subject to fits of despondency, without apparent cause.'[66] Hardie's disillusion had been increased by his isolation, by his erratic behaviour as a party tactician and his unpredictable attitude towards the Liberal alliance, which MacDonald saw as Labour's only lifeline. Yet Hardie had his point also. The distinctiveness of the Labour Party had been lost since 1908; ministers like Lloyd George had all the glamour and all the aura of radical achievement now. Labour stood for little that was uniquely its own. When it did have an independent policy, such as on the Right to Work Bill, its timidity about upsetting the government led to its drawing back. Over a measure like the National Insurance Act, Labour grasped gratefully the sop of 'ninepence for fourpence' and totally rejected the egalitarian and redistributive policy of comprehensive welfare for all, financed out of central social expenditure. On this, Hardie and the Minority Report on the Poor Law made common cause. With all his errors of tactics, Hardie stood for clear-cut principles, even though they might be reconcilable with much of the current Lloyd George programme. Labour under Henderson and MacDonald went in for finessing at the expense of fire. Inspiration, a sense of mission, the motive force that had led Hardie and thousands like him into working-class politics, were being deliberately suppressed in the search for respectability in the finest debating club in the world. It left Hardie bewildered, almost alone. Yet, in the dawning internal and international crisis underlying this Indian summer of Edwardian England, new challenges were looming up which would make Hardie's qualities as crucial for his party as ever in the past.

XII   Class War and the Peace Crusade (1912–14)

The parliamentary manoeuvrings of the Labour Party in 1910–12 took place against a background of social upheaval that dwarfed events at Westminster. In these years Britain experienced industrial conflict of an intensity and extent which was without parallel in her history. As lengthy, and sometimes violent, strikes and lock-outs paralysed the mines, the docks and the railways in 1911, it seemed to many socialists that the class war prophesied by Marx and his followers had finally arrived. In no part of the British Isles was this eruption more dramatic than in South Wales, of which Hardie was one of the parliamentary representatives.[1] In 1908 and 1910 a series of violent strikes broke out, beginning with a stoppage in the Powell-Duffryn collieries in Aberdare, in Hardie's own constituency. A new generation of miners' leaders, younger and more acutely class-conscious, called for the purging of the older generation of Lib-Labs on the South Wales Miners' executive. Older leaders like 'Mabon', the very personification of class collaboration and of the alliance with nonconformist Liberalism, a zealot of the *eisteddfod* and of the *Cymanfa Ganu*, seemed outmoded to militant younger miners' agents like Charles Stanton of Aberdare, one of Hardie's own party organizers. Finally there came the frightening eruptions at the Cambrian collieries, Tonypandy, in early November 1910, which heralded the year-long stoppage by the Cambrian men. In riots which became legendary for their ferocity, a miner, Samuel Boyce, was killed and the Home Secretary, Churchill, sent in Hussars to reinforce the local constabulary and to patrol the coalfield. 'Tonypandy' joined 'Featherstone' in the saga of working-class martyrology. There were equally violent demonstrations in the Aberdare region: 26,000 men were on strike in Hardie's own constituency by the end of November. South Wales seemed to have become the cockpit of industrial conflict of a new and terrifying kind. Stanton called for a 'fighting brigade' of miners to meet the violence of the police with counter-violence.[2] Shortly afterwards two workers were to be shot and killed in a railway strike at Llanelli. In 1912 there was a national miners' strike on behalf of the minimum wage. More insidiously, in the Rhondda and other Welsh valleys, the tutorial classes of the Plebs League and of the Central Labour College movement, together with the militant branches of the Miners' Unofficial Reform Committee, seemed to herald a new surge of revolutionary Marxism throughout the coalfield. New doctrines of direct action, also, were heard – de Leonism, Sorelism, above all the seductive appeal of Syndicalism or other forms of workers' control. *The Miners' Next Step*, published by the Unofficial Reform Committee at Tonypandy in 1912 and written by militant young Welsh Marxists like Noah Ablett and Will Mainwaring, presented a challenge not merely to Liberal capitalism in South Wales but also to the elected leadership of the Welsh Miners' Federation. They offered a threat also to the constitutional social democracy of which Keir Hardie was the supreme symbol. As younger miners permeated the Welsh coalfield, many of them Englishmen like Frank Hodges or A.J. Cook, out of sympathy with the older Welsh appeal of community, the class war in South Wales, as in the East End docks or the Clydeside areas around Glasgow, seemed suddenly naked and complete.

For Keir Hardie this outburst of industrial conflict posed a tremendous challenge. He was instinctively sympathetic to the workers' cause. He well understood the growing unemployment, the decline in real wages, the population pressures, the squalid living conditions that had brought the strikes about. He also recognized the growth of massive combines and cartels in the Welsh coalfield, with their resultant sharpening of the conflict between capital and labour. One notorious example was the Cambrian Combine built up by his old parliamentary colleague, D.A. Thomas, in whose collieries at Tony-pandy the most notorious violence of all had occurred. Inevitably, therefore, Hardie was a vociferous critic of the manner in which the riots there had been handled. On 15 November 1910 he clashed bitterly with Winston Churchill, the Home Secretary, about police brutality during the Tonypandy disturbances.[3] He provided gruesome details of miners who had received severe facial and bodily injuries at the hands of the special constabulary. He severely criticized their officer, Captain Linday, for over-reacting. He called upon Lloyd George to deny that the Welsh collier was naturally violent or disorderly, and asked repeatedly for a public inquiry. Throughout the labour troubles of the next few years Hardie was a constant critic of the handling of industrial affairs by the Liberal government, and by Churchill in particular. An especially alarming feature, as Hardie saw it, was the tendency towards the indiscriminate use of troops in quelling industrial disorder, or alleged disorder. He accused Churchill of the 'Russification' of the country, especially by sending in the Hussars to patrol the Welsh coalfield after the Tonypandy riots. The automatic use of the army to suppress strikes at home was inseparably bound up, Hardie argued, with the dominance of the military spirit in the conduct of international affairs also.[4] Militarism was one and indivisible.

Despite Hardie's passionate protests, troops were employed again during the national railway strike in August 1911. He denounced the calling up of 58,000 troops, on horse and on foot, which amounted to a virtual declaration of martial law. In one notorious episode at Llanelli, as has been seen, two railway workers were shot down and killed. Hardie replied with a searing pamphlet (one which somewhat embarrassed his parliamentary colleagues), *Killing No Murder*: in this, the facts of violence by the military in Llanelli were starkly exposed. To him, these episodes, and other industrial disturbances like them, confirmed anew the exploitation of the workers, and the hollowness of the pretensions of the Liberal government in claiming to be sympathetic with urban and industrial grievances. He laid the blame for the violence at Llanelli and elsewhere entirely at the door of the army to whom the government had given a free hand to suppress industrial strikes, whatever the human cost. He pointed out that the roots of the railway stoppage lay in the inability of the men to get their union recognized, and to establish proper collective bargaining procedures with the management. But instead of putting pressure on the railway companies to negotiate towards a peaceful settlement, the government had intervened in a totally unilateral and brutal fashion.[5] Lloyd George was, in Hardie's view, especially culpable. In the *Labour Leader* (13 March 1913) Hardie accused him of stirring up the domestic crisis during the Agadir confrontation with Germany in July 1911. Lloyd George's belligerently anti-German speech at the Mansion House during the Agadir crisis had caused an immense sensation. Hardie now alleged that the Chancellor had concluded a secret deal with Sir Guy Granet, the chairman of the Midland Railway Company, by which a bargain was struck over the Railway Rates Bill in return for a settlement of the strike. The outcome was that the British army was being employed to protect, in the first instance, the dividends of the railway shareholders and the blacklegs they introduced into the British railways. The *quid pro quo* was that they were then to be released to protect the investments of British speculators in Morocco. The railway strike and the Agadir crisis were, then, inextricably linked together as part of the seamless web of capitalism in its most brutal guise.

In all this, Hardie's reaction to the class conflict of these years was instinctive and predictable. Automatically, his sympathies were wholly with the workers on strike; automatically too, his soul rebelled against the use of coercive military power to suppress domestic disturbance. On the other hand, his reactions were a good deal more uncertain when he considered the underlying causes of industrial turbulence within the trade union world at the time. He approved of strikes as manifestations of class consciousness that would make the workers more aware of their industrial situation and of the instruments at hand to remedy it. He endorsed in particular the coal and railway strikes of 1911 because they would eliminate craft and sectional differences amongst the miners and railwaymen and work towards the creation of one national union (Merthyr *Pioneer*, 26 August 1911). Only with a united policy based on class solidarity would such objectives as a nation-wide minimum wage for the miners be gained.[6] With the miners thus demonstrating their ability to capture power in the mines, they could advance to capture power in the state as well. Hardie elaborated, in tentative terms (19 January 1913), a scheme for public ownership of the mines, with Government Mines Stock issued to redeem the investments of the private share-holders: significantly enough, he never argued for overt expropriation.[7] In many ways, the class conflict of 1912–14 seemed to him a portent of the growing strength and solidarity of the trade unions; the Triple Alliance concluded between the miners, dockers and railwaymen in 1914 was its ultimate expression.

On the other hand, he was disturbed at some of the forms that industrial protest took. He deplored all attempts to agitate for the unions' demands in a violent manner. Cries such as those from C.B. Stanton for the creation of a 'fighting brigade' of miners were totally at variance with Hardie's ethics; he continued to stress the temperate, law-abiding nature of the British miner. Further, efforts to transform the nation-wide industrial struggle into localized campaigns for syndicalism or workers' control were totally against Hardie's commitment to disciplined, coherent class action. In so far as syndicalism lent a new vitality to the fighting spirit of the workers it should be welcomed. But, in threatening to substitute 'direct action' in its industrial form for constitutional pressure through the Labour Party, syndicalism should be rejected. It was tantamount 'to anarchism in its industrial form'.[8] In an American journal, the *Metropolitan*, he elaborated his views still further. Syndicalism had given a massive stimulus to organization, especially of low-paid and unskilled workers. But its tactics and theory were equally mistaken. The syndicalists aimed to sabotage capitalism from within by making peaceful industrial relations impossible. They ignored the state itself, which was there for the working class to capture and control. Instead of localized, spontaneous stoppages, which would inevitably find the capitalist well-entrenched and with superior force at his disposal, the workers should turn to the wider vision of greater political representation and the implementation of democratic socialism. The strike was no substitute for political action. Workers should strive to control the state, not destroy it, and the Labour Party was their predestined instrument.[9]

As so often, then, Hardie's outlook was still basically that of a moderate, who sought constitutional progress with priority accorded to the parliamentary method. He was alarmed by syndicalist manifestations in railway workshops, or by agitations against the national miners' executive through such bodies as the Unofficial Reform Committee. He had little sympathy with the forms of class war preached by the *Miners' Next Step* at Tonypandy. Ironically, to many observers, Hardie, in justifying the rioters at Tonypandy and lending more or less indiscriminate justification to all the strikes of these troubled years, seemed to confirm his well-established reputation as a fanatical extremist. In reality, his message was a call for organization, discipline and courage harnessed on behalf of peaceful protest within the framework of the law – provided that the law was applied with even justice to capitalists and labour alike.

Hardie's dilemmas concerning the industrial warfare of these years were underlined in August–September 1913 when he was caught up in a violent labour struggle that broke out in Ireland. On 31 August 1913 a strike by the Dublin Transport Workers, headed by their charismatic leader, James Larkin, was violently broken up by the police. Baton charges resulted in hundreds of injuries and the death of at least one of the strikers.[10] For a moment, Dublin became the focus of the class struggle throughout the British Isles. A crisis in the city's tramways had long been anticipated, with the declared opposition of W.M. Murphy, the owner of the Dublin Tramways Company and a prominent newspaper magnate, to the militant policy of the unions symbolized by 'Larkinism'. Hardie at once travelled to Dublin and plunged boldly into the controversy. He joined the solemn cortège which attended the funeral of the dead tramway worker at Glasnevin cemetery. He declared the solidarity of the British labour movement with Larkin and his followers. 'He would say that they could never have God's Kingdom upon earth until Socialism had settled the working-class question.'[11] At Dublin and at Belfast he took the opportunity to direct the minds of his working-class audiences away from the sectarian animosities surrounding Irish home rule, and to educate them in the threat facing all labour organizations in Ireland, whether Orange or Green. He detailed many cases of police brutality which he himself had witnessed in Dublin. He contrasted the desperate struggle for elementary rights of trade union organization there with the massive profits being increasingly wrung by international capitalists out of the blood and toil of the workers. The capitalist interest represented by the Liberal government was firmly behind Dublin Castle in its violent campaign to crush the workers' rights.

Once more, Hardie seemed to emerge as an advocate of class war and of industrial extremism. And yet again, in reality, he was trying to argue the constitutionalist case, admittedly with a passion and rhetorical flamboyance that were all his own. He denied that Larkin was an advocate of syndicalism. On the contrary, he was (so Hardie claimed) a supporter of the ILP who sought to create a constitutional Labour Party in the new parliamentary assembly to be set up in the self-governing Ireland that was shortly to arise.[12] The battle in Ireland was for elementary rights of trade union organization. The struggle of Larkin's tramway workers, Hardie argued, was fundamentally a logical continuation of the sufferings of the Tolpuddle martyrs, and of other pioneers of labour organization, down to and beyond the Taff Vale verdict. It was a call for stronger, not for weaker, trade unions; in any case it was capitalists like Murphy, backed up by the police, who were assuming the offensive. Even during the passionate crisis of Larkinism, therefore, Hardie did not deviate from the main outlines of working-class advance that he had championed throughout his career. When the strike of the Dublin Tramway Workers finally petered out in February 1914, after the failure of the British TUC to lend adequate financial support and the refusal of British transport workers to take sympathetic action on behalf of their revolutionary Irish comrades, Hardie saw Larkin as a martyr in another blood-stained act of the working-class tragedy.

Hardie's attitude towards strikes and industrial action generally was clarified in a fierce controversy in which he was engaged with Philip Snowden in October 1913, shortly after the crisis of the Dublin tram-way strike. Snowden, whose attitude towards domestic affairs had become increasingly cautious, argued vehemently against the priority being accorded to strike action. While strikes might still retain their value, for instance amongst unskilled men struggling to gain recognition for their unions, all too often they were counter-productive. Most working men and women suffered from strikes, Snowden claimed. On the contrary, positive advances for the workers, such as the Minimum Wage for miners, invariably sprang from the House of Commons, usually as a result of successful pressure by the Labour Party. Snowden pointed out that the British TUC had been repelled by the violent tactics of the Dublin tramway men under Larkin's command, and that, in any event, industrial violence usually worked to the disadvantage of the Labour Party. He cited recent by-elections at Crewe, Midlothian and Chesterfield to show how Labour candidates had suffered from being identified with violence and industrial unrest instead of with constitutional action.[13] Hardie replied with massive effect in the *Labour Leader*. He poured scorn on Snowden's tendency to cite the 'public' as being opposed to strikes: this was a familiar tactic of the newspaper press, used long before Larkinism was heard of. The vast majority of 'the public' was working class. Strikes, Hardie argued, should not be used wildly or indiscriminately. They should be conducted in a tolerant, peaceful manner. But the strike weapon should always be retained. It was an essential weapon open to the workers: 'every fresh accession of spirit in the trade unions should find its reflexion in the sphere of politics'. Without strikes, parliament would never have made the Minimum Wage a leading priority. Without strike action, the plight of the Dublin Tramway workers would never have captured public attention. The strike and the ballot went hand in hand. 'It is the experience gained by the strike which ultimately filters into the consciousness of the working class and makes political action a triumphant reality.'[14] To most observers, Hardie's simple logic carried the day. He was still advocating constitutional action as the supreme weapon, but urging that class solidarity and disciplined industrial militancy were essential towards making that weapon effective. Hardie, in short, sought a middle route. He steered a consistent course between those who advocated 'direct action', often of a violent nature, and those like Snowden who argued, in effect, that the strike was obsolete and ought to be abandoned. Hardie was endeavouring to show the tactical and theoretical inter-relationship between the political and the industrial wings of a class-conscious labour movement. At a time of supreme class bitterness and fears of total industrial anarchy, it was Hardie's statesmanlike call for the new opportunities for labour to be taken up alongside the old instruments, and above all for a powerful Labour Party, that carried conviction. It enabled labour to find a *via media* between the anarcho-syndicalists and the Lib-Labs. In so far as Hardie was a major architect of this achievement, it was one of his supreme contributions to the effective evolution of the British labour movement.

The arguments over Larkinism and class war took place at a time when Hardie's role as an isolated individual seemed all the more pronounced. Glasier saw Hardie as prematurely old, consumed by ambition and by resentment at being supplanted by MacDonald.[15] This harsh verdict reflected something of Glasier's own disappointment, now that he had lost the editorship of the *Leader* and failed to find an alternative niche within the ILP. T.D. Benson echoed these criticisms of Hardie's political role. 'Hardie,' he wrote, 'by his very nature is incapable of working with a Party. He has always been a lone and a solitary figure and must continue till the end.'[16] On issue after issue until the spring of 1914, Hardie came into conflict with the Labour Party leadership and with MacDonald in particular. His stand in the writing of *Killing No Murder* and his uninhibited endorsement of Larkinism acutely embarrassed his colleagues.[17] He also emerged as a champion of George Lansbury when he took up arms against his parliamentary colleagues. Like Hardie, Lansbury was a vehement partisan of the suffragettes and a passionate critic of the Labour Party's failure to oppose the government adequately over its forcible feeding of imprisoned suffragettes and its unwillingness to introduce a women's enfranchisement measure. In November 1912 Lansbury resigned his seat at Bow and Bromley on the women's issue and announced that he would refuse the Labour whip if he were re-elected. The national executive then declared that his candidature at Bow and Bromley could not be officially supported. Hardie, however, was a pugnacious defender of Lansbury and promptly resigned his seat on the Labour Party executive in protest.[18] Four Labour members (Hardie, Snowden, Thorne and O'Grady) defied the official party view and campaigned for Lansbury in the by-election. Hardie urged that Labour should vote against the government's Franchise Bill, if female suffrage was not included. The whole episode seemed to confirm Hardie's role as a critic and a supporter of party indiscipline. The fact that Lansbury was then defeated in the by-election at Bow and that Labour lost an important beach-head in London added to the impotent fury of MacDonald, Henderson and the leading figures in the party.

For Hardie the whole affair was deeply saddening and disillusioning. Not merely were his relations with his leading colleagues sorely strained despite several Labour members' insistence that the new Franchise Reform Bill of 1912 must be extended to women. He no longer captured the allegiance of the suffragettes, either. Despite his long relationship with the Pankhursts and his record of service to the cause of women's rights, Hardie now found himself frequently heckled by women during his speeches in the country. They regarded him as 'a man of words not deeds', whose gradualism and constitutionalism had produced no tangible results. A suffragette sympathizer (November 1913) found Hardie 'looking very old and weary & he seemed to feel he had lost his power'.[19] Indeed, the suffragette movement itself, deeply rent over tactics after the defection of many moderates from the WSPU, seemed to be running into the ground.

Hardie's fundamental criticism of the Party now was that its relations with the Liberals were becoming dangerously intimate. As the Liberals needed Labour support in pushing through Irish Home Rule and Welsh Disestablishment in 1912–14, Hardie deplored the closer alliance that this implied. He denounced the 'slobbering talk' about 'the friendly understanding between the Liberals and the Labour Party'. Lloyd George he dismissed as 'a pettifogging attorney'.[20] Indeed there was every indication that the alliance between the two parties was tending almost towards a fusion, with Lloyd George insidiously sowing the seeds for a new re-alignment of the left. Josiah Wedgwood, the backbench Liberal member for Newcastle-under-Lyme, was one tentative mediator in June 1913. He sounded out the leading Labour members about the prospects of 'a firmer alliance'. MacDonald, Snowden and, more surprisingly, Barnes, made a sympathetic response. By contrast, Jowett, Anderson and Hardie were amongst those who thought it impossible.[21] Meanwhile every portent seemed to suggest a closer understanding between the government and the Labour Party. Labour seemed notably reluctant to oppose Liberals in critical by-elections: Hardie sharply criticized the failure of Labour to put up a candidate in the Leicester by-election. Difficulty in several mining seats, where the Labour allegiance of miners' candidates was in doubt, also posed awkward questions about relations between the two leftward parties.

The climax was reached, secretly, on 3 March 1914, just prior to the Curragh crisis in Ulster, when Lloyd George saw MacDonald's secretary and directly broached the possibility of a firmer arrangement with Labour, perhaps with MacDonald entering the government.[22] He pointed out the common threat that faced Labour and the Liberals, in the face of an insubordinate military and a revived outcry for tariff reform. MacDonald himself was obviously sympathetic and repeated some of Lloyd George's arguments in his own *Leicester Pioneer*. To Hardie, however, the very idea was anathema, the negation of his basic creed of labour independence. When the NAC met on 17 March 1914 the prospect of accepting Lloyd George's offer was formally discussed. Hardie made known his outright opposition. He agitated throughout the ILP to torpedo MacDonald's scheme of a Lib-Lab alliance at the next general election.[23] He encouraged Fenner Brockway, the youthful new editor of the *Labour Leader*, to fulminate against a Liberal alliance. He also put up Brockway at the 1914 annual conference of the ILP at Bradford, at which Hardie presided, to reject any possible alliance with the Liberals: Brockway's effective speech, Hardie shrewdly told him, was more suitable for an ILP than a Labour

Party audience. Hardie and Brockway had massive support. Snowden, however reformist on other issues, took MacDonald severely to task for negotiating with the Liberal whips behind the backs of his colleagues. The delegates overwhelmingly rejected any idea of a pact.[24] Gradually, throughout the spring and early summer of 1914, the prospect of a fusion receded: in by-elections at North-East Derbyshire and Ipswich, Labour (much to MacDonald's embarrassment) found itself opposing Liberals at the polls. In each case, Unionists captured the seat. Hardie undoubtedly was an instrumental factor in preserving the rigid path of independence. At the cost of severely strained relations with MacDonald in particular, he had carried the day for the traditional policy.

These constant conflicts reinforced Hardie's position of isolation within the Labour Party. He was still a dominant and charismatic figure, playing host at Nevills Court to socialists from all parts of the world. To young idealists like Fenner Brockway or Hugh Dalton he seemed, with his tweed suit, pipe and open-necked shirt, the very epitome of socialism in its most pure and uncorrupted form. More and more he retreated into his own coterie of intimates and advisers. He took solace from the visits of young girl socialists like Rose Davies and Agnes Hughes from South Wales, and struck up strongly emotional relationships with them. More than ever it was noticeable that Hardie's contacts in the House and in his social life outside were entirely bounded by the Labour movement. With the Liberals he virtually suspended all relationships. The consequence was, among other things, a marked deterioration of relations with the Liberal official machine in his own Merthyr constituency. At the end of 1912 the Merthyr Liberals announced that, in response to Hardie's long campaign against them, they would be running two official candidates at the next general election. In July 1913 a second Liberal prospective candidate was duly adopted, in the formidable person of Thomas Artemus Jones, an articulate Welsh-speaking barrister of impeccable nonconformist antecedents.[25] At the next peacetime general election, therefore, Hardie would face outright Liberal antagonism and his seat at Merthyr might well be placed in jeopardy. A vigorous anti-socialist campaign was conducted throughout the coalfield, spearheaded by two Liberal members, Clement Edwards and J. Hugh Edwards, with Hardie as its major target. Hardie himself was sufficiently concerned to ask the

Labour Party for a temporary organizer in his constituency 'to lick the organization into shape again'.[26] Hardie, then, seemed more and more to lapse into a limbo of his own, detached from most of his leading parliamentary colleagues, a lone figure even within the ILP, yet more and more at odds with the Liberals whose political ally he had for so long been forced into being.

What Hardie retained as his major source of strength was a unique position of dominance throughout the international labour movement and a unique hold on the affections of grass-roots party workers. He could still provide an inspirational force denied to any of his associates, even MacDonald. This was shown time and again during these years, and gave his struggles to keep the party sound over an alliance with the Liberals, over strikes, militarism and women's suffrage, added power. He proudly detailed his record for March–August 1913: nine Commons speeches, 75 parliamentary questions, meetings up and down the country that entailed journeys of 11,000 miles.[27] His charismatic authority was never more impressively shown that in July 1912 on the occasion of the King's visit to Merthyr. Hardie addressed to him an open letter, in his finest vein, on conditions in the Dowlais Iron Works. He outlined, with matchless force, industrial relations in the foundry at 'Sweated Dowlais', which had led to an eighteen-weeks' strike of the iron moulders. The total capitalized stock of the Dowlais company amounted to £4,555,500 on which shareholders (who included several leading churchmen) were drawing vast dividends. The obverse was a basic daily wage of 1s 10d a day for the ironworkers, and demoralizing working conditions. He urged the King to avoid visiting the Dowlais works during his visit to Merthyr, and demanded a government inquiry into industrial conditions for employees of Guest, Keen and Nettlefold.[28] Hardie gained some short-term results. The government agreed, on the advice of the Fair Wages Advisory Committee, to regard the steel-makers of Dowlais as being employed on government work. Unskilled men received increased pay awards of up to 3s a day plus percentages. More important was the way in which Hardie, as he had done earlier in the Overtoun affair, used iniquitous working conditions in one foundry as a weapon in a wider critique of the capitalist structure. At a time when commentators were obsessed with 'unrest' in the coalfield, Hardie deflected attention to the squalid reality of actual factory conditions which lay beneath strikes and stoppages. It also served to confirm that he himself was a unique champion of the working-class revolt.

Apart from personal crusades of this kind, Hardie's one institutional weapon was the ILP. Despite all the heart-searching occasioned by the Victor Grayson affair in 1909, he still preserved a working connection with the party at a time when all other channels of protest were denied to him. The ILP was still uniquely identified with Hardie himself. This was dramatically demonstrated in Whitsun 1912 when the annual conference of the party was held at Merthyr. It had been postponed until then because of the miners' strike in April. Kneeshaw, the ILP official who arranged the conference, noted 'The local people are anxious that the Conference should be held at Merthyr, not necessarily as a compliment to Mr Hardie but because the Liberals have decided to adopt two Liberal candidates for the general election, and the Conference in Merthyr would be a great success and help propaganda in the district.' Kneeshaw concluded that the practical difficulties of arranging a conference at Merthyr had been exaggerated and that in any event the desirability of assisting Hardie made it vital to train national publicity on the ILP presence in the constituency.[29] It was, on balance, a triumphantly successful occasion. It was launched by a powerful sermon on 'the message of Jesus' by the Rev. Rowland Jones, a well-known 'new theologian' minister, at Tabernacle Chapel, Merthyr. Closer to the realities of the class struggle, Hardie himself reiterated before a large gathering at the Olympia skating rink that the ILP's ultimate objective remained revolution, not merely reform: he seized the opportunity to denounce any Lib-Lab deviationists who might exist in the party. He criticized 'the retention of Liberal beliefs by some of the Trade Union members who had joined the Labour Party'.[30] At the conference he then carried a resolution which demanded the immediate implementation of an eight-hour day and a minimum living wage by parliament. Younger delegates present noted that MacDonald made only a belated and brief appearance at Merthyr and took this as an indication of his well-known disagreements with Hardie.[31] In general, however, the Merthyr conference confirmed Hardie's dominant position within his own party.

For the year 1913–14 Hardie's role in the ILP was reinforced by his being elected again as party chairman. This was intended as a compliment to Hardie who would, therefore, preside over the 'coming of age' conference which was destined to be held once again in Bradford, the venue of the inaugural meeting twenty-one years earlier. He was an active party chairman, as would have been anticipated. He collapsed in July 1913 while waiting in a train at Euston station, but soon bounced back to health. He served on the Parliamentary, National Organizing, Divisional Organizing and other Committees of the party. He also exerted his influence to secure the appointment of Fenner Brockway, a militant socialist who had once been in the SDF, to the editorship of the *Labour Leader* in 1912 in succession to J.F. Mills. Brockway, as has been seen, proved a useful ally in Hardie's efforts to restrain MacDonald's penchant for a pact with the Liberals, of a formal or informal kind, and Hardie kept in constant touch with him in 1912–14.[32] The most important issue confronting Hardie during his year of chairmanship, however, concerned the British Socialist Party, into which Hyndman's SDF had now merged itself. After years in the wilderness, and after deriving little benefit from its association with the erratic Victor Grayson, Hyndman's party now sought affiliation to the Labour Party. Hardie made a number of unexpectedly sympathetic gestures. At the NAC on 13 December, to Glasier's resentment, he took an unheralded favourable line towards affiliation and rebuffed Hudson who had been put up to argue the case for caution. 'Hardie has in a way betrayed us,' Glasier wrote.[33] In 1914 Hardie appeared on a number of joint socialist unity platforms with Hyndman, and also Bernard Shaw and Sidney Webb. The BSP and the ILP exchanged fraternal delegates at their annual conferences in the spring of 1914.[34] Even so, there is little doubt that Hardie's overall attitude towards the BSP remained one of scepticism, and he did little to hasten on affiliation in any practical sense. He still felt too alienated by the dogmatism of Hyndman, reinforced as it was by a growing nationalism and jingoism which showed itself in fierce BSP denunciations of Germany. When Hardie stepped down from the chairmanship of the NAC in April 1914, the British Socialist Party remained safely in the wilderness, and not until 1916, when Hardie was dead, did Hyndman's party finally merge into the labour alliance which the SDF had so consistently denounced in the past.

Hardie's chairmanship of the ILP came to a climax at the Bradford meeting in April 1914.[35] It was far from being a harmonious occasion. There was severe heckling by suffragettes of Hardie himself and also of Snowden and MacDonald. This was because the ILP had declined either to break with the government or demand the immediate enfranchisement of all women without restriction. On the platform there were fierce conflicts between MacDonald and Snowden, the latter backed up by Fred Jowett and indirectly by Hardie from the chair, over the recurring issue of relations with the Liberals. Nevertheless what remained in the memory of all those present was Hardie's majestic presidency over the coming-of-age of the party which he himself had fostered. The ILP had remained a small organization; its delegates were drawn to an unduly large degree from middle-class activists rather than from trade unionists; its finances remained precarious. It had, nevertheless, survived as the only effective vehicle of democratic socialism in Britain, and as a vindication of Hardie's long-declared policy that they should 'goon our ain gait'. His closing address before an audience of children at St George's Hall, Bradford, was an extraordinary demonstration of the magnetism and spiritual force which he could exert over the party. He appealed to his young listeners to love flowers, animals, their fellow men, to hate injustice and cruelty, never to be mean or treacherous, always to be generous in service. He depicted the loveliness of the world as it could become if poverty and war were to be eliminated. He and those who had worked with him had failed but they – the children – could succeed. 'If these were my last words I would say them to you, lads and lasses. Live for that better day.' Sixty years later observers present could still recapture the thrill of emotion that Hardie's passionate eloquence evoked. Hardie himself wrote of his reactions to his young Welsh socialist friend, Rose Davies:

> The conference was an inspiration. In all my experience I have never felt the same elation of spirit, and that I suppose explained the high tone of my remarks to the children and again at the close of the conference, especially the reference to my wife. The ILP has entered upon a new phase in its wonderful career and will again make history during the next four years.[36]

Hardie's presiding over the Bradford conference, indeed, in many ways restored his old relationship with the ILP rank and file after years of bitter disagreement. His relations with MacDonald were much improved after the conference: no doubt this was assisted by the confrontations of Labour and Liberal candidates at North-east Derbyshire and other by-elections. Indeed it was known that Hardie had resisted pressure from the authors (with whom Fred Jowett was closely associated), of 'the green manifesto', *Let us Reform the Labour Party*, which called into question the basic relationship of the ILP with their Labour colleagues.[37] Things were being patched up with Bruce Glasier also, with whom much of the old cordiality was being restored. Glasier described a wild, gusty night in South Wales on the road to Swansea after a socialist meeting:

> We made merry. Hardie and Williams [Councillor David Williams of Swansea] with two small glasses of Benedictine. We played parlour quotes with the landlord and his wife, and a parrot who showed such friendliness to Hardie that it perched on his shoulder. Hardie was proud of this mark of esteem from the sapient bird. . . . What a vocal time we had in the car driving to Swansea. Hardie and I sang like young students all the way . . . Scottish songs and choruses, 'The Battle of Stirling' etc. It was a prime night out & quite renewed the old attachment between Hardie and myself.[38]

Glasier was again an honoured and frequent guest at 'the prophet's chamber' in Nevills Court. What Hardie was most touched by, though, was the personal warmth he received from ordinary members of the ILP during the Bradford meeting in April 1914. When he was presented with a gong, divided into twenty-one sections, at the end of the meeting (a memento retained at the Cumnock home down to the 1970s), he poured out his heart. He took occasion to pay particular tribute to the courage and dedication of his wife, who had borne so many of the struggles with him and who had kept his home going on twenty-five shillings a week when he was member for West Ham. Throughout that spring and summer letters came in confirming Hardie's unique hold on the love and imagination of British socialists, and his unique ability to touch their hearts. For a man like the Scottish ILP supporter, David Farrell, Hardie stood apart from all other human beings:

> You Dear Old Soul, you don't know a tithe of the lovers you have, aye I might almost say worshippers, so keep your auld heart up, your worth to socialism is more than you will ever realize. You are still the Dear Old Lovable Hardie you always were. My Class right or wrong. Bless you for those words. Our Class, Hardie, would that they would become class conscious, then wars, poverty and all other crimes would be a thing of the past, aye an' its coming up yet for a' that.

Farrell added, 'I have more love & reverence for you than I have for my own father'.[39] Countless others could have echoed these words.

In the British domestic scene, Hardie, secure in his hold on the affections of the ILP and of many working-class people outside its ranks, still saw every prospect for hope. But these later years were overshadowed by the growing threat of militarism which loomed over Hardie's mind like a lowering cloud until the crisis of 1914. His newspaper columns and speeches in these years were full of the menace inherent in the international situation. As has been seen in an earlier chapter, he was unique in his awareness of the world-wide aspect of the socialist movement. He was a passionate advocate of the view that only through united working-class action could the road to peace be preserved. When he returned from his world tour in the spring of 1908, his concern with the menace of events in Europe was intensified. He was foremost among those Labour members who criticized the warlike aspects of British diplomacy during these years. He acted with the backbench foreign affairs group of radicals, including Sir Arthur Ponsonby, J. Allen Baker, Philip Morrell and J. King, in demanding a reduction of military and naval expenditure by Britain and the successful readjustment of the balance of power in favour of a true *entente* between Britain, France and Germany. Hardie added the particular theme that an ailing capitalism and a resurgent military class were threatening the world with renewed armaments races and with the permeation of the psychology of jingoism and violence. The use of troops in labour disputes in Britain, in South Wales and elsewhere, seemed to him clear evidence of the way in which militarism could corrupt society at home. Hardie's views on foreign affairs were simple and clear-cut: no alliances, no increased armaments, no intervention in the Balkans, Morocco or elsewhere, and fraternity with the workers of the world. He reacted with especial fury to the *entente* with Czarist Russia in 1907, which was negotiated while he was abroad on his world tour. To socialists and radicals elsewhere, Russia was the most hateful of all tyrannies, particularly after the suppression of the Duma in 1906; it was in no sense a suitable ally for Britain. Hardie rejected outright the claim that the *entente* with Russia in 1907 was a simple and honourable adjustment of frontier disputes. In the case of Persia, for instance, Hardie argued that the Czar had taken the opportunity to send Cossack troops into north Persia for the sake of Russian usurers and with the connivance of Sir Edward Grey and the British administration in India. The root cause of the *entente* with Russia, Hardie claimed, with populist fervour that radical backbenchers echoed time and again, was the need for protecting British investors in the Near East. 'While Mr Lloyd George keeps the nation in a commotion over the Budget and National Insurance Bills, the Cabinet of which he is a member is doing the will of the big financial houses. The Barings, the Schusters, the Cassels, and the Rothschilds are the real rulers of the nation.'[40] Hardie was amongst those backbenchers, mainly Liberal, who launched a furious attack in June 1908 on the eve of the visit of Edward VII to Czar Nicholas II at Reval on the Baltic. Hardie detailed the shooting down of political and industrial demonstrators in Russia. The King's visit 'was to condone the atrocities for which the Czar's government and the Czar personally must be held responsible'. Hardie was pulled up by the Chairman of Committees for use of the term 'atrocities' and had to withdraw it.[41] Undeterred, he went on to refer to the suppression of national minorities in Finland, Georgia and Poland, and the imprisonment and exile of leaders of the 1905 Duma. He suggested that financial interests behind the scenes had prompted the King's visit. There was a curious aftermath. In a fury, Edward VII struck off Hardie's name, along with those of Ponsonby and Victor Grayson, from the list of MPs eligible to attend Buckingham Palace garden parties. 'We don't want any bloody agitation here,' the King remarked.[42] Although Hardie had no intention of going to any such functions (and although he regretted being mixed up with Grayson), he turned the incident into valuable publicity for the socialist and pacifist cause. He claimed that if he were fit to represent the working class of Merthyr at Westminster, he was equally suitable to represent them at Buckingham Palace also. The Labour Party declared that until Hardie's name was restored to this symbolic list, no Labour member would attend functions at the Palace. The King, embarrassed at being himself the target of a politically-motivated strike, had to climb down, while angry reverberations about the implications of the alliance with Russia raged on.

Hardie was a central figure in every effort to superimpose the moral force of the peace movement throughout each major crisis. During the naval scare of 1908–9, when the 'dreadnoughts' programme was stepped up in response to new pressure from the German navy, he spoke out powerfully against the war hysteria. He chaired a meeting at St James's Hall at which the German socialists Kautsky and Ledebour came and added their pleas to the call for Anglo-German amity.[43] Bernstein came over later on, while MacDonald led a British Labour delegation to Germany – one, unfortunately, financed by anti-socialist politicians and by the Hirsch-Duncker 'Free Trade Unions'. Hardie's voice called powerfully for peace during the next tense years. In December 1913 he presided over a great peace demonstration at the Albert Hall, where the speakers included Jaurès, Molkebuhr, Vandervelde and Anatole France. He argued, as has been seen, that the Agadir confrontation with Germany in July 1911 was partly engineered in order to put pressure on the workers during the national railway strike and partly to sustain British bond-holders in Morocco. He also claimed that it showed anew the perils of secret diplomacy in that it left uneasiness in the minds of the Germans and other great powers. 'Perhaps a Power will one day have the courage to insist upon a clean, honest diplomacy, and should that day come it will usher in a revolution.'[44] During the Balkan Wars of 1912–13 Hardie argued passionately against Hyndman's anti-German hysteria. He called for non-intervention by the great powers in the Balkans. On the other hand, he did acknowledge in the Merthyr *Pioneer* (16 November 1912) that there were legitimate points of conflict in the Balkans, particularly Serbia's yearning for an outlet to the sea, which was denied her by Austrian military domination. He also admitted the reactionary and expansionist nature of the Young Turk regime, which had led it into conflict with neighbouring Balkan states. Originally, he confessed, British socialists had welcomed the Young Turk revolution of 1908 and thought it might alleviate the lot of the working class and peasants in the Turkish empire. But 'Young Turk in office proved to be an Old Turk writ large', with press censorship, the imprisonment of political critics, religious and ethnic persecution as the fruits of government.[45] The military defeats of Turkey in 1912 and of Russia at the hands of the Japanese in 1904–5 were taken by Hardie as evidence of the spiritless, demoralized way in which a military despotism would confront its adversaries on the battlefield – not exactly a pacifist argument, incidentally. It was a further nail in the coffin of the arguments of Lord Roberts, the National Service League and conscriptionists as a whole. In general, though, there was little that Hardie and his radical allies in the House could do to rouse public opinion. After Agadir British naval preparations went ahead, contingency plans were drawn up in collaboration with the French chiefs of staff, should the Germans invade Belgium, and Lloyd George joined the Committee of Imperial Defence as a vigorous new exponent of a strong foreign policy. The new axis of Grey and Lloyd George was a powerful factor in eliminating some of the ambiguities of British diplomacy and strategic planning in 1913–14, and impelling Britain towards war.

If Hardie could do little in Britain itself, save to try to rouse the nation to the threat of international militarism, abroad there was one possible instrument. This was the Socialist International, in which Hardie increasingly placed his hopes of saving the world from the holocaust of Armageddon. In 1910 he attended the Copenhagen conference of the International, and in conjunction with the French delegate, Dr Edouard Vaillant, put forward a proposal that the International should endorse an international strike by the working class in the event of war. This motion was shelved, predictably enough, by the delegates at Copenhagen. There were possible socialist antidotes to militarism that rivalled Hardie's proposal for a general strike. Jaurès, for instance, championed the idea of a national citizens' militia which would replace armies drawn from the military caste. In any case he did not share Hardie's pessimism that the capitalist system would lead to war, while he welcomed the Triple Alliance as a first step towards an international federation. The German socialists, mindful of the threat posed by Czarist Russia, were prepared to argue that wars of national self-defence were still admissible by socialists. Hardie persisted with his scheme of a general strike: along with Vaillant, Jaurès, Bebel, Adler, Rubanovich and Huysman, he served on a committee appointed by the International Socialist Bureau to draft a resolution for the Berne International in 1912. Here again, however, nothing concrete resulted. There was a mood of exultation as Bebel and Jaurès embraced in fraternal comradeship to the background of 'the bells of Basle'. Hardie's 'wonderful and hoary head' caught the imagination of one Russian woman delegate.[46] Finally it was agreed that the Hardie-Vaillant resolution would be placed formally on the agenda of the International due to be convened at Vienna in 1914. Hardie himself continued to crusade for a general strike. He advocated also a triple alliance between the socialist movements in Britain, Germany and France. Meanwhile he tried to mollify trade union members of the Labour Party executive at home by explaining that a general strike was only a measure of the last resort, to be adopted if political action and diplomatic negotations failed. Throughout the early summer of 1914 Hardie was actively involved in negotiations with the International Socialist Bureau in pushing on the concept of a general strike. He managed to enlist the partial support of Jaurès for the cause. He always found promoting the cause of a general strike to be an uphill battle. British Labour men regarded it as impractical; German Marxists like Kautsky saw it as anarchistic and utopian. Even so, in June and July 1914 the socialist movement seemed to be moving steadily nearer to evolving a coherent strategy that would protect the workers of the world from the conflicts and rivalries of the capitalist and militarist interests. Edouard Vaillant, writing to Hardie from Paris, urged that the International Miners' Congress should follow the example of the British miners' strike and adopt a resolution in favour of a general strike against war. 'A similar strike [to the British] would make war impossible in all the states. . . . If the trade unions of the industries which, like the miners and railway workers whose general strike would – internationally made – suffice to prevent the war, dare not tell their decision to prepare this action and international strike against the war, socialism and civilization go certainly to the abyss.' Vaillant concluded, 'I know you, I know how great was ever your desire and will to prevent the crime and danger of war, and I know also your influence on the opinion and will of the English working class and especially of the miners'.[47]

The campaign for a general strike by the workers confirmed that Hardie retained his stature in the socialist world in the summer of 1914. Indeed, his authority among socialist organizations overseas never stood higher. This counteracted the divisive and fractious nature of the Labour Party at home, which found Hardie somewhat peripheral to many of its policies. In the peace crusade, as in the domestic class war, he was a lone campaigner. He had had discussions in the House with Sir Norman Angell, author of the celebrated anti-war tract, *The Great Illusion*, in 1911. Hardie advised Angell not to have a version of his book published under the auspices of the ILP. 'You will be well advised not to associate it too much with men like me.'[48] As always, then, he was the great outsider. But in the difficult years since 1911 he had not laboured in vain. He had helped steer the labour movement away from anarcho-syndicalism and also from overt alliance with the Liberals. He had helped to sustain it as a political movement without compromising its objectives. He had presided over the ILP at a vital period in its history and had rehabilitated his own relationship with it. Above all, in the peace movement he remained a voice of sanity and of pacific tolerance in a world threatened by the juggernaut of war.

XIII   At Gethsemane (1914–15)

In the later weeks of July 1914 Hardie felt little more anxiety than did other political leaders that a world war was approaching. Like most other politicians, he regarded the Austrian-Serbian crisis after the assassination of the Archduke Franz Ferdinand at Sarajevo as essentially a local affair, similar to other Balkan crises in the past. He told the International Socialist Bureau that there was no special urgency that called for his resolution on behalf of a general strike by the working class to be tabled. His columns in the Merthyr *Pioneer*, like those of the press in general, were mainly concerned with the political crisis in Ireland and the threat of civil war between Protestant Ulster, backed up by the Unionist Party, and Catholic southern Ireland. Hardie was on welcome and familiar ground in attacking the role of George v in this emergency. The suggestion that the King should intervene as a mediator, Hardie wrote, meant that 'the King casts his lot with the reactionary peers and rebellious Ulsterities'. As always, Hardie threw his support behind constitutionalism and the democratically-elected representatives of the people. 'King George is not a statesman. He is not the pleasure-loving scapegrace his father was before him, but like his father, he is destitute of even ordinary ability. . . . He is being made the tool of the reactionary classes.'[1] Pacifist though he was, Hardie urged Asquith and the British government to stand firm. He was also involved with trying to amend the Welsh Disestablishment Bill and to provide compensation in the form of life security for the Welsh curates, 'the workmen of the Church'.[2]

But, like politicians generally, Hardie was wrenched away from these familiar domestic controversies. On 25 July Austria-Hungary issued an ultimatum to Serbia; Serbia's mild-tempered reply was rudely rejected. By the end of the month it was apparent that the crisis in the Balkans was threatening to erupt into a major conflict, with

Austria-Hungary relying on German support, and Serbia backed up by Russia, with whom France was also in alliance. Britain herself might even become sucked in, and universal catastrophe ensue. Hardie's initial moves were directed towards the International Socialist Bureau, which held an emergency meeting at Brussels on 29–30 July 1914. This did not go well. Hardie, who attended as one of the British delegates along with Glasier and Dan Irving of the BSP found the discussions confusing, with the specific call for a general strike merged into a wider debate on imperialism as the root cause of war. Glasier commented waspishly that Hardie was 'rather huffed at the seeming lack of attention paid to him'. More basic to Hardie's attitude was that he considered that the Bureau was paying insufficient regard to the views of the British labour movement, which felt quite uninvolved in the international crisis, and was concerned less with doctrinal exegesis than with practical action. Hardie left on the morning of 30 July, and in his absence the Bureau failed to produce any concrete proposals.[3]

It was already becoming clear that the German socialists were generally endorsing the view that the threat to national security from Czarist Russia overrode workers' solidarity. Further, on 31 July, Jaurès was assassinated in Paris, and the fear grew that the French socialists also would merge their internationalism in the 'patriotic' cause of the sacred union, to save the fatherland. In fact, Jaurès himself had already indicated, before his death, that he supported the French government's stand. The mirage of international action by the workers of all countries to frustrate the war policies of the governments dissolved. By 2 August it was evident that Germany and Russia were in confrontation in the east, that France was going to intervene as Russia's ally, and that socialists in the belligerent countries were mostly going to follow the nationalist line. Socialists like Viviani were prominent in the French government. Most shattering of all, the German socialists, now deprived of the mighty leadership of August Bebel who had died the previous year, decided by seventy-eight to fourteen to vote for war credits. Kautsky and Bernstein, the antagonists over the 'revisionist' controversy, later joined the minority. As Hardie wrote in his 'weekly budget' (echoing John Bright during the Crimean War), 'the angel of death with blood-stained wings was hovering over Europe'.[4]

Britain's position still remained ambiguous. Even as late as 1 August it was believed that Lloyd George might head a peace party to insist on British neutrality. By 3 August all this had changed – indeed the dream of a peace party was wholly unreal anyway. The German threat to Belgium united virtually all the British Cabinet in support of Grey's policy of firmness. There was no prospect of Lloyd George's voluntarily taking to the wilderness.[5] Only the ageing Morley and the ineffective Burns (both old opponents of Hardie's) resigned from the cabinet. At midnight on 4 August Britain was at war.

For Hardie this was a shattering experience, the destruction of all the ideals of social progress and international fraternity he had treasured throughout his career. He took part in a great demonstration in Trafalgar Square on 2 August, which called for a general strike by the British workers. The Labour Party issued a manifesto to this effect. But it was clear that the mass of the Labour members and a majority of the party executive were moving towards an endorsement of British involvement in war. When Grey made his epoch-making (and strangely elliptic) statement to the House of Commons on 3 August, Hardie and MacDonald courageously raised their voices in protest. Hardie's speech was a rambling, over-passionate one, but he did provide a note of sharp dissent.[6] His speech, indeed, was more militant than that of MacDonald or any other speaker. He threatened the government with united action by the workers against their policy, action which he himself would do his best to encourage. But his words were in vain. Indeed it was a Labour member, Will Crooks, who led an emotional rendering of the national anthem by the members present. Hardie, reviled and abused as never before, then decided to carry the fight to his Welsh constituency. Here he faced an even more crushing experience. His 'peace' meeting at Aberdare on 6 August was howled down. The demonstrators in the audience were led by Charles Stanton, the local miners' agent, a Welsh Mussolini who turned as naturally to the advocacy of world war as of class war. Hardie had barely time to blurt out a few hurried sentences about the 'poisonous lies' spread about the Germans and Prussianism. He added, 'If there is one man on the face of the earth we ought to help sink into oblivion, it is the great bloodstained Czar of Russia.' The meeting was abandoned in total disorder, to the unbridled glee of the Merthyr and Cardiff press.[7] Hardie was deeply shaken and poured out his sense of depression to Glasier on his return home to Nevills Court. To a Merthyr friend, after the failure of the Aberdare meeting, he reflected sadly, 'I now understand the sufferings of Christ at Gethsemane'. Hardie's self-identification with his Saviour was leading him towards his own crucifixion.

Hardie's attempts to rouse the national conscience in the latter months of 1914 made little headway. He found himself at odds with Henderson and most of the leaders of the Labour Party. He was savagely heckled by working-class audiences at Manchester and other cities. At one time it even looked as if the ILP itself might prove to be uncertain in its attitude to the war. Hardie was disturbed by the qualified nature of the resolutions passed at various ILP demonstrations: 'not so determined in condemnation of the war as I would have liked', he wrote.[8] However on 31 August the NAC did endorse the views of Hardie and MacDonald in their opposition to the war and attacked the participation of ILP members in recruiting rallies with Liberal and Unionist speakers. Hardie and MacDonald then co-operated in sharpening the tone of ILP policy statements, even though Hardie's original draft manifesto on the war had been rejected in favour of a crisper version written by W.C. Anderson.[9] Hardie himself was unmistakably hostile to the war: it affronted every principle he held dear. Yet, with declining physical powers and a crushed spirit, even he found the personal pressures of maintaining a pacifist stance to be almost unbearable. Glasier noted that Hardie preferred to travel up by train from Merthyr to London with him for company; he guessed that Hardie was anxious about the insults he might endure from jingoistic fellow-passengers if he travelled alone.[10] In the press Hardie's views went through various gyrations that reflected his agony of mind. In the *Pioneer* and in *Forward*, he defended himself against charges that he was oblivious to considerations of national security and self-defence:

A nation at war must be united especially when its existence is at stake. . . . With the boom of the enemy's guns within earshot, the lads who have gone forth by sea and land to fight their country's battles must not be disheartened by any discordant note at home. . . . We must see the war through but we must also make ourselves so familiar with the facts as to be able to intervene at the earliest possible moment in the interests of peace.

He denied that the ILP stood for the immediate ending of the war. In the first instance, 'the German troops must be thrown back across their own frontier'.[11] It was an unexpected view from the uncompromising pacifist of pro-Boer days.

Hardie concentrated rather on the way in which the war was being fought, on the dissemination of lies against the German people, on the threats to civil liberties and to the living standards of the working class that the war had brought in its wake. However, in a mass meeting at the Olympia skating rink at Merthyr on 30 October, Hardie, speaking in conjunction with MacDonald, again denounced the outbreak of war.[12] This time he had a relatively peaceful hearing. Germany, he argued, had offered reasonable terms of compromise over Belgium, which Grey had turned down. Russian militarism was a far more dangerous threat to humanity than was the might of Germany. Compulsory military service would be an inevitable consequence of total war, with the resultant 'Russification' of Britain as well. He also condemned the low pay and dismal living conditions of troops at the front and the meagre six-months' allowance for widows guaranteed by the government. Inevitably, then, whatever his qualifications, Hardie found himself popularly abused as a pro-Hun, who spread sedition and who circulated false rumours about the patriotic British troops at the front. He was savagely attacked by his fellow Merthyr MP, the Liberal Edgar Jones, in the House of Commons. Jones alleged that Hardie had tried actively to discourage recruiting for the forces.[13] Hardie denied the charge, but was forced to make the admission that recruiting from the Merthyr area showed that Welsh patriotic zeal had been unaffected by recent political controversies. It all reinforced the impression of him as the defensive, evasive spokesman of an unpatriotic minority who sought to undermine the nation's will to fight without having the courage to admit it openly.

His main hope now was that the ILP and other anti-war agencies would be able to stir the national conscience sufficiently to deflect the government towards peace negotiations. He warmly applauded an anti-war article by Bernard Shaw, 'Commonsense and the War'. 'Only a Celt could have done it,' Hardie wrote.[14] He was restored once again to friendly relations with John Burns and with many anti-war Liberals with whom his contacts had been minimal in the pre-war years. In a talk with Hardie on 15 February, Burns found him 'looking much older, and worried about the war, living a lonely life with little to divert him'.[15] On the other hand, Hardie was less willing than was

MacDonald to merge the ILP into a wider radical alliance of all opposed to the war. In particular, he opposed MacDonald's endeavours to link the ILP campaign with the mainly Liberal members of the Union of Democratic Control, founded now by E.D. Morel. Hardie argued at the NAC meeting of 16 October that the UDC's activities 'took away from the energy and kudos of the ILP'. He also had some disagreement with some of the NAC sub-committee involved with the circulation of anti-war literature. Hardie and MacDonald here argued that the specific political origins of the war should be the main target of ILP propaganda; Glasier preferred to emphasize the socialist objective of the ultimate abolition of war altogether.[16] Hardie, indeed, found it increasingly difficult to sustain any viable line of criticism against the war, so apparently overwhelming was the national support for the government in these early months. He took comfort from simple peaceful episodes like the fraternizing of British and German troops on the western front at Christmas time.[17] He expressed the vain hope that incidents like this might convince the soldiers that the workers of the world were not in a state of war with one another, but were comrades with a common interest in mutual well-being.

By the beginning of 1915, it was apparent that the determining feature of Hardie's public career was that he was now a sick man. His arm had been troubling him. 'I can do very little writing which is a nuisance,' he wrote to Agnes Hughes.[18] On 9 January it was announced that he was partly paralysed by a mild stroke. He returned rapidly to the fray to address a miners' meeting at Hamilton where his life as an agitator had first begun. He chaired a meeting of the International Bureau on 14 February and later presided over the annual dinner of the City of London ILP. At the Bureau a resolution was passed, drafted basically by MacDonald, which was strongly anti-German in tone. Hardie was too feeble to stand out against it. The conference was also marred by a dispute between the ILP delegates and their French colleagues about the invasion of Belgium, a quarrel to which the *Daily News* made reference. In addition, Hardie publicly rebuked Litvinov who had complained of the failure to invite the Russian Bolsheviks: Litvinov stalked out angrily. It was another disillusioning blow to the myth of socialist fraternity. Glasier found Hardie to be 'looking strangely old and speaking with a curious faultiness of articulation – his illness had told on him severely'.[19] W.C.

Anderson noted Hardie's frequent absences from the NAC. 'He is we all fear fading out from the scene'.[20] John Morley was shocked by Hardie's wan appearance when they met in the Commons lobby.[21] Glasier found him 'curiously irritable and feeble' and prone to fall asleep, when they dined out at a London restaurant.[22] Hardie made what was to be his last major intervention in the Commons on 25 February. Appropriately, it dealt with the cause of children who were being withdrawn from schools in agricultural areas for cheap labour on the farms. He asked the government to take a firm stand in abolishing child labour in the countryside.[23] His last parliamentary question was asked on 27 April when he passed on a resolution from the Merthyr Trades Council which asked for an increase in old-age pensions owing to rising prices during wartime.[24] Hardie's columns in the *Pioneer* contained some of the old fire, although it was noticeable that the editor padded them out with nostalgic childhood reminiscences, such as the famous tale of his dismissal by the Glasgow baker at the age of ten. It was as though Hardie was publicly acknowledging that his career was at an end, and that only retrospection remained. His final public appearance came at the ILP annual conference at Norwich in April, a sombre gathering totally overshadowed by the war and the bloody conflict being waged in the trenches. Hardie's one intervention was a typical attack on Czarist Russia for the imprisonment of members of the Russian Seamen's Union and of socialist members of the Duma. The alliance with Russia, he declared was 'a disgrace to civilization and progress', and he denounced the 'bloody cruelty of the Czarist regime'. He also got embroiled in a controversy with Lloyd George who, Hardie alleged, had accused British workers of being drunkards. But, as Jowett wrote, 'the fire of life was burning low'.[25] Immediately afterwards Hardie's health collapsed again and he was sent to Caterham sanatorium to recuperate.

The remaining months were painful in the extreme. In addition to growing physical infirmity, Hardie's mind began to give way. Agnes Hughes was told by Nan Hardie of how her father took an irrational dislike to a specialist called in to examine him, and how the doctor had then to be sent away. 'Don't say anything to *anyone*, Aggie, as we don't want any newspaper fuss.'[26] The strain on Hardie's daughter and on his wife was almost unbearable. He became increasingly irritable and also unable to sleep. He did manage one last visit to Nevills Court at the end of May. He wrote to Sylvia Pankhurst, with whom his relations continued to be cordial, that he wanted to hand over some of her letters written to him from America in 1911. She could use her discretion on what to publish and what to keep. He added that he would like to keep a picture of Sylvia which had been hung over the fireplace. He ended wearily, 'There is much in what you say about the war & the state of my health'.[27] At the start of July his physical and mental deterioration was so acute that he was moved temporarily back to the family home at Cumnock. Here the ordeal was even more painful. Nan Hardie wrote, 'The Dr here doesn't know if F.[ather] has reached the climax yet. He thinks he may get worse mentally and told me sleep and nourishment alone will save him. He sleeps fairly well, only awakens with "visions". It is a dreadful trouble.'[28] Hardie had a final period at Caterham. On 28 July he managed to scrawl a feeble postcard message to Sylvia Pankhurst, probably the last communication received from him. It was appropriate that Sylvia, who had perhaps kindled his most intimate emotions, should be the recipient. 'Dear Sylphia [*sic*]. In about a week I expect to be gone from here with no more mind control than when I came.'[29] To the growing distress of his wife and daughter, he was brought home again to Cumnock. He was able to spend a few days with his son Duncan, at Arran, but then went into a deep coma. The end was evidently near. Finally on 26 September Keir Hardie died at the age of fifty-nine. The cause of death was given as pneumonia.

At a time of crisis during the war, his death went relatively unnoticed in the national press. *The Times* wrote a brief and acid obituary, unforgiving to the last. 'He was probably the most abused politician of his time, though held in something like veneration by uncompromising Socialists, and no speaker has had more meetings broken up in more continents than he.'[30] But in the reactions of socialists and working-class people in Britain and many other lands can be traced the almost irreparable sense of loss that Hardie's death aroused. Bruce Glasier, so often at odds with Hardie yet so often closer to him than almost any other man, gave anguished expression to this passionate emotion: 'A strange feeling of fright – sorrow – I know not what, and we wept together. . . . It was good he was taken away so mercifully soon, and not doomed to live years as a half imbecile, blurring our image of him as the greatest fighter of his day.'[31]

Hardie's funeral was a highly emotional affair. He was cremated in Glasgow at the Maryhill crematorium. British socialists were strongly represented, although the war had kept away all delegates from overseas. After the long procession had wound its way down to the crematorium, a few words were spoken by the Rev. A.M. Forson, an associate of Hardie's in his early days in the Evangelical Union. To Glasier's anger, Forson made no reference to Hardie's work for socialism or for international peace. Glasier himself then blurted out a few passionate words about Hardie's being the greatest agitator of his time.[32] A few days later, on 3 October, a memorial service was held at St Andrews Hall, Glasgow, where Ramsay MacDonald delivered the main address and the 'Red Flag' was solemnly sung. In the Labour and socialist press, tributes and official commemorations of Hardie's death flowed in. Shaw penned a moving tribute in which he linked Hardie's death directly with the shattering effect of the war upon his spirit: 'I really do not see what Hardie could do but die'.[33] Although Hardie's broken body lay mouldering in its grave, like John Brown's body, Shaw wrote, his soul would go marching on. Perhaps the most intensely poignant tribute of all came from Sylvia Pankhurst in her *Woman's Dreadnought* (later to be re-christened the *Workers' Dreadnought*). In this, Sylvia laid stress on the romantic, artistic and religious aspects of Hardie's personality. 'Keir Hardie', she wrote, 'has been the greatest human being of our time.'[34]

There was one disagreeable aftermath to Hardie's death. In his will he left only personal property valued at £426 to his wife and children. He owned the house at Cumnock, plus five £1 shares in the Labour Pioneer Press at Merthyr, valued at 2s 6d; £95 13s 1d was due to him from his salary as an MP. At last the myths of Hardie's private means, the covert gifts from the Misses Kippens or from traffickers in 'Tory gold', were exploded: Hardie's only holding of stock had been £387 in the Ayr and District 'Economic Building Society', the surplus of which was claimed by the trustees.[35] At the ILP council on 22 October 1915, T.D. Benson raised the question of the straitened circumstances of Mrs Hardie and her daughter. It was then agreed that £500 in 4½ per cent City of Montreal Sterling Registered Stock, originally purchased from the legacy of the Misses Kippen, should be transferred to a trust and the income paid to Mrs Hardie and after her death to Agnes Hardie. Hardie's funeral expenses were also to be paid.[36] Embarrassingly, Mrs Hardie objected to these arrangements. She resented the idea of a public appeal which would make her the object of charitable sympathy. More substantially, she claimed that £500 was due to Hardie's dependants directly from the Kippen bequest, and that her husband and T.D. Benson had agreed that this should be carried out, should Hardie lose his seat or become infirm. Glasier had to conduct delicate negotiations with Mrs Hardie and Agnes. They argued that Hardie had always insisted that the ILP had agreed to pay £500 from the ambiguous Kippen legacy to him personally and that Hardie had been deeply anxious about this in his last days. Glasier managed to smooth matters over, and on 25 January 1916 the NAC reported that an appeal was to be launched: in six months it had raised £575, and by January 1917 the total was £2,815. In addition, the transfer of £500 in 4½ per cent stock was approved as the basis of a trust fund. The income to Mrs Hardie from the trust would be not less than £22 10s a year, less income tax. The principal of the fund would be eventually turned over to the ILP itself.[37] To the end, then, Hardie's uncertainty about money matters lingered on, though in the final resort his affairs were straightened out. One other detail was that Glasier was requested to undertake an official biography.[38] After some hesitation, since he was himself in failing health, he declined, and the task was entrusted instead to William Stewart, a former Glasgow colleague of Hardie's in the Scottish Labour Party, whose volume eventually appeared in 1921.

Hardie's death left only a transient imprint on the anti-war movement. His major impact had been in the protest he made at the very outbreak of war itself. Thereafter, through failing health, he had not been a dominating figure in the peace campaign; in any case, he was out of sympathy with attempts to merge socialist anti-war protests with the propaganda of the mainly Liberal Union of Democratic Control. To the end, Hardie fought for rugged independence. It was apparent long before his death that Ramsay MacDonald had emerged as the dominant figure in the ILP campaign against the war. After Hardie's death, MacDonald gained new stature as the principal Labour advocate of a negotiated peace and this was to lend him new authority after war ended as a leader of the left. His earlier flirtations with the Liberal alliance paled by comparison with his courageous campaign against the war in the face of an inflamed nationalistic public opinion. Hardie, then, was removed from the public scene at a time when his influence was in any event declining.

But there was one difficult crisis which his death had now exposed. Hardie's removal meant that there was a vacancy at Merthyr: it was recognized that, despite Hardie's long tenure of the seat, this was no easy constituency for the Labour Party to retain. After some delay, the second Liberal candidate, Artemus Jones, said that he could not contest the seat, in view of the party truce. But he added that no Labour candidate opposed to the war as Hardie had been could possibly be countenanced.[39] It soon became clear that the Merthyr Labour supporters were deeply divided. The miners were to ballot for Bob Smillie, James Winstone (president of the South Wales Miners), Enoch Morrell, John Williams and C.B. Stanton for selection as their nominee. Hardie's former agent, Harry Morris, complained to MacDonald: 'The old game is being played for all it is worth, viz., Welsh Nationalism, by the scribes in the South Wales press, Mr Tom Richards MP [the Labour member for West Monmouthshire] being the chief culprit in this direction, but it is pleasing to find that Mr Vernon Hartshorn is a little wiser at the moment.'[40] The issue roused wider ideological issues than whether the new candidate should be a Welshman. Bob Smillie, a Scots associate of Hardie over the years, shared to the full Hardie's anti-war sentiments. He was also strongly identified with the ILP. Llew Francis, the Merthyr barber, wrote to MacDonald, 'The seat is an ILP seat won by the ILPers and kept by them in spite of all the machinations of the miners' E.C. It has never been earmarked by the miners.' He urged MacDonald to come down and throw his influence behind Smillie.[41] MacDonald did not do so and in the end Winstone was nominated on the ballot of the local miners, by the narrow margin of 1,600 votes. Winstone was not an opponent of the war. He supported the official policy of the Labour Party and had taken part in recruiting campaigns in South Wales. On the other hand, he was the official leader of the Welsh miners who had recently taken part in successful strike action against the government's 'treasury agreement'. He was also a member of the ILP and thus inevitably tarred with the anti-war brush.

As a reaction to Winstone's nomination, C.B. Stanton resigned his post as miners' agent for Aberdare, and decided to fight the election as a pro-war independent Labour candidate. Since his belligerent stand on behalf of war since August 1914, Stanton claimed, he had been ostracized by the Miners' Federation and had been left off the list of candidates considered in the miners' ballot.[42] His nomination as an official Labour candidate, by the Typographical Society, was deemed to be invalid by the local LRC. Winstone and Stanton thus found themselves locked in a bitter internecine struggle. The election was superficially tranquil; but beneath the surface there was a desperate struggle between the call of class and of nation. Stanton fought a stridently anti-German campaign. He emerged as an uninhibited advocate of the war against the 'brutal butchers of Berlin': his own son serving at the front provided a human symbol of his dedication to all-out war. Winstone tried to make it clear that he also supported the war effort, but inevitably he was dubbed unpatriotic and seditious. Stanton freely attacked him as 'pro-German'. In addition, Winstone unwisely called in well-known anti-war ILP men like Ramsay MacDonald and Fred Jowett to speak on his behalf.[43] Winstone vehemently attacked conscription: this could sound all too easily like a half-hearted attitude towards total war. Above all, Winstone laboured under the disadvantage of being apparently the chosen successor to Keir Hardie, in a constituency in which Labour had never topped the poll and had always been somewhat divided within itself. It was noticeable that SWMF executive members kept well clear of the constituency. Stanton triumphed convincingly on polling day, by a majority of 4,206 on a low poll. There were basic local reasons for his victory. He received the support of local Liberals and Unionists, including George Brown, a former Tory agent, as well as of miners' agents such as Captain D. Watts Morgan. He also drew votes from Catholic electors and from ironworkers in the constituency.[44] These parochial details, however, were lost sight of in the light of Stanton's stridently 'patriotic' campaign on behalf of a fight to a finish. He himself claimed that 'the boys in the trenches' would rejoice in his victory. The London press was wild with excitement. The *Daily Express* declared that Winstone was associated with 'wishy-washy, backboneless, cosmopolitanism' while Stanton had fought for 'country and Empire'.[45] Victor Fisher, who had worked for Stanton during the by-election, now turned to forming his British Workers' League of patriotic proletarians. Indeed, Lord Milner and his circle of 'social imperialists' regarded the Merthyr by-election as a vital watershed in the history of the British labour movement, a glowing opportunity to rid trade unionists of their domination by the pacifists and revolutionaries of the ILP.[46] The removal of Hardie alone was of profound symbolic significance. For Hardie's former party workers the result was tragic in the extreme. The champion of peace and of fraternity had been succeeded by a proto-Fascist nationalist of the crudest kind. The Merthyr by-election, coming at a time when the anti-war movement was at its lowest ebb, seemed the final confirmation of the futility and failure that had marked Hardie's career for most of its course. Even in his own Welsh valleys, it appeared, he had left no lasting monument.

XIV Hardie's Legacy

At the time of Hardie's death, socialists of all shades were unanimous in their acknowledgement of his unique contribution to the making of the British Labour movement. In the words of the *Pioneer*, the 'member for Humanity had resigned his seat'.[1] Ramsay MacDonald's passionate tribute claimed that 'Hardie's work and memory were safe in the keeping of time'.[2] The Fabian Sidney Webb wrote of Hardie at the time of his funeral, 'He has not an enemy in the world'.[3] George Lansbury, a product of the SDF who shared much of Hardie's dedicated individualism in the causes of pacifism, colonial liberation and women's rights, also offered an emotion-charged verdict. 'On the banks of the Ganges, the Indian workmen will tell of the death of the great white man who came back from his tour determined to get justice done for that vast dependency. By the Nile, the Egyptian fellaheen will also mourn his loss, and the coloured men of South Africa will remember, too, that they have lost a friend.'[4] These spontaneous judgements, echoed by socialists throughout Europe and the empire, were more than *pièces d'occasion* inspired by the shock news of Hardie's death. As the years went by, as total war gave way to twenty years of uneasy peace, to a second world war and then to renewed hopes for social regeneration and world peace after 1945, the image of Hardie as the dedicated, single-minded champion of idealistic socialism in its purest form became enshrined in the collective memory of the British working-class movement. 'He was at once the Joshua and the Moses of the Labour Movement.'[5] Whatever controversies might surround the memory of MacDonald, Snowden or Henderson, Keir Hardie seemed certain of immortality as the one acknowledged folk-hero of the labour movement and of the under-privileged throughout the world.

Hardie's opponents were equally certain in their judgements also. There were those like H.M. Hyndman who found Hardie, with his gyrations between 'socialist unity' and a radical alliance, to be totally unpredictable:

I have never understood Keir Hardie. Today he will declare in favour of votes for all women. Tomorrow he will be arguing for the limitation of the suffrage to the comparatively few with unsurpassed ardour. One week he will denounce in private certain personal and political treachery as seriously injurious to the movement. The next he will be upholding the individual guilty of this behaviour as the most valuable asset of the socialist movement.[6]

Hyndman had his own doctrinaire position, reinforced by personal disappointment; but many who were far from sympathizing with the SDF also found Hardie erratic and personally difficult. Men like Glasier, close to Hardie in many ways, found his characteristics – his extreme individualism, his tendency to take refuge in a romantic, quasi-spiritualist milieu of his own, his enthusiasm for taking private counsel or communion with Frank Smith rather than participating openly in committee meetings – all hard to bear or to understand. On the other hand, opponents of the socialist movement found Hardie all too predictable and comprehensible. He was marked down as an emotional extremist, with no practical gifts. In A.G. Gardiner's penetrating phrase, he was the one man in the parliamentary Labour Party who was unqualified to lead it.[7] He epitomized a socialist radical all too willing to emit clouds of emotional oratory, but all too reluctant to take part in the pragmatic, piecemeal processes of government. The *Daily Telegraph* dismissed him as 'temperamentally a fault-finder', a 'permanent Ishmaelite'.[8] John Burns once told Hardie 'he would be known as the leader who never won a strike, organized a Union, governed a parish, or passed a Bill'. With heavy punning irony, he summed Hardie up as 'Barren Cumnock in the Duchy of Doctrinaire', a man who preached a Jehad of class hatred as a substitute for progressive reform.[9] Even those who sympathized with Hardie and the ILP tended to echo this view. Hardie was seen as an inspirational force above all, an agitator, a prophet, a seer, but one with an aversion to the operation of power. He symbolized a labour movement happy in permanent opposition, cherishing its doctrinal purity in the wilderness. When Hardie did attain a position of authority, briefly, when he was chairman of the parliamentary Labour Party in 1906–7, he did not enjoy the experience. His spirit rebelled against the constraints of authority and the compromises that had to be made; he never held an official position in the movement again. In the sum, the opinion of critics and of many disciples also was that Hardie finished his career with little positive to show. His brief (and unsuccessful) membership of the Auchinleck school board in the early 1880s was his sole acquaintance with translating socialist theory into practical effect.

However difficult to define, Hardie's influence powerfully permeated the Labour Party at least until the general election of 1945. Even as late as 1964, when Dr Horace King was elected the first Labour speaker of the House, Emanuel Shinwell, an old associate of the Clydeside group of ILP members, declared that Keir Hardie would have been proud to see that day. The Hardie tradition was carried on directly by his youngest brother, George, who represented the Springburn division of Glasgow in 1922–31 and in 1935–7.[10] George Hardie, a trained scientist who worked with a Glasgow firm of engineers, was a more practical man than his elder brother: he was successful in inventing a new form of smokeless fuel. During Keir Hardie's lifetime he had tried to apply business caution to some of his financial dealings. Nevertheless, George Hardie kept his brother's ideals bravely in the forefront of parliamentary attention. He, too, was sympathetic to pacifism. He defended James Maxton when the Glasgow School Board sought to dismiss him in 1916 on the grounds of his being a conscientious objector. George Hardie stood at the 'coupon election' in 1918 as 'an outspoken opponent of militarism'. He collaborated with the Clydeside group in 1922–4 in pushing the cause of unemployment, although he himself was never really a militant. Another brother, David, served briefly as Labour member for the Rutherglen division in 1931, and was also a casualty of the 'doctors' mandate' general election of October 1931 when Labour was crushed by Ramsay MacDonald's recently contrived National Government. George died in 1935, David in 1939.

Hardie's daughter, Nan, remained active in politics and became Provost of Cumnock in the later 1930s. It fell to her to unveil a bust of her father sculpted by Benno Schultz in August 1939, on the eve of another world catastrophe which yet again mocked Hardie's ideals.[11] Nan Hardie married a man who, above all others, was to carry on Hardie's spirit of rebellious crusading throughout successive parliaments until his death in 1969. This was Emrys Hughes, the editor of *Forward*, the brother of Hardie's young Welsh friend, Agnes, and the son of a nonconformist minister in Aberdare who had become converted to socialism. He himself was temporarily a student at a theological college, and was much stirred by the Welsh religious revival of 1904–5 which pushed so many young nonconformists towards social reform. Emrys Hughes served as member for South Ayrshire from 1946 onwards. Like his late father-in-law, he was a dedicated pacifist and party rebel; appropriately, he wrote Hardie's biography, a warm, human appreciation, and also published valuable extracts from Hardie's speeches and pamphlets. Hughes was an incorrigible rebel, whose impish humour sometimes got the better of his judgement. Repeatedly in trouble with the Labour whips, perhaps he won more respect on the Conservative benches than amongst his fellow Labour members. But as long as Emrys Hughes was in parliament, the spirit of Keir Hardie brooded there with him, a permanent touchstone of how far the Labour party under the successive leadership of Attlee, Gaitskell and Wilson had strayed from the socialist faith of the founding father.

In the years after 1918, indeed, Labour's domestic and foreign policies bore the clear imprint of Hardie's influence. As the original jingoism of the war years and the 'coupon election' petered out, his ideals gained a new authority in the post-war world, especially among younger voters, working- and middle-class alike. At the 1918 Labour Party conference Will Thorne, heir to the succession at West Ham, hailed Hardie as the one Labour leader who never made bargains.[12] Ironically, it was Ramsay MacDonald, for so long at odds with Hardie over many aspects of the Liberal alliance, who now emerged as a fresh new champion of Hardie's pristine ideals, at a time when Lloyd George's Coalition government was becoming discredited and the old Liberal opposition appeared fragmented and out-of-date. Like Hardie, the Labour Party in the 1920s concentrated on social issues, on alleviating the poverty and squalid living conditions of the working class. These features of society were linked, as Hardie had linked them, with excessive profits on the part of the capitalist and under-consumption on the part of the worker deprived of adequate purchasing power. Social equality would come through struggle and conflict within a hostile capitalist environment, rather than through indicative planning. The details of public ownership were never spelled out. In some sense, indeed, the ILP's 'Living Wage' proposals in the mid-1920s were a break away from the kind of unsophisticated wages policy advocated by Hardie and his generation: its inflationary, financial proposals and its proposed battery of socialist controls went far beyond anything Hardie had ever proposed.[13] His influence on the Labour Party's domestic thinking was evident, too, in the almost total neglect paid to questions of finance, investment and credit. Under the auspices of Philip Snowden, Hardie's former colleague in the ILP who became established as Labour's financial expert after 1906 and who served as Chancellor of the Exchequer in the Labour governments of 1924 and 1929–31, Labour's views on financial matters were not very different from those of the other parties – free trade, sound finance, balanced budgets, the gold standard restored and currency stabilized. These staple features of Labour's domestic programmes showed little change from the era of Keir Hardie. They met with their disillusioning climax in the economic crisis of 1931 when the system refused to function and the surplus, which the workers were denied, disappeared.

On one issue, indeed, Hardie's influence was particularly direct throughout the post-war period – unemployment. After a temporary post-war boom which finally collapsed in the summer of 1920, the total of unemployed workers rose rapidly and was never less than a million for the remainder of the decade. At the darkest period of the 1931 crisis the total was somewhere over three and a half million, a proportion far more grave than anything Hardie had ever claimed in his crusading on behalf of the unemployed from 1892 onwards. The staple industries of the country – coal, cotton and shipbuilding – on which so much of the Labour Party's electoral strength was based, were in chronic decline as their markets dwindled and world trade contracted. Merthyr Tydfil, Hardie's old constituency, numbered almost seventy per cent of its insured male population among the unemployed in 1934. Ironic critics proposed that the population of Merthyr should be rehoused and that the town should be handed over to some vast open-air industrial museum, a monument to the world we had lost.[14] Faced with this crisis, Labour's proposals for remedying unemployment up to 1931 drew heavily on ideas Hardie had sponsored, especially on the Right to Work Bill of 1907. The setting up of afforced local distress committees, with the main initiative for relief schemes resting with them, with only a co-ordinating committee at the centre and a distrust of outside public works proposals were all echoes of pre-1914 – although, to be just to Hardie, his association with Joseph Fels had made him more receptive than many of his Labour colleagues to schemes for public projects such as land colonies. He had also advocated setting up a Ministry of Labour. George Lansbury, who finally resigned with Mosley from the Labour government in 1930, was to carry on this tradition after Hardie's death. In general, though, Labour's policies towards the unemployed, so cruelly exposed by the events of 1929–31, showed little advance upon the views so powerfully and courageously championed by 'the member for the unemployed' at West Ham and Merthyr before the war. In particular, the financial aspects of a policy for unemployment relief were left in the air and this was to prove a bitter source of contention when the Labour government collapsed in August 1931.

In its foreign policies, also, the Labour Party in the post-war period bore at first the clear imprint of Hardie's influence. MacDonald in particular, rehabilitated in radical eyes after his courageous opposition to the war (which cost him his seat at Leicester in 1918), sponsored the kind of visionary internationalism which Hardie had done so much to foster. Philip Snowden also lent support to this ideal, as did most of his ILP colleagues and all those associated with Morel and the Union of Democratic Control. Throughout the early 1920s the Labour Party gained immense credit in claiming to be a party with a special vision in foreign affairs, to stand for a new international order in place of the 'system of Versailles', and to be in a very distinct sense the party most identified with the new League of Nations. MacDonald's handling of foreign affairs during his first administration was widely and justly praised. Not least admired were the attempt to achieve a rapprochement with the Soviet Union, and the trade treaty of 1924. As Hardie would have done, MacDonald often claimed that new relations with eastern Europe would enable British trade to flourish, quite apart from its political benefits. In that sense, foreign policy was a direct key to alleviating trade depression and unemployment at home. Labour also identified itself in the 1920s with movements for colonial liberation, as Hardie had done, although its attitude to the Simon Commission on India 1927–30 suggested that his successors were less committed than Hardie had been in their sympathies with the Congress movement and its new leader, Gokhale's successor, Mahatma Gandhi.

During the 1929–31 Labour government it became apparent that Hardie's internationalism and fraternalism were losing their appeal to Labour minds. In the supreme economic crisis of 1929–31 the Labour government responded with much of the same fiscal nationalism shown by other countries: it proved all too susceptible to the nostrums of Montagu Norman and the Bank of England. Henderson as Foreign Secretary endeavoured to relieve Franco-German hostility and, with the withdrawal of French troops from the Rhineland in 1930 there was momentarily a gleam of hope in the international scene. By the time of the crash of August 1931 this had disappeared, while Snowden's grim determination that Germany should fulfil her reparations obligations was in itself a symbol of how fiscal orthodoxy and the desire for universal brotherhood conflicted in the Labour mind. After 1931 Labour rapidly retreated from the fraternalism which Hardie had represented. Its contacts with socialist movements overseas became largely a matter of form. In any event, the schism in the socialist world after the 1917 revolution in Russia – the formation of two (or, for a time, two and a half) rival socialist Internationals, the division of the working class in France, Italy and elsewhere into Socialists and Communists – made the prospects for socialist collaboration far more complicated than they had been in Keir Hardie's heyday. The Popular Front movement, pushed on by the Comintern after 1934 in France, Spain and, to some extent, Britain, met with little response from the British Labour movement. 'Socialist unity', dreams that 'left could speak to left' were evaporating. The course of events in Catalonia and elsewhere in the mid-1930s, helped them to disappear that much faster, as Orwell pungently documented. Thereafter, Labour's foreign policy became in key respects increasingly insular even after the experiences of inter-allied co-operation during the second world war. After 1945, even after 1964, Labour viewed with intense suspicion proposals for a closer integration with Europe, notwithstanding Harold Wilson's close involvement with the Socialist International. The prominent support of socialist parties in France and Germany for the European Common Market met with little response from the rank-and-file and the parliamentary majority of the Labour Party, or from the TUC. When Britain entered the Common Market at the start of 1973, Labour spokesmen denounced it as a capitalist club which imperilled British sovereignty. The new Labour government of March 1974 took a hostile attitude towards the European community at the outset. Keir Hardie would probably have done the same. He would have found little common ground with the Brussels' commissariat, although the isolationist spirit in which the internal Labour Party argument was conducted would perhaps have repelled him also.

After the 1931 crisis, then, the Labour Party, for good or ill, began to emerge from the era of Keir Hardie. Its foreign policies shifted in emphasis. At home, new young economists associated with Hugh Dalton – men like Hugh Gaitskell and Evan Durbin, with later disciples like Roy Jenkins and Anthony Crosland – attempted for the first time to provide Labour with a viable social democratic policy for planning and for economic management. The attempt was made to provide Labour with a tough-minded 'non-theological' programme for economic growth. This was translated by the Attlee government after 1945 into a frank acceptance of the mixed economy, and a re-application of the physical and fiscal controls applied during the second world war. Labour spent much time in the 1960s and 1970s attempting to evolve a new philosophy of planning, with a wages-and-prices policy based on considerations of efficiency as well as of social justice. The unsuccessful statutory wages policy of 1969 gave way to a more subtle and more congenial 'social contract' with the trade unions in 1974. But all this was worlds removed from the idealistic essentially non-economic vision of Keir Hardie. Indeed, the recession of working-class support from the Wilson government in 1964–70, the growing disillusion with parliamentary politics, Labour's failure to reclaim many of its disillusioned supporters in 1970, suggested to some that the transition from the generous utopianism of Hardie, fired by the vision of human brotherhood, to the pragmatic 'realism' of the 1964–70 administration (a realism allied with no great success in fiscal management as it happened) was a critical change for a party which was a crusade or was nothing. Symbolically, Merthyr Tydfil was temporarily lost to Labour in 1970 – to an octogenarian independent who cited Hardie in his own support. Labour's narrow election victories in February and October 1974, after the collapse of the Heath government's industrial policies, did not suggest that the tide had turned. Membership of the party continued to decline in numbers, while victory was achieved at the polls on only 37 and then 39 per cent of the vote in these two elections.

As the style of socialism preached by Keir Hardie lost favour amidst the vogue for planning in the 1930s and 1940s, so his chosen instrument, too, was ousted from its central place in the Labour alliance. In 1922, when Ramsay MacDonald was elected leader of the parlia-

mentary Labour Party, in preference to J.R. Clynes, the ILP was
still a powerful element in the party. MacDonald himself made much
of his ILP antecedents and his early association with Hardie, especially
now that the ILP had gained new esteem as the advocate of a
negotiated peace in 1917–18. It was ILP votes that gave MacDonald
the party leadership: he was proposed by Emanuel Shinwell, of Lin-
lithgow, and supported strongly by all the Clydesiders on the militant
left. But in the later 1920s the ILP rapidly became a minor part of the
Labour alliance. In any case the Clydesiders had become identified
with a distinctively Scottish position: Hardie had since 1892 been
linked with British socialism, not with the Glasgow parochialism of
the Clyde or the Celtic Communism of John Maclean. The ILP had
lost its right to earmarked places on the Labour national executive
after the new party constitution in 1918, and this was a grave handi-
cap. More important, the events of the 1920s – the comparative
unfruitfulness of the first Labour government, the failure of the 1926
general strike, MacDonald's heavy emphasis on Labour as a responsible
and parliamentary party – all these alienated the ILP. It became
increasingly marked off on grounds of temperament and doctrine from
the main stream of the party. The 'Living Wage' schemes put forward
by Jimmy Maxton and his mainly Scottish supporters were rejected by
the Labour government in 1929. Meanwhile, the Communists
denounced the ILP, ironically enough, for coming to terms with
capitalism. Finally in 1932 the ILP was disaffiliated from the Labour
Party and now claimed only five Scottish members. Thereafter, the
ILP gradually dwindled away until by the 1960s it no longer con-
tested parliamentary elections. The 'work-in' in the Clyde shipyards
in 1972 brought the party no dividends. It was no longer the grand
central pivot of a Labour coalition, but a small, fragmented splinter-
group. What Hardie's attitude might have been to these developments
remained a theme for debate long after his death. In the 1935 Labour
conference at Brighton, one delegate, R.G. Newton, argued for the
re-affiliation of the ILP, and cited Hardie as one who would have
endorsed this move. This was powerfully rebuffed by George Hardie,
the youngest brother, who argued that Keir Hardie would support only
'the solidarity of all working-class people' and would have opposed a
group 'causing disruption in this Party wherever it can'.[15] Keir
Hardie's attitude to the Grayson movement within the ILP in 1909

suggests that this view has much plausibility; but there can be little doubt that with the declining authority of the ILP in the 1930s, Hardie's direct influence over the Labour Party, now under the watchful leadership of Attlee, was remote indeed.

Even so, Keir Hardie remained a powerful name to conjure with in Labour gatherings in the 1930s, and continued to be for decades to come. After the disillusionment of 1931, when MacDonald, Thomas and Snowden joined a National government and when MacDonald showed a powerful attachment to the aristocratic embrace (literally so in the case of Lady Londonderry, so it was alleged), Hardie was evoked as the symbol of a purer, more natural tradition. The simple ideals of the cloth cap and of the creed of fraternity and equality, cherished beneath the chimney stacks, at the pithead and on the shop floor, lingered on powerfully. They served to keep the trade union alliance intact and to enable the industrial and political wings of the Labour Party to make common cause. Ernest Bevin had much contempt for ILP versions of socialism – they 'let their bleeding 'earts run away with their bloody 'eads' in his judgement. Yet even he remained loyal to the basic vision of the Labour Party as a working-class movement rooted in industrial society: he rebelled equally against middle class 'intellectuals' or party 'apparatchiks' like Herbert Morrison.

Hardie's legacy lived on also in a powerful faith in internal party democracy, one that received new reinforcement after the 1931 crisis when MacDonald's actions recalled all the basic Labour prejudices against 'leadership'. Hardie, by contrast, stood not only for socialism but also for populism in all its aspects. In the 1970s Hardie's protest against centralization and tyrannizing governmental planning was echoed, by Anthony Wedgwood Benn amongst others, in new demands for popular participation in decision-making, for representative assemblies in Wales and Scotland (which Hardie strongly supported) and for workers' control in industry (which as a one-time trade unionist he viewed more sceptically). A resurgent Plaid Cymru cited Hardie's sympathy for Welsh home rule, while Labour declared its support for an elective Welsh assembly.[16]

Hardie's appeal survived in the Labour Party after 1931 in foreign affairs also. Although the pacifist views of his disciple, George Lansbury, were crushed at the hands of Ernest Bevin at the Brighton party conference in 1935, Hardie's anti-militarism lived on to con-

dition the party's reflexes towards rearmament. The Labour Party
voted consistently against arms estimates in the 1930s. This was partly
because of a suspicion that capitalist governments would use them to
crush working-class and colonial liberation movements. Partly, too, it
arose from a powerful revulsion against the 'system of Versailles' and
the punitive terms that Lloyd George and Clemenceau were alleged
to have exacted from Germany. Hardie had always been a powerful
advocate of Anglo-German friendship, even after war broke out in
1914. After 1931 his spirit was evoked to lend support to appeasement
and avoiding another war of the kind he had resisted in 1914. In the
period after the second world war, Labour took a more complicated
view of defence and of strategic policies, and endorsed collective self-
defence through NATO and SEATO. Even so, Hardie's arguments
were echoed time and again in the arguments of Aneurin Bevan and
his followers against the rearmament of Germany and increased arms
budgets at home in the 1950s. In the 1960s the Campaign for Nuclear
Disarmament drew powerfully on Hardie's moral inspiration. Indeed,
men like Emrys Hughes, Bertrand Russell and Fenner Brockway, who
had known Hardie himself, were still there to carry on his message. In
a world threatened with total annihilation by weapons more appalling
than any he could have visualized, Hardie's cry for peace seemed,
especially to younger socialists, more compelling than ever.

Hardie's influence on the Labour Party, then, was a powerful one,
both in its domestic and foreign policies. Directly or indirectly, it has
decisively shaped the Britain of the twentieth century. It was still
called upon by those socialists who followed Hardie's concern with
spiritualism. Frank Smith who finally entered the House, briefly, in
1929–31 as member for Nuneaton, after a round dozen of defeats,
repeatedly claimed that Hardie communicated with him during
seances. 'Oh Democracy! thou hast failed, utterly failed! Democracy
has been a failure without God, but God stands forever,' Hardie was
said to have declared. Smith died in December 1940, anticipating the
fulfilment of his pact on earth with Hardie that their souls would be
eternally reunited in the life thereafter.[17] Agnes Hughes (then Mrs
Hedley Dennis) claimed to have communicated with Hardie on 26
July 1945, on hearing of the Labour victory at Merthyr during the
general election. Hardie expressed his doubts, it was reported, that the
Labour Party was built on firm foundations: 'Success does not always

mean right. The only real success is that which is built upon the teach-
ings of Christ – the Sermon on the Mount.'[18] This kind of evidence
must be left to psychic research not to history. In reality, the general
election of 1945 might be regarded in many ways as the posthumous
climax of Hardie's career. For the first time, Labour captured overwhelming power, with massive working-class support. Revenge was
exacted for the suffering of the thirties, for Jarrow and for Munich,
for Merthyr Tydfil and for appeasement. As one particularly well-
heeled representative of the workers (later created a peer) called out,
'We are the masters now'. Events since then – crippling economic
problems which Hardie would not have easily grasped, the decline of
the working-class presence in politics, the fluctuating contacts between
the trade unions and the Labour Party, the persistence of poverty,
social deprivation and class division even after long years of Labour
government – these would have disillusioned Hardie further. In 1945,
then, we might see his supreme achievement. Then, as never before or
later, Hardie's vision had found fulfilment. The workers seemed close
to capturing power on lines he had prescribed since the foundation of
the ILP back in 1893 at Bradford. As Harold Laski, Labour's party
chairman in 1945, recalled, Hardie had provided the two essential keys
to the party's progress.[19] He had stressed the belief in the solidarity of
the working class. And he had urged that Labour's programmes must
be based firmly on ethical foundations. Socialism as he understood it was
a gospel to Hardie, with or without the language of priorities or the
relativistic philosophy of which Aneurin Bevan later spoke. It was that
gospel that provided the spiritual force behind the triumph, however
short-lived, in July 1945. Hardie's influence was constantly recalled
in those later years. Keir Hardie estates and social centres rose up, at
West Ham amongst other places. In Merthyr, there was a Keir Hardie
Shield for schoolboy football teams. In Legbrannock, his birthplace,
there was a Hardie Memorial Garden. Even in the 1970s, under a very
different style of Labour leadership, Hardie provided the essential myth
that gave party workers and trade unionists, especially in the older
industrial areas in Scotland and South Wales, the mainspring of their
faith. For Wil Jon Edwards and many other young socialists in the
valleys, Hardie seemed a Joshua, a Moses, even a latter-day Christ.[20]

Hardie's career, however, suggests that his achievement was more
practical and specific than merely the provision of a generalized ethical

creed, imperfectly articulated. He left little in the form of specific institutions. His socialism had little to do with the machinery of government and nothing to do with economic management. More pervasive than these, it has resulted in the vast majority of the causes for which Hardie crusaded making massive progress in the years after his death. Complete women's suffrage was finally implemented in 1928, while in the 1970s more fundamental issues relating to the subjection of women (usually middle-class women) were being ventilated anew. India, Ceylon and Burmah received their independence from the Labour government in 1947–8. Thereafter, Conservative and Labour governments recognized the 'winds of change' and engaged in colonial liberation, as Hardie had so long demanded, against such overwhelming odds. On the subjection of the coloured majority in South Africa also, Hardie's was a prophetic voice, as a Conservative prime minister, Harold Macmillan, implicitly acknowledged in 1960. At home, Hardie's campaigns on behalf of the unemployed helped rouse the public conscience. The solutions ultimately adopted owed more to Keynes than to Keir Hardie; but Hardie takes his place amongst the founders of the welfare state, of policies to alleviate the lot of the low-paid, and to produce a humanized, socialized capitalism with happier expectations for more and more citizens. His 'Merrie England', the Socialist Commonwealth that was to be, was so ill-defined that it could add little to practical politics. It appealed to the heart, not the head. But the many specific measures that he advocated along the way in terms of social reform have largely borne fruit. In most respects, indeed, it is Hardie whose judgement has stood the test of time; it is his critics who appear bigoted and parochial. He was the prophet of a mass egalitarian welfare democracy. Only world peace, his supreme objective, remains as remote as ever. It would have been a supreme irony to Hardie, perhaps, that much of the social progress for which he called was the product of wartime rather than of peacetime conditions. The two world wars materially improved working-class living standards, and extended social and sexual equality for those that survived. For Hardie this would have been the saddest paradox of all.

Hardie's contribution to the British Labour movement was a unique one. First, he was its supreme strategist. He created not a narrow sect but an outward-looking alliance of the dispossessed. He steered his comrades between the shoals of Marxist dogma and of Fabian permeation. The Communist, William Gallacher, in reviewing Emrys Hughes's biography in 1950, criticized Hardie's utter ignorance of socialist theory, especially of Marxism.[21] Perhaps this was a source of strength. Hardie, in reality, had something far more substantial than dogma to offer – a gift for harmonizing the Labour Party with the British political tradition. He defined socialism in such flexible terms that it was always capable of making common cause with late-nineteenth-century radicalism and with the Liberal left. Hardie would co-operate with radicals on anything – on unemployment, women's rights, peace movements, colonial freedom – however he might distrust the official Liberal party leadership and however much he would treasure the concept of Labour's independence. He enabled the Labour Party to merge into the gradualist, peaceful evolution of British society, however pugnaciously he might champion the workers' cause. In this way, he created a party free from the dogmatic sterility of most other European socialist parties since 1918. The comparative fortunes of the Labour and Communist parties since his death are testimony to his genius as a political strategist.

Secondly, Hardie was the supreme prophet. More than any other politician of his time, he threw out a lifeline from the narrow world of London politics to the inarticulate cloth-cap masses he saw crowding into Villa Park for an international football match.[22] He made the British working-class politically conscious – without alienating those middle-class sympathizers whom he welcomed by the score into the ILP. He communicated to the industrial masses directly, emotionally, as a working man whose life since childhood had been scarred by conflict and by tragedy. But the character of Keir Hardie's political appeal, and his contribution to the Labour movement in Britain and elsewhere, can never be understood if it is not emphasized that in outlook, as in outward appearance, he was very far from being a typical working man. He was a lonely, isolated individual, who fitted in with difficulty into any mass organization. His religious mysticism, his concern with spiritualism and with thought transference, his belief in a previous incarnation for humans and for beasts alike, his attachment to old folk myths, to the Druids, to oral tradition, to the sustaining force of mother earth – these were facets of the essential Hardie too. In his newspaper columns he would inform his startled readers of his belief that 'city life is inherently destructive' and of the need to return to nature, of his faith in the druidic rites, in fairies, magic and faith-healing, of his instinct for prophecy.[23] Socialism for Hardie had little ultimately to do with economic systems or governmental machinery. Socialism for him was only partially about power. It was a secular religion or magic by which man grasped at the mystery and joy of life, in the face of the hideous terrors of a brutalizing world. This mystical aspect of Hardie was central to his make-up. It gave an added dimension to his stature as a prophet of a new social order. It was a part of his unique appeal as an agitator that he was both deeply involved in the industrial scene, as a former miner, and yet basically detached from it, to the despair of the party regulars and the organized committee men. He was a secular prophet in an age of waning faith, yet one with a sure instinct for compromise and for common-sense. In the inspiration he kindled and equally in the practical instruments he created, he would always remain for countless unknown working people, no less than for Sylvia Pankhurst, 'the greatest human being of our time'. It can still be said of Keir Hardie that he belongs to the ages.

Abbreviations

BSP	British Socialist Party
ILP	Independent Labour Party
LEA	Labour Electoral Association
LRC	Labour Representation Committee
MFGB	Miners' Federation of Great Britain
NAC	National Administrative Council
SDF	Social Democratic Federation
TUC	Trades Union Congress
UDC	Union of Democratic Control
WSPU	Women's Social and Political Union

Notes

CHAPTER I THE LEGEND AND THE REALITY
(1856–87)

1 Wil Jon Edwards, *From the Valley I Came* (London, 1956), p. 111.

2 MacDonald's introduction to William Stewart, *J. Keir Hardie: a Biography* (London, 1921), p. xxi.

3 William Paul (ed.), *Keir Hardie Special* (1924).

4 A.G. Gardiner, *Prophets, Priests and Kings* (Wayfarers' Library edition, London, 1917), p. 86.

5 The various biographies of Hardie are listed in section E of the Bibliography. Those of most use are the books by William Stewart (London, 1921), and David Lowe (London, 1923), both of which contain valuable information on Hardie's activities, and Emrys Hughes, *Keir Hardie* (London, 1956), which is helpful on the personal side (Hardie was the author's father-in-law). Dr Fred Reid's unpublished thesis 'The Early Life and Political Development of James Keir Hardie, 1856–92' (Oxford University D.Phil., 1968) is admirably full on Hardie's career in Scotland up to the Mid-Lanark by-election.

6 A.A. Durward, 'The Truth about James Kerr, alias James Keir Hardie, and the ILP' (MS. copy in Nuffield College library, Oxford).

7 Sylvia Pankhurst Papers 73a (Institute of Social History, Amsterdam).

8 *Labour Leader*, 24 August 1906.

9 Merthyr *Pioneer*, 26 December 1914.

10 There is a particularly vivid account in the *Ardrossan and Saltcoats Herald*, 23 December 1882.

11 Hardie diary fragment, foreword (Transport House library).

12 Robert Smillie, *My Life for Labour* (London, 1924), p. 33.

13 See Hardie's account in 'The Labour Party and the Books that helped to make it', *Review of Reviews*, June 1906, pp. 570–1.

14 William Adamson, *The Life of the Rev. James Morison D.D.* (London, 1898), pp. 238ff.

15 Ibid., p. 352.

16 *The Labour Prophet*, November 1892.

17 Hardie diary fragment, 13 March 1884.

18 Fred Reid, 'Keir Hardie's Conversion to Socialism' in Asa Briggs and John Saville (eds), *Essays in Labour History, 1886–1923* (London, 1972), p. 23. He later founded 'Crusaders' clubs' for children.

19 *Ardrossan and Saltcoats Herald*, 20 May 1882.

20 Ibid., 22 February 1884.

21 R. Page Arnot, *A History of the Scottish Miners* (London, 1955), pp. 62–71.

22 Hardie's relations with McDonald are described in the *Ardrossan and Saltcoats Herald*, 12 August 1887; William Small Papers (Nat. Lib. of Scotland, Acc. 3350), f. 5; and *Scottish Leader*, 3 April 1888.

23 Katherine Bruce Glasier, 'J. Keir Hardie: the Man and his Message' (MS. in Glasier Papers).

24 Hardie diary fragment, 13 February 1884.

25 Rules of the Ayrshire Miners' Association, 22 March 1881 (Scottish Record Office, Edinburgh, FS 7/3).

26 *Ardrossan and Saltcoats Herald*, 22 July 1882.

27 Ibid., 30 December 1882.

28 Ibid., 14 August 1885.

29 *Review of Reviews*, loc. cit., p. 571.

30 *Ardrossan and Saltcoats Herald*, 27 March 1885.

31 Hardie diary fragment, 11 March 1884.

32 *Ardrossan and Saltcoats Herald*, 20 November 1885.

33 Rules of Ayrshire Miners' Union and Guild of Comrade Colliers (October 1886) (Scottish Record Office, FS 7/18).

34 For Small, see the essay by Belle Small, 'William Small, Memories, Visions and Work' (1951), in the Small Papers (Nat. Lib. of Scotland), f. 5.

35 Smillie, op. cit., p. 32. Hardie and Smillie had met in Larkhall v. Quarter cricket matches.

36 *Ardrossan and Saltcoats Herald*, 22 October, 3 December 1886.

37 A complete set of this very rare journal exists in the Burns Collection, TUC Library. There is, I am told, another in the ILP archive, Bristol.

38 *Scottish Leader*, 9 February 1887; *North British Daily Mail*, 9 February 1887.

39 *The Miner*, May 1887, p. 72.

40 *Ardrossan and Saltcoats Herald*, 21 January 1887.

41 Smillie, op. cit., p. 74.

42 *Report of the Twentieth Annual Trades Union Congress held at Swansea, September 1887*, pp. 29–31.

43 *Ardrossan and Saltcoats Herald*, 16 September 1887.

44 As is argued in F. Reid, 'The Early Life and Political Development of

James Keir Hardie', pp. 181ff. Dr Reid further claims that Hardie was a committed Marxist thereafter, but that circumstances forced him to keep the fact concealed (ibid., p. 344).

45 *Ardrossan and Saltcoats Herals*, 27 May 1887.

46 *The Miner*, December 1887, pp. 185–6.

47 Ibid., July 1887, pp. 97–8.

48 Hardie, *From Serfdom to Socialism* (London, 1907), p. 26.

CHAPTER II MID-LANARK AND AFTER (1888–90)

1 *Scottish Leader*, 3 September, 1 October 1887.

2 Ibid., 11 November 1887.

3 For an excellent discussion of Champion's career, see Henry Pelling, 'H.H. Champion – Pioneer of Labour Representation', *Cambridge Journal*, January 1953, pp. 222ff.

4 Donald Weeks, *Corvo* (London, 1971), pp. 112–13.

5 Henry Pelling, *The Origins of the Labour Party, 1880–1900* (Oxford, new edn 1965), p. 59. See Champion's letter to *The Times*, 23 January 1888.

6 Kenneth O. Morgan, *Wales in British Politics, 1868–1922* (Cardiff, new edn 1970), p. 113.

7 *Scottish Leader*, 19 and 20 March 1888.

8 *Glasgow Herald*, 23 March 1888.

9 Hardie to Baillie Burt, (?) March 1888 (ILP archive). Copies of Hardie's election addresses are contained in the ILP archive, Bristol.

10 *The Scotsman*, 23 March 1888.

11 Champion to Hardie, 16 March 1888 (ILP archive).

12 Champion to Hardie, 22 March 1888; Maltman Barry to (?) Hardie, 16 April 1888 (ibid.).

13 Champion to Hardie, 22 March 1888 (ibid.); Champion's letter to *The Times*, 18 April 1888; Dona Torr, *Tom Mann: his life and times* (London, 1956), Vol. I, pp. 270–2.

14 Hardie to Home Government Branch, 24 March 1888 (Nat. Lib. of Scotland, MS. 1809, ff. 71–3); *Glasgow Observer*, 31 March 1888; James Handley, *The Irish in Modern Scotland* (Cork, 1947), pp. 277–8.

15 Minute-book of the Scottish Home Rule Association, London Branch, 1888–91 (J. Ramsay MacDonald Papers, 5/54); J. Galloway Weir to Hardie, 28 March 1888 (ILP archive).

16 T.R. Threlfall to Hardie, 19 March 1888 (ILP archive); Edward Harford to Hardie, 13 April 1888 (ibid.).

17 John Wilson to T.R. Threlfall, 6 April 1888 (ibid.).

18 J.T.T. Brown to Hardie, 17 March 1888; 'Diary of the Mid-Lanark Campaign', *sub.* 19 March 1888 (ibid.); *The Scotsman*, 21 March 1888.

19 *North British Daily Mail*, 10 April 1888.

20 *The Scotsman*, 6 April 1888.

21 Ibid.

22 *Glasgow Observer*, 21 April 1888.

23 John Ferguson to Cunninghame Graham, 11 April 1888 (ILP archive).

24 *North British Daily Mail*, 20 April 1888.

25 Quoted in *Scottish Leader*, 14 April 1888.

26 T. McNaught to F. Schnadhorst, 21 April 1888 (ILP archive). Hardie sought to sue the *Scottish Leader* for misreporting his meeting with Schnadhorst.

27 *The Scotsman*, 23 April 1888.

28 *Scottish Leader*, 21 April 1888; F. Schnadhorst to T. McNaught, 23 April 1888 (ILP archive).

29 *Labour Leader*, 12 March 1914.

30 Threlfall to Hardie, 17, 24 April 1888 (ILP archive).

31 Conybeare to Cunninghame Graham, 20 April 1888; Conybeare to Hardie, 24 April 1888 (ibid.).

32 *The Scotsman*, 26 April 1888.

33 T. McNaught to Hardie, 25 April 1888 (ILP archive).

34 *The Miner*, May 1888, p. 49.

35 (?) to Hardie (from Aberdeen), 30 April 1888 (ILP archive); James Mavor to Bruce Glasier, 13 May 1888 (Glasier Papers).

36 *The Commonweal*, 12 May 1888, p. 149.

37 Threlfall to Hardie, 2, 11 May 1888 (ILP archive).

38 *Glasgow Herald*, 16 April 1888.

39 For an informative account of these developments, see David Lowe, *Souvenirs of Scottish Labour* (Glasgow, 1919). Also see Hardie's article on the Scottish Labour Party in *The Democrat*, 1 September 1888.

40 Ferguson to Hardie, 17 May 1888 (ILP archive).

41 *The Miner*, June 1888, p. 62.

42 Ibid., September 1888, p. 97; *Scottish Leader*, 27 August 1888.

43 *Scottish Leader*, 19 September 1888.

44 *The Miner*, June 1888, p. 63.

45 Pelling, 'H.H. Champion', loc. cit.

46 *North British Daily Mail*, 1 March 1890. These developments are fully discussed in J.G. Kellas, 'The Mid-Lanark By-Election (1888) and the Scottish Labour Party (1888–1894)', *Parliamentary Affairs*, Summer 1964, pp. 325ff.

47 *North British Daily Mail*, 6 March 1890.

48 Hardie to Lord Randolph Churchill, 6 December 1889 (Nat. Lib. of Scotland, Emrys Hughes Papers, Dep. 176, Box 1).

49 *The Voice of Labour: being the Report of the first annual Labour Electoral Congress* (1888).

50 *Report of the Twenty-first Annual Trades Union Congress held at Bradford, September 1888*, p. 26.

51 *Report of the Twenty-second Annual Trades Union Congress held at Dundee, September 1889*, pp. 22ff.; cf. Lowe, *Souvenirs*, pp. 46–9.

52 Charles Brown to Broadhurst, 6 September 1889; Enoch Bourne to Broadhurst, 5 September 1889 (London School of Economics Library, Broadhurst Papers, Vol. III, ff. 48, 52).

53 See José Harris, *Unemployment and Politics* (Oxford, 1972), pp. 58ff.

54 TUC Parliamentary Committee minutes, 1, 5 November 1888 (microfilm in TUC Library).

55 *Labour Elector*, 15 November 1888.

56 *Congrès International Ouvrier Socialiste de Paris* (Paris, 1889).

57 Hardie to Engels, 21 May 1889 (Institute of Social History, Amsterdam, Marx/Engels Archive, L 2158).

58 *The Commonweal*, 10 August 1889.

59 Keir Hardie, 'Revisionism versus Radicalism in Germany', *Socialist Review*, November 1910, pp. 193–6.

60 Hardie to Engels, 27 May 1889 (Institute of Social History, Amsterdam, Marx/Engels Archive), L 2159.

61 Engels to F. Sorge, 10 November 1894 (ibid.).

62 *Labour Elector*, 23 November 1889.

63 Hardie to ?, 17 October 1888 (Hull University Library).

CHAPTER III THE EMERGENCE OF THE CLOTH CAP (1890–2)

1 *Labour Elector*, 1 February 1890.

2 Paul Thompson, *Socialists, Liberals and Labour* (London, 1967), pp. 130–5. For Thorne, see his autobiography, *My Life's Battles* (London, n.d. [1925]) and Joyce M. Bellamy and John Saville (eds), *Dictionary of Labour Biography*, Vol. I (London, 1972), pp. 314–19.

3 *Labour Elector*, 29 March 1890.

4 For Smith, see E.A. Champness, *Frank Smith M.P.* (London, 1943). Hardie describes his first meeting with Smith in *Labour Leader*, 17 December 1898.

5 *Borough of West Ham and Stratford Express*, 27 January 1892.

6 *Unemployment and Politics*, especially chapter II.

7   *Borough of West Ham and Stratford Express*, 20 February 1892.

8   *Minutes and Evidence taken before Group 'A' of the Royal Commission on Labour* (P.P. 1892, XXXVI, part I), Vol. II, pp. 190–1 (Hardie's evidence, qu. 12,590).

9   Hardie to Burns, 23 May 1891 (BM, Burns Papers, Add. MSS, 46,287, ff. 169–70).

10 *Borough of West Ham and Stratford Express*, 20 February 1892.

11 Kellas, op. cit., p. 326.

12 *Borough of West Ham and Stratford Express*, 18 June 1892.

13 Ibid., 2 July 1892.

14 Ibid., 29 June 1892.

15 Bernard Shaw to Burns, 12 August 1892 (BM, Burns Papers, Add.MSS, 46,287, f. 311).

16 *Borough of West Ham and Stratford Express*, 23 July 1892; cf. D.A. Hamer, *John Morley: Liberal Intellectual in Politics* (London, 1968), pp. 275–7.

17 Hardie to Burns, 22 July 1892 (BM, Burns Papers, Add.MSS, 46,287, ff. 183–4).

18 *Report of the Twenty-third annual Trades Union Congress held at Liverpool, September 1890*, pp. 37, 53.

19 *Report of the Twenty-fourth annual Trades Union Congress, held at Newcastle, September 1891*, pp. 53–4.

20 *The Miner*, December 1888, p. 133.

21 *The Times*, 4 August 1892. Hardie gave his version in the *Manchester Guardian*, 18 April 1914.

22 *Evening Standard*, 4 August 1892.

23 W.G.R. Kent, *John Burns: Labour's Lost Leader* (London, 1950), p. 51.

24 Ibid.

25 *I.L.P. News*, March 1902.

26 *Borough of West Ham and Stratford Express*, 13 July 1895.

27 Arthur Ponsonby to Queen Victoria, 20 July 1892 (Nat. Lib. of Scotland, Rosebery Papers, Box 114).

28 Letter from Hardie in *Borough of West Ham and Stratford Express*, 20 August 1892.

29 Hardie to Thomas Cape, 14 June 1914 (NUM, Cumberland Area, archives). I am indebted to Mr Hywel Francis for this reference.

CHAPTER IV   MEMBER FOR THE UNEMPLOYED (1892–5)

1   *Labour Leader*, 26 February 1914.

2   National Library of Scotland, Acc. 4494.

3 Ibid. The letters from Hardie to Annie Hines are largely undated, but appear to have been posted between 18 May and 5 July 1893.

4 *Parl. Deb.*, 4th ser., Vol. VII, 450–2; cf. *The Times*, 19 August 1892.

5 *Parl. Deb.*, 4th ser., Vol. VIII, 724–32.

6 Ibid., Vol. XIV, 1580–2.

7 Hardie to Herbert Lewis, 22 August 1893; Hardie to Speaker Peel, 24 August 1893 (ILP archive); *Borough of West Ham and Stratford Express*, 19 December 1894.

8 Keir Hardie, 'The case for an Independent Labour Party', *New Review*, June 1894, pp. 718–25. This journal was edited by Archibald Grove, Hardie's Liberal parliamentary colleague who represented West Ham North.

9 L. Atherley-Jones, *Looking Back* (London, 1925), p. 68.

10 Burns's Diary, 12 April 1893 (BM, Add. MSS, 46,313); J.A. Murray MacDonald to Hardie, 3 January 1894 (ILP archive).

11 Henry Pelling, *The Origins of the Labour Party*, pp. 110–12; *Borough of West Ham and Stratford Express*, 13 August 1892.

12 *The Labour Prophet*, November 1892.

13 *Bradford Observer*, 13–16 January 1893.

14 NAC minutes, 1894 (LSE library); *Annual Conference of the Independent Labour Party, 1894*, pp. 4ff.

15 *Labour Leader*, 21 April 1905; cf. Bruce Glasier's diary, 30 August 1897 (ILP archive).

16 David Lowe, *From Pit to Parliament* (London, 1923), p. 45.

17 *Labour Leader*, 31 March 1894.

18 Laurence Thompson, *The Enthusiasts* (London, 1971), gives an attractive account of Glasier's career.

19 *Labour Leader*, 5 May 1894.

20 Ibid., 21 April 1894.

21 Ibid., 26 May 1894.

22 Ibid., 14 April 1894; Hardie to J. Lister, 21 December 1894 (ILP, archive).

23 Ibid., 28 July 1894; cf. Keir Hardie, 'The Independent Labour Party', *Nineteenth Century*, January 1895, pp. 1–14.

24 MacDonald to Hardie, 15 July 1894, quoted in L. McNeill Weir, *The Tragedy of Ramsay MacDonald* (London, n.d. [1938]).

25 *Report of Twenty-seventh Trades Union Congress held at Norwich, September 1894.*

26 *Report of Twenty-eighth Trades Union Congress held at Cardiff, September 1895*; Beatrice Webb diary, 9 September 1895 (LSE library, Passfield Papers I).

27 *Royal Commission on Labour* (P.P. 1892, XXXVI, Part I), Vol. II, p. 208 (qu. 13,038–40).

28 *Parl. Deb.*, 4th ser., Vol. XIX, 1179–85.

29 Ibid., Vol. XXX, 1174 (a debate on the importation of foreign prison-made goods).

30 *Bradford Observer*, 1 February 1893, citing *The Star*.

31 Engels to Bebel, 26 September 1892, 4 January 1893; Engels to F. Sorge, 10 April 1894 (Institute of Social History, Amsterdam).

32 *Labour Leader*, 30 June 1894.

33 *Parl. Deb.*, 4th ser., Vol. XXVI, 462–4.

34 *Borough of West Ham and Stratford Express*, July–August 1893.

35 *Ibid.*, 19 December 1894.

36 José Harris, op. cit., p. 88n.

37 *Parl. Deb.*, 4th ser., Vol. XXX, 637–42.

38 *First Report from the Select Committee on Distress from Want of Employment* (P.P. 1895, VIII), pp. 68–98. Cf. *Daily Chronicle*, 26 February 1895; *The Speaker*, 2 March 1895; S. G. Hobson, *Pilgrim on the Left* (London, 1938), p. 47.

39 *First Report from Select Committee*, pp. 128–55 (Alden's evidence) and 155–73 (Hills's evidence); cf. *Daily Chronicle*, 1, 2 March 1895.

40 Hardie to David Lowe, 30 March 1895 (ILP archive).

41 José Harris and Cameron Hazlehurst, 'Campbell-Bannerman as Prime Minister', *History*, Vol. 55, No. 185 (October 1970), pp. 360–83.

42 *First Report from Select Committee*, p. xii.

43 *Labour Leader*, 12 December 1896; *Justice*, 5 December 1896.

44 Kenneth O. Morgan, *Wales in British Politics*, pp. 151–6.

45 *Third Report from Select Committee on Distress from Want of Employment* (P.P. 1895, IX), p. 820.

46 On this see Peter Clarke, *Lancashire and the New Liberalism* (Cambridge, 1971); and H.V. Emy, *Liberals, Radicals and Social Politics, 1892–1914* (Cambridge, 1973).

47 NAC minutes, 28 May 1894 (LSE library).

48 *The Speaker*, 20 April 1895.

49 *Borough of West Ham and Stratford Express*, 29 December 1894.

50 *Daily Chronicle*, 29 June 1895.

51 *Borough of West Ham and Stratford Express*, 17 July 1895.

52 Ibid., 13 July 1895; *Labour Leader*, 20 July 1895.

53 *Borough of West Ham and Stratford Express*, 17 July 1895; *The Labour Chronicle*, 1 August 1895.

54 *Daily Chronicle*, 15 July 1895; *Labour Leader*, 20 July 1895.

55 Hardie to (?) Zinfandel 9 July 1895 (ILP archive); Engels to L.

Lafargue, 23 July 1895 (Institute of Social History, Amsterdam); Beatrice Webb, *Our Partnership* (London, 1948), p. 127; *Daily Chronicle*, 16 July 1895.

56 Pelling, op. cit., p. 167.

57 *Labour Leader*, 3 August 1895.

CHAPTER V TOWARDS THE LABOUR ALLIANCE (1895–9)

1 *Labour Leader*, 14 December 1895.

2 *J. Keir Hardie versus the Labour Literature Society: a Reply to the Article signed 'Keir' in the 'Labour Leader' of August 17th 1895* (Glasgow, 1895). There is a copy of this rare pamphlet in the Burns collection, TUC library.

3 Bruce Glasier's notebook for 1895 (ILP archive).

4 Hardie's accounts of his American tour appeared in the *Labour Leader*, 24 August–21 December 1895.

5 The 'psychic crisis' that the United States underwent in the early 1890s is brilliantly discussed in Richard Hofstadter, *The Paranoid Style in American Politics* (New York, Vintage books edition 1967), pp. 147–56.

6 *Labour Leader*, 7 September 1895.

7 Ray Ginger, *Eugene V. Debs: a Biography* (New York, new edition 1962), pp. 189–90.

8 *Labour Leader*, 26 February 1914.

9 Adam Birkmyre to Keir Hardie, 6 January 1896 (Nat. Lib. of Scotland, Emrys Hughes Papers, Box 1).

10 *Labour Leader*, 9 May 1896; Hardie to David Lowe, 20 May 1896 (ILP archive); Kenneth D. Buckley, *Trade Unionism in Aberdeen, 1878–1900* (Edinburgh, 1955).

11 John Gerrie to Ramsay MacDonald, 21 September 1896 (MacDonald Papers, 5/6).

12 *Labour Leader*, 8, 15 August 1896; T.D. Benson to Hardie, 19 September 1896 (ILP archive).

13 *Justice*, 22 August 1896; *Liberty*, March 1896. The latter journal attacked the 'journalistic cuteness' which led Hardie to ask Kropotkin to contribute to the *Labour Leader*.

14 Hardie to Viktor Adler, 28 August, 18 December 1896, 9 January 1897 (Institute of Social History, Amsterdam); John Gerrie to Ramsay MacDonald, 26 September 1896 (MacDonald Papers, 5/6).

15 *Labour Leader*, 8 August 1896.

16 *Justice*, 7 August 1897.

17 NAC minutes, 9 October 1897 (LSE library).

18 *Justice*, 18 December 1897; *Labour Leader*, 2 April 1898.

19 Bruce Glasier's diary, 30 August, 19 September, 13 December 1897 (ILP archive).

20 Hardie to John Penny, 16 August 1897 (ILP archive).

21 *Report of the Annual Conference of the Independent Labour Party held at Birmingham, April 1898*, pp. 23–7; *Labour Leader*, 16 April 1898.

22 Hardie, *The ILP and all about it* (London, 1909), p. 11. Hardie explained Curran's low poll partly in terms of the intimidation of miners by local Liberal coalowners (*Labour Leader*, 6 November 1897).

23 Keir Hardie, *Young Men in a Hurry, Why they are in Hurry, and What they are in a Hurry about* (n.d. – 1898), p. 9.

24 Bruce Glasier's diary, 17 October 1897 (ILP archive).

25 *Bradford Observer*, 17 October 1896.

26 Ibid.

27 *Westminster Gazette*, 1 August 1896.

28 *Bradford Observer*, 24 October 1896.

29 Ibid., 30 October 1896.

30 Bruce Glasier's diary, 11 November 1896.

31 Hardie's election address, East Bradford 1896. Copies of Hardie's election literature are to be found in the Transport House library (which also contains copies of *Hardie's Herald*) and in the Bradford Public library.

32 *Bradford Observer*, 5 November 1896.

33 Bruce Glasier's diary, 11 November 1896 (ILP archive).

34 *Bradford Observer*, 11 November 1896.

35 Bruce Glasier's diary, 14 November 1896 (ILP archive).

36 *Labour Leader*, 17 December 1898.

37 NAC minutes, 23 July 1898 (LSE library).

38 Neville Masterman, *The Forerunner* (Llandybie, 1972), pp. 230–4.

39 J. Keir Hardie and J. Ramsay MacDonald, 'The Independent Labour Party's Programme', *Nineteenth Century*, LIII, January 1899, 20–38.

40 NAC minutes, 28 January 1899 (LSE library).

41 *Labour Leader*, 7 January 1899.

42 Hardie to David Lowe, (?) January 1898 (ILP archive).

43 Hardie to Lowe, 21 September 1898 (ibid.); *Labour Leader*, 28 August 1897.

44 *Justice*, 1 February, 29 April 1899; *Labour Leader*, 18 February, 4 March 1899; NAC minutes, 6 May 1899 (LSE library); Hardie to Thorne, n.d., cited in Thorne, *My Life's Battles*, pp. 263–4.

45 H. Clegg, A. Fox and A.F. Thompson, *A History of British Trade Unions since 1889* (Oxford, 1964), Vol. I, pp. 294–304.

46   Hardie to Dr Stanton Coit, 25 November 1899 (ILP archive); Pelling, *Origins of the Labour Party*, p. 229.

47   *Labour Leader*, 18 July 1896; Sylvia Pankhurst, *The Suffragette Movement* (London, 1931), pp. 136–7.

48   *Lord Overtoun, More about Overtoun, The Overtoun Horrors* and *Overtoun Fictions* (1899). Overtoun was described as a 'moral leper' whose life was 'a living lie'.

49   Hardie to Lowe, 1 December 1896 (ILP archive 1896); Hardie to Sam Higenbottam, 5 May 1897 (Blackburn Public Library).

50   Hardie to David Lowe, (?) June 1898 (ILP archive).

51   *Labour Leader*, 25 June, 2, 9 July 1898; Hardie to Ll. Francis, 1 July 1898 (ILP archive). Cf. Kenneth O. Morgan, *Wales in British Politics*, pp. 204–5.

52   *Labour Leader*, 12 November 1898.

53   Scottish TUC Parliamentary Committee minutes, 26 September 1898 (microfilm in Nat. Lib. of Scotland, Acc. 4682); Hardie to Miss W.H. Irwin, 3 October 1898 (ILP archive).

54   Scottish TUC Parliamentary Committee minutes, 4 March, 26 April 1899; *Glasgow Herald*, 28 April 1899.

55   NAC minutes, 6 May 1899 (LSE library).

56   Miss W.H. Irwin to Ramsay MacDonald, 4 May 1899 (MacDonald Papers, 5/6).

57   Pelling, op. cit., p. 205.

58   Philip, Viscount Snowden, *An Autobiography*, Vol. I (London, 1934), p. 88. The truth of Snowden's assertion cannot be tested.

59   Cf. *Progressive Review*, No. 1, October 1896.

60   *Justice*, 8 April 1899.

61   Bruce Glasier, *The Meaning of Socialism* (London, 1920). Cf. Thompson, *The Enthusiasts*, pp. 90–1.

62   This concerned a legal action against Mrs Ramsay MacDonald brought by George Belt, a member of the ILP accused of sexual impropriety. Hardie had to act as arbiter.

63   *Labour Leader*, 29 April 1899.

64   Glasier's diary, 5, 9, 11 March 1897 (ILP archive); Thompson, op. cit., p. 101.

65   Glasier's diary, 10 April 1898 (ILP archive).

66   Hardie to Glasier, 28 December 1899 (ibid.).

CHAPTER VI   BOER WAR AND KHAKI ELECTION (1899–1901)

1   Hardie's views were recorded in the *Labour Leader*, October 1899–

May 1902, *passim*. See also, 'Some Economic and Industrial Aspects of the War', *New Liberal Review*, August 1901, pp. 50–5.

2   *Labour Leader*, 17 March, 6 January 1900.

3   Ibid., 4 November 1899.

4   Ibid., 3 February, 16 June 1900.

5   Ibid., 5, 19 October 1901; C. Desmond Greaves, *The Life and Times of James Connolly* (London, new edition 1972), p. 131; E. Stewart to Hardie, 6 November 1898 (Nat. Lib. of Scotland, Emrys Hughes Papers, Box 1).

6   Hardie to Ensor, 18 January, 20 February 1900 (Corpus Christi College library, Oxford, Ensor Papers, I).

7   *Labour Leader*, 20 January 1900.

8   Ibid., 10 March 1900.

9   *Report of the Conference held in the Memorial Hall, 1900*, pp. 15–24.

10   Hardie to Ensor, 2 March 1900 (Ensor Papers, I).

11   Glasier to Hardie, 28 February 1900 (ILP archive).

12   Glasier's diary, 28 February 1900 (Glasier Papers).

13   *Eighth annual report of the Independent Labour Party, 1900*, pp. 26–7; Glasier to Hardie, 22 April 1900 (ILP archive).

14   See Kenneth O. Morgan, 'The Merthyr of Keir Hardie', in Glanmor Williams (ed.), *Merthyr Politics: the making of a Working-Class Tradition* (Cardiff, 1966), pp. 67ff.

15   Hardie to Llew Francis, 1 July 1898 (ILP archive).

16   NAC minutes, 28 May 1900 (LSE library).

17   Hardie to Glasier, 21 July 1900 (ILP archive).

18   *Labour Leader*, 9 July 1898.

19   Ibid., 4 November 1899.

20   NAC minutes, 28 July 1900, Glasier to Hardie, 8 August 1900.

21   S.G. Hobson, *Pilgrim to the Left*, p. 75.

22   T. Charteris to MacDonald, 2 May 1900 (Transport House library, LRC letter-files, 1/95/1).

23   *Lancashire Daily Post*, 26 September 1900.

24   Hardie to David Lowe, ? September 1900 (ILP archive).

25   *South Wales Daily News*, 24 September 1900.

26   *Lancashire Daily Post*, 26 September 1900.

27   Ibid.

28   Ibid., 28 September 1900.

29   Ibid., 1 October 1900.

30   Ibid., 29 September 1900.

31   *Labour Leader*, 13 October 1900.

32   Ibid.

33 Kenneth O. Morgan, op. cit. See also Kenneth O. Morgan, 'Wales and the Boer War – a Reply', *Welsh History Review*, IV, No. 4 (December 1969).

34 See Kenneth O. Morgan, 'D.A. Thomas: the Industrialist as Politician', in Stewart Williams (ed.), *Glamorgan Historian* (Barry, Glamorgan, 1966), III, pp. 33ff.

35 *Labour Leader*, 13 October 1900.

36 *South Wales Daily News*, 4 October 1900.

37 Morgan, *Wales in British Politics*, p. 265.

38 *Labour Leader*, 24 November 1900, 17 August 1901.

39 See Keir Hardie, *The Red Dragon and the Red Flag* (Merthyr, 1912). Cf. T.E. Nicholas, 'Y Ddraig Goch a'r Faner Goch', *Y Geninen*, January 1912.

40 Hardie to MacDonald, n.d. (Transport House library, LRC letter-files, 1/288); *Labour Leader*, 24 November 1900.

41 Glasier's diary, 3, 28 October 1900 (Glasier Papers).

42 *Labour Leader*, 20 October 1900; *Llais Llafur*, 27 October 1900. The victorious Liberal was J. Aeron Thomas.

43 *I.L.P. News*, October 1900, p. 4.

44 Ibid., September 1901, pp. 1–2.

45 *Parl. Deb.*, 4th ser., Vol. XCI, 1204–6; speech at Bradford Labour Church, *Bradford Observer*, 4 February 1901.

46 *Manchester Daily Dispatch*, quoted in *I.L.P. News*, April 1902, p. 5.

47 Russell Smart to E.R. Pease, ? January 1901 (LSE library, Pease collection, Vol. I, ff. 33–4); memorandum by Smart on 'Keir Hardie Parliamentary Fund' (MacDonald Papers 5/12).

48 *Can a Man be a Christian on a Pound a Week?* (1901).

49 Hardie to Glasier, 23 August 1901 (ILP archive).

50 Ibid.

51 Ibid.

52 Glasier's diary, 26 August, 27 December 1901 (Glasier Papers).

53 *Woolwich Labour Journal*, October 1901.

54 *Labour Leader*, 21 December 1901. Lloyd George's views are given in his article, 'Lord Rosebery and Peace', *New Liberal Review*, January 1902, pp. 767–74.

55 Ibid., 30 November 1901.

CHAPTER VII THE NEW PROGRESSIVISM (1902–6)

1 Hardie to Glasier, 26 December 1901 (ILP archive).

2 *Labour Leader*, 3 May 1902.

3   Glasier's diary, 9 January 1902.

4   *Labour Leader*, 24 October 1903.

5   Ibid., 21 June 1902.

6   Glasier's diary, 9 September 1909, 4 November 1911.

7   Hardie to J. Middleton, ? 1905 (Transport House library, LRC/25/156).

8   Hardie to J. Penny, 3 April 1901 (ILP archive); Hardie to Glasier, 1 April 1903 (ibid.).

9   *Parl. Deb.*, 4th ser., Vol. XCII, 1175–80.

10 Glasier to Hardie, 23 January 1903 (ILP archive).

11 Bell to Hardie, 9 March 1903, Hardie to Bell, 9 March 1903 (LRC/7/208).

12 LRC minutes, 12–13 March, 13–14 April 1904 (Transport House library); Dai Davies, Pant, to MacDonald, 26 October 1902 (LRC/10/288); *Labour Leader*, 16 January 1904; *Merthyr Express*, September–October 1903 *passim*.

13 Woods to MacDonald, 10 April 1902; Hardie to MacDonald, ? April 1902 (LRC/Misc.); LRC minutes, 8–9 May 1902.

14 John Ward to MacDonald, 29 March 1904 (LRC/15/268); Hardie to Glasier, 24 January 1902 (ILP archive).

15 Glasier's diary, 27 December 1901, 7, 9 January 1902 (Glasier Papers); Hardie to Glasier, 26 January 1901 (ILP archive).

16 Glasier to Hardie, 15 July 1902 (ILP archive).

17 Hardie to MacDonald, 17 July 1902 (LRC/APP); A.B. Newall to MacDonald, 17, 28 July 1902 (LRC/4/39, 41); *Labour Leader*, 26 July 1902.

18 *Labour Leader*, 15 February, 6 September 1902.

19 Hardie to MacDonald, 23 October 1902 (LRC/5/108); Glasier to Hardie, 21 October 1902 (ILP archive); NAC minutes, 29–30 September 1902 (LSE library).

20 Glasier's diary, 14 October 1902.

21 See F. Bealey and Henry Pelling, *Labour and Politics, 1900–1906* (London, 1958), pp. 125ff.

22 *Labour Leader*, 21 February, 7 March, 28 March 1903.

23 Hardie to Glasier, ? 1903 (Glasier Papers).

24 *Parl. Deb.*, 4th ser., Vol. CXXXVIII, 983–6.

25 Hardie to Glasier, 22 October 1903 (ILP archive).

26 H.W. Massingham to Hardie, ? April 1903 (ILP archive); *Labour Leader*, 4 April 1903.

27 *Fourth Annual Conference of the Labour Representation Committee: Report* (1903), pp. 27–35.

28 Hardie to Glasier, 1 April 1903 (ILP archive).

29 Hardie to Glasier, 30 April 1903, Glasier's diary, 4 June 1903 (Glasier Papers); John Hodge to MacDonald, 19 May 1903 (LRC/9/189).

30 MacDonald to Henderson, 3 July 1903 (Transport House library, LRC out-letters, f. 280); Hardie to Glasier, 15 July 1903 (ILP archive).

31 H.M. Hyndman, *Further Reminiscences* (London, 1912), pp. 266–7.

32 Hardie to Glasier, 28 April 1903 (Glasier Papers).

33 W.T. Stead (ed.), *Coming Men on Coming Questions* (London, 1905), pp. 1–5.

34 Ibid.

35 Ben Tillett to MacDonald, 5 October 1903; Lillie Hardie to Mac-Donald, 26 October 1903; Frederick Rogers to MacDonald, 27 July 1903; Hardie to MacDonald, 16 December 1903 (LRC 10/132, 226; LRC/9/360; LRC/12/133). For Tillett's candidature in Swansea District, see Henry Davies to Hardie, 3 August, 18 September 1902 (ILP archive).

36 George Barnes to MacDonald, 31 August 1903 (LRC/10/142).

37 *Labour Leader*, 25 April 1903.

38 Glasier's diary, 24 September 1903 (Glasier Papers); Hardie to Glasier, 22 October 1903 (ILP archive).

39 Hardie to Glasier, 1 November 1903 (ibid.).

40 Hardie to Glasier, 'Hogmanay', 1902 (ibid.); Glasier's diary, 2 March 1903.

41 Glasier's diary, 20 October 1902; *Labour Leader*, 17 January 1903. W.F. Black succeeded Lowe.

42 Glasier to Hardie, 25 June 1902 (ILP archive); Glasier's diary, 26 May 1902; NAC minutes, 8 April 1898 (LSE library).

43 MacDonald to Glasier, 24 January 1903 (ILP archive); MacDonald to Hardie, 21 December 1903 (Transport House library, LRC out-letter books, ff. 179–80).

44 NAC minutes, 22 May 1903 (LSE library).

45 Ibid., 11 November 1903.

46 Glasier's diary, 22 December 1903.

47 NAC minutes, 25–6 January, 21–2 March 1904.

48 Hardie to Glasier, 28 January 1904 (ILP archive); Glasier's diary, 28 January 1904; Glasier to Hardie, 28 January 1904.

49 *Labour Leader*, 20 February 1904.

50 Glasier's diary, 7 October 1904.

51 Ibid., 13 February 1905.

52 Viscount Snowden, 'Keir Hardie', *The Listener*, 18 December 1935.

53 Pete Curran to MacDonald, 9 November 1904; Hardie to MacDonald, 19 October 1904 (LRC/17, 108, 408). Letters in the ILP archive show

that Hardie was also much concerned with selecting a Labour candidate in the South Wales constituencies of Gower and Swansea District.

54 Hardie to MacDonald, ? 1904 (MacDonald Papers, 5/14); Hardie to Glasier, 10 April 1904 (ILP archive).

55 There is a good discussion of this question in Kenneth D. Brown, *Labour and Unemployment 1900–1914* (London, 1971).

56 Hardie to MacDonald, 21 January 1904 (LRC/12/199).

57 *Parl. Deb.*, 4th ser., Vol. CLIII, p. 1155 (13 March 1906).

58 Mary Fels, *Joseph Fels: his life work* (London, 1920), pp. 46–80; George Lansbury, *My Life* (London, 1928), p. 101.

59 Hardie, *The Unemployed Problem with some suggestions for solving it* (1904).

60 *Labour Leader*, 21 October, 16 December 1904; Public Record Office (CAB 37/74).

61 Hardie to G. Balfour, 23 June 1905 (ILP archive); Burns's diary, 19 May 1905 (BM, Add. MSS, 46,323).

62 Glasier's diary, 17 May 1905; LRC executive minutes, 2 June 1905 (Transport House library): letters from Hardie and Russell Smart in G.W. Balfour Papers, Scottish Record Office, Box 121; Hardie to Henderson, 16 May 1905 (LRC/24/447).

63 Glasier to Hardie, 17 June 1904; Hardie to Glasier, 'Sunday Eve, 1904' (ILP archive).

64 *Labour Leader*, 25 August 1905; Brown, op. cit., p. 58.

65 *Labour Leader*, 18, 25 August 1905.

66 Burns's diary, 24 July 1905 (BM, Add. MSS, 46,323).

67 MacDonald to Hardie, 30 October 1905 (LRC/27/376).

68 Hardie to Glasier, 'Sunday Eve', 1904 (ILP archive).

69 *Labour Leader*, 22 December 1905.

70 LRC minutes, 14–15 December 1905 (Transport House library).

71 MacDonald to Hardie, 5 January 1906 (LRC/29/194/i).

72 Marion Coates Hansen to George Lansbury, 24 May, 26 June 1906 (LSE library, Lansbury Papers II, ff. 254, 263).

73 *South Wales Daily News*, 9 January 1906.

74 Smith to J. Middleton (telegrams), 12, 15 January 1906 (LRC/30/402–3); Hardie to Middleton, ? January 1906 (ibid., 403); MacDonald to Middleton, 11 January 1906 (ibid., 29/285/i); Middleton to Hardie, 11 January 1906 (ibid., 31/139–140).

75 *Merthyr Express, South Wales Daily News, Tarian y Gweithiwr*, January 1906, *passim*: Hardie to Dai Davies, 3 January 1906 (ILP archive).

76 *Labour Leader*, 26 January 1906.

CHAPTER VIII LEADER OF THE PARTY (1906–7)

1   LRC executive minutes, 4 October 1905 (Transport House library); *Labour Leader*, 9 February 1906.

2   Glasier to Hardie, 11 February 1906 (ILP archive); Hardie to R.B. Cunninghame Graham, 5 December 1905 (ibid.).

3   MacDonald to Glasier, 21 July 1906 (ibid.); Lord Elton, *The Life of James Ramsay MacDonald* (London, 1939), p. 132.

4   *Labour Leader*, 16 February 1906; G. Dallas to M. Macarthur, 7 February 1906 (ILP archive), where MacDonald is accused of plotting against Hardie becoming chairman.

5   Bruce Glasier, *J. Keir Hardie M.P.: a Memorial* (n.d.), p. 50.

6   *Parl. Deb.*, 4th ser., Vol. CLVIII, pp. 139ff.; Vol. CLXVII, pp. 439–42.

7   Burns's diary, 10 April 1906, 30 May 1906, 28 August 1907 (BM, Add. MSS, 46,324, 46,325).

8   *Parl. Deb.*, 4th ser., Vol. CLII, p. 196.

9   MacDonald to Glasier, 21 July 1906 (ILP archive).

10 *Select Committee on the Procedure of the House of Commons, 1906* (P.P. 1906, VIII, 531); Hardie to Dilke, 21 March 1906 (BM, Add. MSS, Dilke Papers, 43, 919, f. 48).

11 *Select Committee on the Income Tax, 1906* (P.P. 1906, IX, 659); Dilke's memorandum on 'Advanced Radicals', 31 January 1906, Sir Edward Hamilton to Dilke, 4 May 1906 (BM, Add. MSS, 43, 919, ff. 16–17, 24–6, 61–2).

12 W.C. Bridgeman, *Political Notes*, p. 31 (Bridgeman Papers). I am indebted to Dr Cameron Hazlehurst for this reference.

13 Glasier to Hardie, 1 June 1906 (ILP archive).

14 Snowden to Benson, cited in Glasier's diary, 21 July 1906.

15 Ibid.; MacDonald to Glasier, 21 July 1906.

16 Henderson to Hardie, 29 August 1906 (Transport House library, Labour Party General Correspondence, 7/184).

17 Glasier's diary, 27 August 1906.

18 Hardie, *From Serfdom to Socialism* (London, 1907), p. 63.

19 Hardie, *The Citizenship of Women: a Plea for Women's Suffrage* (1905); *Parl. Deb.*, 4th ser., Vol. CLXIV, pp. 511–12.

20 Hardie, *The Queenie Gerald Case. A Public Scandal. White Slavery in a Piccadilly Flat* (1913).

21 Hardie to Glasier, 25 July 1903 (Glasier Papers).

22 *Labour Leader*, 29 February 1896.

23 Glasier's diary, 2 November 1913; Frank Smith to MacDonald, 30 April 1907 (MacDonald Papers, 5/17); MacDonald to Glasier, 3 May 1907 (ILP archive).

24 I am very grateful to Miss E.M.W. Schreuder, of the Institute of Social History, Amsterdam, for her help in investigating the career of Sylvia Pankhurst.

25 MS. notes, Sylvia Pankhurst MSS 1C (Institute of Social History, Amsterdam); Sylvia Pankhurst, *The Suffragette Movement* (London, 1931), op. 174.

26 Hardie to Sylvia Pankhurst, 27 February 1907 (Sylvia Pankhurst Papers, 1C).

27 Hardie to Sylvia Pankhurst, 10 March 1911 (ibid.).

28 *Parl. Deb.*, 4th ser., Vol. CLIX, pp. 365ff., 461ff. (21 June 1906).

29 Glasier's diary, 27 August 1906.

30 Ibid., 30 November 1906, 19 January 1907.

31 *Report of the Seventh Annual Conference of the Labour Party, 1907*, pp. 49–50.

32 Ibid., pp. 61–3, Thompson's account (*The Enthusiasts*, p. 149) is erroneous.

33 Glasier's diary, 26, 28 January 1907.

34 Hardie to Glasier, 4 March, 5 April 1907 (ILP archive).

35 Ibid., 7 May 1907.

36 W.W. Price to MacDonald, 28 April 1907 (Labour Party GC/14/1). I have benefited from discussions with the late Mr Price.

37 Hardie to Glasier, 5 April 1907 (ILP archive).

38 Hardie to Glasier, ? June 1907 (ibid.). Hardie had severely criticized the alienation of land in Natal which had led to a Zulu uprising there in 1906.

39 NAC minutes, 29–30 March 1907 (LSE library); Labour Party Emergency Committee minutes, 29 June 1907 (LSE Pease Collection, II, f. 56); MacDonald to Glasier, 20 or 21 July 1907 (ILP archive).

40 NAC minutes, 5–6 July 1907.

41 Hardie to MacDonald, 11 July 1907 (Transport House library, LP/CAN/06/2/66).

42 MacDonald to Glasier, 20 or 21, 30 July 1907 (ILP archive).

43 LRC minutes, 20 May 1908 (Transport House library).

CHAPTER IX THE INTERNATIONALIST

1 Philip Snowden, introduction to Keir Hardie, *India: Impressions and Suggestions* (London, new edition 1917), p. vii.

2 See the early chapters of Henry Pelling, *America and the British Left* (London, 1956).

3 *Parl. Deb.*, 4th ser., Vol. CXLV, pp. 778–82.

4 Ibid., p. 782. Cf. John A. Garrard, *The English and Immigration* (London, 1971), chapters IV and V.

5 See above, p. 88.

6 *Labour Leader*, 26 August 1904.

7 Georges Haupt, *Socialism and the Great War* (Oxford, 1972), pp. 160–8.

8 E.g. *Labour Leader*, 4 November 1899.

9 R.J. Crampton, 'August Bebel and the British Foreign Office', *History*, Vol. 58, No. 193 (June 1973), pp. 218–32.

10 Keir Hardie, 'Revisionism versus Radicalism in Germany', *Socialist Review*, November 1910, pp. 193–6; *Labour Leader*, 14, 21 October 1910.

11 Hardie to Glasier, 8 November 1902 (ILP archive); *Labour Leader*, 6 December 1902; Keir Hardie, 'The French Socialist Congress', *Socialist Review*, April 1912, pp. 111–19.

12 *Labour Leader*, 19 October 1906.

13 See above, p. 88.

14 V.I. Lenin, *British Labour and British Imperialism* (London, new edition 1969), pp. 101–2.

15 Richard Hofstadter, 'Charles A. Beard' in *The Progressive Historians* (New York, Vintage Books edition 1970), p. 175.

16 *Daniel de Leon: a Symposium* (New York, 1920), II, pp. 40–1.

17 Samuel Gompers, *Seventy Years of Life and Labor*, Vol. II (New York, 1924), chap. XXVII; there is an admirable collection of Gompers's writings in Gerald E. Stearn (ed.), *Gompers* (Englewood Cliffs, New Jersey, 1971).

18 Keir Hardie, 'Socialism in America', *Socialist Review*, April 1909, pp. 89–94; *Labour Leader*, 25 September, 2, 9 October 1908.

19 Keir Hardie, 'America Revisited', *Socialist Review*, December 1912, pp. 257–65; *Labour Leader*, 21 November 1912–6 February 1913.

20 *Labour Leader*, 12 July 1907.

21 Ibid., 4–25 October 1907.

22 *The Voice* (Winnipeg), 2 August 1907.

23 *Proceedings of the Twenty-Fourth Annual Convention of the Trades and Labor Congress of Canada*, 1908, pp. 80–1.

24 *Halifax Herald* (Nova Scotia), 23 September 1908. Cf. an interview with Hardie in *The Morning Chronicle* (Halifax), 21 September 1908. The *Herald* was Conservative, the *Chronicle*, Liberal.

25 *Proceedings*, p. 81.

26 *Labour Leader*, 26 November 1909.

27   Kenneth McNaught, *A Prophet in Politics* (Toronto, 1959), pp. 54–5; *Parl. Deb.*, 5th ser., Vol. XXVI, pp. 1038, 1186.

28   See M.N. Das, *India under Morley and Minto* (London, 1964), pp. 88ff.; Stanley A. Wolpert, *Tilak and Gokhale* (Berkeley, California, 1962).

29   Philip Snowden, op. cit., p. vii.

30   *Parl. Deb.*, 4th ser., Vol. CLXI, pp. 594–7.

31   *The Times*, 2 October 1907.

32   Ibid., 2–14 October 1907.

33   M.N. Das, *India under Morley and Minto* (London, 1964), p. 72.

34   Ibid., p. 85.

35   *Daily News*, 18 October 1907; Shackleton to MacDonald, 27 October 1907 (Transport House library, LPGC/20/366).

36   Hardie to Glasier, 8 October 1907 (wrongly written as 1909) (ILP archive).

37   Hardie to Glasier, 11 April 1908 (Glasier Papers); Das, op. cit., p. 119.

38   E.g. *Parl. Deb.*, 4th ser., Vol. CLXXXVII, pp. 1347ff.; Vol. CXCIII, pp. 171ff.; Vol. CXCVIII, pp. 193ff.; ibid., 5th ser., Vol. III, pp. 594ff.; Vol. VIII, pp. 2076ff.; Vol. XVII, pp. 663ff.; Vol. XIX, pp. 2045ff. etc. Gokhale sent Hardie much information.

39   This correspondence is contained in the Crewe Papers, C/18a nd I/16 (11, 12) in the Cambridge University Library. Cf. *Labour Leader*, 31 July 1908.

40   Lenin, op. cit., p. 52.

41   ILP Publications Department Report, April 1909 (NAC minutes, LSE library).

42   *India: Impressions and Suggestions* (London, 1909), p. 71.

43   *Labour Leader*, 28 February, 6, 13, 20 March, 10 April 1908.

44   Ibid., 27 March, 3 April 1908, 2 April 1909, 22 May 1913.

45   Jack Griffiths to Keir Hardie, 12 August 1914 (Nat. Lib. of Scotland, Emrys Hughes Papers, Box 1, f. 1).

46   *Parl. Deb.*, 4th ser., Vol. CXIX, pp. 1529ff. (19 March 1903).

47   Ibid., Vol. CLXVII, pp. 1107–11 (17 December 1906).

48   H.W. Sampson to MacDonald, 17 October 1907 (Transport House library, LPGC/18/203).

49   *Labour Leader*, 17 April 1908.

50   *Parl. Deb.*, 5th ser., Vol. LVI, pp. 814ff. (31 July 1913), and Vol. LVIII, pp. 385ff. (2 February 1914).

51   *Labour Leader*, 10 April 1908.

52   Ibid., 24 September 1909.

53   Fred Lewisohn to R.C.K. Ensor, 22 April and 8 August 1909, from Rangoon (Corpus Christi College library, Oxford, Ensor Papers I).

CHAPTER X THE POLITICAL THEORIST

1 *Labour Leader*, 30 March 1906.

2 *Report of the Annual Conference of the Independent Labour Party held at Birmingham*, 1911, pp. 82ff.

3 Hardie, 'Karl Marx – the Man and his Message', *Labour Leader*, 26 August 1910; cf. H.M. Hyndman to Hardie, 11 July 1905 (Transport House library).

4 Hardie, 'Karl Marx', loc. cit.; Hardie, *From Serfdom to Socialism* (London, 1907), pp. 92–4.

5 E.g. *Labour Leader*, 24 December 1898.

6 Ibid., 2 September 1904.

7 *From Serfdom to Socialism*, pp. 25–6.

8 Ibid., p. 1.

9 Ibid., p. 36; Hardie, *The Red Dragon and the Red Flag* (Merthyr, 1912), p. 12.

10 *From Serfdom to Socialism*, p. 25.

11 *Labour Leader*, 12 December 1896.

12 Hardie, 'Christ and the Modern Movement', in C.G. Ammon (ed.), *Christ and Labour* (London, 1913), pp. 77–91.

13 *From Serfdom to Socialism*, p. 26.

14 *Labour Leader*, 1 August 1896.

15 Merthyr *Pioneer*, 11 May 1912.

16 *Labour Leader*, 21 October 1910, 25 September 1913; Hardie, 'August Bebel', *Socialist Review*, September 1913, pp. 501–4; *The I.L.P. and all about it* (London, 1909), pp. 12–13.

17 *Labour Leader*, 25 August 1905, 6 November 1908.

18 Hardie, 'The British Labour Party', *International Socialist Review*, May 1910, pp. 985–8; idem., 'The General Election', *Socialist Review*, November 1909, pp. 172–9.

19 Hardie, *My Confession of Faith in the Labour Alliance* (London, 1909), p. 12.

20 Hardie, *The I.L.P. and all about it*, pp. 6, 11–12; *Labour Leader*, 2 September 1904.

21 Hardie, 'The Labour Movement', *Nineteenth Century*, LX (November 1906), p. 879.

22 Hardie, 'The French Socialist Congress', *Socialist Review*, April 1912, pp. 111–19.

23 Hardie, 'History repeats itself', *Socialist Review*, October–December 1914, pp. 354–60.

24 Hardie, *My Confession of Faith in the Labour Alliance*, pp. 11–12.

25 Fenner Brockway, *Socialism over Sixty Years* (London, 1946), p. 108.

26 Hardie, 'Christ and the Modern Movement', loc. cit.; idem, 'The Christianity of Christ', *The Labour Prophet*, November 1892; Hardie's 'confession of faith', cited in *Aberdare Leader*, 21 April 1906; *Merthyr Pioneer*, 9 March 1912.

27 *Keir Hardie Special* (1924).

28 Hardie to Shaw, 14 February 1912 (BM, Shaw Papers, Add. MSS, 50, 538, ff. 22–3).

CHAPTER XI   FREELANCE RADICAL (1908–11)

1 *Labour Leader*, 10, 17 April 1908; souvenir material in R.C.K. Ensor papers (Corpus Christi College library, Oxford).

2 Glasier to MacDonald, 12 March 1908 (MacDonald Papers, 5/18); MacDonald to Glasier, 29 August 1908 (ILP archive).

3 Glasier to MacDonald, 1 September 1908 (MacDonald Papers, 5/18).

4 Glasier to MacDonald, 5 November 1908 (ibid.).

5 *Labour Leader*, 5 July 1908.

6 There is considerable correspondence between Hardie and Herbert Gladstone in the Herbert Gladstone Papers (BM, Add. MSS, 46066–46067).

7 Hardie to Glasier, 11, 16 May 1908 (Glasier Papers).

8 *Daily Mail*, 14 October 1908; Christabel Pankhurst to Mrs Travers Symons, 20 January 1911; E. Hills to Keir Hardie, 20 July 1909; draft letter from Mrs Travers Symons, ? 1910 (Nat. Lib. of Scotland, Emrys Hughes Papers, Box 2, f. 2).

9 Minutes of City of London ILP, 28 May 1909 *et seq.* (LSE library).

10 John Burns's diary, 26 October 1908 (BM, Add. MSS, 46, 325).

11 *Parl. Deb.*, 4th ser., Vol. CXCIV, pp. 1646–56 (26 October 1908).

12 Ibid., Vol. CXCVIII, pp. 259–62.

13 MacDonald to Glasier, 26 October 1908 (ILP archive).

14 Mary Fels, *Joseph Fels*, pp. 129–48.

15 Hardie to Glasier, 27 December 1908 (Glasier Papers).

16 See W. Thompson, *The Life of Victor Grayson* (Sheffield, 1910).

17 Laurence Thompson, *Robert Blatchford: Portrait of an Englishman* (London, 1951), p. 204.

18 *Labour Leader*, 28 October 1908; notes of speeches at Holborn Town Hall (Transport House library, LP/CAN/06/2/143).

19 MacDonald to Glasier, 26 October, 31 December 1908 (ILP archive).

20 Glasier to MacDonald, 16 November 1908 (MacDonald Papers, 5/18); Glasier's diary, 16 February 1909 (Glasier Papers).

21 Glasier's diary, 30 November 1908 (ibid.).

22 *Labour Leader*, 9 April *1909*; *Report of the Annual Conference of the Independent Labour Party, 1909*, pp. 42ff.

23 Glasier's diary, 13 April 1909 (Glasier Papers).

24 *Labour Leader*, 16 April 1909.

25 NAC minutes, 30 September 1909 (LSE library).

26 W. Thompson, op. cit., p. 206.

27 NAC minutes, 26 November 1909 (LSE library).

28 Glasier's diary, 27 July 1909.

29 Keir Hardie, *The Party Pledge and the Osborne Judgement* (London, 1911).

30 Glasier's diary, 18 July 1909.

31 Hardie to Glasier, 25 November 1909 (Glasier Papers).

32 Labour Party executive minutes, 3 November 1909 (Transport House library).

33 Hardie to Glasier, 25 November 1909 (Glasier Papers).

34 *Merthyr Express*, 21 August, 23 October 1909.

35 Ibid., December 1909–January 1910 *passim*.

36 Glasier's diary, 17, 18 January 1910.

37 See Kenneth O. Morgan, 'The Merthyr of Keir Hardie', in Glanmor Williams (ed.), *Merthyr Politics*, pp. 76–7; Hardie to MacDonald, 26 December 1909 (MacDonald Papers, 5/19).

38 Hardie to MacDonald, ? February 1910 (ibid., 5/20).

39 MacDonald to Glasier, 30 March 1909 (ILP archive).

40 Barnes to MacDonald, 1 February 1910 (MacDonald Papers, 5/20); Hardie to T.D. Benson, 22 February 1910 (Glasier Papers).

41 *Labour Leader*, loc. cit.; *Report of the Annual Conference of the Independent Labour Party, 1910*, pp. 58–9.

42 Hardie to T.D. Benson, 22 February 1910 (Glasier Papers).

43 Hardie to Benson, ? February 1910; Glasier's diary, 28 February 1910 (ibid.).

44 *Labour Leader*, March–April 1910 *passim*; Hardie, 'Labour and Liberalism in Wales', ibid., 13 May 1910.

45 *Report*, pp. 58–9.

46 Glasier's diary, 10 December 1910 (Glasier Papers).

47 Ibid., 15 March 1910; Earl Winterton, *Orders of the Day* (London, 1953), p. 44.

48 Kenneth O. Morgan, op. cit., pp. 76–7.

49 Barnes to MacDonald, ? 1911 (MacDonald Papers, 5/21).

50 NAC minutes, 15 March 1911.

51 E. Whiteley to MacDonald, 25 January 1911 (MacDonald Papers, 5/21).

52 W.C. Anderson to MacDonald, 20 May 1911 (ibid.).

53 NAC minutes, 11 May 1911 (LSE library).

54 Ibid., 25 May 1911.

55 Hardie to Glasier, 1 January, 17 May 1911; Glasier's diary, 5 May 1911 (Glasier Papers).

56 Glasier's diary, 14 August 1911.

57 Ibid., 3 January 1912.

58 Merthyr *Pioneer*, 3 June 1911 *et seq*. It was initially published by the Labour Pioneer Press, which had been partly financed by D.A. Thomas, MP, the owner of the Cambrian Collieries. Hardie obtained a donation towards the £250 needed to extend the *Pioneer*'s plant and machinery from a wealthy woman socialist (Hardie to Miss S. Seruya, n.d. 1911, Nat. Lib. of Scotland, MS. 4461).

59 An obituary and photograph of Nicholas (1880–1971) appeared on the front page of the *Morning Star*, 21 April 1971.

60 Hardie to Glasier, 13 February 1911 (Glasier Papers).

61 *Report of the annual conference of the Independent Labour Party, 1911*, pp. 82–4.

62 Glasier's diary, 5 September 1911.

63 *Report of the Eleventh Annual Conference of the Labour Party, 1911*, pp. 81–2.

64 Merthyr *Pioneer*, 3 June, 8 July, 29 July 1911; Henderson to Mac-Donald, 30 September 1911 (MacDonald Papers, 5/21).

65 *Labour Leader*, 15 December 1911: 'Why We Opposed the Insurance Bill'.

66 Hardie to Glasier, 4, 5 January 1912 (Glasier Papers).

CHAPTER XII CLASS WAR AND THE PEACE CRUSADE (1912–14)

1 For discussion of these developments, see Kenneth O. Morgan, *Wales in British Politics*, pp. 247–55, and 'The Merthyr of Keir Hardie', loc. cit., pp. 73–7.

2 *Merthyr Express*, 19 November 1910.

3 *Parl. Deb.*, 5th ser., Vol. XX, pp. 10–18, 262–4, 404–16, Vol. XXI, pp. 214ff.

4 *Merthyr Express*, 14 October 1911; Hardie to G. Lansbury, 9 August 1913 (LSE library, Lansbury Papers, VII, ff. 121–2).

5 Merthyr *Pioneer*, 26 August 1911. Cf. Lucy Masterman, *C. F. G. Masterman* (London, 1939), p. 233.

6 Ibid.

7   Ibid., 19 January 1913.

8   Ibid., 11 May 1912.

9   *The Metropolitan*, June 1912 (pp. 13–14): copy in Tamiment library, New York.

10 Emmet Larkin, *James Larkin: Irish Labour Leader, 1876–1947* (London, 1965), pp. 126ff., 149ff.

11 Ibid., p. 127; *The Times*, 3 September 1913.

12 'The Truth about Dublin', Merthyr *Pioneer*, 13 September 1913; *Labour Leader*, 11 September 1913.

13 *Labour Leader*, 9 October 1913.

14 Ibid., 2, 23 October 1913.

15 Glasier's diary, 6 January 1912 (Glasier Papers).

16 T.D. Benson to MacDonald, 26 January 1911 (MacDonald Papers, 5/21).

17 Glasier's diary, 10 October 1911 (Glasier Papers).

18 Labour Party executive minutes, 14 November, 5 December 1912 (LSE library, Pease Collection II); cf. Hardie, 'Women and the Vote', *Labour Leader*, 12 December 1912.

19 Glasier's diary, 26 November 1913.

20 *Merthyr Express*, 14 October 1911, citing Hardie's speech at Dowlais.

21 Josiah Wedgwood to MacDonald, 12 June 1913 (MacDonald Papers, 5/23).

22 Memorandum in MacDonald Papers, 8/1.

23 NAC minutes, 17 March 1914.

24 *Report of the Annual Conference of the Independent Labour Party, 1914*; Fenner Brockway, *Inside the Left* (London, 1942), pp. 36–7; interview with Lord Brockway, 19 March 1974.

25 *Merthyr Express*, 26 July 1913.

26 Hardie to A. Peters, 'Sunday' (October 1913); A. Peters to Matt Lewis, 4 November 1913 (Transport House library, LP/CAM/13/1/245, 250).

27 'An M.P.'s work', Merthyr *Pioneer*, 30 August 1913.

28 Ibid., 29 July 1911; *Merthyr Express*, 26 August 1911.

29 Francis Johnson, 'Report from Head Office, 4 July 1911', NAC minutes, July 1911 (LSE library).

30 *Merthyr Express*, 1 June 1912.

31 Interview with Rt Hon. James Griffiths PC, 19 November 1972.

32 NAC minutes, 1913–14 *passim*; interview with Lord Brockway, 19 March 1974. Brockway's salary as editor was £3 10s a week.

33 NAC minutes, 13 December 1913; Glasier's diary, 13 December 1913.

34 C. Tsuzuki, *H.M. Hyndman and British Socialism* (Oxford, 1961), pp. 177–8.

35 *Report of the Annual Conference of the Independent Labour Party, 1914;
   Yorkshire Observer Budget*, 18 April 1914.

36 Brockway, *Inside the Left*, p. 39; interview with Lord Brockway, 19
   March 1974; Hardie to Rose Davies, n.d. (1914) (Glamorgan Record
   Office, Cardiff, D/Dxik/30/27).

37 Brockway, *Socialism over Sixty Years*, pp. 104–6. This pamphlet was
   written by McLachlan, Hall, Douthwaite and Belcher: cf. Leonard Hall
   et al., *Let Us Reform the Labour Party* (London, 1910).

38 Glasier's diary, 4 December 1913 (Glasier Papers).

39 David Farrell to Hardie, 1, 6 October 1914 (Nat. Lib. of Scotland,
   Emrys Hughes Papers, Box 1, f. 1).

40 Merthyr *Pioneer*, 25 November 1911.

41 *Parl. Deb.*, 4th ser., Vol. CXC, pp. 252–61: cf. A.J. Anthony Morris,
   Radicalism against War, 1906–1914 (London, 1972), pp. 175–81.

42 Glasier's diary, 7 May 1910 (Glasier Papers).

43 *Labour Leader*, 16 December 1910.

44 Merthyr *Pioneer*, 2 December 1911.

45 Ibid., 9, 16 November 1912.

46 Georges Haupt, *Socialism and the Great War* (Oxford, 1972), p. 92.
   The delegate was Alexandra Kollantay.

47 Vaillant to Hardie, 1 August 1912 (ILP archive).

48 Sir Norman Angell, *After All* (London, 1951), p. 170. Angell himself
   was reluctant to be linked to the 'extremists' of the ILP.

CHAPTER XIII   AT GETHSEMANE (1914–15)

1 Merthyr *Pioneer*, 25 July 1914.

2 *Parl. Deb.*, 5th ser., Vol. XLVI, pp. 1549ff.

3 Glasier's diary, 29, 30 July 1914 (Glasier Papers); Haupt, op. cit., pp.
   202, 208, 250; Hardie to Troelstra, 13 November 1914 (Institute of
   Social History, Amsterdam: Troelstra Archive, 550/18).

4 Merthyr *Pioneer*, 8 August 1914.

5 See Cameron Hazlehurst, *Politicians at War* (London, 1971), pp. 54ff.;
   and Kenneth O. Morgan (ed.), *Lloyd George: Family Letters, 1885–
   1936* (Oxford, 1973), pp. 166–7.

6 *Parl. Deb.*, 5th ser., Vol. LXV, pp. 1839–41.

7 *Merthyr Express*, 8 August 1914; *Western Mail*, 8 August 1914. Cf.
   Wil Jon Edwards, *From the Valley I Came*, pp. 120–1.

8 Hardie to Agnes Hughes, 26 August 1914 (Hedley Dennis Papers,
   Abercynon).

9 NAC minutes, 31 August 1914 (LSE library); Hardie to MacDonald,

10 October 1914 (MacDonald Papers, 5/98); interview with Lord Brockway, 19 March 1974.

10 Glasier's diary, 26 October 1914.

11 Merthyr *Pioneer*, 15 August, 28 November 1914; *Forward*, 2 January 1915.

12 *Merthyr Express*, 31 October 1914.

13 *Parl. Deb.*, 5th ser., Vol. LXVIII, pp. 286–7, 305–8; *Merthyr Express*, 14, 21 November 1914.

14 Hardie to Shaw, 26 November 1914 (BM, Add. MSS, 50,538, ff. 24–5).

15 Burns's diary, 15 February 1915 (BM, Add. MSS, 46,337).

16 NAC minutes, 16 October 1914.

17 Merthyr *Pioneer*, 9 January 1915.

18 Hardie to Agnes Hughes, 15 February 1915 (Dennis Papers).

19 City of London ILP annual report for 1915 (LSE library); Glasier's diary, 2, 22 February 1915. Cf. Walter Kendall, *The Revolutionary Movement in Britain, 1900–21* (London, 1969), pp. 92–3.

20 Glasier's diary, 11 March 1915.

21 Stewart, *J. Keir Hardie*, p. 365.

22 Glasier's diary, 15 April 1915.

23 *Parl. Deb.*, 5th ser., Vol. LXX, pp. 402–8.

24 Ibid., Vol. LXXI, p. 593.

25 *Report of the Annual Conference of the Independent Labour Party, 1915*; Brockway, *Socialism over Sixty Years*, p. 133; *Merthyr Pioneer*, 10, 17 April 1915.

26 Nan Hardie to Agnes Hughes, n.d. (1915) (Dennis Papers).

27 Hardie to Sylvia Pankhurst, 27 May 1915 (Institute of Social History, Amsterdam, Pankhurst Papers, 1/C).

28 Nan Hardie to Agnes Hughes, 18 July 1915 (Dennis Papers).

29 Hardie to Sylvia Pankhurst, 28 July 1915 (Institute of Social History, Amsterdam, Pankhurst Papers, 1/C).

30 *The Times*, 27 September 1915.

31 Glasier's diary, 27 September 1915.

32 Ibid., 29, 30 September 1915.

33 Merthyr *Pioneer*, 9 October 1915; *Woman's Dreadnought*, 16 October 1915.

34 *Woman's Dreadnought*, 2 October 1915. The Institute of Social History at Amsterdam includes various notes for this obituary in the Pankhurst Papers, B/12.

35 *The Times*, 6 January 1916; *Manchester Guardian*, 6 January 1916; Emrys Hughes Papers, National Library of Scotland, Box 1, f. 2. I am

indebted to Mr R. Bruce Aubry for assistance in discovering the details
of Keir Hardie's will.

36 NAC minutes, 22 October 1915 (LSE library).

37 Ibid., 24–25 January, 11–12 May, 6–7 July 1916.

38 Thompson, *The Enthusiasts*, pp. 217–18. Glasier did write a brief
    'memorial' of Hardie, published in 1919.

39 *Merthyr Express*, 2 October 1915.

40 Mary Morris to MacDonald, 10 October 1915 (MacDonald Papers,
    5/25).

41 Llew. Francis to MacDonald, 20 October 1915 (ibid.).

42 *Merthyr Express*, 6 November 1815.

43 Ibid., 27 November 1915.

44 Ibid.

45 Ibid., 4 December 1915; *Labour Voice*, 4, 11 December 1915. The latter
    journal, formerly *Llais Llafur* of Ystalyfera, the main Welsh-language
    organ of the ILP, had changed its political stance after the outbreak of
    war and was now violently hostile to anti-war socialists.

46 See J.O. Stubbs, 'Lord Milner and Patriotic Labour, 1914–1918',
    English Historical Review, LXXXVII (October 1972), pp. 723–5.

CHAPTER XIV HARDIE'S LEGACY

1   Merthyr *Pioneer*, 2 October 1915.

2   Ibid.

3   Ibid.

4   Ibid.

5   *Commonwealth*, October 1915 ('Keir Hardie: In Memoriam', by F.
    Lewis Donaldson).

6   Hyndman, *Further Reminiscences*, pp. 257–8.

7   Gardiner, *Prophets, Priests and Kings* (London, Wayfarer's Library
    edition 1917), p. 86.

8   *Daily Telegraph*, 27 September 1915.

9   Burns's diary, 26 September 1915 (BM, Add. MSS, 46,337).

10 See S.V. Bracher (ed.), *The Herald Book of Labour Members* (London,
    1923).

11 *Daily Herald*, 21 August 1939.

12 Sylvia Pankhurst's notebook (Institute of Social History, Amsterdam,
    Pankhurst Papers, 83b). Sylvia Pankhurst noted, 'The conference was
    awed for a moment by the mention of its founder. The stern and
    beautiful figure seemed to loom over us.'

13 Robert Skidelsky, *Politicians and the Slump* (London, 1968), pp. 47–50.

14 J.W. England, 'The Merthyr of the Twentieth Century: a Postscript', in Glanmor Williams (ed.), *Merthyr Politics*, p. 82.

15 *Thirty-fifth Annual Report of the Labour Party, 1935*, pp. 139–40.

16 In the Merthyr by-election of April 1972, the Plaid Cymru candidate stressed that 'Henry Richard, Keir Hardie and S.O. Davies supported a Parliament for Wales'. He was right about the last two.

17 E.I. Champness, *Frank Smith*, p. 60; diary of Mrs Hedley Dennis, 24 September 1940.

18 Diary of Mrs Hedley Dennis, 26 July 1945. Hardie, Smith and Mrs Dennis all communicated through the medium, Abdul Latif.

19 *Daily Herald*, 20 August 1932.

20 Cf. Wil Jon Edwards, op. cit., pp. 110–11.

21 *Daily Worker*, 13 April 1950.

22 *Labour Leader*, 29 April 1899.

23 Ibid., 18 July 1903.

Select Bibliography

The sources for late nineteenth- and early twentieth-century British labour history are of overwhelming bulk. A complete bibliography would fill several volumes. I have confined myself here, particularly in sections E and F, strictly to works that proved directly useful in studying Hardie's career.

A. MANUSCRIPT COLLECTIONS

B. OFFICIAL PAPERS

C. NEWSPAPERS, PERIODICALS and REPORTS

D. KEIR HARDIE'S PUBLISHED WRITINGS

E. BIOGRAPHIES

F. OTHER WORKS

A. MANUSCRIPT COLLECTIONS

1. *In Libraries, Museums and Record Offices*
Blackburn Public Library
    Higenbottam correspondence
Bristol University Library (by courtesy of Mr Bruce Aubry)
    Independent Labour Party Archives: Glasier Diaries, 1895–99
                              Hardie-Adler correspondence
                              Hardie-Glasier correspondence
                              Hardie-Lowe correspondence
                              Hardie-Penny correspondence
                              Mid-Lanark MSS
                              Miscellaneous correspondence
British Museum
    Burns Papers (Add. MSS, 46,287, 46,312–337)
    Campbell-Bannerman Papers (Add. MSS, 41,239)
    Dilke Papers (Add. MSS, 43,919)
    Herbert, Viscount Gladstone Papers (Add. MSS, 46,066)
    Shaw Papers (Add. MSS, 50,538)
Cambridge University Library
    Crewe Papers (C/18 and I/16)

Corpus Christi College, Oxford, Library
  R.C.K. Ensor Papers
Glamorgan County Record Office, Cardiff
  Aberdare ILP Minute Books (D/DX Lj 2)
  Alderman Rose Davies Papers (D/D 1k, 30–1)
Hull University Library
  Hardie correspondence (six cards and letters)
Institute of Social History, Amsterdam
  Bernstein Archive
  Marx-Engels Archive
  Robert Murray Archive
  Socialist International Papers
  Sylvia Pankhurst MSS
  Troelstra Archive
Labor Department Archive, Ottawa
London School of Economics Library
  Broadhurst Papers, Vols II–V
  ILP (City of London Branch) Minute Books, 1909–15
  ILP (National Administrative Council) Minute Books, 1893–1917
  Lansbury Papers, vols I–III
  Passfield Papers, vols I–III
  Pease Collection, vols I and II
National Library of Scotland
  Acc. 3350 (William Small Papers)
  Acc. 4461 (Hardie-Seruya correspondence)
  Acc. 4494 (Hardie-Hines correspondence)
  Acc. 5121 (National Labour Daily, 1911)
  Acc. 5234 (Hardie letter)
  MSS 1809 and 7198
  Emrys Hughes Papers (Dep. 176)
  Rosebery Papers, Box 114
  Scottish TUC Parliamentary Committee minutes, 1897–1900 (on micro-
    film)
National Library of Wales
  Lloyd George Papers (MSS 20,430 C)
Public Record Office
  Cabinet Papers (CAB 37/74 and 37/91)
Scottish Record Office, Edinburgh
  Rules of Ayrshire Miners Association, 1881 (FS 7/3)
  Rules of Ayrshire Miners Association, 1886 (FS 7/18)
  G.W. Balfour Papers, 121

Tamiment Library, New York City
 Algernon Lee Papers
Trades Union Congress Library
 TUC Parliamentary Committee minutes 1887–1900 (on microfilm)
Transport House Library
 Hardie MSS and Diary fragment
 Labour Representation Committee executive minute books, 1900–6
 Labour Representation Committee General Correspondence, 1900–5
  (files 1–31)
 Labour Representation Committee out-letter copy-books, 1900–5
 Labour Party General Correspondence, 1906–8 (files 1–22)
 Labour Party campaign files, 1908–13
 Frederick Pickles collection
University College of Swansea Library
 Cumberland Area National Union of Mineworkers' Archives

2. *Privately Owned*
Colne Valley Labour Party records (by courtesy of Mr Arthur Belcher,
 Huddersfield)
Papers of Mrs Agnes Dennis (by courtesy of Mr Hedley Dennis, Abercynon)
Papers and Diaries (1900–20) of J. Bruce Glasier and papers of Mrs
 Katherine Bruce Glasier (by courtesy of Mr Malcolm Bruce Glasier, West
 Kirby)
Papers of Francis Johnson (transcripts by courtesy of Dr Henry Pelling,
 Cambridge):
  Aberdeen Trades Council Minutes
  Glasier correspondence
  Hardie correspondence
  MacDonald correspondence
Papers of J. Ramsay MacDonald (by courtesy of Mr David Marquand MP)

B. OFFICIAL PAPERS

Hansard, *Parliamentary Debates*, Third and Fourth Series
Minutes and Evidence with Appendices taken before Group 'A' of Royal Com-
 mission on Labour, Second Report and Minutes of Evidence, 1892, Vol. II
 (H. of C. 1892, XXXVI, pt. I, p. 1)
Select Committee on Distress from Want of Employment, 1895. *First Report*
 and Minutes of Evidence (H. of C. 111/1895, VIII, p. 1); *Second Report*
 and Minutes of Evidence (H. of C. 253/1895, VIII, p. 215); *Third Report,*
 Evidence and Appendices (H. of C. 365/1895, IX, p. 1)

Select Committee on the Procedure of the House of Commons, 1906. First and Second Reports, with Minutes of Evidence, Appendix and Index (H. of C. 89, 181/1906, VIII, p. 429)

Select Committee on Income Tax, 1906 (H. of C., 365/1906, IX, p. 659). *Report, Proceedings, Minutes of Evidence, Appendices and Index*

Railway Strike (Employment of Military): Correspondence between Home Office and Local Authorities, 1911, (H. of C. 323/1911, XLVII, p. 691)

C. NEWSPAPERS, PERIODICALS and REPORTS

1. *Newspapers*
Aberdare Leader
Aberdare Times
Appeal to Reason (Girard, Kansas)
Ardrossan and Saltcoats Herald
Baner ac Amserau Cymru (Denbigh)
Borough of West Ham and Stratford Express
Bradford Daily Telegraph
Bradford Observer
Clarion
Commonweal
Daily Chronicle
Forward
Y Genedl Gymreig (Caernarvon)
Glasgow Herald
Glasgow Observer
Halifax Herald (Halifax, Nova Scotia)
Hardie's Herald (Bradford)
I.L.P. News
Industrial Banner (Ottawa)
Justice
Labour Chronicle (Edinburgh)
Labour Elector
Labour Leader
Labour Prophet (Bradford)
Lanarkshire Examiner
Lancashire Daily Post (Preston)
Llais Llafur: Labour Voice (Ystalyfera)
Manchester Guardian
Merthyr Express
Merthyr *Pioneer*

The Miner: a Journal for Underground Workers (in Burns Collection, TUC Library)
Morning Chronicle (Halifax, Nova Scotia)
North British Daily Mail
Preston Guardian
Rhondda Leader
The Scotsman
Scottish Leader
South Wales Daily News
South Wales Echo
The Speaker
Tarian y Gweithiwr (Aberdare)
The Times
The Voice (Winnipeg, Alberta)
Western Mail
Woman's Dreadnought
Yorkshire Observer Budget (in Bradford Public Library)

2. *Other Periodicals*
Contemporary Review
Y Geninen
The Nation
Progressive Review
Socialist Review
Use was also made of the press cuttings departments of the Transport House Library and of the Canadian Public Archives, Ottawa.

3. *Reports*
Annual Reports of the following organizations:
    Independent Labour Party, 1893–1916
    Labour Electoral Association, 1887–9
    Labour Representation Committee, 1900–5
    Labour Party, 1906–15, 1935
    Socialist International, 1889–1912
    Trades and Labor Congress of Canada, 1908–9
    Trades Union Congress, 1887–95
American Labor Annual

D. KEIR HARDIE'S PUBLISHED WRITINGS

1. *Hardie's Books*
From Serfdom to Socialism (London, 1907, reprinted 1974)
India: Impressions and Suggestions (London, 1909, 2nd edition 1917)

2. *Hardie's Pamphlets*

The Mines Nationalization Bill (1893)

Jack Clears the Way (1896)

Young Men in a Hurry. Why they are in a hurry and what they are in a hurry about (1898)

The Pru in the Pillory (1899)

Lord Overtoun, Chrome, Charity, Crystals and Cant (1899)

More about Overtoun (1899)

The Overtoun Horrors (1899)

Overtoun Fictions. A lame defence. A pulverising reply (1899)

Can a Man be a Christian on a Pound a Week? (1901)

Labour Politics: a Symposium (with Philip Snowden and David Shackleton) (1903)

The Unemployed Problem and some suggestions for Solving it (1904)

John Bull and his Unemployed. A Plain Statement on the Law of England as it affects the Unemployed (1905)

The Citizenship of Women: a Plea for Women's Suffrage (1906)

Socialism, the hope of Wales (1908)

Indian Budget Speech, Delivered in the House of Commons on July 22nd, 1908 (1908)

The I.L.P. and all about it (1909)

My Confession of Faith in the Labour Alliance (1909)

Socialism and Civilisation (1910)

The Common Good: an Essay in Municipal Government (1910)

Labour and Liberalism in Wales (1910)

Labour and Christianity (1910)

The Party Pledge and the Osborne Judgement (1910)

Killing no Murder! The Government and the Railway Strike (1911)

The Labour Unrest. Its Causes, Effects and Remedies (with Ramsay Mac-Donald) (1912)

Radicals and Reform (1912)

The Red Dragon and the Red Flag (1912)

The Queenie Gerald Case. A Public Scandal. White Slavery in a Piccadilly Flat (1913)

A Force to be Reckoned With (1914)

Hardie also wrote six 'coming of age' leaflets for the ILP in 1913.

3. *Hardie's Articles*

'The Scottish Labour Party', *The Democrat*, September 1888.

'The Christianity of Christ', *The Labour Prophet*, November 1892.

'The Case for an Independent Labour Party', *The New Review*, June 1894.

'The Independent Labour Party', in Andrew Reid (ed.), *The New Party* (London, 1894).

'On the Independent Labour Party', *Progressive Review*, December 1896.

'The Independent Labour Party's Programme', *Nineteenth Century*, LIII (January 1899) (jointly written with J. Ramsay MacDonald).

'On Labour and Politics in Great Britain', *Forum*, August 1900.

'Some Economic and Industrial Aspects of the War', *New Liberal Review*, August 1901.

'The Aims of the Independent Labour Party', ibid., November 1901.

'The Independent Labour Party', *Nineteenth Century*, April 1903.

'Socialism', *Manchester Medical Students' Gazette*, November 1905.

'Socialism and the Political Future', *Vanity Fair*, 8 February 1906.

'A Labour Budget', *Review of Reviews*, April 1906.

'The Labour Party and the Books that helped to make it', ibid., June 1906.

'The Labour Movement', *Nineteenth Century*, LX (December 1906).

'Women and Politics', in Brougham Villiers (ed.), *The Case for Women's Suffrage* (London, 1907).

'Sir Henry Campbell-Bannerman', *Socialist Review*, May 1908.

'Michael Davitt: I. The Democrat', ibid., August 1908.

'Socialism in America', ibid., April 1909.

'The General Election', *Socialist Review*, November 1909.

'Modern Brigands', *Christian Commonwealth*, 14 July 1909.

'The British Labour Party', *International Socialist Review*, May 1910.

'Revisionism v. Radicalism in Germany', *Socialist Review*, November 1910.

'The French Socialist Congress', ibid., April 1912.

'Labour's Victory in England: the Minimum Wage Bill and the Social Revolution', *The Metropolitan*, June 1912.

'America Revisited', *Socialist Review*, December 1912.

'The Red International', ibid., February 1913.

'The Pioneer of the I.L.P.', ibid., April 1913.

'August Bebel', ibid., September 1913.

'Christ and the Modern Movement', in C.G. Ammon (ed.), *Christ and Labour* (London, 1913).

'History Repeats Itself', *Socialist Review*, October–December 1914.

Hardie also published weekly columns in the *Ardrossan and Saltcoats Herald* (1881–7), *Labour Leader* (1893–1904, and more sporadically thereafter) and the Merthyr *Pioneer* (1911–15). In addition, he wrote scores of leaflets, occasional pieces and tracts, mainly for the ILP. The Burns Collection at the TUC Library includes many pamphlets etc. relating to the Labour movement this period.

E. BIOGRAPHIES (arranged in order of subject; place of publication London unless otherwise stated)

ABRAHAM, William, *Mabon*, by Eric Wyn Evans (Cardiff, 1959).

ANGELL, Sir Norman, *After All* (1951).

ATHERLEY-JONES, L., *Looking Back* (1925).

BLATCHFORD, Robert, *Robert Blatchford: Portrait of an Englishman*, by Laurence Thompson (1951).

BROCKWAY, A. Fenner, *Inside the Left* (1942).

BURNS, John, *John Burns: Labour's Lost Leader*, by W.G.R. Kent (1950).

CHAMPION, H.H., 'H.H. Champion – Pioneer of Labour Representation', by H. Pelling, *Cambridge Journal*, January 1953.

CLYNES, J.R., *Memoirs*, 2 vols. (1937).

CONNOLLY, James, *The Life and Times of James Connolly*, by C. Desmond Greaves (1961).

CUNNINGHAME GRAHAM, R.B., *Don Roberto*, by A.S. Tschiffely (1927).

DEBS, Eugene V., *The Bending Cross*, by Ray Ginger (New Brunswick, New Jersey, 1949).

DE LEON, Daniel, *Daniel de Leon: a Symposium* (New York, 1920).

EDWARDS, Wil Jon, *From the Valley I Came* (1956).

ELLIS, Tom, *The Forerunner*, by Neville Masterman (Llandybïe, 1972).

FELS, Joseph, *Joseph Fels: his life work* (New York, 1916).

GLASIER, Bruce and Katherine Bruce, *The Enthusiasts*, by Laurence Thompson (1971).

GOMPERS, Samuel, *Seventy Years of Life and Labor* (New York, 1924), 2 vols.

GRAYSON, Victor, *The Life of Victor Grayson*, by W. Thompson (Sheffield, 1910).

HADDOW, W.M., *My Seventy Years* (Glasgow, 1943).

HARDIE, J. Keir, *J. Keir Hardie: the Man and the Message*, by J. Bruce Glasier (1919).

— *J. Keir Hardie*, by William Stewart (1921).

— *Keir Hardie's Socialism*, by Francis Johnson (1922).

— *From Pit to Parliament: the story of the early life of Keir Hardie*, by David Lowe (1923).

— *Keir Hardie's Speeches and Writings*, edited by Emrys Hughes (1928).

— *Keir Hardie*, by Hamilton Fyfe (1935).

— *Keir Hardie: Prophet and Pioneer*, by James Maxton (1939).

— *Keir Hardie*, by G.D.H. Cole (1941).

— *A Pictorial Biography of Keir Hardie*, by Emrys Hughes (1950).

— *Keir Hardie*, by Emrys Hughes (1956).

— *The Hungry Heart: a romantic biography of Keir Hardie*, by John Cockburn (1956).

— *Keir Hardie*, by Kenneth O. Morgan (Oxford, 1967).

— 'The Early Life and Political Development of James Keir Hardie', by F. Reid (unpublished Oxford University D.Phil. thesis, 1968).

HOBSON, S.G., *Pilgrim to the Left* (1938).

HYNDMAN, H.M., *The Record of an Adventurous Life* (1911).

— *Further Reminiscences* (1912).

— *H.M. Hyndman and British Socialism*, by C. Tsuzuki (Oxford, 1961).

JONES, Jack, *My Lively Life* (1928).

JOWETT, Fred, *Socialism over Sixty Years*, by A. Fenner Brockway (1946).

LANSBURY, George, *My Life* (1928).

LARKIN, James, *James Larkin: Irish Labour Leader*, by Emmet Larkin (1965).

MACDONALD, J. Ramsay, *The Tragedy of Ramsay MacDonald*, by L. McNeill Weir, n.d. (1938).

— *The Life of James Ramsay MacDonald*, by Lord Elton, Vol. I (1939).

MANN, Tom, *Tom Mann and his Times*, by Dona Torr, Vol. I (1956).

MASTERMAN, C.F.G., *C.F.G. Masterman*, by Lucy Masterman (1939).

MAVOR, James, *My Windows on the Street of the World*, Vol. I (1923).

MAXTON, James, *James Maxton: the Beloved Rebel*, by John McNair (1955).

MORLEY, John, *Recollections*, Vol. II (1917).

MORISON, Rev. James, *The Life of the Rev. James Morison D.D.*, by William Adamson (1898).

PANKHURST, Sylvia, *The Suffragette Movement* (1931).

— *The Fighting Pankhursts*, by David Mitchell (1967).

SMILLIE, Robert, *My Life for Labour* (1924).

SMITH, Frank, *Frank Smith: Pioneer and Mystic*, by E.I. Champness (1943).

SNOWDEN, Philip, *An Autobiography*, Vol. I (1934).

— *Philip Snowden*, by Colin Cross (1966).

THORNE, Will, *My Life's Battles*, n.d. (1925).

TILAK, B.G., *Tilak and Gokhale*, by Stanley A. Wolpert (Berkeley, 1962).

WEBB, Beatrice, *Our Partnership* (1948).

— *Beatrice Webb's Diary 1912–24*, edited by Margaret Cole (1952).

WOODSWORTH, J.S., *A Prophet in Politics: a Biography of J.S. Woodsworth*, by Kenneth McNaught (Toronto, 1959).

F. OTHER WORKS (place of publication London, unless otherwise stated)

Arnot, R. Page, *The Miners* (1949).

Bealey, F. and Pelling, Henry, *Labour and Politics, 1900–1906* (1958).

Bellamy, Joyce, and Saville, John (eds), *Dictionary of Labour Biography*, Vol. I (1972), Vol. II (1974).

Blewett, Neil, *The Peers, the Parties and the People: the General Election of 1910* (1972).

Bracher, S.V. (ed.), *The Herald Book of Labour Members* (1923).

Braunthal, Julius, *History of the International, 1864–1914* (1966).

Briggs, Asa, and Saville, John (eds), *Essays in Labour History*, Vol. II (1972).

Brown, Kenneth D., *Labour and Unemployment, 1900–1914* (1971).

— 'Conflict in Early British Welfare Policy: the Case of the Unemployed Workmen's Bill of 1905', *Journal of Modern History*, Vol 43 (December 1971).

Buckley, Kenneth D., *Trade Unionism in Aberdeen, 1878 to 1900* (1955).

Carswell, Donald, *Brother Scots* (1927).

Clarke, P.F., *Lancashire and the New Liberalism* (Cambridge, 1971).

Clegg, Hugh, Fox, Alan, and Thompson, A.F., *A History of British Trade Unions since 1889*, Vol. I (Oxford, 1964).

Craik, W.W., *The Central Labour College* (1964).

Cole G.D.H. *The History of Socialist Thought: the Second International*, Vol. III, Book II (1956).

Das, M., *India under Morley and Minto* (1964).

Dowse, R.E., *Left in the Centre* (1966).

Duffy, A.E.P., 'Differing Policies and Personal Rivalries in the Origins of the Independent Labour Party', *Victorian Studies*, September 1962.

Durward, Alan A., 'The Truth about James Kerr, alias Keir Hardie and the I.L.P.', n.d. (unpublished MS. in Nuffield College Library, Oxford).

Emy, H.V., *Liberals, Radicals and Social Politics, 1892–1914* (Cambridge, 1973).

Fox, K.O., 'Labour and Merthyr's Khaki Election of 1900', *Welsh History Review*, Vol. 2, No. 4 (1965).

Gardiner, A.G., *Prophets, Priests and Kings* (1914).

Hall, Leonard *et al.*, *Let Us Reform the Labour Party* (1910).

Handley, James, *The Irish in Modern Scotland* (Cork, 1947).

Harris, José, *Unemployment and Politics* (Oxford, 1972).

Haupt, George, *Socialism and the Great War* (Oxford, 1972).

Hyman, Richard, *The Workers' Union* (Oxford, 1971).

Johnston, Thomas, *History of the Working Classes in Scotland* (Glasgow, 1946).

Keir Hardie versus the Labour Literature Society Limited: a Reply to the Article signed 'Keir' in the 'Labour Leader' of August 17 1895 (Glasgow, 1895).

Kellas, James G., 'The Mid-Lanark By-election (1888) and the Scottish Labour Party (1888–1894)', *Parliamentary Affairs*, Summer 1965.

Kendall, Walter, *The Revolutionary Movement in Britain, 1900–21* (1969).

Koss, Stephen, *John Morley at the India Office* (Newhaven, Connecticut, 1969).

Lean, Garth, *Brave Men Choose* (1961).

Lenin, V.I., *British Labour and British Imperialism* (1969).

McBriar, A.M., *Fabian Socialism and English Politics, 1884–1918* (Cambridge, 1966).

McKibbin, Ross, 'James Ramsay MacDonald and the Problem of the Independence of the Labour Party', *Journal of Modern History*, Vol. 42 (June 1970).

Moody, T.W., 'Michael Davitt and the British Labour Movement', *Transactions of the Royal Historical Society* (1953).

Morgan, Kenneth O., *Wales in British Politics, 1868–1922* (Cardiff, 2nd edition 1970).

— *The Age of Lloyd George* (1971).

Pelling, Henry, *The Origins of the Labour Party* (Oxford, new edition 1965).

— *Popular Politics and Society in Late Victorian Britain* (1967).

— *Social Geography of British Elections, 1885–1910* (1968).

Poirier, Philip, *The Advent of the Labour Party* (1958).

Skidelsky, Robert, *Politicians and the Slump* (1968).

Smart, H. Russell, *The Independent Labour Party: its Programme and Policy* (1893).

Solberg, C.T., 'The Independent Labour Party' (unpublished Oxford University B.Litt. thesis, 1939).

Stonelake, Edmund, *Aberdare Trades and Labour Council 1900–1950: Jubilee Souvenir*, Aberdare, n.d. [1950].

Taylor, A.J.P., *The Troublemakers* (1957).

— *Englishmen and Others* (1964).

Thompson, Paul, *Socialists, Liberals and Labour* (1967).

Williams, Glanmor (ed.), *Merthyr Politics: the making of a Working-class Tradition* (Cardiff, 1966).

Weinroth, Howard, 'The British Radicals and the Balance of Power', *Historical Journal*, XIII (December 1970).

— 'Norman Angell and *The Great Illusion*', *Ibid.*, XVII (September 1974).

Welsh History Review, Vol. 6, No. 3 (Welsh Labour History number, June 1973).

Wolpert, Stanley, *Morley and India, 1906–1910* (Berkeley, 1967).

Index